Responding to Individuals with Mental Illnesses

Editors

Michael T. Compton, M.D., M.P.H.
Assistant Professor, Department of Psychiatry and Behavioral Sciences
Emory University School of Medicine
Atlanta, Georgia

Raymond J. Kotwicki, M.D., M.P.H.
Assistant Professor, Department of Psychiatry and Behavioral Sciences
Emory University School of Medicine
Atlanta, Georgia

JONES AND BARTLETT PUBLISHERS
Sudbury, Massachusetts
BOSTON   TORONTO   LONDON   SINGAPORE

M000278458

World Headquarters

Jones and Bartlett Publishers
40 Tall Pine Drive
Sudbury, MA 01776
978-443-5000
info@jbpub.com
www.jbpub.com

Jones and Bartlett Publishers
Canada
6339 Ormindale Way
Mississauga, Ontario L5V 1J2
Canada

Jones and Bartlett Publishers
International
Barb House, Barb Mews
London W6 7PA
United Kingdom

Jones and Bartlett's books and products are available through most bookstores and online booksellers. To contact Jones and Bartlett Publishers directly, call 800-832-0034, fax 978-443-8000, or visit our website www.jbpub.com.

Substantial discounts on bulk quantities of Jones and Bartlett's publications are available to corporations, professional associations, and other qualified organizations. For details and specific discount information, contact the special sales department at Jones and Bartlett via the above contact information or send an email to specialsales@jbpub.com.

Production Credits

Chief Executive Officer: Clayton E. Jones
Chief Operating Officer: Donald W. Jones, Jr.
President, Higher Education and Professional Publishing: Robert W. Holland, Jr.
V.P., Sales and Marketing: William J. Kane
V.P., Production and Design: Anne Spencer
V.P., Manufacturing and Inventory Control: Therese Connell
Publisher, Public Safety Group: Kimberly Brophy
Acquisitions Editor: Jeremy Spiegel
Editor: Jennifer S. Kling
Production Supervisor: Jenny L. Corriveau
Director of Marketing: Alisha Weisman
Interior Design: Anne Spencer
Cover Design: Kate Ternullo
Composition: Arlene Apone
Cover and Interior Image (blue siren): © Comstock Images/Alamy Images
Cover Image: © Mikael Karlsson/Alamy Images
Text Printing and Binding: Malloy, Inc.
Cover Printing: Malloy, Inc.

Library of Congress Cataloging-in-Publication Data

Responding to individuals with mental illnesses / [edited by]
  Michael T. Compton and Raymond J. Kotwicki.
    p. ; cm.
  Includes bibliographical references.
  ISBN-13: 978-0-7637-4110-5 (pbk.)
  ISBN-10: 0-7637-4110-8 (pbk.)
  1. Mental illness—Handbooks, manuals, etc. 2. Psychiatry—Handbooks, manuals, etc. 3. Criminal justice personnel—Handbooks, manuals, etc.   I. Compton, Michael T. II. Kotwicki, Raymond J.
  [DNLM: 1. Mental Disorders. 2. Law Enforcement.   WM 140
R434 2007]
  RC456.R47 2007
  616.89—dc22
                                        2006030484

6048

Printed in the United States of America
14 13 12 11 10   10 9 8 7 6 5 4 3 2

CONTENTS

Part 1 - Recognizing the Need

Chapter I: The Myths of Mental Illness | 2

Introduction 3
The Prevalence of Mental Illnesses and Addictive Disorders
    in the United States. 5
Social Consequences of Untreated Serious Mental Illnesses 6
The Myth of Dangerousness and Violence in People with
    Severe Mental Illnesses. 7
The Problem of Stigma 8
Conclusion 9
Chapter Wrap-Up 10

Chapter 2: Criminalization of Mental Illnesses | 13

Introduction 13
Purpose of the Criminal Justice Process 13
Mens rea and Criminal Intent 14
Consideration of Mental Illnesses in the Criminal Justice Process 14
Links Between Mental Illnesses, Socioeconomics, and Criminalization 15
    Education 15
    Economics 15
    Substance Use 16
    Race and Other Social Factors 16
Consequences of Incarceration of People with Mental Illnesses. 16
Decriminalization of Mental Illnesses 17
Conclusion. 17
Chapter Wrap-Up 19

Chapter 3: Mental Health Care in Detention | 21

Introduction 21
Background: Where Have All the Psychiatric Hospitals Gone? 21
The Number of People with Mental Illnesses in Jails and Prisons. 22
Factors Contributing to the Increase in Incarceration of Persons
    with Mental Illnesses 22
    Civil Commitment Laws 22
    Treatment in the Community 23
    Tougher Sentencing Laws and the Cost Factor 23
Right to Treatment of Inmates with Mental Illnesses. 24
Mental Health Services Offered in Jails and Prisons 24

Managing Mental Health Problems. **25**

    Recognizing the Problem. 25

    Adjustment Difficulties of Inmates with Mental Illnesses. 26

    Respect and Awareness 26

    Inmates Faking a Mental Illness 27

Transfers of Inmates to a Psychiatric Hospital. **27**

    Nonadherence with Psychiatric Medications 27

    Incompetence to Stand Trial 28

    Not Guilty by Reason of Insanity 28

Conclusion **29**

Chapter Wrap-Up. **30**

Chapter 4: Crisis Intervention Team (CIT) Programs   33

Introduction **33**

The Complexity of Law Enforcement Work **33**

Law Enforcement Responses to Family Crises **34**

Types of Partnerships Between Law Enforcement and Mental Health. **34**

Development of the Memphis CIT Model **35**

Local and State CIT Programs **36**

Personal Characteristics of CIT Officers **37**

The CIT Curriculum **37**

The Importance of Crisis Centers and Emergency Receiving Facilities **38**

The Effectiveness of CIT. **39**

    CIT Provides Specialized Responses for Mental Health Emergencies. 39

    CIT Decreases Use of Force and Arrests, While Enhancing Referral to Treatment 40

    CIT Officers Refer People Who Are in Need of Treatment 40

An Example of a Statewide CIT Program: Georgia's Experience **40**

Families' Perspectives on CIT and Legal Issues. **41**

Chapter Wrap-Up. **43**

Chapter 5: Collaborations Between Mental Health and Law Enforcement   46

Introduction. **46**

Points of Intervention. **46**

    Dispatch. 46

    Scene of the Incident 47

    Police Station. 47

    Pre-arraignment Custody 47

    Arraignment and Pretrial Release/Detention Hearing 48

    Jail 48

    Adjudication 49

Existing Models of Collaboration **50**

    CIT Training for All Officers 50

    CIT and Medical Bracelet Program 50

    New Recruit Education 50

    Psychiatric Emergency Response Team 51

    Community Mental Health Officer 51

    Mobile Crisis Teams with Police Collaboration. 51

    Forensic Assertive Community Treatment 52

Unmet Needs and Future Directions 52

    Inadequate Mental Health Resources. 52

    Housing Issues. 53

    Social Security Benefits, Medicaid, and Medicare 53

    Professional Education 54

Chapter Wrap-Up. 55

Part II - Understanding Mental Illnesses

Chapter 6: Recognizing Signs and Symptoms of Mental Illnesses   58

Introduction. 59

Signs and Symptoms Involving Emotions 60

Signs and Symptoms Involving Thoughts or Beliefs 61

Signs and Symptoms Involving Perceptions or Senses 62

Signs and Symptoms Involving Behavior. 62

Conclusion 63

Chapter Wrap-Up. 64

Chapter 7: Schizophrenia and Related Disorders   67

Introduction. 68

Common Signs and Symptoms. 68

    Positive Symptoms. 68

    Negative Symptoms 69

    Disorganized Symptoms 70

    Cognitive Signs and Symptoms. 70

    Other Signs and Symptoms 71

    Diagnostic and Statistical Manual of Mental Disorders. 71

Course. 72

    Disability Caused by Schizophrenia 72

    Aggression and Suicide in People with Schizophrenia 72

Treatment. 73

    Antipsychotic Medications 73

    Psychosocial Treatments 74

**Engaging and Assessing Individuals with Schizophrenia and
    Related Disorders 76**

Chapter Wrap-Up. 78

Chapter 8: Mood Disorders: Major Depression and Bipolar Disorder   82

Introduction. 83
Common Signs and Symptoms of Major Depression. 83
Common Signs and Symptoms of Bipolar Disorder. 84
Other Mood Disorders. 85
    Dysthymic Disorder and Cyclothymic Disorder 85
    Mood Disorders Due to a General Medical Condition and Substance-Induced
       Mood Disorders. 85
Biopsychosocial Treatment of Mood Disorders. 86
    Biological Treatments. 86
    Psychological and Social Treatments. 87
Engaging and Assessing Individuals with Mood Disorders. 88
Conclusion 88
Chapter Wrap-Up. 89

Chapter 9: Substance Abuse and Dependence   92

Introduction. 93
An Overview of Specific Substances of Abuse 94
    Alcohol 94
    Amphetamines and Amphetamine-Like Substances 95
    Cannabis 96
    Cocaine 96
    Hallucinogens 97
    Inhalants 98
    Opiates. 98
    Phencyclidine and Related Substances 99
    Sedatives, Hypnotics, and Anxiolytics. 99
Treatment of Substance Abuse and Dependence 100
Comorbidity and Dual Diagnosis 101
Chapter Wrap-Up 102

Chapter 10: Delirium and Dementia   104

Introduction 104
What Is Delirium?. 105
    Delirium Due to a Medical Condition 106
    Delirium Related to Substance Use 106
Common Signs and Symptoms of Delirium 106
Course of Delirium 107
Treatment of Delirium 108
Dementia. 109
Alzheimer's and Non-Alzheimer's Types of Dementia 110
Common Signs and Symptoms of Dementia. 111
Course of Dementia 111
Treatment of Dementia. 112
Engaging and Assessing Individuals with Dementia 112
Chapter Wrap-Up. 114

Chapter 11: Responding to Children and Adolescents with Emotional and Behavioral Disorders   116

Introduction...117
Engaging Caregivers in Children's Mental Health Treatment...............117
Developmental Milestones 118
Self-injurious Behavior and Suicidal Ideation in Children 118
Aggressive and Disruptive Behavior in Children 120
Childhood Abuse and Neglect...121
Substance Use Disorders in Adolescents................................123
Conclusion 124
Chapter Wrap-Up 125

Chapter 12: Responding to Individuals with Developmental Disabilities   128

Introduction 129
What Are Developmental Disabilities?..................................129
Mental Retardation...132
Autism..133
How to Identify People with Developmental Disabilities
    in Emergencies..134
Communicating with People with Developmental Disabilities 135
Chapter Wrap-Up 137

Chapter 13: Anxiety Disorders   139

Introduction 140
Common Signs and Symptoms 140
    Panic Disorder..140
    Social Anxiety Disorder..141
    Obsessive-Compulsive Disorder 141
    Generalized Anxiety Disorder 142
    Post-traumatic Stress Disorder 142
Course of Anxiety Disorders 143
Treatment of Anxiety Disorders 144
Engaging and Assessing Individuals with Anxiety Disorders...............145
Chapter Wrap-Up 147

Chapter 14: Maladaptive Coping Skills, Personality Disorders, and Malingering   149

Introduction 150
Borderline Personality Disorder.......................................151
Antisocial Personality Disorder 152
Malingering..153
Engaging and Assessing Individuals with Personality Disorders............154
Chapter Wrap-Up 156

Chapter 15: De-escalation Techniques   160

Introduction..161
Cochran and Dupont's Continuum of Escalation..........................163
    Uncertainty...163
    Questioning...163
    Refusal...163
    Demanding...164
    Generalized Acting Out..164
    Specific Acting Out...164
    Recovery..164
    Rapport...165
    Cooperation...165
Levels of Crisis Complexity...166
    Low-Complexity Crisis...166
    Moderate-Complexity Crisis......................................166
    High-Complexity Crisis..167
How to De-escalate a Crisis Situation...............................167
    Listening...168
    Minimal Encouragers...168
    Reflecting/Mirroring..168
    Restating or Paraphrasing.......................................169
    Emotional Labeling..169
    "I" Statements..169
Putting It All Together...170
Conclusion..172
Chapter Wrap-Up...173

Chapter 16: Responding to Special Populations   175

Introduction..176
Responding to Homeless Persons with Mental Illnesses................176
Responding to People with Suicidal Thinking or Behavior.............179
Engaging and Assessing Individuals Who Are Paranoid or Aggressive........180
Conclusion..182
Chapter Wrap-Up...184

Chapter 17: A View of Law Enforcement– Consumer Interactions Through the Lens of Psychosis   186

Introduction..186
Cultural Competence...186
How Are We Different?...187
    Delusions...188
    Hallucinations..189

Heightened Sensitivity...190
Good Drugs and Bad Drugs..190
Cognitive Difficulties...191
**A Second Perspective on Dealing with a Person with
Schizophrenia in Crisis...191**
Chapter Wrap-Up 194

Chapter 18: Emergency Receiving Facilities and Other Emergency Resources   196

Introduction 197
Options to Obtain a Mental Health Assessment 197
Emergency Receiving Facilities.....................................197
Other Options...198
The Law Enforcement–Mental Health Interface 198
Management of Agitation in the Emergency Department 200
Weapons in Secure Areas...200
Arrests in the Emergency Department..............................201
Determining How Best to Obtain a Mental Health Assessment.............201
Dangerousness to Self or Others...................................202
Inability to Care for Oneself 202
Challenges and Frustrations..203
Conclusion 203
Chapter Wrap-Up..205

Chapter 19: Mental Health Resources and Levels of Care   207

Introduction...208
National-Level Resources...208
Local Crisis and Access Service Systems 210
Levels of Care 211
Secure Residential Inpatient Care 212
Nonsecure Residential Treatment 212
Intensively Managed Nonresidential Service.......................212
Intensive Outpatient Care..212
Outpatient Care...213
Recovery Maintenance and Health Management Services........213
Chapter Wrap-Up 214

Index   216

CONTRIBUTORS

Michael T. Compton, M.D., M.P.H.
Assistant Professor
Emory University School of Medicine
Department of Psychiatry and
  Behavioral Sciences
Atlanta, Georgia

Jocelyn Smith Cox, M.D.
Staff Psychiatrist
Cumberland Mental Health Services, Inc.
Bowling Green, Kentucky

David W. Covington, N.C.C., L.P.C., M.B.A.
Chief Operating Officer
Integrated Health Resources
Behavioral Health Link
Atlanta, Georgia

Barbara D'Orio, M.D., M.P.A.
Associate Professor
Emory University School of Medicine
Department of Psychiatry and
  Behavioral Sciences
Atlanta, Georgia

Glenn J. Egan, Ph.D.
Assistant Professor
Emory University School of Medicine
Department of Psychiatry and
  Behavioral Sciences
Atlanta, Georgia

Leesha Ellis-Cox, M.D.
Child and Adolescent Psychiatry Fellow
  and Community Psychiatry /
  Public Health Fellow
Emory University School of Medicine
Department of Psychiatry and
  Behavioral Sciences
Atlanta, Georgia

Frederick J. Frese, III, Ph.D.
Assistant Professor of Psychology in
  Clinical Psychiatry
Northeastern Ohio Universities College
  of Medicine
Akron, Ohio

Denise Garrett, M.S.W.
Fulton County Department of Health
  and Wellness
Office of Emergency Preparedness
Atlanta, Georgia

Milt Greek
Senior Systems Analyst
Ohio University
Athens, Ohio

Patrick J. Haggard, M.D.
Assistant Professor
Emory University School of Medicine
Department of Psychiatry and
  Behavioral Sciences
Atlanta, Georgia

Nzinga Ajabu Harrison, M.D.
General Psychiatry Resident
Emory University School of Medicine
Department of Psychiatry and
  Behavioral Sciences
Atlanta, Georgia

Nora Haynes, Ed.S.
President
National Alliance on Mental Illness (NAMI)
  of Georgia
Atlanta, Georgia

Karen M. Hochman, M.D.
Assistant Professor
Emory University School of Medicine
Department of Psychiatry and
  Behavioral Sciences
Atlanta, Georgia

Manjula Kallur, M.D.
Fellow in Geriatric Psychiatry
Emory University School of Medicine
Department of Psychiatry and
  Behavioral Sciences
Atlanta, Georgia

Raymond J. Kotwicki, M.D., M.P.H.
Assistant Professor
Emory University School of Medicine
Department of Psychiatry and
    Behavioral Sciences
Atlanta, Georgia

David J. Lushbaugh
Advisory Board Chair
Georgia Crisis Intervention Team Program
Atlanta, Georgia

Janet R. Oliva, Ph.D.
Inspector
Office of the Director
Georgia Bureau of Investigation
Atlanta, Georgia

Kevin J. Richards, Ph.D.
Forensic Psychologist
Northwest Georgia Regional Hospital
Adult Outpatient Forensic Services
Rome, Georgia

Carol M. Schall, Ph.D.
Director
Virginia Autism Resource Center at
    Grafton School
Richmond, Virginia

Ruth S. Shim, M.D.
Community Psychiatry/Public Health Fellow
Emory University School of Medicine
Department of Psychiatry and
    Behavioral Sciences
Atlanta, Georgia

Monica Taylor-Desir, M.D., M.P.H.
Staff Psychiatrist
Winslow Indian Health Center, Inc.
Winslow, Arizona

Keith Wood, Ph.D.
Associate Professor
Emory University School of Medicine
Department of Psychiatry and
    Behavioral Science
Atlanta, Georgia

ACKNOWLEDGEMENTS

We have been extremely impressed and delighted with the compassion and commitment of the large group of contributors to this book. They have dedicated considerable time and effort to writing chapters that we believe are particularly relevant to law enforcement officers and other public safety and criminal justice professionals. From the outset, we figured that more than 20 minds would be more effective and meaningful than just two. We are honored to have worked with talented contributors representing diverse perspectives, including counseling, criminal justice, psychiatry, psychology, and social work, as well as perspectives from family members and people living with major mental illnesses. We are indebted to a number of individuals who kindly volunteered to review chapters and provide advice—psychology and public health students, law enforcement officers, and others—including: Masuma Bahora, Victoria Chien, Elizabeth Gallu, Sonya Hanafi, Paul Michaud, Janet Oliva, Ken Riley, and Charles Westbrook. We are especially grateful to Lauren Franz and Jessica Rutland who provided assistance with formatting, writing vocabulary words and review questions, and compiling the various chapters during the last days and hours of our work on the book. Nadine Kaslow supported this effort from its inception, and gave guidance and encouragement during every step along the way, and Florrie Kaslow was very helpful in advising us on the administrative tasks of compiling and editing a book. At Jones and Bartlett Publishers, we are particularly appreciative of the kindness of Kimberly Brophy and Jennifer Kling. Most importantly, we are grateful to Kendrick Hogan and Todd Pouwels for their unending support and caring as we spent many hours on this endeavor.

Michael T. Compton & Raymond J. Kotwicki

Former First Lady, Mrs. Rosalynn Carter

De-stigmatizing mental illness has long been one of my foremost concerns. During our years in the White House, Jimmy and I worked to encourage people to talk about mental health and mental illness and to get mental health care when they needed it. I was proud to serve as honorary chair of the President's Commission on Mental Health, which resulted in passage of the Mental Health Systems Act of 1980.

Since leaving the White House, I have continued my work through the Carter Center Mental Health Program. Unfortunately today, despite the fact that mental illnesses now can be diagnosed and treated effectively, our nation's mental health system is in shambles. That was the conclusion of the 2004 President's New Freedom Commission on Mental Heath.

Today the largest "mental health" facility in our country is not a hospital or a state-run mental institution. Rather, America's largest mental health treatment facility is the Los Angeles County Jail. It is clear that people with mental illnesses are not receiving timely, appropriate mental health services to aid in their recovery. Many who may be symptomatic and untreated end up incarcerated, often for non-violent crimes and misdemeanors.

This problem has two causes: an inadequate mental health infrastructure and misplaced priorities of people who can help. Imagine if police officers and other first responders within a community could divert people with mental illnesses away from jail and toward treatment. What a tremendous difference that would make to countless individuals and their families. This is why, in addition to advocating for improved mental health services funding, training, and research, I think it is important to encourage the development of programs where first responders identify people in crises with mental illnesses and take them to treatment instead of jail. While police officers and other first responders are too busy to act as mental health providers, I am certain these well-intentioned professionals want the best care for individuals with mental illnesses they encounter in the community.

The State of Georgia has embraced one way to do this: Crisis Intervention Team (CIT) training. The Carter Center convened important stakeholders in the state several years ago to strategize methods to train police officers on how to best work with offenders with mental illnesses in the community. The Carter Center and I fully support CIT training and the idea that recovery from mental illnesses is most possible outside jails and prisons.

This publication, *Responding to Individuals with Mental Illnesses*, is one important tool to ensure that people with these illnesses can access necessary treatment. Drs. Compton and Kotwicki have compiled information about the signs and symptoms of mental illnesses, methods to de-escalate potentially volatile situations involving people who suffer from them, social circumstances that influence mental illnesses in the community, as well as consumers' own accounts of interactions with law enforcement officers. I believe in the social justice issues at the core of CIT training and recommend this handbook to CIT trainees and other law enforcement/public safety/criminal justice students.

Today we have mental health treatments that are accessible and effective. Unlike years ago when people with mental illnesses were warehoused in state mental institutions, individuals treated for severe mental illnesses like schizophrenia or bipolar disorder can lead happy, productive lives in recovery. However, these individuals do not recover from their illnesses in jails and prisons. Diversion of offenders with mental illnesses toward treatment outside jail will facilitate their recovery as well as strengthen the communities in which they live.

This text is designed to be a guide for recognizing mental illnesses and responding to people affected by these disorders, especially during times of crisis. Our goal is to describe the signs and symptoms of a variety of psychiatric illnesses, substance use disorders, and developmental disabilities, especially those that may be most frequently encountered by first responders and public safety officials, as well as professionals in the criminal justice system. Many of the chapters deal with specific categories of mental illnesses and provide basic skills to enhance interactions with people with these disorders who may be facing stressful situations. This is not a comprehensive textbook about psychiatric disorders, but rather a practical guide that aims to enhance knowledge and skills for non-mental health professionals who interact with individuals with such illnesses.

The intended audience for this text is relatively broad, but generally falls into two categories. First, the book is written primarily for public safety officials, including law enforcement officers, fire fighters, security agents, and emergency medical personnel. Second, this text may also be very useful for criminal justice professionals, such as corrections officers, probation and parole officers, attorneys, and judges. Given the complex interface between the criminal justice field and the mental health professions—especially as it concerns people with serious mental illnesses—people working in the public safety and criminal justice fields will benefit from specialized knowledge about mental illnesses.

The inspiration for this book arose from several sources. First, as community psychiatrists, we work with socially disadvantaged people with severe and persistent mental illnesses, and we have observed that nearly all of our patients have had significant interactions with both public safety officials and criminal justice professionals. The outcomes of these interactions are often linked to the extent of knowledge that the public safety officials and criminal justice professionals have about mental illnesses. We believe that the lives of our patients, and patients with serious mental illnesses across the country, can be improved by enhancing knowledge and strengthening collaborations between first responders/criminal justice professionals and mental health professionals. Thus, this book is primarily inspired by the complex and often challenging lives of our patients, especially our patients at Grady Health System in downtown Atlanta, Georgia. Second, we have been invigorated by a number of compassionate family members of people with serious mental illnesses. The Georgia chapter of the National Alliance on Mental Illness (NAMI) has been a particularly strong advocate for training law enforcement officers about mental illnesses, reducing stigma toward those with mental illnesses, and diverting their loved ones from incarceration to treatment. Several of these family members have been an integral part of the development of this book, and have contributed to the writing of it. Third, having been involved in Georgia's Crisis Intervention Team (CIT) training program, we have witnessed the great interest in learning more about mental illnesses by many of the police officers that we have had in our classes. We salute these officers who want to know more about mental illnesses and how to help people living with these disorders who are in crisis. Many of these officers have a true compassion, and indeed a tender side, and we hope that this text will enhance their knowledge and skills so they can embrace their call to be informed and caring public safety officials who promote recovery for people with major mental illnesses. The remarkable attendance at the First National CIT Conference in Columbus, Ohio in 2005, and the Second National CIT Conference in

Orlando, Florida in 2006 testifies to the broad and growing interest in mental health from the public safety and criminal justice fields.

The book is divided into three sections. Part I, *Recognizing the Need for an Informed Public Safety / Criminal Justice Community*, provides a foundation for the subsequent two parts by introducing mental illnesses and establishing reasons why public safety and criminal justice professionals need to know about mental illnesses. In the first chapter, we give a brief introduction to the prevalence of mental illnesses in the United States and the social consequences of these illnesses. We also present the myth of dangerousness and violence, as well as the broader problem of stigma, which contributes to the high rates of untreated mental illnesses and the unfairness that society continues to heap upon people who are innocently affected by serious mental illnesses. The second chapter, by Dr. Keith Wood and Dr. Raymond Kotwicki, provides a community mental health perspective on the problem of criminalization, or the excessive involvement in the criminal justice system of people with serious mental illnesses. The next chapter, by Dr. Glenn Egan, presents a discussion of deinstitutionalization, factors contributing to the increase in incarceration of people with mental illnesses, and mental health services provided in some detention facilities. Chapter 4 describes one very important approach for collaborations between public safety, criminal justice, and mental health professionals—the Memphis model of Crisis Intervention Team (CIT) training. This chapter was written by several leaders of Georgia's CIT program, including Dr. Janet Oliva, Ms. Nora Haynes, Mr. David Covington, Mr. David Lushbaugh, and Dr. Michael Compton. CIT is the leading model for providing specialized training to law enforcement officers, and is being implemented in localities across the country. The chapter that follows, by Dr. Karen Hochman, provides a discussion of other important models of collaboration between public safety/criminal justice and mental health, including mobile crisis units and innovative forensic assertive community treatment programs.

Part II, *Understanding Mental Illnesses*, gives detailed information on symptoms and modern treatment approaches for a number of psychiatric illnesses, substance use disorders, and developmental disabilities. The chapters of this section contain extensive advice about how to respond to and interact with people with specific disorders, especially during times of crisis. In Chapter 6, Dr. Monica Taylor-Desir defines and discusses the importance of the terms signs, symptoms, syndromes, and diagnoses. This chapter serves as a foundation for understanding the diseases described in the subsequent chapters of Part II. Chapter 7 focuses on schizophrenia, one of the most severe and oftentimes disabling psychiatric illnesses. Though this illness is relatively rare, it is one that is commonly encountered by first responders dealing with mental health crisis situations. Chapter 8, by Dr. Nzinga Ajabu Harrison, provides information on the major mood disorders—major depression and bipolar disorder. Dr. Jocelyn Smith Cox provides an overview of a number of substances of abuse in the following chapter, and describes signs and symptoms commonly encountered during intoxication and withdrawal from a variety of drugs. Delirium and dementia—disorders affecting memory and orientation—are discussed by Dr. Manjula Kallur and Dr. Raymond Kotwicki in Chapter 10. Emotional and behavioral disorders of childhood and adolescence—including attention-deficit/hyperactivity disorder, oppositional defiant disorder, and conduct disorder—are described by Dr. Leesha Ellis-Cox in the next chapter. Chapter 12 focuses on developmental disabilities, especially mental retardation and autistic disorder. In that chapter Dr. Carol Schall gives many useful, practical tips for interacting with people with these disabilities. The major anxiety disorders—including panic disorder, social anxiety disorder, obsessive-compulsive disorder, generalized anxiety disorder, and post-traumatic stress disorders—are discussed in Chapter 13, by Dr. Ruth Shim. Next, Dr. Patrick Haggard describes maladaptive coping strategies and personality disorder. He particularly focuses on borderline personality disorder, antisocial personality disorder, and malingering.

Part III, *Responding with Enhanced Knowledge and Skills*, offers detailed information on de-escalation techniques and a number of other important issues that will allow public safety and criminal justice professionals to connect people affected by serious mental illnesses to appropriate treatment services. In Chapter 15, Dr. Kevin Richards presents an important discussion of de-escalation techniques. This chapter describes Cochran and Dupont's continuum of escalation, the levels of complexity of crisis incidents, and how to de-escalate a crisis situation. The next chapter provides information on responding to several special populations, including people who are homeless, people with suicidal thinking or behavior, and people who are paranoid and/or aggressive. In Chapter 17, Dr. Frederick Frese and Mr. Milt Greek offer thoughtful first-person accounts of interactions between individuals experiencing psychotic symptoms and law enforcement officers. The following chapter, by Dr. Barbara D'Orio and Ms. Denise Garrett describe emergency receiving facilities that law enforcement officers may frequently utilize when assisting people with mental illnesses, as well as commonly encountered scenarios during emergency evaluations. Chapter 19, by Mr. David Covington provides information on a number of national and local crisis resources. This chapter also presents the various levels of care with which individuals with mental illnesses may be engaged.

Throughout the book, we sometimes refer to people with mental illnesses as *patients*. This is a traditional term used by health professionals for people who are receiving medical or psychiatric care. In other instances, we use the terms *consumers* or *clients*. This terminology is increasingly common as health professionals recognize that patients are receiving services, have rights and autonomy, and are equal partners in medical decision-making. In other places, the term *subjects* may be used to refer to someone who is the focus of an interaction under discussion. Generally, and even in the book's title, we use the term *individuals with mental illnesses* or *people with mental illnesses*, because this person-first terminology seeks to minimize the use of potentially stigmatizing words and phrases such as "mentally ill person," "bipolar patient," or "schizophrenic."

Concepts are often best illustrated through stories. Many of the case vignettes that are presented in the various chapters relate to interactions, particularly those between individuals with mental illnesses and law enforcement officers. While this may have been convenient for writing the vignettes, the intended audience includes not only police officers, but other public safety officials and criminal justice professionals. Many of the chapters begin with or incorporate case vignettes to illustrate the illnesses under discussion and the special issues involved when interacting with people with the various mental illnesses. Chapters end by highlighting important concepts, defining vocabulary words to underscore specific important words and terms, and presenting a series of questions for review and discussion.

One may make the argument that efforts to decriminalize mental illnesses and people who behave inappropriately as a result of mental illnesses should be focused on the mental health system and not the criminal justice system. While we agree that the mental health system holds primary responsibility for treating and preventing individuals with mental illnesses from decompensating in the community, we also acknowledge that the overburdened, under-funded, and fragmented mental health system in America may not have the capabilities to face this challenge alone. Involving law enforcement officers, other public safety officials, and criminal justice professionals in the mental health system's goal of decriminalizing mental illnesses is of utmost importance. We believe that just as jails and prisons have become *de facto* mental health facilities, so must criminal justice and law enforcement officials become *de facto* mental health agents. This evolving role should not supplant the involvement of mental health professionals or advocates, nor should such collaborations threaten other initiatives—from within the mental health system, the public policy arena, or even social justice organizations— to divert people with mental illnesses away from incarceration and into appropriate, collaborative, recovery-oriented treatment.

It is our sincere hope that this book will serve to enhance knowledge and skills of our nation's highly valued public safety and criminal justice professionals. We hope that partnerships between these officials and mental health professionals will continue. Ultimately, it is our hope that the lives of people affected by psychiatric illnesses, substance use disorders, and developmental disabilities, will be improved, and that the promising goals of achieving recovery are promoted.

Michael T. Compton & Raymond J. Kotwicki

Recognizing the Need

1 **The Myths of Mental Illness**
Raymond J. Kotwicki, M.D., M.P.H.
Michael T. Compton, M.D., M.P.H.

2 **Criminalization of Mental Illnesses**
Keith Wood, Ph.D.
Raymond J. Kotwicki, M.D., M.P.H.

3 **Mental Health Care in Detention**
Glenn J. Egan, Ph.D.

4 **Crisis Intervention Team (CIT) Programs**
Janet R. Oliva, Ph.D.
Nora Haynes, Ed.S.
David W. Covington, N.C.C., L.P.C., M.B.A.
David J. Lushbaugh
Michael T. Compton, M.D., M.P.H.

5 **Collaborations Between Mental Health
and Law Enforcement**
Karen M. Hochman, M.D.

The Myths of Mental Illness

Case Vignette: Keith

Keith was diagnosed with schizophrenia at 19 years of age. In conjunction with his supportive parents and a case manager from the local peer support center, Keith learned masonry at a trade school, obtained Medicaid and mental healthcare services, applied for Supplemental Security Income (which provided him with approximately $500 per month), and found a one-room apartment in a Section 8 housing high-rise apartment complex. Keith felt good about his life. One day, on his way home from registering to vote in the next presidential election, he realized that while he had brought money for bus fare to the registration office, he had forgotten to bring the return fare. Keith thought he could scrape together the fare through panhandling and began asking passers-by for change to accumulate enough money for his return trip home.

The city in which Keith lives has a panhandling ordinance within its downtown district, in an effort to limit aggressive panhandling that may frighten away visitors and hurt the local economy. Officer Johnson witnessed Keith's behavior and arrested him for this misdemeanor. Keith was taken to the city jail, where he could not post bail. He was kept in jail for 34 days awaiting the appointment of a public defender so that his case could be heard by a judge. He could not afford a private attorney with his fixed and very limited income. Keith did not recall the name of his antipsychotic medication, so he could not inform the psychiatrist at the detention center, and he was not given his medication for the month. Moreover, Keith's Medicaid and Social Security income were discontinued due to federal regulations. Keith's employer needed help immediately; because Keith was unavailable, the contractor hired a replacement mason. Keith wanted to vote for his choice for the presidential race, but because he lacked identification and was incarcerated during the election, Keith was not allowed to cast his vote in the election.

After Keith was finally released from jail, he returned to his apartment only to learn that he was being evicted for failure to pay rent. Paranoid, disorganized, off his medications, now homeless, disconnected from his family and supports, and without mental health care and income, Keith decided to stay at the downtown overflow shelter. There he met Les, the resident cocaine dealer and pimp. Keith began using crack as a way to attempt to cope with his hallucinations and paranoia. Eventually, he started "turning tricks" to earn drug money and ultimately he contracted human immunodeficiency virus (HIV).

■ Introduction

Mental illnesses are biological diseases affecting the brain that cause a variety of symptoms and affect one's feelings, thinking, and behaviors. Mental health professionals make a diagnosis of a mental illness based on the specific symptoms experienced, the length of time for which they have been present, and the ways in which they vary over time. Presently, mental health professionals rely on the *Diagnostic and Statistical Manual of Mental Disorders,* fourth edition (American Psychiatric Association, 2000), for a complete description of all of the various mental illnesses that affect children and teenagers, adults, and the elderly. Although a complete review of all mental illnesses is beyond the scope of this chapter, some of the disorders that law enforcement officers and other public safety and criminal justice professionals are likely to encounter are briefly mentioned here and then described in detail in later chapters. These and some other illnesses are shown in **Table 1.1.**

For the purposes of this overview, mental illnesses can be simplified and lumped into eight broad categories:

1. Disorders usually first diagnosed in infancy, childhood, and adolescence
2. Disorders mostly affecting the elderly
3. Substance use disorders
4. Schizophrenia and other psychotic disorders
5. Mood disorders, including major depression and bipolar disorder
6. Anxiety disorders
7. Personality disorders
8. A large group of miscellaneous mental illnesses

The disorders usually first diagnosed in children and teenagers include illnesses such as autistic disorder, learning disorders, attention-deficit/hyperactivity disorder, and conduct disorder. Disorders that first begin in later life include Alzheimer's disease and other forms of dementia.

Substance use disorders are classified as either abuse or dependence, with the latter being roughly equivalent to the popular term "addiction." Schizophrenia and related disorders are a group of illnesses that lead to a variety of symptoms, including delusions and hallucinations; these disorders are often quite disabling.

Table 1.1 Broad Categories of Mental Disorders and Some Examples in Each Category	
Disorders Usually First Diagnosed in Infancy, Childhood, and Adolescence Autistic disorder Learning disorders Attention-deficit/hyperactivity disorder Conduct disorder	**Mood Disorders** Major depressive disorder Bipolar disorder
	Anxiety Disorders Panic disorder Social anxiety disorder Obsessive-compulsive disorder Post-traumatic stress disorder
Disorders That Begin in Later Life Alzheimer's disease Dementia associated with Parkinson's disease	
	Personality Disorders Paranoid personality disorder Antisocial personality disorder Borderline personality disorder
Substance Use Disorders Alcohol abuse and dependence Marijuana abuse and dependence Cocaine abuse and dependence	
Schizophrenia and Other Psychotic Disorders Schizophrenia Schizoaffective disorder	

Mood disorders primarily affect one's emotional state. They include several varieties of depression and bipolar disorder. Bipolar disorder can be thought of as the opposite of depression. It is characterized by episodes of mania in which the mood is too elevated and the energy level is too high.

A number of anxiety disorders are distinguished, including panic disorder, social anxiety disorder, obsessive-compulsive disorder, and post-traumatic stress disorder. Personality disorders can be thought of as long-term difficulties in relating to other people due to an over-reliance on problematic coping strategies. Finally, the large group of other disorders (which we consider "miscellaneous" here because they are less commonly encountered by public safety and criminal justice professionals) includes illnesses such as dissociative disorders, sleep disorders, and eating disorders.

Mental illnesses also can be classified into three groups:

- **Psychiatric illnesses** include most of the previously mentioned disorders, such as schizophrenia, bipolar disorder, post-traumatic stress disorder, and personality disorders.
- **Addictive diseases**, also called substance use disorders, include abuse of or dependence on a number of drugs.
- **Developmental disabilities** encompass mental retardation and serious emotional disturbances present from a very early age, such as autism.

Many psychiatric illnesses and addictive disorders first appear in the mid-teens to late twenties. Research conducted in recent decades suggests that most psychiatric illnesses result from both genetic and environmental factors, such as early life experiences. Currently, most of these illnesses can be effectively treated with a variety of mental health treatments, including both medications and psychosocial treatments (i.e., counseling, educational programs, and vocational rehabilitation). Because these treatments rarely bring about a complete cure, the model currently embraced by the mental health community is one of recovery.

> *Recovery* means a process in which people affected by mental illnesses are able to participate as fully as possible in their communities. Mental health professionals focus on recovery by working collaboratively with patients to assist them in regaining the highest level of functioning and quality of life possible, based on the patient's own life goals.

Recovery means a process in which people affected by mental illnesses are able to participate as fully as possible in their communities. Mental health professionals focus on recovery by working collaboratively with patients to assist them in regaining the highest level of functioning and quality of life possible, based on the patient's own life goals. Several different types of **mental health professionals** work with people with mental illnesses, including mental health associates or psychiatric technicians, pastoral counselors, marital and family therapists, professional counselors, case managers, addiction counselors, social workers, psychiatric nurses, psychologists, and psychiatrists.

Several major health authorities, including the Centers for Disease Control and Prevention (CDC), have stated that mental health is integral to overall health and well-being and should be accorded the same urgency as physical health. Although mental health treatments are effective, they are greatly underused—the majority of people with a mental illness or addictive disorder do not receive treatment. The CDC suggests that a number of public health challenges exist with regard to mental illnesses:

- Identifying risk factors for these disorders
- Increasing awareness about these disorders and the treatments for them
- Eliminating stigma about mental illnesses and their treatments
- Eliminating **health disparities**, which occur when some people (such as the poor and ethnic minorities) do not have equal access to treatments compared to other groups
- Improving access to mental health services

In its 2003 report to the U.S. President, the New Freedom Commission on Mental Health also emphasized these issues as well as ongoing problems with the current mental health treatment system, which is very complex and fragmented.

In recent years, it has been increasingly recognized that mental illnesses and addictive disorders are more costly and cause more disability (such as time off work, decreased productivity, and interference with life activities) than most medical conditions. In fact, of the 10 leading causes of disability in developed countries (including the United States), six are mental illnesses or addictive disorders (depression, alcohol use, schizophrenia, bipolar disorder, drug use, and obsessive-compulsive disorder). Another of the 10 leading causes of disability is self-inflicted injuries, which are usually related to the presence of a mental illness, such as major depression, bipolar disorder, or borderline personality disorder.

■ The Prevalence of Mental Illnesses and Addictive Disorders in the United States

Unfortunately, mental illnesses and addictive disorders are very common. Two large-scale research studies were conducted in the 1980s and the 1990s—the Epidemiologic Catchment Area study and the National Comorbidity Survey—in an effort to discover exactly how common these disorders are in the United States. These studies surveyed thousands of people to determine the **prevalence** of these disorders—that is, the percentages of people affected by each condition. Other studies have sought to determine how common mental illnesses are in children and teenagers and in the elderly population. Some of the statistics turned up by this research are alarming. In particular, nearly 50% of all people will experience a mental illness or addictive disorder at some point during their lives.

> Nearly 50% of all people will experience a mental illness or addictive disorder at some point during their lives.

Some of the most common illnesses are major depression and anxiety disorders (**Table 1.2**). Approximately 17% of the U.S. population will experience an episode of major depression at some time during their lives, and this percentage is even higher for women. Whereas men have a lifetime prevalence of major depression of about 12%, more than one in five women (21%) will experience an episode of major depression. Social phobia, which is also called *social anxiety disorder*, occurs in approximately 13% of people at some point over the course of a lifetime, and post-traumatic stress disorder occurs in nearly 8%. In general, women are more likely than men to develop depression or an anxiety disorder. The more severe disorders are less common. For example, bipolar disorder is found in less than 2% of people and schizophrenia in about 1%. Men and women are affected by bipolar disorder and schizophrenia about equally.

In children and teenagers, psychiatric disorders are also very common: In any given 3- to 6-month period, one in four children will have a psychiatric disorder (Table 1.2). *Disruptive behavior disorders,* such as oppositional defiant disorder, attention-deficit/ hyperactivity disorder, and conduct disorder, occur more frequently in boys than in girls.

Table 1.2	Approximate Lifetime Prevalences of Select Mental Illnesses and Addictive Disorders
Children and Teenagers	**Adults**
Major depression: 4.6%	Major depression: 17.0%
Substance use disorders: 4.5%	Alcohol abuse: 9.4%
Oppositional defiant disorder: 3.6%	Alcohol dependence: 14.1%
Conduct disorder: 3.5%	Social anxiety disorder: 13.3%
Attention-deficit/hyperactivity disorder: 2.7%	Post-traumatic stress disorder: 7.6%
Separation anxiety disorder: 2.4%	Drug abuse: 4.4%
	Drug dependence: 7.5%
	Bipolar disorder: 1.6%
	Schizophrenia: 1.0%

In older adults and the elderly, mental illnesses and addictive disorders tend to be less common than in the young and persons in middle adulthood. However, major depression continues to be common even in later life, and the prevalences of diseases causing dementia, such as Alzheimer's disease, increase with advancing age. Furthermore, in the United States, suicide rates are highest among white men older than age 65 years, as compared to the rates in any other demographic group.

Alcohol and drug abuse and dependence are also quite common, and their prevalences peak in the late teens and young adulthood. Approximately 24% of people will experience alcohol abuse or dependence at some point in their lifetime, and 12% will develop drug abuse or dependence involving marijuana, cocaine, heroin, or other illegal drugs. Men are more likely than women to have addictive disorders. Rates of substance abuse are higher among individuals with lower educational levels, lower income, and unemployment, and in those with limited social supports. Based on results of the 2000 National Household Survey on Drug Abuse, 14.5 million Americans aged 12 years and older have a substance use disorder, or approximately 6.5% of the population. About 12 million Americans have alcohol abuse or dependence, 3 million have marijuana abuse or dependence, 1 million abuse or are dependent on prescribed addictive medicines, and nearly 1 million have cocaine abuse or dependence.

One of the major findings of the large-scale epidemiologic research studies relates to **comorbidity**—a problem in which two or more disorders occur together in the same person at the same time. For example, many people with major depression also have an anxiety disorder such as panic disorder, generalized anxiety disorder, or post-traumatic stress disorder. Many people with bipolar disorder or schizophrenia also have a substance use disorder.

Oftentimes, one substance use disorder is accompanied by another. Comorbidity also can involve a mental disorder and a medical disease. In such a case, the mental illness often negatively influences the medical disease and leads to poorer outcomes. Likewise, the medical disease can have negative effects on the mental illness.

Another important issue discovered in the large-scale studies is the fact that only one-third of people who had a mental disorder during the past year received any sort of professional treatment. Some of the reasons underlying this phenomenon include the belief that "I don't have a problem," the desire to try to solve the problem on one's own, the belief that the problem will improve by itself, financial or situational barriers to receiving treatment, and the myth that treatments are not effective. Because of the unacceptably low rates of treatment in people who have mental illnesses and addictive disorders, interventions are needed to improve mental health awareness and treatment-seeking in the general population.

> Because of the unacceptably low rates of treatment in people who have mental illnesses and addictive disorders, interventions are needed to improve mental health awareness and treatment-seeking in the general population.

■ Social Consequences of Untreated Serious Mental Illnesses

In the absence of appropriate, timely mental health treatment, individuals with mental illnesses often face a major decline in their social functioning and quality of life. Symptoms of mental illnesses may appear odd to other people, preventing formation of supportive friendships and relationships. Relationship difficulties contribute to limited social support during times of stress. Limited social support, in turn, brings about other serious life problems. People with untreated mental illnesses may become socially isolated, relying exclusively on their own strengths to function in society. Of course, everyone requires help from others at times. People with **serious mental illnesses** (psychiatric illnesses that cause functional impairment that substantially interferes with major life activities) may require help more often than others. Research suggests that one of the best indicators of successful work, personal fulfillment, and quality of life is the amount of social support a person enjoys. Individuals with untreated mental illnesses, who face social isolation and must rely on themselves, become vulnerable to further "social drift" into despair, poverty, and perhaps crime.

Persons with untreated serious mental illnesses who face life alone tend not to do very well. Individuals with psychotic or mood symptoms may have difficulties attending school or making it to work every day. Without help from family and friends, such people likely will not thrive in these tasks. The resultant unemployment and limited education perpetuate the social isolation frequently experienced by people with untreated serious mental illnesses. Lack of income or job opportunities limits the ability of these people to break out of the cycle of low educational attainment, poverty, and social isolation.

When incarceration is added to this mix, social outcomes for people with untreated serious mental illnesses plummet. Being in jail for a month or longer often leads to loss of entitlements such as Medicaid, general assistance, food stamps, and perhaps even Social Security income benefits. Unpaid rent and other bills during the period of incarceration similarly can result in eviction, poor credit, or repossession of belongings. In sum, the combination of the social isolation that results from untreated serious mental illnesses and incarceration positions individuals for an uphill battle in life.

In the case vignette at the beginning of this chapter, Keith experiences many of these losses. He goes off his medication and begins experiencing psychotic symptoms that were controlled prior to his arrest. He loses his job, his housing, and his social entitlements because of his incarceration. Keith even loses his right to participate in an election in which he could have voted for candidates who might have changed the policies that led to his hardships. Most significantly, Keith became disconnected from the friends and other social supports that were important for his recovery from his mental illness. This led him to reach out to Les, who then exploited Keith, ultimately leading to his contracting HIV. Untreated serious mental illnesses affect most aspects of one's life, including relationships, economics, health care, civil liberties, entitlements, and length and quality of life. Researchers estimate that people with the most serious mental illnesses have significantly more physical illnesses than other people, and they die on average 10 years before similar groups of people without mental illnesses.

> Researchers estimate that people with the most serious mental illnesses have significantly more physical illnesses than other people, and they die on average 10 years before similar groups of people without mental illnesses.

■ The Myth of Dangerousness and Violence in People with Severe Mental Illnesses

Despite the frequent arrests of people with serious mental illnesses, it is clear that most major crimes are committed by people without mental illnesses, and most people with mental illnesses do not commit crimes. In his 1999 Surgeon General's Report, Dr. David Satcher unequivocally concluded that there is no more risk of violence from someone with a mental illness than from any general member of our society. In fact, many people with severe mental illnesses are too disorganized or fearful to perpetrate crimes. Nevertheless, many people assume that individuals with symptoms of mental illnesses who act strangely or who think unusually are dangerous. Unknown ideas or unusual characteristics that may not be understood tend to be misinterpreted as threats.

Mental health professionals who work with individuals with severe mental illnesses commonly observe that such people are amazingly resilient and clever. For most people who are used to having stable incomes and creature comforts, it would be nearly impossible to survive even one night on the streets with serious psychiatric symptoms, such as hearing voices (hallucinations) or being convinced of a frightening government plot (a delusion). Yet some individuals with untreated serious mental illnesses accomplish this daily. Within the context of having limited resources and symptoms of a mental illness, it is remarkable how well many people with serious mental illnesses have adapted to their environment. Urinating in an abandoned lot when there are no public toilets available, performing songs for money on the streets next to tourist attractions, and even using substances to avoid the pain and anxiety of derogatory hallucinations or reexperiencing past traumas make a great deal of practical sense given the contexts of living with limited supports and symptoms of serious mental illnesses. Although these behaviors might be judged by some as oppositional, they often serve as practical solutions given the experiences of some people with untreated severe mental illnesses.

Are such behaviors in the face of harsh circumstances crimes? Strict interpretation of local, state, and federal policies often suggests that they are. In truth, given the contexts of the lives of people with untreated severe mental illnesses whose intent is to do the best they can, such actions may actually represent **resilience**, not criminal intentions. While people with mental illnesses are extremely overrepresented in U.S. jails and prisons, this trend does not indicate that they are more dangerous or aggressive. Rather, such an overrepresentation exists because our social policies and priorities force certain individuals to act civilly disobedient to survive. People with untreated severe mental illnesses and limited resources interact more frequently with the penal system not because they are more dangerous or malicious than other individuals, but because they have unmet needs.

> People with untreated severe mental illnesses and limited resources interact more frequently with the penal system not because they are more dangerous or malicious than other individuals, but because they have unmet needs.

■ The Problem of Stigma

In addition to explicit policies and laws that make life tougher for people with untreated severe mental illnesses, stigma often further limits possibilities. The term **stigma**, which refers to an attribute that is "deeply discrediting," was originally used to describe "bodily signs designed to expose something unusual and bad about the moral status of the signifier" (Goffman, 1963). Today, stigmatizing characteristics of mental illnesses may be less visually apparent, but most commonly consist of personal, psychological, and social attributes that lead to prejudice and discrimination.

Mental illnesses are among the most highly stigmatized conditions, and numerous studies have revealed negative views toward both psychiatric disorders and the people who suffer from them (Wahl, 1999). The attachment of stigma to people with mental illnesses affects both the public and the individual, resulting in stereotypes and unfair attitudes and actions. Further, stigma harms the self-esteem of many people who have serious mental illnesses (Link, Struening, Neese-Todd, Asmussen, & Phelan, 2001).

On a widespread level, stigma leads to loss of opportunities, difficulties in the workplace and the criminal justice system, and disparities in access to health care (Corrigan, Markowitz, & Watson, 2004; Corrigan & Kleinlein, 2005). Recent public attention has focused on how this stigma affects those seeking mental health treatment. The 1999 Surgeon General's report on mental mealth (U.S. Department of Health and Human Services, 1999) explains that stigma "deprives people of their dignity and interferes with their full participation in society."

In addition, the U.S. President's New Freedom Commission on Mental Health (U.S. Department of Health and Human Services, 2003) discusses the necessity of reducing the stigma associated with mental illnesses. This goal is especially urgent given that myths suggesting that individuals with mental illnesses are violent or frightening have increased—rather than decreased—in recent decades (Phelan, Link, Stueve, & Pescosolido, 2000). Knowing that someone has a mental illness suggests to many people that such individuals are dangerous; unconnected with reality; and unable to work, love, enjoy life, have sex, or even think for themselves. These stereotypes are inaccurate. Nevertheless, the stigma associated with mental illnesses causes some people to form opinions about the worth and capabilities of individuals who have mental illnesses based on a diagnosis of a brain disease rather than on their characters.

> The stigma associated with mental illnesses causes some people to form opinions about the worth and capabilities of individuals who have mental illnesses based on a diagnosis of a brain disease rather than the content of their characters.

Case Vignette: Tony

Tony is a 44-year-old homeless man with schizoaffective disorder. One winter morning, in an underground subway station in a large, bustling city, several people notified a subway attendant that this man was both asking for money and stating that he had a bomb in his bags. The transportation authority's police department was called, and an officer was dispatched. This particular officer had an uncle with schizophrenia and also had been through a training program on responding to people with mental illnesses.

Upon arrival, the officer observed that Tony was clearly agitated, loud, and delusional. Tony did not appear to be dangerous, however, and it was very doubtful that he actually had a bomb in his bags, which from a distance appeared to contain only scraps of clothing and newspapers. After some perseverance, the officer was able to engage Tony in a conversation about how cold it was outside and how several people had been frightened earlier by his loud and threatening statements. Although charges could have been pressed (such as panhandling, loitering, and making terroristic threats), the officer was able to calm Tony and safely transport him to a mental health/social services assistance center. Although Tony might be unlikely to follow treatment recommendations due to the severity of his illness and social deterioration, in this instance reconnection with helping agencies seemed more appropriate to the officer than yet another incarceration.

■ Conclusion

Individuals with serious mental illnesses are disproportionately represented in U.S. jails and prisons. While a significant proportion of people will experience a mental illness during their lifetime, people with mental illnesses generally pose no increased risk of danger to others in society. Public policies that do not help people with mental illnesses succeed in life coupled with the stigma attached to mental illnesses may prompt people who could do well with mental health treatment from seeking such care. Untreated severe mental illnesses may lead to a downward spiral in functioning, social support, and quality of living that may prompt what appear to be inappropriate or even misdemeanor behaviors. Such behaviors may lead to incarcerations that further limit possibilities for success in the future. First responders who understand the myth of dangerousness of people with severe mental illnesses and who choose to reject the stigma associated with mental illnesses can dramatically affect the futures of such people and promote social justice rooted in knowledge and compassion.

> First responders who understand the myth of dangerousness of people with severe mental illnesses and who choose to reject the stigma associated with mental illnesses can dramatically affect the futures of such people and promote social justice rooted in knowledge and compassion.

Chapter Wrap-Up

- Most mental illnesses and addictive disorders can be effectively treated with a variety of mental health therapies, including both medications and psychosocial treatments. Recovery means a process in which people affected by mental illnesses are able to participate as fully as possible in their communities. Mental health professionals focus on recovery by working collaboratively with patients to assist them in regaining the highest level of functioning and quality of life possible, based on the patient's own life goals.

- Major public health challenges related to mental illnesses include eliminating the stigma associated with mental illnesses, increasing awareness about these disorders and their treatments, and improving access to effective treatments.

- Mental illnesses and addictive disorders are very common, especially depression, anxiety disorders, and alcohol abuse and dependence. Nearly 50% of all people in the United States will experience a mental illness or addictive disorder at some point. Research suggests that only one-third of people who have a mental disorder actually receive any sort of professional treatment.

- People with severe mental illnesses typically have significantly more physical illnesses than other people, and they die on average 10 years before similar groups of people without mental illnesses.

- People with untreated mental illnesses and limited resources interact more frequently with the criminal justice system not because they are inherently more dangerous or malicious, but because they have unmet needs that may cause them to commit misdemeanor "quality of life crimes" or other minor infractions.

- The stigma associated with mental illnesses causes some people to form opinions about the worth and capabilities of individuals who have mental illnesses based on their psychiatric diagnoses rather than the content of their characters. Consciously rejecting the stigma that has been attached to mental illnesses is essential to fair treatment of all citizens.

- First responders who understand the myth of dangerousness of people with severe mental illnesses and who choose to reject the stigma associated with mental illnesses can dramatically affect the futures of such people and promote social justice rooted in knowledge and compassion.

Vital Vocabulary

addictive diseases: also called substance use disorders; disorders characterized by psychosocial impairment due to abuse of or dependence on addictive substances (alcohol or drugs)

comorbidity: a situation in which two or more disorders occur together in the same person at the same time

developmental disabilities: mental impairments that affect a person's abilities to think, communicate, interact with others, remember facts and details, and take care of oneself; all developmental disabilities, such as mental retardation and autistic disorder, appear before the age of 18 and remain with the person throughout his or her life

health disparities: when people, such as the poor and ethnic minorities, do not have equal access to treatments compared to other groups

mental health professionals: people who work with individuals with mental illnesses, including mental health associates or psychiatric technicians, pastoral counselors, marital and family therapists, professional counselors, case managers, addiction counselors, social workers, psychiatric nurses, psychologists, and psychiatrists

prevalence: the percentage of people affected by a condition

psychiatric illnesses: mental disorders such as schizophrenia, bipolar disorder, posttraumatic stress disorder, and personality disorders

recovery: the process in which people are able to live, work, learn, and participate fully in their communities, living fulfilling lives despite a disability

resilience: personal and community qualities that allow one to rebound from difficult situations, trauma, tragedy, or other stress, and to go on with life with a sense of mastery and hope

serious mental illnesses: psychiatric illnesses that cause functional impairment that substantially interferes with major life activities

stigma: negative attitudes and beliefs that cause the general public to fear, reject, avoid, or discriminate against people with mental illnesses

Questions for Review and Discussion

1. What are some of the broad categories of mental illness?
2. What are some of the public health challenges with regard to mental illnesses?
3. What factors can affect the future of a person with a mental illnesses?
4. How does stigma generally affect the life of an individual with a mental illness?

Resources

American Psychiatric Association. *Diagnostic and statistical manual of mental disorders* (4th ed). Washington, DC: American Psychiatric Association, 2000.

Corrigan PW, Kleinlein P. The impact of mental illness stigma. In: Corrigan P (Ed.). *On the stigma of mental illness: practical strategies for research and social change.* Washington, DC: American Psychological Association, 2005.

Corrigan PW, Markowitz FE, Watson AC. Structural levels of mental illness stigma and discrimination. *Schizophr Bull* 2004;30:481–491.

Goffman E. *Stigma: notes on the management of spoiled identity.* Englewood Cliffs, NJ: Prentice-Hall, 1963.

Link BG, Struening EL, Neese-Todd S, Asmussen S, Phelan JC. The consequences of stigma for the self-esteem of people with mental illnesses. *Psychiatr Serv* 2001;52:1621–1626.

Phelan JC, Link BG, Stueve A, Pescosolido BA. Public conceptions of mental illness in 1950 and 1996: what is mental illness and is it to be feared? *J Health Soc Behav* 2000;41:188–207.

U.S. Department of Health and Human Services. *Mental health: a report of the Surgeon General.* Rockville, MD: U.S. Department of Health and Human Services, 1999.

U.S. Department of Health and Human Services. President's New Freedom Commission on Mental Health. Achieving the promise: transforming mental health care in America. Final report. Rockville, MD: U.S. Department of Health and Human Services, 2003.

Wahl OF. *Telling is risky business: mental health consumers confront stigma.* Piscataway, NJ: Rutgers University Press, 1999.

Acknowledgements and Disclosures

Raymond Kotwicki has received grant support from the American Psychiatric Institute for Research and Education (APIRE/GlaxoSmithKline Research Award in Severe Mental Illness), the United Way of Metropolitan Atlanta, and the Woodruff Foundation. He also served as a consultant for Pfizer Pharmaceutical Company in 2005, and is a member of the Speakers' Bureau for AstraZeneca Pharmaceuticals, Janssen Pharmaceuticals, and Pfizer Pharmaceutical Company. Dr. Kotwicki is President of the Board of Directors for Positive Impact, Inc., an HIV and AIDS prevention and mental health services organization, and has provided consulting to the Atlanta Regional Commission on Homelessness. Dr. Kotwicki and Dr. Compton are Co-directors of the Post-doctoral Fellowship in Community Psychiatry/Public Health at the Emory University School of Medicine.

Michael Compton has received research grant support from the Emory Medical Care Foundation, the American Institute for Research and Education/GlaxoSmithKline, the American Institute for Research and Education/AstraZeneca, and the National Institute of Mental Health. He has served as a consultant for AstraZeneca Pharmaceuticals, WebMD Health, and Medscape.

Criminalization of Mental Illnesses

■ Introduction

Individuals with serious mental illnesses sometimes look and act as if they could be dangerous. Their different thoughts and actions often make those around them uncomfortable and afraid. People with severe mental illnesses frequently do not follow the social norms of dress and grooming, speech and thought, interactions and behaviors, and perception and judgment. They are sometimes considered odd or "crazy," and often they are considered dangerous. If someone thinks that he is the real president of the world or that she is the true Virgin Mary; if someone says that she causes plane crashes or that he will destroy those doing evil; if someone responds to questions about his or her identity by speaking about planets and fish or by singing the "Star-Spangled Banner," one might assume that he or she would be dangerous. These individuals' unpredictable, often impulsive, apparently uncontrollable behaviors are understandably considered a threat to community functioning. Society fears for both its potential victims, as well as the safety of the odd or crazy person.

This chapter describes ways in which people with mental illnesses may be inappropriately thought to be dangerous and explores how incarceration can be particularly damaging to the futures of people with mental illnesses. The goal of this discussion is not to argue that incarcerations have no place in our society; rather, this chapter aims to help public safety and criminal justice professionals appreciate that some people with mental illnesses can be better served through diversion away from jail and toward treatment.

■ Purpose of the Criminal Justice Process

In general, people with serious mental illnesses do not carry a sign, wear a label, or go around announcing their condition. To the casual observer, those people with mental illnesses when living and functioning in communities may initially appear much like anyone else. When they do something the community finds strange or dangerous, the initial assumption usually is "Here is a 'normal' person doing something 'bad or wrong'," not "Here is a person with a mental illness who is having symptoms of his or her illness." This variability of perspective affects how law enforcers view individuals' culpability for their actions.

Normal people who do something bad or wrong against society are considered "criminals." They break the laws that societies create to maintain and govern good and safe communities. People who break societal laws are to be identified, stopped, punished—often by being removed from the community—and, ideally, rehabilitated prior to regaining full and free access to the community. The goal in creating laws to protect communities and societies is to catch criminal behavior early so as to eliminate criminal tendencies, thereby preventing big, horrendous crimes that might happen if early

> When individuals with mental illness do something the community finds strange or dangerous, the initial assumption usually is "Here is a 'normal' person doing something 'bad or wrong'," not "Here is a person with a mental illness who is having symptoms of his or her illness."

criminal tendencies were not properly handled. This arrangement of rules and consequences prevents anarchy that results in unproductive, unruly societies.

The problem for many people with serious mental illnesses is that many laws created to protect and improve communities and societies may also target actions and behaviors that are actually symptoms of their mental illnesses. Their symptoms, when not understood as part of an illness, are considered illegal, criminal, and a threat to society. As a result, individuals with serious mental illnesses account for roughly one in five persons in criminal justice settings even though they number only one in thirty people in most communities. Such an overrepresentation of people with serious mental illnesses in jails and prisons may stem from our culture's assumption that behaviors must be assessed outside the context of who is behaving. For individuals with mental illnesses, behaviors must be considered in light of the psychiatric disorder, substance use disorder, or developmental disability that is present.

■ *Mens rea* and Criminal Intent

> The problem for many people with serious mental illnesses is that many laws created to protect and improve communities and societies may also target actions and behaviors that are actually symptoms of their mental illnesses.

The U.S. criminal justice process usually begins with an officer of the law—often with the help of reporters in the community—"catching" a person in the act of breaking a societal law. Identification of actions and behaviors as being criminal requires that there was some intent to do wrong (the concept of *mens rea*). Sometimes, even though a bad action occurred, if there was no intent for ill will, the officers of law may deem that a crime has not been committed. For example, when U.S. Vice-President Dick Cheney shot his hunting companion, Mr. Cheney was not arrested or fined. Mr. Cheney perpetrated a bad and dangerous act, but because he had no intention of shooting and hurting his friend, the incident was considered an accident and not a crime. Consequently, motivation for behavior is considered in many potential criminal actions in general society.

Even before the possibility of *mens rea* is considered, however, the initial identification of criminal behavior results in an arrest and detention. While it is considered a continuation of the identification process (the person is accused of engaging in criminal behavior, but the judgment of whether it is officially criminal behavior has not yet occurred), detention is used to immediately stop the problematic acts and behaviors in the community and to begin the adjudication and punishment of those acts. Even if officers merely escort individuals under suspicion of a crime to a holding facility and not jail, the person is isolated from his or her community, prevented from engaging in normal daily activities and functions, involuntarily confined in a highly secured environment, and required to follow very controlling rules and orders. From the start of the identification and arrest process, individuals who are suspected of criminal behavior—whether or not criminal intent exists—are treated like criminals.

■ Consideration of Mental Illnesses in the Criminal Justice Process

For people with serious mental illnesses, entering the criminal justice system is particularly challenging, especially when that entry occurs because of illness-related symptoms. When a person, owing to his or her mental illness, acts on the belief that he or she owns property that others claim to possess; or when a person, owing to his or her mental illness, states intent to harm persons (possibly including oneself) or property, it is understandable that citizens who are unaware of the mental conditions of such individuals would prefer to have such socially deviant acts and behaviors addressed in the criminal justice system. Untreated, inappropriately treated, and inadequately treated individuals with serious mental illnesses likely experience unusual perceptions about what is happening in the community around them. They may believe there is a conspiracy to get them. They may be convinced that governmental leaders are stealing their thoughts. They may think they are powerless and already dead. They may be following the direction of voices that others can't hear. Behaviors that may initially appear to be defiant or criminal may, indeed, result from symptoms of mental illnesses.

For people with mental illnesses, arrest and incarceration may be more distressing than they are for people without equivalent mental health concerns. Many times individuals with mental illnesses deal with their symptoms by isolating themselves—that is, by actively avoiding confinement, crowded settings, controlling environments, and external controls. Being arrested and jailed can be a destabilizing experience for them, because holding facilities are often crowded, confined, controlled, and closely observed environments. The resulting mismatch between preferred coping mechanisms and true experiences during incarcerations often worsens their conditions. In fact, some of the most bizarre mental illness-related behaviors occur in incarceration settings. These behaviors can lead to aggression that can create additional legal and social problems for the incarcerated person with a mental illness. Not only are individuals with serious mental illnesses more likely to be arrested, but they are also more likely to be housed with more serious offenders requiring closer observation, more likely to act out in these settings, and more likely to remain in jail for longer periods of time.

> Behaviors that may initially appear to be defiant or criminal may, indeed, result from symptoms of mental illnesses.

> Not only are individuals with serious mental illnesses more likely to be arrested, but they are also more likely to be housed with more serious offenders requiring closer observation, more likely to act out in these settings, and more likely to remain in jail for longer periods of time.

■ Links Between Mental Illnesses, Socioeconomics, and Criminalization

Education

Several social factors are frequently associated with serious mental illnesses in industrialized countries that are likewise associated with being overrepresented in the criminal justice system. The majority of individuals with a serious mental illness have less education; the less formal education a person has, the more likely he or she will be involved in the criminal justice system. Research suggests that more than 75% of students with a serious mental illness do not graduate from high school. In many areas of the United States, one of every five (20%) men in their twenties who have a high school or less education is incarcerated; one of every two (50%) men in their thirties with limited education has a criminal record. Limited formal education is a risk factor for criminal justice system involvement, and people with serious mental illnesses often have extremely limited formal education histories. Such an interrelationship makes it much more likely that individuals with severe mental illnesses will eventually interact with the criminal justice system.

> Limited formal education is a risk factor for criminal justice system involvement, and people with severe mental illnesses often have extremely limited formal education histories.

Economics

Financial variables also contribute to the overrepresentation of people with serious mental illnesses in jails and prisons. The majority of individuals with a serious mental illness are classified as belonging to low socioeconomic groupings. Some sociologists suggest the illnesses cause people to increasingly become less able to handle the stresses of higher-paying positions. The less income a person has, the more likely he or she will become involved in the criminal justice system. Limited income is a risk factor for criminal justice system involvement. In fact, in many areas of the United States, nearly 80% of the individuals in jail meet the poverty criteria defined for warranting a public defender. Low income is an important risk factor for incarceration itself, and it likely contributes to lengthier stays in jail and fewer opportunities for reintegration back into society after release.

Substance Use

The majority of individuals with a serious mental illness have associated substance abuse or dependence. Substance use is clearly associated with being in the criminal justice system: As many as 85% of arrests and incarcerations in the United States result from either substance use itself or behaviors connected to using substances (e.g., selling sex for drugs, dealing). Substance use is a major risk factor for criminal justice system involvement, and people with a mental illness are at increased risk for using these illegal substances. The cycle continues.

Race and Other Social Factors

A disproportionate number of individuals with a serious mental illness are members of disenfranchised groups that experience increased rates of arrest and incarceration. Racial and cultural minorities such as African Americans, people who are homeless, and individuals living in poor, "crime-infested" neighborhoods have increased rates of imprisonment. Perhaps citizens watch individuals from these groups more closely than others. Perhaps people from these disadvantaged groups have fewer opportunities to attain quality lives and turn to illegal behaviors to cope with that disappointment. At any rate, being part of a disenfranchised subgroup is a risk factor for criminal justice system involvement.

In summary, criminalization of people with mental illnesses is not simply related to the illnesses themselves. Criminalization of people with sub-optimally treated mental illnesses also pivots on issues of social justice. Individuals with severe, persistent mental illness are more likely than others to be less educated, poorer, using illegal substances, from minority groups, homeless, from broken families with histories of multiple arrests, and living in less stable neighborhoods or housing facilities. All of these factors culminate in increased arrests and incarcerations for people with mental illnesses. Jail diversion is one tool by which we can undo this injustice. Challenging social disparities and institutionalized barriers to equal social services and rights is another key ingredient in ensuring people with mental illnesses do not inappropriately enter the penal system.

■ Consequences of Incarceration of People with Mental Illnesses

For individuals with a serious mental illness, arrest and incarceration not only are likely to make their condition worse, but also increase the chances that they will be involved in the criminal justice system in the future. Several consequences of being incarcerated increase the likelihood of individuals with serious mental illness entering the criminal justice system's revolving door.

Being arrested increases the likelihood of being rearrested for a multitude of reasons. For example, associating with individuals who are engaging in illegal acts increases the likelihood that a person will learn antisocial behaviors. Becoming familiar with the "incarceration culture" in jail or prison predisposes someone with mental illness to act like other members of that peer group. Losing benefits such as Medicaid, Supplemental Security Income, other entitlements, or a job while incarcerated also increases the likelihood of future criminal justice involvement. Having a criminal record narrows one's job options and possible housing opportunities (especially government-subsidized housing), and makes it more difficult to secure loans and other future possibilities. Likewise, being kept apart from families and support systems leads to distant relationships and decreases support for individuals after release. If children are involved, having an incarcerated parent predisposes the children to future arrests as well.

■ Decriminalization of Mental Illnesses

It would seem obvious that the best approach to addressing individuals with serious mental illness who are being disruptive in the community would be to identify those persons and have them appropriately treated in the mental health system, not the criminal justice system. Because individuals with a serious mental illness are no more likely to commit serious crimes than members of the population without mental illness, it would seem that their high arrest and incarceration rates are unnecessary mistakes. Borrowing a phrase from the National Alliance on Mental Illness, the goal should instead be to use "Treatment, Not Jails."

> Because individuals with a serious mental illness are no more likely to commit a serious crime than members of the population without mental illness, it would seem that their high arrest and incarceration rates are unnecessary mistakes.

Mental health treatment plans that combine the use of psychiatric medications, psychological understanding and direction, and social support and rehabilitation have proven to be very effective. Such treatments are quite valuable not only in controlling and managing disruptive behaviors of incarcerated people with mental illnesses, but also in assisting individuals with a serious mental illness to become active, positive contributors while bettering their lives and the communities in which they and we all live.

While arresting and detaining individuals with a serious mental illness through the criminal justice system temporarily free the community from their disruptive behaviors, they often worsen the person's immediate and long-term personal and community functioning. Since they have become aware of the many negative effects that traditional incarceration can have on individuals with serious mental illness, many criminal justice systems have begun creatively teaming up with community mental health treatment providers through early screening and referral, the use of mental health courts and alternative sentencing models, and specialized programming and treatment access. In addition, many criminal justice systems are providing more comprehensive psychiatric services in jail and prison settings. Policy makers and politicians are beginning to understand that treatment—not incarceration—of people with mental illness makes economic, ethical, and even clinical sense.

> Policy makers and politicians are beginning to understand that treatment—not incarceration—of people with mental illness makes economic, ethical, and even clinical sense.

The most effective methods of decriminalizing serious mental illness and maintaining and attaining safer and more productive communities have involved the cooperative inter-workings of the criminal justice and mental health systems described in this book. When mental illness-related acts and behaviors are identified, and officers have the option of placing individuals in community-based mental health treatment settings where people with mental illness can receive timely and appropriate mental health care, the futures of people with mental illnesses are dramatically improved. In addition to mental health care, support for attaining housing, entitlements, substance abuse treatment, education, and socialization may allow many individuals with mental illnesses to recover from their illnesses instead of spending years in jail or prison. Public safety and criminal justice professionals represent essential components in this referral process.

■ Conclusion

There is a tendency to see people who are "different" as being "dangerous." Too often, because a person is stuck with a label and its associated stigma of having a mental illness, it is assumed that the individual is prone to violence. Most of the media reports about mental illness focus on danger and violent crime, so our culture feeds this danger myth. Individuals with severe mental illness, who may be hallucinating and delusional and unable to function well in their daily lives, may actually pose a reduced risk for violence relative to their normal counterparts; they may not be able to organize themselves well enough to behave dangerously toward others through planning and organizing an assault.

All too often, people's expectations become self-fulfilling prophecies. Approaching someone with a mental illness with anxiety, being standoffish and cold, and acting apprehensively or responding with confusion may create a more upsetting and agitated environment for the person who has a mental illness, perhaps even eliciting dangerousness. Our individual approaches to people with serious mental illnesses, coupled with societal and institutional racism, classism, and stereotype-related disadvantages, all contribute to the overrepresentation of people with mental illnesses in prisons and jail. While we understand that people with mental illnesses are no more dangerous than anyone else, our culture has created a system in which we are meant to believe that they are.

Chapter Wrap-Up

- For many individuals with a serious mental illness, the criminal justice system is deeply flawed, in that many laws created to protect and improve communities and societies include actions and behaviors that are symptoms of their mental illnesses.

- Although individuals with a serious mental illness account for one of every 30 people in most communities, they represent one of every five persons in criminal justice settings.

- Identification of actions and behaviors as being criminal requires that the perpetrator had some intent to do wrong, a concept called *mens rea*. People with severe mental illnesses may have no intention of wrongdoing, because their illegal actions are frequently based on their symptoms and not intent to harm.

- Not only are individuals with a serious mental illness more likely to be arrested, but they are more likely to be housed with more serious offenders requiring closer observation, more likely to act out in these settings, and more likely to remain in jail for longer periods of time.

- Criminalization of people with mental illnesses is not simply related to the illnesses themselves; it is an issue of social justice. Income, education, race, substance use disorders, social modeling, and community structure are all factors that contribute to the overrepresentation of people with mental illnesses in the criminal justice system.

- For individuals with a serious mental illness, arrest and incarceration not only are likely to make their condition worse, but also increase the chance that they will be involved with the criminal justice system in the future.

- Because individuals with a serious mental illness are no more likely to commit a serious crime than those in the population without mental illness, it would seem that their high arrest and incarceration rates are unnecessary mistakes. Mental health–criminal justice partnerships are key ways to avoid making the same mistakes in the future.

Vital Vocabulary

mens rea: identification of actions and behaviors as being criminal with intent to do wrong

Questions for Review and Discussion

1. How might someone with a serious mental illness show illegal behavior that is not criminal?
2. Which socioeconomic factors associated with serious mental illnesses also contribute to illegal behaviors?
3. From a societal point of view, is it more economical and helpful to the United States to incarcerate someone who has a mental illness or to treat that person with the goal of recovery and reintegration into society?
4. Which unique characteristics of people with mental illnesses might make their experiences in jail or prison unlike others' experiences?

Resources

Fisher WH, Packer IK, Simon LJ, et al. Community mental health services and the prevalence of severe mental illness in local jails: are they related? *Admin Policy Ment Health* 2000;27:371–382.

Lamb HR, Weinberger LE. Persons with severe mental illnesses in jails and prisons: a review. *Psychiatr Serv* 1998;49:1094–1095.

Lamberti JS, Weisman RL, Schwartzkopf SB, et al. The mentally ill in jails and prisons: toward an integrated model of prevention. *Psychiatr Quart* 2001;72:63–77.

Primm AB, Osher FC, Gomex MB. Race and ethnicity, mental health services and cultural competence in the criminal justice system: are we ready to change? *Comm Ment Health J* 2005;41:557–569.

Acknowledgements and Disclosures

Keith Wood works with the Georgia Department of Human Resources and has received service contracts and grants from the State of Georgia, Fulton and DeKalb Counties, and the Department of Human Resources.

Raymond Kotwicki has received grant support from the American Psychiatric Institute for Research and Education (APIRE/GlaxoSmithKline Research Award in Severe Mental Illness), the United Way of Metropolitan Atlanta, and the Woodruff Foundation. He also served as a consultant for Pfizer Pharmaceutical Company in 2005, and is a member of the Speakers' Bureau for AstraZeneca Pharmaceuticals, Janssen Pharmaceuticals, and Pfizer Pharmaceutical Company. Dr. Kotwicki is President of the Board of Directors for Positive Impact, Inc., an HIV and AIDS prevention and mental health services organization, and has provided consulting to the Atlanta Regional Commission on Homelessness. Dr. Kotwicki and Dr. Compton are Co-directors of the Post-doctoral Fellowship in Community Psychiatry / Public Health at the Emory University School of Medicine.

Mental Health Care in Detention

■ Introduction

In 1992, the National Alliance on Mental Illness (NAMI, previously called the National Alliance for the Mentally Ill) and the Public Citizen's Health Research Group produced a report called *Criminalizing the Seriously Mentally Ill: The Abuse of Jails as Mental Hospitals*. This report called national attention to the fact that large numbers of persons with serious mental illnesses were being held in jails. In most cases, these individuals were charged with minor crimes often stemming from symptoms of their mental illnesses rather than intentional malice. Over the years, the number of people with mental illnesses in U.S. jails and prisons has continued to escalate out of proportion to growth of the general population. The inescapable reality is that jails and prisons have become the new asylums of the twenty-first century, as was poignantly depicted in the 2005 Public Broadcasting System's *Frontline* special, "The New Asylums."

This chapter examines some historical events that resulted in this troublesome relocation of people with mental illnesses from treatment facilities to the criminal justice system. It also identifies potential barriers and suggests some solutions to providing appropriate and timely mental health care to individuals with mental illnesses in the U.S. penal system. While the statistics presented in this chapter paint a somewhat bleak picture regarding the shunting of individuals with mental illnesses out of the criminal justice system and into treatment, law enforcement officers play key roles in making a difficult situation more tolerable.

■ Background: Where Have All the Psychiatric Hospitals Gone?

Before the nineteenth century, people with serious mental illnesses in the United States often spent many years in almshouses, jails, and prisons. In the 1800s, concern for the well-being of people with mental illnesses encouraged the creation of mental institutions or psychiatric hospitals. For example, the Central State Hospital in Milledgeville, Georgia (originally called the Georgia Lunatic Asylum), was opened in 1846 and grew to become the largest mental institution in the world, occupying about 1,750 acres. In the 1960s, the number of hospitalized psychiatric patients at the Milledgeville Central State Hospital alone totaled some 13,000 patients.

Since the late 1950s, however, a gradual shift in the housing of individuals with serious mental illnesses has occurred. For example, in Georgia's state and county hospitals, the total number of hospitalized psychiatric patients in 2000 was 2,916 people, even though the state's general population had doubled from about 4,000,000 in 1960 to more than 8,000,000 in 2000. Clearly, psychiatric institutionalization did not parallel population trends.

A National Association of State Mental Health Program Directors Research Institute study in 2003 indicated that from 1972 until 1990, state and county psychiatric beds in the United States decreased more than 70%, with many state psychiatric hospitals closing during this period. In the 1990s, additional hospitals were closed, leading to a further decline of more than 40% in the number of hospitalized patients. Although the current closure rate seems to be slower than it was during the 1990s, states continue to eliminate psychiatric hospitals. In the late 1990s, approximately 70,000 persons with severe mental illnesses resided in public psychiatric hospitals in the United States, with 30% of these patients being in forensic units (Steadman & Veysey, 1997). (In the context of mental health, **forensics** refers to a branch of psychology and psychiatry that specializes in the interface between these professions and the law, and **forensic units** admit patients who have legal problems affected by their mental illnesses.) By the end of 2000, there were only 55,000 people in public psychiatric hospitals.

This reduction in the number of hospital beds continues to occur despite the fact that half of all states report shortages in psychiatric beds due to hospital downsizing. While the rates of mental illnesses remain constant, the number of psychiatric beds has decreased dramatically. Where, then, are people with serious mental illnesses treated today?

■ The Number of People with Mental Illnesses in Jails and Prisons

In 1999, the U.S. Department of Justice released a report indicating that nearly 283,800 inmates and 547,800 probationers reported having a mental illness. These statistics were based on the number of jail and prison inmates reporting a history of mental illness (10%) or a history of an overnight stay in a mental institution (10%) in studies conducted between the years 1995 and 1997. The report concluded that approximately 16% of inmates in state and federal jails and prisons have a serious mental illness, such as major depression, bipolar disorder, or schizophrenia (Ditton, 1999). It is important to recognize that this report is not based on an actual assessment of the mental status of the inmates or verification of their histories. Indeed, some inmates with mental illnesses—especially those who do not want to take psychiatric medications—are reluctant to reveal anything about their mental health histories.

According to NAMI, approximately 500,000 of the nearly 2,000,000 U.S. inmates have a mental illness, with 16% of the prison population and 25% of the jail population classified as having a severe mental illness. If less serious psychiatric disorders and substance use disorders are considered, then the percentage of inmates who would be classified as having a mental illness is likely more than 50%. The proportion of inmates with mental illnesses is also likely to be higher in large cities.

■ Factors Contributing to the Increase in Incarceration of Persons with Mental Illnesses

Civil Commitment Laws

During the past 40 years, significant changes in civil commitment laws have occurred and have had a major impact on the U.S. psychiatric hospital system. Before 1966, mental hospitals were able to keep patients with mental illnesses for almost as long as they wanted regardless of the patients' desires. In 1966, a landmark federal court case (*Lake v. Cameron*) mandated that committed patients need to be treated in the least restrictive environment possible. In 1972, the federal court established procedural requirements for commitment (*Lessard v. Schmidt*). Commitment came to require evidence of an overt act demonstrating dangerousness within the 30 days preceding commitment. Patients also had to be notified of their right to a jury trial and the right to counsel. In addition, proof of the need for commitment was set to "beyond a reasonable doubt."

In 1975, the U.S. Supreme Court decided that a nondangerous patient cannot be confined without meeting criteria such as an inability to care for oneself. That is, a patient cannot be committed just on the basis of a healthcare provider's or officer's opinion of a need for treatment (*O'Connor v. Donaldson*). Additionally, in 1979, clear and convincing evidence was set as the standard of proof for civil commitment (*Addington v. Texas*).

The end result of the various court decisions during the past 40 years is that it has become increasingly difficult for doctors to involuntarily commit individuals with mental illnesses to a psychiatric hospital, and modern commitment standards almost inevitably revolve around dangerousness criteria.

> The end result of the various court decisions during the past 40 years is that it has become increasingly difficult for doctors to involuntarily commit individuals with mental illnesses to a psychiatric hospital, and modern commitment standards almost inevitably revolve around dangerousness criteria.

Treatment in the Community

During the decades in which these court decisions were made, a fervent belief grew among many in the mental health professions that persons with mental illnesses do much better when they live in the general community. Spurred by the emphasis on personal freedom in the 1960s, widespread support developed for **deinstitutionalization**, the process of gradually releasing patients from institutions to treatment in outpatient community settings, with less reliance on hospital care.

Although deinstitutionalization was a great principle that promoted the civil liberties of people with major mental illnesses, the problem became that people with serious mental illnesses were often returned to the community with insufficient supervision and support to succeed on their own. Most people were placed in low-cost housing in neighborhoods that had high rates of crime and substance abuse. Many individuals who were regularly given medication for a long period of time often became solely responsible for their own medication adherence. Some stopped taking their psychiatric medications, sometimes because of side effects, impaired insight, or costs, and started using alcohol and illegal drugs, perhaps as an attempt at self-medication.

When people with mental illnesses had a problem requiring immediate attention, they were now more likely to encounter a law enforcement officer than a mental health professional. Thus began the trend toward incarcerating individuals with mental illnesses rather than diverting them into the mental healthcare system. Many of these individuals were unnecessarily incarcerated due to the arresting officer's lack of specialized training. In many instances, deinstitutionalization was actually **transinstitutionalization**, meaning that patients were shifted from one type of institution (i.e., the state psychiatric hospital) to another (e.g., board-and-care facilities, nursing homes, and jails and prisons).

Tougher Sentencing Laws and the Cost Factor

Tougher sentencing laws enacted in the 1980s and 1990s led to a major increase in the prison population as a whole, a trend that has often overwhelmed the court system. Many defendants with mental illnesses who are awaiting trial remain in jail for long periods of time because of their dependence on the public defender system and inability to pay a bond. Socioeconomic factors such as poverty, race, and the strength of one's social support system all influence who is initially incarcerated as well as how long one waits for trial.

It is expensive for states to house and treat individuals with mental illnesses in psychiatric hospitals, and studies show that jail or prison sentences are cheaper. Mental hospitals also have faced the need to adhere to accreditation and performance standards over the years, and this has driven up costs. These reasonable regulations, such as mandated staff-to-patient ratios and required qualifications for the staff, greatly inflated costs of treating people with mental illnesses. The cost difference between keeping someone in a mental hospital as opposed to a jail or prison is now dramatic. For example, the cost of housing an inmate in a Georgia jail varies from about $35 to $72 per day (without consideration of providing psychiatric medications or care), depending largely on the facility's proximity to a large urban area. In contrast, inpatient psychiatric hospitalization, especially for forensics services, can cost more than $550 per day. These figures do not account for differences in quality of life between the two settings.

■ Right to Treatment of Inmates with Mental Illnesses

Mental health treatment—and medical treatment more generally—is not a right guaranteed by the U.S. Constitution for all citizens. However, inmates in detention facilities have been granted the right to mental health treatment as well as medical treatment during their incarcerations. In 1981, the U.S. Supreme Court decided that the government must provide medical care for prisoners and that deliberate indifference to a prisoner's medical needs is cruel and unusual punishment, a violation of the Eighth Amendment (*Estelle v. Gamble*). In 1994, the Supreme Court determined that prison officials can be found liable for not providing an inmate with humane conditions of confinement if they know of and disregard an excessive risk to inmate health or safety (*Farmer v. Brennan*). This may at first seem like an unfair protection for those in detention compared to those in the general population, but it is important to understand the reasoning: Inmates' rights to treatment are based on the fact that they cannot, by the nature of their incarceration, obtain treatment on their own. Because the government has assumed custody of them, the government also has the responsibility to provide them with adequate care.

> Inmates in detention facilities have been granted the right to mental health treatment as well as medical treatment during their incarcerations.

■ Mental Health Services Offered in Jails and Prisons

According to the American Psychiatric Association (APA), "the fundamental policy goal for correctional mental health treatment is to provide the same level of mental health services to each patient in the criminal justice process that should be available in the community" (APA, 2000, pp. 16–17). The purposes of the treatment can vary but often include the following goals:

- Making the institution safer for everyone
- Reducing the suffering caused by mental illnesses
- Preventing suicide by identifying high-risk inmates and by providing treatment
- Enabling inmates to make use of the programs and services offered, which could help a person with a mental illness function in a general population area or prepare for release
- Helping the inmate participate in the court proceeding and obtain a fair trial or plea bargain, which may involve restoring the inmate's competency to be arraigned or to stand trial

The APA also states that "mental health treatment is more than mere prescribing of psychotropic medication, and psychiatrists should resist being limited to this role" (2000). Although the APA does not spell out exactly which mental health treatments should be provided, it does state that the treatment should be consistent with generally accepted psychiatric practices and institutional requirements.

The actual mental health treatments available in detention facilities vary widely, with fewer services generally available in smaller institutions (Steadman & Veysey, 1997). According to the Bureau of Justice Statistics of the U.S. Department of Justice, in 2000, mental health services were provided in 1,394 of the nation's 1,558 state public and private adult correctional facilities. Approximately 70% of facilities housing state prison inmates screened inmates at intake for mental illnesses, distributed psychotropic medications when needed, and provided counseling by trained mental health professionals. Some 65% conducted psychiatric assessments and helped released inmates obtain community mental health services, and 50% provided 24-hour mental health care. Mental health counseling was received by about 12.5% of state prisoners, with almost 10% receiving psychiatric medications (Beck & Maruschak, 2000). Of course, the mere availability of services and medications does not necessarily mean that people who need care actually receive it.

It is generally accepted that all inmates should be screened at intake for any history of psychiatric treatment, symptoms, and medications. Screening for suicidal and homicidal ideation is especially important, given the adversarial nature of incarceration. Forms are often developed for this purpose, often with trained intake workers—rather than licensed mental health professionals—asking the questions. Anyone reporting a history or current symptoms of a mental illness should be evaluated as soon as possible by a mental health professional. The facility should provide crisis counseling, suicide prevention plans, and psychiatric medications when needed. Maintaining a separate, dedicated area in the facility for housing inmates with mental illnesses is often helpful. Continuous availability of mental health professionals to perform clinical evaluations and arrange for the prescription of emergency medications is needed. In addition, discharge planning should be done by the mental health staff to aid individuals with serious mental illnesses in securing housing and services upon release.

> It is generally accepted that all inmates should be screened at intake for any history of psychiatric treatment, symptoms, and medications. Screening for suicidal and homicidal ideation is especially important, given the adversarial nature of incarceration.

The availability of psychotherapy in detention facilities appears to be extremely limited. During the 1960s and 1970s, considerable attention was given to the management and rehabilitation of prison inmates in general through behavioral principles and techniques. Although the term "correctional institution" is still used, the reality is that jails and prisons—for the most part—now function just as "penal institutions." After the 1970s, a pro-punishment movement eliminated most of the research on and funding for anything involving a psychological approach to reducing criminal behavior through rehabilitation (Milan, 2004). The stark difference between treating people with mental illnesses in psychiatric hospitals compared to incarcerating them reflects this underlying philosophy: Treatment implies recovery, whereas incarceration implies punishment.

■ Managing Mental Health Problems

Recognizing the Problem

Anyone who works in a jail or a prison is likely to encounter inmates who are "slow" and may be given a diagnosis of mental retardation if the problem existed since they were children. When working with older inmates, memory difficulties may be recognized, such as early dementia resulting from Alzheimer's disease. Inmates with advanced human immunodeficiency virus infection are often at risk for dementia and other psychiatric conditions. Many other brain disorders, such as tumors and head traumas, can also cause mental problems. Thus it is important to recognize that signs and symptoms of mental illnesses can be caused by serious medical conditions.

Several major psychiatric illnesses, including **major depressive disorder**, **bipolar disorder**, and **schizophrenia**, are among the most frequent diagnostic categories encountered in jails and prisons, besides **substance use disorders**. Severely depressed inmates may appear withdrawn, lack energy, and have poor appetites and difficulty sleeping. Inmates with bipolar disorder in a **manic episode** may talk constantly, pace frantically, have excessive energy, and become angry very quickly. Individuals with schizophrenia may appear to be interacting with someone who is not there (often as a response to auditory hallucinations), have paranoid delusions, show little communication ability, or have markedly disorganized thinking. In addition, **personality disorders**, which are patterns of attitudes, behaviors, and maladaptive coping strategies that interfere with one's relationships, are often seen in people in jails and prisons. These include <u>**antisocial personality disorder**</u>, <u>**narcissistic personality disorder**</u>, and <u>**borderline personality disorder**</u>. These illnesses will be described in more detail in subsequent chapters.

An important difference between recognizing these disorders in jailed individuals compared to people within the community centers on functionality. Each of these disorders negatively affects one's community functioning, which is an essential feature of any mental illness. Given the limited functioning that occurs in prisons initially, inmates with mental illnesses may not come to providers' or officers' attention early, as declining functionality may be difficult to observe in controlled jail or prison settings.

Adjustment Difficulties of Inmates with Mental Illnesses

For most people, incarceration would be a very stressful experience. For persons with severe mental illnesses, it can be a terrifying ordeal and may even provoke a worsening of the signs and symptoms of psychiatric disorders. Often, inmates with serious mental illnesses do not understand their charges, their rights, and the length of time they could be held in jail. They usually have no ability to hire an attorney and must rely entirely on the public defender system. In many cases, inmates with severe mental illnesses do not meet with their attorneys until they appear in court. They can become very depressed, paranoid, and disorganized. <u>**Hallucinations**</u> may increase. Individuals with alcohol or drug dependence may experience signs and symptoms of withdrawal, which often require medical attention. In short, inmates with mental illnesses face extra difficulties navigating the penal system in addition to those experienced by others.

When inmates with mental illnesses are experiencing <u>**psychotic symptoms**</u> such as hallucinations or <u>**paranoid delusions**</u>, which result in serious distortions of reality or marked mood symptoms, agitated and aggressive behaviors can occur. In a psychotic state, an inmate may look upon even a simple touch that is meant to show caring as a threat. Unless detention officers have been trained in recognizing and responding to inmates with mental illnesses, their responses to psychotic symptoms could quickly—albeit inadvertently—escalate a situation. What on the surface appears to be just an unwillingness to cooperate—a behavioral problem—could, in fact, be the result of hallucinations or paranoid delusions.

Speaking in a calm voice at a safe distance while trying to alleviate their fears or distract them can often defuse the situation for people with mental illnesses under the stress of incarceration. Although placing out-of-control inmates in physical restraints or isolation (administrative segregation) may be needed for a short period because of safety issues, the process should not be used as a punishment. Punishing an inmate for showing psychotic symptoms makes no more sense than punishing someone for having a heart attack.

Respect and Awareness

The cooperation of inmates with mental illnesses is best obtained by showing them respect as human beings. It is important to get to know them well, working to understand their strengths and vulnerabilities. Carefully observing their behaviors will help in recognizing subtle signs of tension, depression, and psychotic experiences. Goals should be set to ensure a timely response and referral to the mental health staff when problems become apparent. Learning strategies to defuse a tense situation involving a person with a mental illness is important, such as speaking with a firm but calm voice, moving the inmate to a quiet and safe place, and listening. Additionally, many problems with inmates with mental illnesses can be avoided if they are protected from inmates who exploit their weaknesses.

Suicide prevention is an essential part of working with inmates with mental illnesses. Strategies to prevent suicide involve: (1) identification of high-risk inmates; (2) recognition of stressful situations, such as new charges, sentencing, denial of parole, institutional changes, and bad news about family and friends; (3) establishing clear lines of referral for mental health services; and (4) planning for housing options upon release. If an inmate completes suicide, several actions must be taken to assist the staff who worked with the inmate. Reviewing the facts surrounding the suicide may help to avoid future occurrences, and allowing corrections staff to discuss and process their feelings in the event of a suicide attempt or completion are two necessary responses within the justice system.

In addition, maintaining inmate confidentiality is important. The stigma surrounding mental illnesses pervades jails and prisons just as it does the rest of society. All inmates have a right to privacy of their medical or psychiatric conditions as well as a right to privacy regarding the facts of their criminal cases. Discussion of inmates should be done only with those who have a need to know. Cultural competence is similarly important. Factors such as race, religion, gender, and sexual orientation should not be the cause for belittling an inmate or a source of gossip.

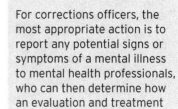

For corrections officers, the most appropriate action is to report any potential signs or symptoms of a mental illness to mental health professionals, who can then determine how an evaluation and treatment plan should proceed.

Inmates Faking a Mental Illness

Even the most experienced mental health professionals are sometimes fooled by an inmate faking the symptoms of a mental illness. An observant inmate who has been around people with mental illnesses, perhaps while incarcerated, can often imitate their symptoms for personal gain. It is not easy for a person without a mental illness to consistently act depressed, manic, or psychotic, however. Inmates may feign mental illnesses for reasons related to **secondary gain**, such as obtaining special privileges, seeking the effects of psychotropic medications, or obtaining transfer to a less restrictive psychiatric setting. For corrections officers, the most appropriate action is to report any potential signs or symptoms of a mental illness to mental health professionals, who can then determine how an evaluation and treatment plan should proceed.

■ Transfers of Inmates to a Psychiatric Hospital

Having a mental illness, even a serious one, does not excuse a person from hurting other people or stealing or damaging property. When laws are broken, there must be consequences, which sometimes involve detention in a penal institution. Nevertheless, some people break laws unintentionally and without malice due to symptoms of mental illnesses or out of perceived necessity, such as public urination when one is homeless and living in a crowded shelter with only one restroom. In such situations, and when psychiatric signs and symptoms are severe, transfer to a psychiatric hospital for treatment rather than punishment in the penal system may be appropriate. This approach is not a form of jail diversion, because the patient remains a detainee during his or her hospitalization. (Various forms of jail diversion are discussed in other chapters.)

Nonadherence with Psychiatric Medications

Inmates experiencing psychosis or mania frequently refuse to take psychiatric medications, often due to **impaired insight**. In a facility that does not have the authority to force an individual to take medications, this can be quite a problem. In cases where inmates present a danger to themselves or others or cause serious disruptions to the operations of the detention facility, mental health professionals often write orders sending these inmates to a psychiatric hospital, where they can receive appropriate treatment. Psychiatric medications usually cannot be forcibly administered in a jail, except in an emergency situation. By contrast, prisons may have the authority to force medications on a more regular basis. Psychiatric staff members at a detention facility are usually knowledgeable about the laws in specific states regulating forced psychiatric medication. In general, healthcare professionals attempt to engage patients in treatment to avoid coerced or forced treatment in an effort to avoid collapse of the essential provider–patient trusting relationship.

Nonadherence with psychiatric medications also may be related to issues other than one's mental illness. Jails and prisons have cultures of their own, with unique methods of defiance. Sometimes inmates may not swallow their medications—called "cheeking" the medication—so that they can either trade the pills to someone else who plans to abuse the effects of the medication or stockpile the pills for a suicide attempt by overdose. Every effort must be made by corrections officers who note medication nonadherence to ensure that the behavior does not result in catastrophic consequences.

Some inmates may adhere to their medication regimens but still show severe symptoms. These inmates are sometimes sent to a hospital that has the capability of trying other medications in the hope of finding the one (or more) needed to alleviate the symptoms.

Incompetence to Stand Trial

Psychiatrists and psychologists often evaluate defendants in detention facilities to help determine whether the inmate is competent to stand trial. Most jurisdictions lacked standards for incompetency until 1960, when the U.S. Supreme Court defined competency to stand trial as more than just being oriented and having some recollection of the recent events. The Court held that the accused must have "sufficient present ability to consult with a reasonable degree of rational understanding" and "a rational as well as factual understanding of the proceeding against him" (*Dusky v. the United States*). Mental health professionals may be helpful in determining if these indicators have been met.

Defendants found incompetent are usually not released but rather are confined to a forensic unit of a psychiatric hospital until competency is restored. This provision was widely abused, with individuals spending an average of 4.3 years in confinement, which was in many cases far longer than the sentence that would have been imposed after conviction. In fact, before the 1970s, about half of these unconvicted defendants who were deemed incompetent spent the rest of their lives in confinement. In 1972, however, the Supreme Court ruled that long pretrial confinement in a mental institution was unconstitutional (*Jackson v. Indiana*).

Today, if defendants do not meet the criteria for competency, they are usually sent to a psychiatric institution for a specific period of time so that an attempt can be made to restore competency. If the person does become competent, he or she would be returned to the jail to await trial. If competency cannot be restored after a reasonable period of time—often a year—defendants usually have to be released or civilly committed to a psychiatric hospital.

Not Guilty by Reason of Insanity

Inmates are also transferred from a jail to a psychiatric hospital rather than to a prison when they are found not guilty by reason of insanity (NGRI). Each state, as well as the federal government, determines the criteria for "insanity," which is a legal term and not a psychiatric term. A few states, in fact, do not recognize the "insanity defense" at all and use other pleas to accommodate defendants with serious mental illnesses. Notwithstanding, the concept of insanity implies that society should not punish persons for a crime if they lacked the mental capacity to understand what they were doing or if they were incapable of controlling their behavior due to a mental illness at the time of the alleged crime.

The recognition of insanity as a valid defense in this country has been around since at least the mid-nineteenth century. Despite the availability of this defense, a judgment of NGRI is relatively rare. Insanity is raised as an issue in only 2% of criminal cases. In cases in which the insanity plea is raised, estimates place the success rate at about 1 person per 1,000 cases. Most cases involving an insanity plea are resolved through plea bargains rather than by going to trial. If a person is found NGRI, he or she will likely spend many years—if not the rest of his or her life—in a forensic unit of a psychiatric hospital. Consequently, NGRI is not a "ticket out of jail," because it often leads to confinement longer than would have occurred by a conviction.

■ Conclusion

Detention officers are not trained or paid to provide mental health treatment but rather are charged with keeping the institution safe and functioning properly. Nevertheless, their actions can have an enormous impact on the mental state of inmates. Officers are encouraged to keep the following guidelines in mind:

1. When inmates with mental illnesses repeatedly refuse to take their prescribed psychiatric medications, there should be more frequent observations of the inmates and consultations with the mental health staff.

2. Mental health professionals should be notified as soon as possible if there is a threat of suicide or an inmate is discovered hoarding medications for a potential suicide attempt by overdose.

3. In addition to noticing inmates who have prominent behavioral disturbances, officers should be aware of inmates who are quiet, because they may be in a great deal of psychological pain but not expressing it in a way that gets them into trouble until they attempt suicide.

4. Anyone who works with individuals with mental illnesses needs to develop good communication skills. Orders have to be given frequently in a detention facility. However, the ways in which orders are presented, such as the tone of voice, can make a tremendous difference in obtaining the cooperation of inmates with mental illnesses.

5. Rewarding positive behavior is often much more effective in changing behavior than punishing negative behavior.

6. Frequent communication with the mental health staff is essential.

7. The procedures and guidelines of an institution should be followed, but it is equally important to be alert for unanticipated problems.

8. Additional training and support should be offered to detention officers who regularly work with defendants with mental illnesses.

9. Working with people who are living with mental illnesses is not easy but can be very rewarding.

Chapter Wrap-Up

Chapter Highlights

- In part owing to failures of community mental health systems that stem largely from insufficient funding, detention facilities have become de facto psychiatric institutions for many people with serious mental illnesses. As many as one-fourth of jail and prison inmates may have major psychiatric illnesses; when minor mental conditions and substance use disorders are included, this proportion may approach one-half.

- The increase in the number of people with serious mental illnesses in jails and prisons is partly related to deinstitutionalization (or transinstitutionalization), a trend that has occurred over recent decades. Deinstitutionalization, which aimed to provide outpatient treatment in the community rather than institutional settings, was partly stimulated by the civil rights movement, changes in civil commitment laws, rising costs associated with hospital care, the advent of effective psychiatric medications, and the principle of providing care in the least restrictive setting.

- Detainees have a right to receive appropriate medical and mental health care of the same standard that would be available in community settings. In reality, mental health treatments available in detention facilities vary widely.

- All inmates should be screened at intake for any history of psychiatric treatment, symptoms, and medications. Screening for suicidal and homicidal thoughts is especially important.

- Corrections officers will be better prepared to interact with detainees with serious mental illnesses if they have received training on recognizing signs and symptoms of mental illnesses, understanding the adjustment difficulties of inmates with mental illnesses, and interacting with inmates with mental illnesses in a respectful manner.

- In some instances, inmates may be transferred to psychiatric facilities because of treatment nonadherence, incompetence to stand trial, or receiving the court designation of not guilty by reason of insanity.

Vital Vocabulary

antisocial personality disorder: a mental illness in which individuals repeatedly engage in criminal, aggressive, irresponsible behavior

bipolar disorder: an illness characterized by abnormalities of mood along two extremes, depression and mania

borderline personality disorder: a mental illness in which individuals have unstable and intense relationships, and demonstrate impulsivity and emotional instability

deinstitutionalization: the process of gradually releasing patients from institutions to treatment in outpatient community settings

forensics: a branch of psychology and psychiatry that specializes in the interface between these professions and the law

forensic units: psychiatric units in which patients who have legal problems affected by their mental illnesses can be admitted for evaluation and treatment

hallucination: a perception that occurs in the absence of an external stimulus, such as hearing a voice when there is no one there (auditory hallucinations)

impaired insight: a lack of a clear understanding about the nature of the mental illness

major depressive disorder: a psychiatric disorder that includes symptoms such as excessive sadness, difficulty sleeping or sleeping too much, preoccupation with guilty thoughts, decreased energy, decreased enjoyment in pleasurable activities, poor memory and concentration, isolation from friends and family, hopelessness, and thoughts of suicide

manic episode: a period of at least one week when a person experiences a state of euphoria or elation that may be manifested as impaired judgment, excessive spending, decreased need for sleep, rapid speech, racing thoughts, functional impairment, irritability, and anger

narcissistic personality disorder: a mental illness in which individuals have an exaggerated sense of self-importance and difficulties in relationships

paranoid delusions: false beliefs that one is being followed, watched, or maliciously pursued

personality disorders: mental disorders consisting of patterns of attitudes, behaviors, and maladaptive coping strategies that interfere with one's relationships with others

psychotic symptoms: symptoms such as hallucinations or delusions that indicate an impairment in reality testing

schizophrenia: a mental illness that often causes psychosis (hallucinations or delusions)

secondary gain: the benefit that one is seeking when faking an illness

substance use disorders: also called addictive diseases; disorders characterized by psychosocial impairment due to abuse of or dependence on addictive substances (alcohol or drugs)

transinstitutionalization: patients being shifted from one type of institution to another

Questions for Review and Discussion

1. Explain some ways in which an officer can defuse a situation when an individual with a mental illness is acting out while incarcerated.
2. Under what conditions would an officer use restraints or isolation for an individual with a mental illness who is incarcerated?
3. How is the cooperation of inmates with mental illnesses best obtained?
4. Explain some strategies that can be taken to prevent suicide in inmates with mental illnesses.
5. In what instances should inmates be transferred from a jail to a psychiatric facility?

Resources

American Psychiatric Association. *Psychiatric services in jails and prisons* (2nd ed). Washington, DC: American Psychiatric Association, 2000.

Beck AJ, Maruschak LM. Mental Health Treatment in State Prison, 2000. Bureau of Justice Statistics special report, July 2001, NCJ 188215.

Ditton PM. Mental health and treatment of inmates and probationers. Washington, DC: U.S. Department of Justice, Bureau of Justice Statistics, 1999 (NCJ 174463).

Milan MA. *Behavioral approaches to correctional management and rehabilitation: the essential handbook of offender assessment and treatment.* Hoboken, NJ: John Wiley & Sons, 2004.

Steadman HJ, Veysey BM. Providing services for jail inmates with mental disorders. National Institute of Justice, Research in Brief, January 1997.

Acknowledgements and Disclosures

Glenn Egan has received research grant support from the Emory Medical Care Foundation as well as salary support from a grant held by Dr. Erica Duncan (Emory University School of Medicine).

Crisis Intervention Team (CIT) Programs

■ Introduction

Law enforcement officers are increasingly called upon to perform social service functions, and the importance of partnerships between law enforcement professionals and mental health professionals is more apparent today than ever. This chapter begins with a brief discussion of the complex nature of police work, which inevitably involves human behavior. For example, law enforcement officers frequently serve as first responders for family crisis situations, and some of these encounters relate to the presence of a mental illness that requires treatment.

While several types of collaborations between law enforcement officers and mental health professionals have been developed, the most widely disseminated model is the Crisis Intervention Team (CIT) model, which originated in Memphis, Tennessee. This chapter describes the CIT program in terms of its initial development, local and state implementations of CIT, personal characteristics of CIT officers, the typical curriculum used by CIT training programs, important principles for CIT to be useful as a form of pre-booking jail diversion, and research that has shown CIT to be effective. Experiences of the statewide CIT implementation in Georgia are then described in detail. Finally, the chapter provides some family members' perspectives on CIT.

■ The Complexity of Law Enforcement Work

Throughout the United States, the apprehension of criminals has been and will continue to be an integral function of the law enforcement community. For many years, various media and sources of entertainment (e.g., newspapers, magazines, radio, television, movies, and plays) have glamorized the role of the police officer in arresting criminals while engaging in exciting and dangerous behavior. Undue emphasis on this aspect of an officer's duties can lead to a general lack of understanding of the complex tasks carried out by a police officer and the skills necessary to perform those tasks (Russell & Beigel, 1990).

According to Russell and Beigel (1990), those who often refer to the "good old days" in law enforcement may be recalling the past when many believed that a police officer needed only a badge, a gun, and "plenty of guts" to perform his or her duties. It is doubtful that those items alone sufficed to carry out all of the officer's responsibilities. Undeniably, these officers possessed other equipment and human traits that contributed to their abilities to accomplish assigned tasks then, in the same manner that officers possess traditional tools and personal attributes necessary to effectively execute their duties now. Police officers historically have performed many social service functions, such as distributing charity to people in need. In modern society, police officers confront a variety of problems, few of which relate to serious criminal activity. Instead, most of their duties involve functions that may include rendering aid to a homeless person, rescuing a lost child, resolving a family dispute, intervening in a suicidal act, securing protective custody and transporting a person who has a mental illness to an emergency evaluation facility, or assisting a confused elderly person.

The increasing complexity of the tasks performed by police officers, combined with evolving societal opinions about unlawful behavior and the lack of desire by the general public to become involved in addressing serious criminal activity, have contributed to some police officers' perceptions that they are isolated when enforcing the law. They often perform their duties in the midst of apathetic, indifferent, and frequently hostile surroundings, and they must address situations in which emotions are volatile and danger poses a constant threat. Although the responsibilities of the police officer are complex, a core element relating to an officer's duties remains constant: "The one thing police officers deal with—not just during duty hours, but during the entire waking day—is human behavior" (Russell & Beigel, 1990, p. 7).

Russell and Beigel (1990) further point out that police officers' routine transactions involve the behavior of criminals, citizens, fellow officers, and themselves. The behavior may or may not be of a criminal nature, it may sometimes be related to an illness, and it may be conscious or unconscious. These encounters may involve behavior resulting from conditions of emotional stress or situations involving life-and-death decisions and personal danger. Therefore, police officers and other public safety officials often must respond to others in a mental health capacity, becoming "devoted students of human behavior" (p. 7) who must practice this psychology on the street. Today, police officers must possess significant knowledge about human behavior and are indeed expected to be "practical, street-level psychologists" (p. 7).

■ Law Enforcement Responses to Family Crises

> When a law enforcement officer responds to a crisis that involves a person with a serious mental illness who is not receiving treatment, the safety of both that person and the police officer may be compromised, particularly when the officer has received little or no training about mental illnesses and crisis intervention.

One of the more difficult duties in law enforcement involves police officers' responses to family crises. The officer generally must enter into these situations with limited or no information about the nature of the family or the crisis and reestablish peace. The manner in which the officer responds to these situations will determine whether a peaceful, even therapeutic, resolution to the problem is achieved (Miller & Braswell, 2002). According to Miller and Braswell, "More officers are assaulted while responding to family disturbance calls than for any other single category of police work" (2002, p. 41).

Family crisis situations sometimes involve a person with a mental illness. When a law enforcement officer responds to a crisis that involves a person with a serious mental illness who is not receiving treatment, the safety of both that person and the police officer may be compromised, particularly when the officer has received little or no training about mental illnesses and crisis intervention.

■ Types of Partnerships Between Law Enforcement and Mental Health

Given the frequency with which they encounter people with serious mental illnesses, law enforcement, public safety, and criminal justice professionals clearly need to know about mental illnesses. To provide this knowledge, a variety of collaborations between the mental health system and law enforcement have been developed. To learn more about these partnerships, Deane and colleagues (1999) surveyed police departments in 194 U.S. cities, each with a minimum population of 100,000 citizens, to identify the strategies used to solicit assistance from the mental health system in addressing crises that involve persons with mental illnesses. The majority of police departments in these cities had not identified a specialized strategy to respond to people in crisis who might have a mental illness. Among the departments that had taken this step, three primary approaches could be identified:

- The **police-based specialized police response** strategy involves the use of sworn officers who have special mental health training to provide crisis intervention services and to serve as liaisons to the formal mental health system. CIT is an example of this type of response.
- The **police-based specialized mental health response** strategy involves the use of mental health consultants employed by the police department. These consultants are not officers, but provide on-site or telephone consultations to officers in the field.
- The **mental health-based specialized mental health response** strategy includes programs that rely on mobile crisis teams, a component of the local community mental health system, which develop a special relationship with the police department to respond to special mental health needs at the site of an incident.

In 1999, a very small proportion (3%) of departments indicated that they had implemented a specialized unit of officers who were trained to address crisis calls involving persons with mental illnesses. According to Deane et al., "This innovative strategy appears to be a relatively new type of police response developed under community policing initiatives" (1999, p. 100).

■ Development of the Memphis CIT Model

The original CIT model was developed in Memphis, Tennessee, beginning in 1988. The Memphis program was established in response to a crisis in which a person with a history of a mental illness and substance abuse was fatally shot by law enforcement while holding a knife. Using the work of family advocates from the Memphis Chapter of the Alliance for the Mentally Ill to provide the basic foundation for the CIT model, a community task force made up of law enforcement, mental health and addiction professionals, and consumer advocates was established (Dupont & Cochran, 2000).

Prior to developing the CIT model, the Memphis Police Department provided eight hours of academy-based training in crisis intervention related to mental illnesses, which surpassed the national average. Nevertheless, the perceived needs of the community had exceeded the scope of this training. Therefore, the Memphis CIT task force identified four basic objectives when developing the CIT model: (1) to provide advanced training for officers, (2) to ensure immediacy of the crisis response, (3) to promote safety of the officer and consumer involved in the crisis, and (4) to deliver proper care for the person in crisis. According to Dupont and Cochran, "Addressing these goals set into motion a dynamic relationship between community policing, mental health service delivery, and advocacy that focused on issues of police use of force and jail diversion" (2000, p. 339).

Officers trained by the Memphis CIT program were required to be assigned to the uniform patrol division, which allowed them to serve as front-line officers who responded to emergency calls for assistance generally dispatched through their 9-1-1 system. During their regularly assigned shifts, these officers responded to an entire range of emergency calls, but were specifically assigned to disturbances involving individuals with mental illnesses, **substance use disorders**, or **developmental disabilities**. To ensure that sufficient numbers of trained officers were accessible throughout the city—available for every precinct and every shift—approximately 15% to 20% of the entire patrol division eventually was trained. Procedures for dispatching trained CIT officers were standardized by a protocol used by the 9-1-1 operators when dispatching crisis calls to the patrol division (Dupont & Cochran, 2000). **Table 4.1** shows the potential benefits of the Memphis model of CIT.

Table 4.1	Potential Benefits of the Memphis Model of CIT

- Crisis response is immediate.
- Arrests and use-of-force incidents decrease.
- Under-served consumers are identified by officers and referred to care.
- Patient violence and use of restraints in emergency rooms decrease.
- Officers are better trained and educated in verbal de-escalation techniques.
- Officers' injuries during crisis events decline.
- Officer recognition and appreciation by the community increase.
- Fewer "victimless crimes" (minor infractions) arrests occur.
- The program contributes to cost savings.

Source: Memphis Police Department, www.memphispolice.org/Crisis%20Intervention.htm

According to Dupont and Cochran (2000), referral of persons in crisis to proper care requires changes in attitude for both police officers and mental health professionals. Officers continue to be frustrated by the ongoing barriers to mental health care. Unfortunately, in many instances, the criminal justice system (and ultimately incarceration) has become the alternative to a mental health referral. If this problem is perpetuated, "the process of criminalization of mental illnesses is reinforced, and the benefits of jail diversion are ignored" (Dupont & Cochran, 2000, p. 340).

■ Local and State CIT Programs

The Memphis CIT training program eventually became recognized throughout the United States for its training of police officers in crisis intervention techniques (Addy & James, 2005). Indeed, according to Addy and James (2005), the Memphis program is considered the "gold standard" for training police officers in crisis intervention. Its CIT model has since been replicated in many localities and states. The model appears to bring about good results:

- A reduction in the risk of danger posed to the police officers and the persons who have a mental health crisis
- Diversion of persons with mental illnesses in need of treatment to mental health treatment centers in lieu of incarceration
- Decreased trauma and stigma associated with police contact and criminal justice system involvement
- Increased officer awareness and interest in mental health advocacy

Prior to the implementation of CIT programs throughout the United States, many persons with mental illnesses who were in crisis were transported to local jails because law enforcement officers were frequently unaware of how mental illnesses might influence the situations to which they responded. In those jurisdictions where CIT programs have been established, police officers have been specially trained to assist persons in mental health crises in obtaining appropriate services to address their specific needs. Officers who have received specialized CIT training are often recognized not only by the persons they directly serve, but also within the entire community through the CIT pins or patches displayed on their uniforms. The First National CIT Conference (held in Columbus, Ohio, in April 2005) and the Second National CIT Conference (which took place in Orlando, Florida, in September 2006) demonstrated the large number of CIT programs being implemented in localities and states across the country.

■ Personal Characteristics of CIT Officers

CIT programs are designed to train police officers in a manner that will equip them to respond both compassionately and effectively. Officers who possess certain personal traits or characteristics are better suited than other officers to effectively intervene in crisis situations. These traits include kindness, empathy, compassion, maturity, and leadership, in addition to patience, flexibility, and creativity. CIT officers must be observant, be able to exercise good judgment, and demonstrate respect for—and preserve the dignity of—individuals who have mental illnesses, addictive disorders, or developmental disabilities and who are in crisis (Reuland, 2004).

■ The CIT Curriculum

In the CIT model, experienced officers volunteer for advanced training in crisis intervention techniques. Many of the 40 hours of intensive training focus on scenarios developed from actual incidents. These scenarios are used to illustrate crisis de-escalation principles, and intensive feedback from fellow officers and mental health professionals ensures mastery of the skills (Dupont & Cochran, 2000). One of the most important objectives of CIT centers on safety—the safety of officers, of individuals with mental illnesses, and of the entire community.

Modeled after the Memphis CIT program, the CIT training programs used in many states usually include a full week of both classroom and practical law enforcement training provided by mental health professionals and trained CIT law enforcement instructors. The instructional content addresses mental illnesses, addictive diseases, and developmental disabilities. In addition, visits to state or local mental health agencies or emergency receiving facilities are included in the CIT curriculum, and de-escalation strategies and techniques are taught and practiced. Realistic role-play scenarios are instrumental teaching tools used by CIT programs, allowing officers the opportunity to learn, develop, and master effective crisis intervention skills.

> Realistic role-play scenarios are instrumental teaching tools used by CIT programs, allowing officers the opportunity to learn, develop, and master effective crisis intervention skills.

Some of the topics covered in the classroom portion of CIT training are shown in **Table 4.2**. **Table 4.3** lists potential sites that CIT classes may visit to get first-hand exposure to local mental health agencies and the consumers whom they serve.

Table 4.2 CIT Training Program Course Curriculum: Recommended Topics

Understanding Mental Illnesses	Co-occurring Disorders/Dual Diagnoses
Criminalization of People with Mental Illnesses	Developmental Disabilities
Signs and Symptoms of Mental Illnesses	Neurological Disorders
Schizophrenia and Other Psychotic Disorders	Dementia/Alzheimer's Disease
Mood Disorders	Mental Health Services/Community Resources
Anxiety Disorders	Cultural Differences
Personality Disorders	Consumer Perspectives
Childhood Emotional and Behavioral Disorders	Family Perspectives
Suicide Prevention, Intervention, and Aftercare	Crisis Intervention Strategies
Diagnosis and Treatment of Psychiatric Illnesses	De-escalation Techniques/Performance-Based Role-Play Scenarios
Medications, Side Effects, and Adherence	Mental Health Law/Legal Issues
Posttraumatic Stress Disorder	Departmental Policy and Procedures
Substance Use Disorders	

Table 4.3	CIT Training Program Course Curriculum: Site Visits *	

Crisis access hotline triage center	Crisis stabilization program
Outpatient services provider	Psychiatric hospital/residential facility
Emergency receiving facility	Veterans Administration hospital

* Interactions between consumers and police officers at these facilities are recommended to convey the consumers' perspectives about mental illnesses and their experiences with law enforcement (when legally permitted and approved by the facility and consumers).

■ The Importance of Crisis Centers and Emergency Receiving Facilities

In conjunction with CIT training, some communities have developed pre-booking diversion programs that involve specialized crisis response sites where police officers can deliver persons in psychiatric crisis for evaluation and then return to their regular patrol duties. Obviously, CIT programs will be ineffective if officers do not have knowledge of social service and mental health agencies to which patients can be referred, or if emergency receiving facilities do not exist. Likewise, the work of CIT officers will be impeded if emergency receiving facilities create lengthy delays for officers who bring patients for evaluation.

Steadman et al. (2001) conducted a study that examined three jail diversion programs in an effort to identify important program operating principles. The Montgomery County, Pennsylvania, program was characterized by a pre-booking and post-booking diversion program based in the local county psychiatric hospital. In that setting, when officers encountered a person with a suspected mental illness, either they could transport that person directly to the hospital's emergency services or the hospital's ambulance service—whose staff members were both emergency medical technicians and psychiatric crisis specialists—could be dispatched to assist the person in crisis. The Memphis, Tennessee, pre-booking jail diversion program possessed two distinct features—a police team consisting of specially trained CIT officers and a crisis center. The crisis triage center, based in the emergency department at the regional medical center, established a no-refusal policy and a 15- to 30-minute "turnaround" time for police officers who transported people to the center. The Multnomah County, Oregon, pre-booking jail diversion program also included a crisis triage center and a police CIT program modeled after the Memphis CIT program. Police officers could access the "one-stop" centralized crisis services at the center, which had also implemented a no-refusal policy for police referrals (Steadman et al., 2001).

Steadman et al. (2001) found that each of the three programs afforded a centralized site, accessible 24 hours per day, which allowed police officers the opportunity to bring a person in psychiatric crisis to the facility. The no-refusal policy for law enforcement, accompanied by the mutual respect that existed between law enforcement and mental health personnel, assured officers that crisis staff uniformly accepted police referrals at all three sites. The researchers noted that the specialized crisis response units "streamlined" their referral process to minimize officers' time at the center. In addition to performing evaluations, the specialized crisis response sites linked consumers to both mental health and substance abuse services in the community (Steadman et al., 2001).

Dupont and Cochran (2000) suggest that the comprehensive nature of the CIT program presents a challenge to both criminal justice and mental health systems because it focuses on issues that require the mental health emergency system to respond in an efficient, "user-friendly" manner. Police officers are more apt to use a program that can assist them in performing their tasks in an effective and timely manner. When officers are confronted with extensive barriers to or delays in obtaining services for persons they are transporting to a medical facility in lieu of incarceration, they may be discouraged from continued involvement in the program. Therefore, the CIT model is not simply an intervention program that addresses mental illness emergencies, but also "a process of addressing system change for crisis care within a community as a whole" (p. 339).

■ The Effectiveness of CIT

The CIT program is an effective means of identifying appropriate alternatives to incarceration for individuals who have a mental illness and may have committed a minor penal offense or pose a danger to themselves or others, but who are generally nonviolent and in need of treatment. CIT assists officers in identifying available resources for people in need of services, encourages local collaborations to address local mental health needs, and provides education and training about mental illnesses to reduce the stigma associated with these disorders. The program is effective largely because it forges community partnerships among professionals (i.e., law enforcement professionals, mental health clinicians, consumers, and family members) who are committed to helping people with mental disorders.

Following the development and implementation of CIT programs in various localities and states, several studies have been conducted to determine the effectiveness of these programs.

CIT Provides Specialized Responses for Mental Health Emergencies

Steadman and colleagues (2000) conducted a study that compared three models of police responses to incidents involving persons with suspected mental illnesses. The researchers examined the frequency in which specialized professionals responded to these incidents and determined how often they were able to resolve the crisis without executing arrests. The study, which took place in 1996–1997, involved three sites: Birmingham, Alabama; Knoxville, Tennessee; and Memphis, Tennessee.

The Birmingham program was a police-based specialized mental health response that involved a team of community service officers—non-sworn police employees possessing professional training in social work or related fields—who assisted police officers in mental health emergencies by providing crisis intervention and some follow-up assistance. The Knoxville program relied on mobile crisis units to respond to mental health crises and to make telephone calls and referrals from the local jail that lacked an inpatient mental health program. The Memphis program consisted of the CIT program—a police-based program utilizing specially trained officers to respond to mental health crises (Steadman et al., 2000).

The results of the study revealed important differences across the three sites with regard to the proportion of mental disturbance calls eliciting a specialized response. In Birmingham, the number of mental disturbance calls receiving a specialized response was restricted by the availability of the community service officers, which was particularly evident at night and during the weekends. In Knoxville, the mobile crisis unit's lengthy response times might have posed a significant barrier for its use by police officers. Officers often expressed concern and frustration about the delays of the mobile crisis team and, therefore, may have decided to incarcerate persons or transport them to services or other locations without requesting the unit. The proportion of calls that resulted in a specialized response was significantly higher in Memphis than in the other two cities. Indeed, the Memphis CIT program included the most active procedures for linking persons with mental illnesses to mental health treatment resources (Steadman et al., 2000).

CIT Decreases Use of Force and Arrests, While Enhancing Referral to Treatment

The Albuquerque, New Mexico, Police Department instituted a CIT program based on the Memphis model in 1997. Following its implementation, Bower and Pettit (2001) found that almost half of the police contacts (48%) with individuals suspected of having mental illnesses resulted in transportation to a local mental health facility where they received professional care. Fewer than 10% of the persons contacted were arrested or placed in protective custody. Also, since the inception of the CIT program in Albuquerque, special weapons and tactics calls involving a crisis intervention component were reduced by 58%. Police shootings involving persons in crisis have also declined since 1997, even though the population of Albuquerque has increased. The study lends support to the premise that CIT officers use skill and discretion in resolving potentially lethal situations (Bower & Pettit, 2001).

In 2002, the University of Louisville, in Louisville, Kentucky, in partnership with the Louisville Metro Police, established a CIT program to enhance police interactions with citizens with mental illnesses and to improve mental healthcare delivery to those in acute distress. During the program's first year, the number of patients treated by the local emergency psychiatric service increased substantially—from an average of 500 patients per month to 600 patients per month. The arrest rate among all crisis calls decreased to 2.1%, which was dramatically lower than the national average of 20%, and significantly lower than the entire police department's rate of 6.2% (Strauss et al., 2005).

> Research suggests that CIT officers are able to identify psychiatric emergencies and refer patients who require evaluation and treatment to services.

CIT Officers Refer People Who Are in Need of Treatment

The study by Strauss et al. (2005) in Louisville also determined the characteristics of the persons transported to the emergency facility by CIT officers. Data were collected for one month, beginning six months after the institution of the program. The research suggests that CIT officers are able to identify psychiatric emergencies and refer patients who require evaluation and treatment to services. Although the study examined only one month of data, the researchers demonstrated that patients referred by CIT officers are ill and benefit from psychiatric evaluation and care in a manner similar to those who are referred by health professionals.

■ An Example of a Statewide CIT Program: Georgia's Experience

Like many other states, Georgia historically provided some training to law enforcement officers to better equip them to respond to persons with mental illnesses who are in crisis. However, until 2004, few formal programs that established community collaborations between police departments and mental health providers existed in the state. In early 2002, the Georgia Chapter of the National Alliance on Mental Illness (NAMI Georgia) initiated coordinated efforts to develop a partnership among leaders across the state to facilitate a major jail diversion program. This project was labeled "Partners in Crisis," and through this partnership an analysis was conducted on jail overcrowding and the successes of mental health or drug courts in specific counties.

In October 2003, a state CIT summit was held in Georgia. In January 2004, an inaugural group of officers and professionals, primarily from the metropolitan areas of the state, went to Memphis, Tennessee, to meet with CIT officers, talk with 9-1-1 dispatchers, and participate in a "ride-along" program to observe directly the dynamics of the entire Memphis program. Twenty-two representatives from this original group in Georgia later returned to Memphis to attend the 40-hour CIT course in July 2004.

Following the summer of 2004, a Georgia CIT Advisory Board expanded the program from its initial scope, which included only metropolitan Atlanta, to the entire state. An advisory board steering committee made up of representatives from the Atlanta Police Department, Emory University School of Medicine/Grady Health System, Georgia Bureau of Investigation, Georgia Department of Corrections, Integrated Health Resources, and NAMI Georgia worked closely with the Georgia Public Safety Training Center to develop a CIT curriculum. The Georgia Peace Officer Standards and Training (P.O.S.T. Council) approved the CIT curriculum for use by communities throughout the state. This official approval allowed for increased uniformity and improved quality in the training delivered to law enforcement officers so that the core tenets of the Memphis model were maintained while programs were individualized for the needs of various localities. CIT training programs began in Georgia in December 2004.

In 2005, the CIT Advisory Board focused on specific program objectives that included a plan to train 20% of Georgia law enforcement officers in CIT by the end of 2007. In 2006, the Georgia CIT program received funding from the Georgia Department of Human Resources Division of Mental Health, Developmental Disabilities and Addictive Diseases to achieve this ambitious objective.

The Georgia CIT program includes attempts to evaluate its effectiveness and the quality of its training. For example, Compton and colleagues (2006) conducted a study of the Georgia CIT program to determine whether the program was effective in reducing stigmatizing attitudes of police officers toward people with schizophrenia. From December 2004 to July 2005, surveys were administered to 159 police officers both immediately prior to and after their 40-hour CIT training programs. The results of the study revealed that, compared with baseline surveys, after the training officers reported improved attitudes concerning aggressiveness among individuals with **schizophrenia**, became more supportive of treatment programs for schizophrenia, evidenced greater knowledge about schizophrenia, and reported less social distance (a form of stigma) toward persons with schizophrenia.

> The CIT program is successful because of its strong partnerships among law enforcement officers, health professionals, the local business community, advocates, individuals with mental illnesses, and their family members and friends.

The Georgia CIT program has become an exemplary community initiative because of the number of different agencies that are dedicated to a common mission: communities within which persons with serious mental illnesses receive treatment, not criminal incarceration, when possible. The CIT program is successful because of its strong partnerships among law enforcement officers, health professionals, the local business community, advocates, individuals with mental illnesses, and their family members and friends.

■ Families' Perspectives on CIT and Legal Issues

Mental illnesses are common in the United States, with approximately 57.7 million adults and children having a diagnosable mental disorder each year (U.S. Department of Health and Human Services, Centers for Disease Control and Prevention, 2005). Similar to cancer or heart disease, mental disorders can be very disabling in terms of lost productivity and even premature death. However, research has improved the ability of mental health professionals to recognize, diagnose, and treat mental illnesses effectively, and 80% to 90% of mental disorders are treatable using medication and other therapies (U.S. Department of Health and Human Services, Centers for Disease Control and Prevention, 2005). Unfortunately, many people with diagnosable mental illnesses do not seek treatment. For those who have not received treatment, for those whose treatment has been ineffective for various reasons, and for those who have otherwise not been rehabilitated or able to successfully recover, the understanding and support of family members is particularly critical to their safety and welfare.

Families of persons who have mental illnesses and are in crisis sometimes have to contact law enforcement for intervention because of their loved one's refusal to seek or receive treatment. Laws pertaining to involuntary commitment of persons with mental illnesses in many states mandate that individuals must pose a danger to themselves or others to warrant the initiation of any treatment without their consent. Therefore, police officers may become involved in potentially dangerous or violent situations in which persons may have deteriorated mentally and pose a significant risk of harm to themselves or others. Additionally, police officers may be requested to provide assistance in situations when a person with a mental illness presents with serious symptoms, but the mental health system cannot respond because the person is not considered dangerous. In several states, the laws do not allow police officers to transport a person with a mental illness who refuses to accept treatment unless that person has committed a penal offense. Consequently, officers are challenged with the decision either to initiate an arrest to ensure the person's safety or to refrain from initiating an arrest, but without assurance that the person will not succumb to harm.

In jurisdictions that require commission of a penal offense before a person who may have a mental illness can be transported for a psychiatric evaluation, police officers frequently elect to charge persons with or arrest them for criminal violations to facilitate legal transportation to an emergency facility for help. Charging or arresting a person who has a mental illness for the sole purpose of acquiring treatment and services for that individual commences a cycle of criminalization that affects both the person and his or her family. The lives of family members soon become intertwined with the criminal justice system, and they may become consumed with court costs and loss of income due to court appearances or other legal proceedings. In cases involving the incarceration of a person who has a mental illness, the detention facility becomes the surrogate provider of mental health services. The institutionalization of persons who have mental illnesses in a criminal justice facility contributes to continued criminalization of those persons, and it may present additional risks for this vulnerable population if they are further victimized by other inmates.

Many states do not have sufficient resources for providing treatment in community settings. Therefore, a significant percentage of people with mental illnesses may wander the streets or become incarcerated in detention facilities. These facilities do not provide an effective environment for treatment or recovery, but are nevertheless forced to house those who have mental disorders because the mental health system is unable to accommodate them for various reasons. For many family members whose loved ones have been subjected to the criminal justice system, the development of CIT represents a promising solution to a difficult problem: obtaining treatment for persons who have mental illnesses and are in crisis in lieu of incarceration.

Family members are essential components of the CIT program, and during CIT training sessions they often describe their past interactions with law enforcement in times of crisis. Family members provide support for other families affected by a mental illness, and these families often network to share their experiences and knowledge of available resources. Many families are members of their local NAMI chapters. NAMI is a family-based, support and advocacy organization that comprises spouses, parents, children, siblings, and friends of persons with severe mental illnesses, as well as treatment professionals. The members of this national organization are dedicated to improving the quality of life of all whose lives are affected by these mental illnesses, through advocacy, education, research, and support (NAMI, 2006).

Chapter Wrap-Up

- The complex tasks performed by police officers and the challenges that often arise when officers respond to family crises have contributed to the identification of a police response strategy for safely and appropriately intervening in these situations.
- The CIT model was initially developed in Memphis, Tennessee, after an incident in which an armed person who had a history of mental illness was killed by law enforcement. Since then, CIT programs have been established throughout the United States to train police officers in a manner that will equip them to respond safety, effectively, and humanely to situations involving persons in mental health crisis.
- Local jails and detention centers have become surrogate providers of mental health services for persons with mental illnesses who have been arrested for a crime, because the mental health system is not equipped to accommodate a significant percentage of those in need of treatment. The institutionalization of these persons in a criminal justice facility contributes to their continued criminalization and allows for further victimization by other inmates. Entry of these persons into the criminal justice system affects not only the individual but also his or her family due to the accumulation of legal fees, absences from employment for court appearances, and other demands.
- CIT provides an alternative to incarceration for persons who have mental illnesses and may pose a danger to themselves or have committed minor penal offenses. Generally, these persons are nonviolent and in need of services in a mental health setting. Through CIT programs, local communities are able to identify available health resources, encourage local collaboration to address local mental health needs, and provide education about mental illnesses to reduce the stigma attached to them.
- CIT programs succeed because they forge a strong community partnership between local law enforcement and corrections officers; health professionals; business leaders; and individuals with mental illnesses, their family members, and their friends.

Vital Vocabulary

developmental disabilities: mental impairments that affect a person's abilities to think, communicate, interact with others, remember facts and details, and take care of oneself; all developmental disabilities, such as mental retardation and autistic disorder, appear before the age of 18 and remain with the person throughout his or her life

mental health-based specialized mental health response: programs that rely on mobile crisis teams—a component of the local community mental health system—which develop a special relationship with the police department to respond to mental health needs at the site of an incident or crisis

police-based specialized mental health response: the use of mental health consultants employed by the police department who are not officers, but who provide on-site or telephone consultations to officers in the field

police-based specialized police response: the use of sworn officers who have special mental health training to provide crisis intervention services and to serve as liaisons to the formal mental health system; the Crisis Intervention Team model is an example of this type of response

schizophrenia: a biological brain disease that often causes psychosis

substance use disorders: also called addictive diseases; disorders characterized by psychosocial impairment due to abuse of or dependence on addictive substances (alcohol or drugs)

Questions for Review and Discussion

1. Why is it important for law enforcement officers to learn about, understand, and be able to identify mental illnesses?
2. Explain some potential benefits of the Memphis model of CIT.
3. Explain how the CIT program contributes to breaking the cycle of criminalization of serious mental illnesses.
4. What role do strong community partnerships play in the success of a program like CIT?

Resources

Addy C, James RK. Finding the best crisis intervention team practices for law enforcement agencies in the United States. Paper presented at the First National CIT Conference–Capitol University Law School, Columbus, OH, May 2005.

Bower DL, Pettit WG. The Albuquerque Police Department's crisis intervention team: a report card [Electronic Version]. *FBI Law Enforcement Bull* 2001;February:1–6.

Compton MT, Esterberg ML, McGee R, Kotwicki RJ, Oliva JR. Crisis intervention team training: Changes in knowledge, attitudes, and stigma related to schizophrenia. *Psychiatr Serv* 2006; 57:1199–1202.

Deane MW, Steadman HJ, Borum R, Veysey BM, Morrissey JP. Emerging partnerships between mental health and law enforcement. *Psychiatr Serv* 1999;50(1):99–101.

Dupont R, Cochran S. Police response to mental health emergencies: barriers to change. *J Am Acad Psychiatry Law* 2000;28(3):338–344.

Memphis Police Department, Crisis Intervention. Retrieved October 17, 2006 from http://www.memphispolice.org/Crisis%20Intervention.htm.

Miller L, Braswell M. *Human relations and police work* (5th ed.). Prospect Heights, IL: Waveland Press, 2002.

National Alliance on Mental Illness. (2006). *About NAMI.* Retrieved October 17, 2006, from: http://www.nami.org/Content/NavigationMenu/Inform_Yourself/About_NAMI/About_NAMI.htm

Reuland M. A guide to implementing police-based diversion programs for people with mental illness. TAPA Centre for Jail Diversion, January 2004.

Russell HE, Beigel A. *Understanding human behavior for effective police work* (3rd ed.). New York: Basic Books, 1990.

Steadman HJ, Deane MW, Borum R, Morrissey JP. Comparing outcomes of major models of police responses to mental health emergencies. *Psychiatr Serv* 2000;51(5):645–649.

Steadman HJ, Stainbrook MA, Griffin P, Draine J, Dupont R, Horey C. A specialized crisis response site as a core element of police-based diversion programs. *Community Serv* 2001;52(2):219–222.

Strauss G, Glenn M, Reddi P, Afaq I, Podolskaya A, Rybakova T, et al. Psychiatric disposition of patients brought in by crisis intervention team police officers. *Community Ment Health J* 2005;41(2):223–228.

U.S. Department of Health and Human Services Centers for Disease Control and Prevention–Office of Minority Health. (2005, October 19). *Eliminate disparities in mental health*. Retrieved October 17, 2006, from http://www.cdc.gov/omh/AMH/factsheets/mental.htm.

Acknowledgements and Disclosures

Janet Oliva is employed by the Georgia Bureau of Investigation, a state law enforcement agency, and manages federal grant funding received through a Children's Justice Act grant, which is administered by the Georgia Department of Human Resources, Division of Family and Children Services. The funds were awarded to the Georgia Bureau of Investigation for specific application to the Georgia CIT Program, to address the needs of families and children who have mental illnesses and are in crisis. Dr. Oliva also serves in the capacity of Statewide CIT Coordinator in Georgia, and is a Georgia CIT Advisory Board member.

Nora Haynes is an education specialist who is retired from the Georgia Department of Education. She is co-chair of the Georgia CIT Advisory Board and president of the Georgia chapter of NAMI.

David Covington is a Georgia CIT Advisory Board member, and is employed by the Behavioral Health Link in Atlanta, Georgia. Behavioral Health Link is a service of Integrated Health Resources and is funded by the Georgia Department of Human Resources, Division of Mental Health, Developmental Disabilities and Addictive Diseases to provide screening, triage, and referral services and mobile crisis teams in 15 counties, which include the cities of Atlanta and Augusta. Behavioral Health Link is also the Southeast Regional Crisis and Access Call Center for the 1-800-273-TALK National Suicide Prevention Lifeline Network administered by the Substance Abuse and Mental Health Services Administration's Center for Mental Health Services.

David Lushbaugh is Training Support Services manager for the Georgia-Pacific Corporation in Atlanta, Georgia. He is the former president of NAMI-Georgia and currently chairs the Georgia CIT Advisory Board, which provides oversight for the Georgia CIT Program.

Michael Compton is a Georgia CIT Advisory Board member and is employed by the Emory University School of Medicine. He has received research grant support from the Emory Medical Care Foundation, the American Institute for Research and Education/GlaxoSmithKline, the American Institute for Research and Education/AstraZeneca, and the National Institute of Mental Health. He has served as a consultant for AstraZeneca Pharmaceuticals, WebMD Health, and Medscape.

Collaborations Between Mental Health and Law Enforcement

■ Introduction

This chapter explores ways in which public safety and criminal justice professionals might collaborate with mental health providers to assist individuals with mental illnesses who come in contact with law enforcement. The chapter begins by identifying the various points of intervention starting with the initial call for assistance to a law enforcement agency, tracing the path that would be taken by a **defendant** with a mental illness in the judicial process. Next, it outlines models of collaboration other than the Memphis Crisis Intervention Team (CIT) model (which is described in detail in Chapter 4). Finally, the chapter addresses unmet needs and proposes future directions for promoting jail-diversion programs for people with mental illnesses.

■ Points of Intervention

People with mental illnesses residing in the community often come in contact with law enforcement. The most common scenarios may include one or more of the following: being victimized by another individual, bearing witness to a crime, as the suspect or perpetrator of a crime, as the subject of a mental health crisis (such as suicidal or aggressive behavior), or as the object of complaints of public nuisance. When law enforcement becomes involved in any such event, the typical scenario is that an officer is on patrol and witnesses an event, or law enforcement officers are sent to respond to a call for assistance that is relayed to them by a dispatcher. Law enforcement officers and mental health professionals who work closely together can positively influence the outcomes for individuals with mental illnesses who interact with the legal system. Points of intervention at which offenders with mental illnesses may be diverted away from incarceration and toward appropriate mental health treatment include at the time of dispatch, at the police station, during pre-arraignment custody, or during the **arraignment** itself. Each of these points is described briefly in this section.

Dispatch

Dispatchers, who speak with individuals calling 9-1-1, represent the first point at which law enforcement and mental health professionals may collaborate. Dispatchers may be trained to ask questions to determine whether a mental illness might be a factor in the situation. Mental health professionals may be involved in designing protocols such as a structured questionnaire or flowchart that dispatchers may use to elicit the mental health and substance abuse history of the individuals involved in the call. Detailed records should be kept by law enforcement agencies, especially for locations where there are repeated calls or unresolved problems. Computer-aided dispatch is an example of a computerized system for storing and retrieving detailed information about calls for service. Call histories may be extremely useful if the same individuals with known mental illnesses are repeatedly involved in community crises.

Scene of the Incident

When officers arrive on the scene, they must first ensure the safety of all the persons involved and then bring a resolution to the crisis situation. They also need to determine whether a crime has been committed and whether a mental illness is a significant factor in the incident. Adequate training in recognizing the signs of mental illnesses is obviously essential. Officers frequently consult with knowledgeable professionals to determine whether an emergency mental health evaluation is warranted, and they ultimately decide on a disposition for the individual involved. Mental health professionals—either at the scene itself or when consulted by officers at the scene—may be helpful in determining whether the person's behavior results from malice or symptoms of an untreated mental illness. While on the scene, officers should document their observations of the appearance, behavior, and speech of individuals with mental illnesses, in addition to gathering other relevant information concerning the incident. This documentation could have a huge effect on the legal disposition and the mental health treatment of the person involved.

> While on the scene, officers should document their observations of the appearance, behavior, and speech of individuals with mental illnesses, in addition to gathering other relevant information concerning the incident.

Police Station

If an officer determines that a crime has been committed and that it serves the public interest for a person with a mental illness to be taken into custody, the officer may bring the person (now a defendant) to a holding facility or jail. The defendant is held in this location until an arraignment takes place.

During this time, it is critical that detainees be adequately screened for suicide risk and to determine whether an emergency psychiatric evaluation is needed. Any of the following issues can cause a sudden deterioration in an individual's mental state: substance intoxication or withdrawal, unrecognized physical health problems, sleep deprivation, medication side effects, and need for continuation of prescribed psychiatric medication. Most suicides occur during the first few days in custody. People with mental illnesses often need continued access to their prescribed medications and, like all detainees, they should be offered adequate food, water, and access to toilet facilities. Mental health professionals may become involved in many aspects of the course of action at the police station, from initial suicide assessment to prescribing psychiatric medications to individuals who are being detained.

> Any of the following issues can cause a sudden deterioration in an individual's mental state: substance intoxication or withdrawal, unrecognized physical health problems, sleep deprivation, medication side effects, and need for continuation of prescribed psychiatric medication.

Pre-arraignment Custody

The next stage at which mental health professionals and law enforcement officers might interact occurs during the pre-arraignment custody period. While the defendant is in custody waiting for the first appearance in front of a judge (the arraignment), the prosecuting attorney reads the police report and reviews the defendant's criminal history, frequently called the "rap sheet." The defendant is given the opportunity to hire a lawyer; if he or she does not have the financial means to do so, a public defender is appointed.

Defense attorneys need to have adequate information about their clients' mental illness and treatment. In some states, attorneys can access state mental health records with a client's consent. Defense attorneys also need to be aware of available mental health resources and alternatives to incarceration, including pretrial diversion treatment options, which occur at the discretion of the prosecutor at this point in the process of arrest. Generally, after being charged with a nonviolent misdemeanor, the defendant may be offered participation in pretrial diversion, wherein he or she may undergo intensive mental health and/or substance abuse treatment for a period of 6 to 12 months. Upon successful completion of this program, charges may be dropped. If treatment is not completed successfully, the prosecution process resumes.

Mental health providers play essential roles during this pre-arraignment phase of arrest. These professionals may provide thorough outpatient mental health records that lay the groundwork for jail-diversion treatment requests. Similarly, mental health professionals may partner with defense or even prosecuting attorneys to petition for jail-diversion treatment alternatives rather than incarceration for offenders with mental illnesses. The more clear and detailed the jail-diversion plan is, the more likely a judge will approve it. Pre-arraignment mental health and law enforcement partnerships are crucial in avoiding incarceration of individuals with mental illnesses.

Arraignment and Pretrial Release/Detention Hearing

At the arraignment, defendants are formally advised of the charges against them and asked how they wish to plead. At the pretrial release/detention hearing, the judge decides whether the defendant will be released or held in jail until the case can be adjudicated. This decision is based on information available to the judge, who weighs the risk of the defendant failing to appear in court as well as the potential threat to the safety of the community should the defendant be released.

Each jurisdiction assigns some kind of neutral entity (pretrial services, in some places) to gather information relevant to the pretrial release decision. Defendants should be advised that they have the right to speak with an attorney before answering any questions. The neutral entity is charged to advise the judicial officer on the defendant's mental health history and, with permission from the defendant, the defendant's current mental state. Then the judicial officer makes a decision to either release the defendant or continue legal proceedings based on that evidence. The neutral entity also researches and develops a list of available options to address the defendant's mental health needs. Mental health professionals may be very helpful in assessing the defendant's mental status and even in devising jail-diversion treatment alternatives.

> Pretrial release treatment options for defendants with mental illnesses may include inpatient and outpatient treatment programs, assertive community treatment, intensive case management, crisis residential services, recovery-oriented psychosocial rehabilitation programs, treatment for co-occurring substance use disorders, assistance with housing and finances, access to transportation, and vocational counseling.

It is often in the best interest of the defendant to release mental health information to the judge to facilitate release into a pretrial diversion treatment program. Pretrial release treatment options for defendants with mental illnesses may include the following options: inpatient and outpatient treatment programs, assertive community treatment, intensive case management, crisis residential services, recovery-oriented psychosocial rehabilitation programs, treatment for co-occurring substance use disorders, assistance with housing and finances, access to transportation, and vocational counseling. Strong liaison relationships between law enforcement and mental health professionals assist in determining the most appropriate and expeditious placement of defendants into these treatment options.

Defendants who would otherwise be entitled to pretrial release should not be detained solely to conduct a competency evaluation. A pretrial release decision and the assessment of competency are legally separate issues.

Jail

Defendants who are not released at the pretrial release hearing are sent to the local city or county jail until they can post bail or the case is adjudicated. This point is a critical juncture for the well-being of defendants with mental illnesses. Jails should have policies and procedures in place to screen for, evaluate, and treat the mental illnesses and **substance abuse** or **withdrawal** syndromes of detainees. Observation of new inmates should last for at least 72 hours—the period of greatest risk for mental deterioration precipitated by stress or substance withdrawal syndromes. Jails should also develop specific policies and procedures to screen for mental illnesses and suicidal thinking, under the supervision of qualified mental health professionals. When jail staff detect signs of a possible mental illness, referral to a mental health professional should occur.

Jail staff should also be trained to recognize mental health crises. Mental health professionals including psychiatrists should be available 24 hours a day, seven days a week, to evaluate potential crises and prescribe emergency medications in detention facilities. In addition, specialized housing units should be available for inmates who require close medical supervision.

Discharge planning—the development of a transition plan from jail back into the community—should be included among the mental health services provided in jails and prisons. Failure to do so may precipitate a rapid deterioration in mental status with acute psychiatric hospitalization or re-incarceration following release from jail. Psychiatric social workers and case managers may be extremely useful in discharge planning.

Adjudication

Just like cases in which a mental illness is not a factor, charges against a defendant with a mental illness may be dropped, the defendant can plead guilty, or the defendant can be found guilty or not guilty by trial. In addition, the law allows other options specific to defendants with severe mental illnesses: They may be found incompetent to stand trial, not guilty by reason of insanity, or guilty but insane. The latter two rulings are very rarely used. Although many people assume that the legal findings "not guilty by reason of insanity" and "guilty but insane" absolve defendants of their responsibilities altogether, the mandated forensic mental health treatment alternatives associated with these rulings can be even more restrictive than incarceration.

A judge also may exercise discretion in pursuing alternatives to conviction and sentencing for people with mental illnesses. For example, in some states, a court may defer or withhold **adjudication** and order a defendant to abide by conditions such as mental health and/or substance abuse treatment. Generally, if these conditions are met, the charges are dismissed. Consequently, several court strategies are available to divert offenders with mental illnesses away from incarceration and toward mental health treatment.

In addition to rulings in traditional courts used to divert individuals with mental illnesses toward treatment, other courts have been developed to specifically address mental health issues among defendants. Mental health and drug courts are specialized courts that operate in some jurisdictions, albeit with widely varying procedures and methods. Their purpose is to effectively address the needs of persons with serious mental illness and substance use disorders. Typical sentencing options within mental health or drug courts may include charging a fine and imposing a period of probation or incarceration in a jail or prison. Ideally, by the time a case has reached this point, there is sufficient information to assist the sentencing judge in formulating an individualized sentence aimed at addressing the mental health disorders that were present during the illegal behaviors.

If a pre-sentencing investigation report is generated, it should include information about the defendant's medical and mental health histories. This information is to be disclosed only to defense counsel, the prosecution, the court, and any supervising correctional institution or probation, and only with the consent of the defendant. When an offender is known to suffer from a mental illness, the following information should be made available to the court at the time of sentencing: diagnoses including co-occurring substance use disorders, current and past treatment histories, and available community resources. A sentencing judge in the mental health or drug court should be able to order mental health treatment as a condition of release. Defendants should have the same options available to them as in pretrial diversion. Nevertheless, mental health or drug courts differ from traditional courts in that the former courts have greater leeway to order mental health treatment for convicted defendants.

> Discharge planning—the development of a transition plan from jail back into the community—should be included among the mental health services provided in jails and prisons. Failure to do so may precipitate a rapid deterioration in mental status and acute psychiatric hospitalization or re-incarceration following release from jail.

> The law allows several options specific to defendants with severe mental illnesses: They may be found incompetent to stand trial, not guilty by reason of insanity, or guilty but insane. The legal findings "not guilty by reason of insanity" and "guilty but insane" do not absolve defendants of their responsibilities altogether, because the mandated forensic mental health treatment alternatives associated with these rulings can be even more restrictive than incarceration.

■ Existing Models of Collaboration

Given the various points at which jail diversion is possible for defendants with mental illnesses, it should come as no surprise that various municipalities have developed unique programs focusing on different stages of arrest. This section briefly describes several of these programs.

CIT Training for All Officers

The Athens-Clarke Crisis Intervention Program in Athens, Georgia, trains every officer using the CIT model. This universal approach to training all police officers implies that all officers require skills to effectively respond to persons with mental illnesses in the community. All new recruits are required to attend post-academy training in mental health crisis intervention. The police department intends to eventually train all sworn personnel in the CIT model. Training all law enforcers in a department has obvious advantages. Possible disadvantages include cost, the lack of interest some officers may have in learning CIT, and the lack of generalizability of this model to larger departments.

CIT and Medical Bracelet Program

Seminole County, Florida, assigns a CIT-trained officer to every shift. In addition, CIT staff create and maintain files of information on every person with whom they have contact. This department also participates in the Medical Bracelet Program, which offers free, voluntary registration to people with mental illnesses. An individual's bracelet or identification card alerts law enforcement officers to important medical or mental health conditions, just like the bracelet that people with diabetes often wear to alert first responders to their disease. This information is stored in the department's communication center and is available at any time.

This model has advantages of constant CIT availability as well as the ready availability of mental health information on the bracelets. However, consumers who lose their bracelets or who choose not to wear them do not realize these potential benefits from the program. Emergency first responders similarly may not observe the bracelets if they do not look for them, limiting their usefulness. Perhaps most important, wearing a bracelet—an outward sign of a mental illness—may exacerbate the stigma felt by persons with these conditions.

New Recruit Education

In 1976, the Birmingham, Alabama, police department developed a Community Service Officer (CSO) unit. This unit responds to situations involving any of the following elements: elder abuse, child endangerment, domestic abuse incidents, and situations involving survivors of violent crimes, missing persons, and mental illness crises. In addition, when a patrol officer responds to a call involving someone with a mental illness, he or she can ask for secondary response from a CSO.

The CSO unit is staffed by six social workers. These social workers are not sworn police officers, nor do they carry weapons or have the authority to arrest. They dress in civilian clothes, drive unmarked cars, and carry police radios. The CSOs can provide crisis intervention, make referrals, and transport individuals to a mental health facility for evaluation and treatment.

Specialized mental health professionals on the CSO unit may use their expert knowledge to triage and de-escalate community-based situations involving individuals with mental illnesses. Separating CSO staff from the rest of the department may create several challenges, however. While the CSO staff thoroughly understand mental health concepts, they may have limited legal or safety knowledge. This disparity may result in unsafe aggressive circumstances, limited authority, or even a "hierarchy" within the department in which CSO staff are viewed to be less important because they cannot make arrests or carry weapons.

Psychiatric Emergency Response Team

San Diego County, California, has formed 24 Psychiatric Emergency Response Teams composed of trained officers or deputies paired with mental health professionals. These teams are specially selected, and all must complete an 80-hour course of training. They respond to calls that may involve mental illnesses throughout the county.

Community Mental Health Officer

The Florence, Alabama, Police Department uses a modified CIT approach in its law enforcement partnership with mental health professionals. In this model, one officer (who has received approximately 100 hours of mental health training) serves as a community mental health officer (CMHO) and is the second responder to all calls involving people with mental illnesses. The CMHO, who is available on an around-the-clock basis, determines whether the person needs an urgent psychiatric evaluation and has the authority to order an involuntary commitment for 48 hours, similar to the role of many probate judges. He or she also reviews arrest reports on a weekly basis to check on the status of arrestees who have been identified as having a mental illness. The CMHO also determines whether the arrestees are adherent with medications, whether their conditions are deteriorating, and whether they may be in need of emergency treatment. This officer maintains close ties with the local mental health facility and the local hospital emergency room, where arrestees are taken for injuries or treatment of other medical conditions. In 2001, the CMHO and the Alabama State Department of Mental Health collaborated to develop a 40-hour, statewide, post-academy training program in mental health and substance abuse for all officers.

The continuity of care and information a CMHO provides to a municipality is remarkable. Unfortunately, employing such a health officer can be costly. Moreover, the use of a second responder may consume valuable time. Coordination of arrival of one officer to a scene can be difficult enough; adding a second may be prohibitive.

Mobile Crisis Teams with Police Collaboration

Mobile Crisis Teams (also referred to as Mobile Crisis Units), like those in Anne Arundel County, Maryland, are generally part of a local community mental health service system, are staffed with licensed mental health clinicians, and work closely with law enforcement. The Mobile Crisis Team is working or on call throughout every day and night in most areas. The team acts as second responders who are called to assist once the scene has been secured by law enforcement. Staff members may be contacted to assist police officers in any of the following situations: mental health crises, incidents involving individuals with **developmental disabilities**, and incidents involving victims of domestic abuse or sexual assault. Mobile Crisis Team staff may become involved in transporting individuals to a mental health facility or to substance abuse treatment programs. Mobile Crisis Teams may also be important when outpatient commitments—court-mandated, monitored mental health or substance abuse treatment—are involved. In addition, they are responsible for being aware of and connecting individuals with community resources.

Mobile Crisis Teams become involved in a mental health crisis only after scene safety has been established by law enforcement officers. This approach has both positive and negative aspects. On the one hand, it is helpful for mental health professionals not to be involved in potentially dangerous situations so that attention can be focused on mental health care instead of public safety. On the other hand, much therapeutic value can be lost during de-escalation attempts that do not include professionals with mental health training. The success of Mobile Crisis Teams also depends on family or law enforcers' willingness to involve the teams in particular situations. If the Mobile Crisis Team is not contacted during a crisis, this model of law enforcement–mental health partnering cannot work.

Forensic Assertive Community Treatment

Assertive Community Treatment (ACT) was originally developed to help people with severe mental illnesses, who are at high risk of homelessness and hospitalization, become successfully reintegrated into the community. ACT programs are designed to engage high-risk individuals using mobile services that are available 24/7 using active outreach. They offer a broad range of services, including mental health and addiction treatment, transportation, financial services, and vocational support. ACT teams also employ **peer specialists**—that is, consumers who have recovered from their mental illnesses and are willing to share their personal experiences with others.

Forensic Assertive Community Treatment (fACT) programs, such as Project Link in Rochester, New York, aim both to engage consumers who have not done well in traditional outpatient mental health settings and to prevent re-arrest and re-incarceration. Project Link requires a history of arrest for admission to the program, uses the jail as its primary referral source, partners with multiple criminal justice agencies to divert clients from further criminal justice involvement, and provides residentially based addiction treatment, if needed. Preliminary research suggests that this program may be effective at improving community adjustment and reducing the rates of arrest, incarceration, and hospitalization.

The virtues of fACT are manifold. Consumers have increased psychosocial support and services to aid in their recoveries. The program's incorporation of peer specialists reduces the stigma associated with severe, persistent mental illnesses and repeated incarcerations. The multidisciplinary team approach ensures that most areas of consumers' lives are considered in treatment planning. Unfortunately, the relatively steep costs of fACT (roughly $500,000 per team annually treating 30 consumers) combined with the paucity of mental health professionals trained in this model limit the number of other communities that can support this model of care. Additionally, a law enforcement officer is not directly included as part of a fACT team. Such an omission may create challenges in acute safety crises or when consumers are arrested.

■ Unmet Needs and Future Directions

Inadequate Mental Health Resources

Unfortunately, the mental health system in the United States is underfunded, complicated, and fragmented. It comprises both private and public systems of care and is funded by a wide variety of payment sources, including Medicaid, Medicare, state general revenue funds, local matches, federal mental health block grants, patient fees, and payments from private health insurance companies. It can be quite challenging to determine what resources exist in a given locality and how they can be accessed by people with mental illnesses who are involved with the criminal justice system.

It is particularly problematic to find appropriate diversion treatment alternatives in rural communities, where medical and mental health services are in extremely short supply. Despite the fact that the prevalence of mental health and substance use disorders is similar in rural and urban areas, there is a shortage of mental health providers, including both psychiatrists and licensed social workers, in rural areas. In addition, people who live in rural areas may experience more difficulties in finding adequate transportation and obtaining health insurance, even when mental health resources exist in the community. Residents of small towns or rural areas also may have greater concerns about the stigma associated with being diagnosed with and seeking help for a psychiatric illness. Indeed, the ability to maintain confidentiality is questionable in these sparsely populated areas—a consideration that can affect opportunities for housing, insurance, and employment.

Solutions to these problems need to address issues related to training and recruitment of mental health professionals in underserved localities, reimbursement issues, and models of collaboration between primary care providers and specialized mental healthcare systems. Innovative approaches, including telemedicine and mobile clinics, may also be required to overcome these obstacles. Other unresolved problems include shortages in personnel and systems that can provide culturally competent services, child and adolescent services, geriatric services, services for people with developmental disabilities, treatment programs for sex offenders, and integrated treatment programs for individuals with co-occurring mental illnesses and substance use disorders.

Housing Issues

Successful reintegration of the person with a mental illness into the community depends on the availability of safe, supportive, and affordable housing. Some research shows that retention rates are higher in housing that is part of an integrated mental health services program rather than independent housing without attached services. Every correctional facility's release/transition planning process should include assistance with housing, if needed.

Unfortunately, it can be extremely difficult to obtain housing for individuals who are stigmatized by having both a mental illness and a criminal history. For example, individuals convicted of certain violent, drug-related, or sexual offenses are not eligible for federal housing assistance. In addition, unemployment, poverty, and disruptions in Social Security benefits—including Supplemental Security Income (SSI) and Social Security Disability Insurance (SSDI)—related to incarceration make obtaining adequate housing even more challenging. Accessing health care also may be more difficult for persons who have been incarcerated because after 30 days of imprisonment, Medicaid benefits, including mental health benefits, are suspended. Integrated treatment programs (such as the fACT program described earlier) that offer comprehensive services such as intensive case management, psychiatric care, substance abuse treatment, housing, assistance with finances and prevocational services can provide much needed services for this vulnerable population, which remains at high risk of re-arrest, homelessness, or acute mental status deterioration.

Social Security Benefits, Medicaid, and Medicare

People who are disabled, including many individuals with mental illnesses, are eligible for monthly income support through the SSDI and/or SSI programs. SSDI is meant to provide income for people who have worked and paid Social Security taxes. When a person's SSDI income is low because he or she has not worked very long, that individual also may be eligible for SSI. SSI is awarded to low-income individuals who do not have substantial work histories. Once someone is found to be eligible for SSI, in most states that individual also automatically becomes eligible for Medicaid. Medicaid is a government-sponsored medical insurance for disabled and low-income individuals. Persons who receive SSDI become eligible for Medicare 24 months after they qualify for SSDI income.

Arrest and incarceration can cause significant disruptions in income and health insurance coverage. One cannot continue to receive SSI or SSDI benefits while incarcerated. Generally, SSI payments are suspended for incarcerations of up to 12 months. The individual then has to apply to have benefits reinstated when he or she is released, so long as the person still meets the low-income eligibility requirements. However, individuals who have been incarcerated for more than 12 months must start the application process all over. People who have been incarcerated for one year or longer must reapply for SSI benefits and demonstrate that they currently meet the federal definition of "disabled." This process is lengthy, time-consuming, and often unsuccessful the first time around. Incarceration very definitely affects one's income and corresponding ability to successfully reintegrate into society after release from jail or prison.

Inmates who had not received SSI or SSDI before incarceration may apply for benefits in anticipation of their release. These individuals often need assistance with completing the forms and submitting information to support their applications. Corrections staff should actively assist inmates with mental illnesses with applying for benefits to which they may be entitled, including SSI, SSDI, Temporary Assistance for Needy Families (e.g., food stamps, infant support), Veterans Administration programs, Medicaid, and Medicare. Because many inmates with mental illnesses have such limited resources, linking them with available social programs in a timely manner can mean the difference between successful reintegration versus re-arrest and re-incarceration.

Professional Education

There is an ongoing need for improved understanding and collaboration among professionals working in mental health, law enforcement, and corrections. Mental health professionals are often unaware of the specific paths that their clients may take in traversing the criminal justice system or the points at which their involvement/advocacy can have a positive impact on these individuals' welfare. Improved understanding of the roles of the various professionals and organizations might lead to enhanced collaboration between law enforcement and mental health professionals, program development, and innovative patient-advocacy initiatives. Further research on the effectiveness of educational programs and models of collaboration are needed. Like everyone else, individuals with mental illnesses have families, friends, hopes, dreams, and, in many cases, a great and unrealized potential to contribute to our society in meaningful ways.

Chapter Wrap-Up

- Collaboration between criminal justice/law enforcement professionals and mental health professionals is essential to ensure appropriate diversion of individuals with mental illnesses away from incarceration and toward treatment.

- There are several key points at which law enforcement–mental health collaborations can make dramatic differences—namely, dispatch, at the scene, at the police station, in the pre-arraignment custody period, in the arraignment period, at a trial, during incarceration, and especially in jail or prison discharge planning.

- In addition to CIT training, a variety of other models of collaboration between law enforcement officials and the mental health community have been developed. Each model has its own virtues and limitations.

- Forensic ACT teams are multidisciplinary, intensive support teams that include peer specialists and produce positive outcomes for people with histories of multiple incarcerations and difficulties accessing traditional mental health services.

- An incarceration history poses challenges to successful reintegration of the inmate with a mental illness into society after release. Entitlements such as Social Security benefits, Medicaid, and general assistance may be lost during imprisonment, and past incarceration limits subsidized housing and employment opportunities.

Vital Vocabulary

adjudication: legal ruling of the punishment or retribution for the perpetrator of a crime

arraignment: a defendant's first appearance in front of a judge at which time the defendant is formally advised of the charges against him or her, and asked how he or she wishes to plead

defendant: an individual taken into police custody as result of possible criminal activity. Designation given to someone prior to an official legal verdict

developmental disabilities: mental impairments that affect a person's abilities to think, communicate, interact with others, remember facts and details, and take care of oneself; all developmental disabilities, such as mental retardation and autistic disorder, appear before the age of 18 and remain with the person throughout his or her life

discharge planning: the development of a plan for transitioning from jail to the community

peer specialists: consumers who have recovered from their mental illnesses and are wiling to share their experiences with others

substance abuse: a maladaptive pattern of substance use that causes repeated problems

withdrawal: a physiological and/or psychological syndrome that occurs when someone who has been regularly using a drug stops abruptly; different addictive substances are associated with different withdrawal syndromes

Questions for Review and Discussion

1. Why is it essential that, while on the scene, officers document their observations of the appearance, behavior, and speech of individuals with mental illnesses, in addition to gathering other relevant information concerning the incident?
2. Explain the importance of discharge planning for individuals with mental illnesses, as well as the possible consequences of failure to undertake discharge planning.
3. Why is collaboration between criminal justice/law enforcement professionals and mental health professionals essential for individuals with mental illnesses?

Resources

Council of State Governments. Criminal Justice/Mental Health Consensus Project. New York: Council of State Governments, June 2002.

Handbook for working with defendants and offenders with mental disorders (3rd ed.). Federal Justice Center, October 2003.

Lamb HR, Weinberger LE, DeCuir WJ. The police and mental health. *Psychiatr Serv* 2002;53:1266–1271.

Lamberti SJ, Weisman RF, Dara I. Forensic assertive community treatment: preventing incarceration of adults with severe mental illness. *Psychiatr Serv* 2004;55:1285–1293.

Massaro J. *Working with people with mental illness involved in the criminal justice system: what mental health service providers need to know* (2nd ed.). Delmar, NY: Technical Assistance and Policy Analysis Center for Jail Diversion.

Steadman HJ, Williams-Deane M, Borum R, Morrissey JP. Comparing outcomes of major models of police responses to mental health emergencies. *Psychiatr Serv* 2000;51:645–649.

Acknowledgements and Disclosures

Karen Hochman has received research grant support from the Emory Medical Care Foundation. She is grateful to Judge Winston P. Bethel, chief magistrate in DeKalb County, Georgia, for assistance in reviewing this chapter and for introducing her to the concept of "therapeutic jurisprudence." This chapter is dedicated to the memory of Dr. Hochman's brother, Mark Dickof. He was initially diagnosed with schizophrenia while undergoing a fitness assessment for a misdemeanor charge in Toronto, Canada, in 1989.

Understanding Mental Illnesses

PART

II

6 **Recognizing Signs and Symptoms of Mental Illnesses**
Monica Taylor-Desir, M.D., M.P.H.

7 **Schizophrenia and Related Disorders**
Michael T. Compton, M.D., M.P.H.

8 **Mood Disorders: Major Depression and Bipolar Disorder**
Nzinga Ajabu Harrison, M.D.

9 **Substance Abuse and Dependence**
Jocelyn Smith Cox, M.D.

10 **Delirium and Dementia**
Manjula Kallur, M.D.
Raymond J. Kotwicki, M.D., M.P.H.

11 **Responding to Children and Adolescents with Emotional and Behavioral Disorders**
Leesha Ellis-Cox, M.D.

12 **Responding to Individuals with Developmental Disabilities**
Carol M. Schall, Ph.D.

13 **Anxiety Disorders**
Ruth S. Shim, M.D.

14 **Maladaptive Coping Skills, Personality Disorders, and Malingering**
Patrick J. Haggard, M.D.

Recognizing Signs and Symptoms of Mental Illnesses

Case Vignette: Mac

Mac is a 58-year-old, African American male veteran. Since his discharge from the U.S. Army in his early twenties, Mac has spent the majority of his life being homeless. Although he never witnessed military combat, he was discharged from the army due to a mental illness that developed during his service. Mac has been in and out of hospitals over the years. Most of the people in his urban neighborhood know Mac by name.

One evening a teenaged girl in the neighborhood places a 9-1-1 call. She reports that a scruffy-looking man has wandered into her yard and is acting bizarrely, waving his arms. Upon arrival at the scene, officers notice that Mac appears to be wearing four or five layers of clothing even though it is summertime. He is pacing back and forth in the front yard of the home and appears to be carrying on a conversation with unseen persons. When the officers try to engage Mac, he tells the officers that they already know what he has been thinking and that they found him because of the radio waves that are coming out of the microchip that was placed in his heart when he entered the military. A crowd is beginning to gather around the home and some neighbors are taunting Mac, but his facial expression appears to be blank and set in stone. He continues to tell the officers, while pacing, that the government is after him and that they have come for him because they are agents of the army.

■ Introduction

In today's society, police officers are increasingly asked to perform a type of street triage. Police officers are often the first—and many times the only—community resource called to respond to situations involving persons with mental illnesses. The community has an expectation that the responding officer will accurately recognize an individual with mental health needs and refer that person to the appropriate resources. The officer must determine whether an individual's criminal activity is the primary concern and warrants making an arrest, or whether the person exhibits evidence of a mental illness, indicating a need for referral to an evaluation facility. In many communities, the police force has the only 24-hour emergency transport capability for a person with a mental illness. If a person does not want to be evaluated, the police department is oftentimes the only agency that can involuntarily transport a person to an evaluation facility. Thus one of the most valuable tools an officer can possess is a basic understanding of the signs and symptoms of mental illnesses.

> One of the most valuable tools an officer can possess is a basic understanding of the signs and symptoms of mental illnesses.

An illness, whether physical or mental, presents with both signs and symptoms. For medical and mental health professionals, a **sign** is an objective observation indicating that something is out of the ordinary or that a disease process might be present. Signs may be observed in a routine encounter or they may be elicited through laboratory tests or other examinations. Examples of signs of illnesses include fever, agitation, elevated blood pressure, high blood glucose (blood sugar), or a slowing of one's movements. A person does not complain about signs, such as high blood pressure or elevated blood glucose. Rather, these signs are observed by a healthcare provider and may indicate the presence of a medical problem such as hypertension (high blood pressure) or diabetes.

A **symptom**, by contrast, is a subjective experience that may not necessarily be observed by an onlooker. Examples of symptoms reported by patients include fatigue, headaches, nausea, and hallucinations. Symptoms often cause a person to go to a healthcare provider, whereas signs of an illness are discovered through tests and examinations.

Most medical and psychiatric illnesses consist of clusters of both signs and symptoms. Such a cluster is called a **syndrome**. An example of a medical syndrome is diabetes, which consists of both signs—such as elevated blood glucose—and symptoms—such as increased thirst, increased hunger, frequent urination, and numbness and tingling in the fingers and toes. Other common medical syndromes include a heart attack, an ear infection, the flu, coma, and stroke. An example of a psychiatric syndrome is mania, which likewise consists of both signs—excessive speech and irritability—and symptoms—a decreased need for sleep, increased energy, and racing thoughts. The many other psychiatric syndromes include depression, panic, psychosis, and dementia.

The word **diagnosis** refers to the specific medical terminology given to an illness by healthcare professionals—that is, a medical term that describes a specific syndrome. Examples of specific medical diagnoses include diabetes mellitus (diabetes), acute myocardial infarction (heart attack), and cerebrovascular accident (stroke). Psychiatric diagnoses include bipolar disorder, major depressive disorder, and Alzheimer's disease, among many others. Mental health professionals make psychiatric diagnoses based on patients' signs and symptoms according to specific criteria outlined in the *Diagnostic and Statistical Manual of Mental Disorders,* fourth edition (*DSM-IV*), a book developed by leading psychiatric researchers. To be diagnosed with a psychiatric illness, a person must exhibit various combinations of signs and symptoms over a specified period of time. Symptoms that may be due to drugs, medical conditions, or other psychiatric illnesses may not meet full diagnostic criteria.

Mental illnesses can affect almost all areas of a person's life. They cause combinations of signs and symptoms that may include emotional changes (affecting one's feelings), cognitive changes (affecting one's thinking or beliefs), perceptual changes (affecting one's senses), and behavioral changes (affecting one's movements or actions). Whereas the other chapters in Part 2 focus on specific psychiatric diagnoses, this chapter presents some of the many psychiatric signs and symptoms that form these diagnoses. These signs and symptoms are important indicators, or clues, that a mental illness may be present. As such, public safety and criminal justice professionals can observe signs and listen for symptoms to assist in accessing care so that formal diagnoses can be made by mental health professionals.

■ Signs and Symptoms Involving Emotions

Mental health professionals use the word __mood__ to indicate the subjective report of one's inner emotional state. Therefore, a mood problem is subjective and is designated as a symptom. Examples of mood symptoms include sadness, depression, mood swings, excessive happiness, irritability, and anxiety. Feelings of sadness or mild depression are often appropriate responses to a disappointment or a loss. However, depression that causes problems in one's life is a mood that is characterized by persistent sadness (lasting two weeks or longer), loneliness, despair, low self-esteem, helplessness, hopelessness, and an inability to cope with the stresses of everyday life. Severely depressed individuals may find it very difficult to become motivated to carry out even the most mundane day-to-day tasks.

On the opposite end of the emotion spectrum, a person's mood may be elevated. Normal feelings of well-being, expansiveness, optimism, and pleasure are experienced when life is going very well and in states of love. Sometimes, however, mood elevations develop that are unrelated to experiences and become dysfunctional. Elevated moods include euphoria, elation, and ecstasy. Euphoria is an exaggerated feeling of well-being that is inappropriate and unrelated to one's circumstances. Elation is a mood consisting of joy, triumph, and intense self-satisfaction or optimism. Euphoria or elation may be present in __mania,__ which is a syndrome that occurs in people who have bipolar disorder (see Chapter 8). During an episode of mania, an individual may exhibit impairments in judgment, excessive spending, decreased need for sleep, rapid speech, racing thoughts, and functional impairment. As mania increases, irritability and anger often increase. Abnormally elevated moods are primarily seen in manic states, but they may result from the use of certain medications or street drugs as well. __Hypomania__ is a milder form of mania that can be characterized as cheerful and brimming with self-confidence, though it also can be irritable.

Mental health professionals use the term __affect__ to describe the external expression of an individual's inner emotional state. It is possible to observe a person's external expressions; therefore problems with one's affect are usually signs rather than symptoms. Whereas mood is a person's own report of how the individual is feeling emotionally, affect is the observation that others can make about the person's emotions. A person's affect may be described in several ways. For example, saying that the affect is "blunted or flat" means that a person's expression remains static even when his or her internal mood varies. It remains stable regardless of what is happening in the environment, almost as if no emotions are felt. This kind of __blunted or flat affect__ is sometimes seen in schizophrenia (see Chapter 7). An __inappropriate affect__ describes situations in which a person's facial expression and outward emotion do not match the individual's thoughts. An example may be inappropriate laughter when discussing something sad. A person who has a rapidly changing affect, such as laughing one minute and crying the next, is described as having a __labile affect__. A labile affect is often present during a manic episode of bipolar disorder.

Psychiatric signs and symptoms must always be considered within the context of the individual's ethnic background and culture. Some behaviors or symptoms that may be mistaken as psychiatric signs and symptoms may truly be appropriate in unique cultures. For example, many fundamentalist Christian churches support the idea that parishioners having spiritual experiences are able to talk in languages they have never studied or that do not exist. Such beliefs may appear disorganized or delusional to someone unaware of the context in which they occur. Cultural influences determine appropriateness of certain behaviors.

Anxiety is often a normal, transient feeling that helps a person adapt to a situation that may pose a threat. As such, anxiety can be thought of as the basis for the "fight or flight" response that drives all sorts of physiological changes, such as elevated heart rate, sweating, or diversion of blood toward muscles. In contrast to fear, the emotional state that exists when the source of a threat is evident, anxiety may occur when a perceived threat is not well defined but still anticipated. Persons with anxiety often find it difficult to describe the feeling of anxiety. Anxiety is characterized by a host of physical and psychological responses to a threatening situation (real or fantasized), and some mental illnesses cause excessive anxiety that is associated with impairments in functioning. A person describing feelings of anxiety may state that he or she is tense, panicky, terrified, jittery, nervous, wound up, unable to relax, or unable to sleep. An individual with anxiety may also complain of dizziness, chest pain, headache, tingling in the fingers or toes, nausea, restlessness, or fidgetiness.

A **panic attack** is a specific syndrome of anxiety that consists of a circumscribed episode of severe anxiety usually lasting 10 to 30 minutes. Associated symptoms usually peak within 10 minutes, including the subjective experience that one may be dying or losing control. Signs of a panic attack may include chest pain, difficulty breathing, shortness of breath, sweating, and tremors of the hands. It has been estimated that as much as 30% of the general population experiences at least one panic attack each year. When panic attacks are recurrent and unexpected, the person may be diagnosed with panic disorder, which is a specific psychiatric diagnosis for which effective treatments have been developed.

■ Signs and Symptoms Involving Thoughts or Beliefs

Usually a person's thought process is effortless, clear, and easy to follow—one thought logically connects to the next in a linear fashion. Occasionally, however, a person's thoughts may be scattered, and he or she may experience difficulty sticking to one topic. The majority of people have briefly experienced periods of losing one's train of thought, not being able to identify a word, or having racing thoughts during times of extreme stress. A person's speech pattern provides clues to his or her thought patterns. Thoughts may be either unusually slow or excessively accelerated. **Thought blocking** is a sign that appears as a break in the train of thought. A person may abruptly stop his or her conversation in mid-sentence and be unable to express the next thought. Thought blocking is sometimes seen in individuals with schizophrenia. Accelerated types of thinking are exhibited through racing thoughts, rapid speech, and **flight of ideas** (a rapid flow of thought with frequent changes of topics). A person exhibiting **pressured speech** talks in a rapid, excessive, and loud fashion. Racing thoughts, flight of ideas, and pressured speech are often characteristic of mania in bipolar disorder.

A person's thought process may also be described by its direction and continuity. A person may have **circumstantial thinking**, in which the thoughts digress from the topic, include excessive detail, but eventually return to the initial topic of conversation. A person who is **tangential** will depart from the topic of conversation and continue to wander farther and farther from the topic, never returning to the initial topic of conversation. The term **loose associations** describes a collection of thoughts that do not have a clear relation. **Word salad** consists of words that are strung together, but have no clear relation. These signs, which make up a syndrome called a **formal thought disorder**, may be present in some subtypes of schizophrenia.

Whereas the **thought process** refers to how the thoughts are put together (and can be disorganized as described earlier), **thought content** consists of what the person is thinking about. Thus, when mental health professionals assess their patients' thought content, they may ask questions to determine whether ideas of reference, obsessions, paranoia, or delusions are present. **Ideas of reference** are false ideas that events or statements refer specifically to oneself when they actually do not. **Delusions** are fixed, false beliefs. These beliefs are usually not congruent with the person's educational, social, or cultural background. Many types of delusions are distinguished, including delusions of grandeur and paranoid delusions. **Delusions of grandeur** are beliefs that one holds special powers or is extremely important (for example, "I am Jesus Christ"). **Paranoid delusions** are beliefs that one is being followed, watched, or maliciously pursued (e.g., "There are harmful x-ray beams coming through my apartment floor from the neighbor downstairs"). Paranoid delusions are probably the most common delusions that a law enforcement officer encounters. Persons experiencing paranoia can be extremely suspicious and tense and can appear very frightening to others.

■ Signs and Symptoms Involving Perceptions or Senses

The most common perceptual symptoms are **hallucinations**. A hallucination is a perception that occurs in the absence of an external stimulus. The most commonly encountered perceptual disturbances are **auditory hallucinations**, which are often reported as "hearing voices." Some auditory hallucinations are **command hallucinations** that instruct a person to do something. These hallucinations may vary in intensity, and patients vary in their abilities to resist acting on such commands. Auditory hallucinations are relatively common among individuals with schizophrenia, but can also occur in the context of depression, bipolar disorder, dementia, and delirium. **Visual hallucinations**—seeing things when nothing is really there—are rarer. A **flashback**, which may occur in post-traumatic stress disorder, is similar to a visual hallucination, but it is an intense visual reliving of an emotionally charged experience. **Olfactory hallucinations** involve the sense of smell, and **gustatory hallucinations** pertain to the sense of taste; both forms of hallucinations are extremely rare. A **tactile hallucination** occurs when a touch is misperceived on the skin. A common tactile hallucination is formication, which is the sense that bugs are crawling on one's skin. Tactile hallucinations may occur during delirium, especially delirium tremens resulting from severe alcohol withdrawal.

■ Signs and Symptoms Involving Behavior

Aggressive behavior may occur when a person becomes hypervigilant in response to a perceived threat. Aggression may be exhibited as a continuum of behaviors that range from irritability to verbal threats to assault. Irritability also often occurs in response to hunger, pain, or frustration.

Aggressive behaviors may also be directed inward, rather than toward someone else. For example, some adolescents struggle to cope with extreme levels of stress in school, in their families, and in their peer relationships, and they often find themselves frustrated. In recent years, the number of adolescents who engage in self-harming behaviors appears to have increased dramatically. Teens who practice such self-harming behaviors experience tremendous tension and anxiety before the act, along with an intense preoccupation with injuring themselves. Many who engage in such behaviors, including **cutting** (making intentional superficial cuts with a blade or razor on one's skin), report that the impulse to cut is irresistible and cannot be avoided. The person may feel little or no pain as the cut, burn, or scratch is inflicted. In fact, the individual may even have feelings of relief, comfort, and arousal after the act.

Sometimes, behavioral signs and symptoms may result from the medications used to treat psychiatric disorders. For example, **akathisia** is a motor restlessness that may be seen when a person is taking an antipsychotic medication. A person exhibiting akathisia may report difficulty finding a comfortable position, an inability to stop moving, restlessness, or feeling like he or she has dancing feet or has to walk around. Objectively, an officer may observe a person rocking back and forth from one foot to another while standing, anxiously pacing or walking, or crossing or uncrossing the legs when seated. **Tardive dyskinesia**, which is also caused by certain psychiatric medications, consists of facial movements, lip puckering or smacking, eye blinking, or writhing finger movements. Such movements are involuntary medication side effects, not signs of aggression or defiance.

■ Conclusion

Many emotional, cognitive, perceptual, and behavioral cues can signal to a public safety officer or criminal justice professional that a person may be experiencing a mental illness. When an officer takes into account a person's ethnic and social background—along with the environmental cues from the scene—the officer's ability to recognize the signs and symptoms of mental illnesses will prove invaluable. Identifying the possible signs and symptoms of mental illnesses is the first step to thoroughly assessing a potentially volatile situation and determining the most appropriate actions.

Chapter Wrap-Up

- In many communities, the police force has the only around-the-clock emergency transport capability for a person with a mental illness. One of the most valuable tools for an officer when triaging behavioral emergencies in the community is a basic understanding of the signs and symptoms of mental illnesses.

- An illness, whether physical or mental, presents with both signs and symptoms. Signs are the observable clues that an illness might be present. Symptoms describe the subjective verbal reports made by someone who may be dealing with an illness. Mental illnesses involve a combination of changes in feelings, thinking, perceptions, and behaviors.

- Paranoid delusions are the form of delusions that a police officer is most likely to encounter. Auditory hallucinations (hearing things others cannot hear) are the most common perceptual symptoms of mental illnesses, especially schizophrenia.

- Aggression may be exhibited as a continuum of behaviors that range from irritability to verbal threats to assaults. Aggression related to mental illnesses may originate from illness symptoms rather than intended malice.

Vital Vocabulary

affect: the external expression of one's inner emotional state

akathisia: motor restlessness that may be a side effect of antipsychotic medications

anxiety: an unpleasant emotion that is experienced in anticipation of a usually ill-defined event; nervousness

auditory hallucinations: hearing sounds or voices when no one is there

blunted or flat affect: mildly and severely reduced expression of emotional intensity; the person may appear to be bland, unemotional, or even devoid of feelings

circumstantial thinking: thoughts digress from the topic and include excessive detail, but eventually return to the initial topic of conversation

command hallucinations: auditory hallucinations that instruct a person to do something

cutting: intentional superficial cuts made with a blade, razor, or other sharp object on one's skin

delusions: fixed, false beliefs

delusions of grandeur: fixed, false beliefs that one holds special powers or is extremely important

diagnosis: a medical term for a specific syndrome

flashback: an intense visual reliving of an emotionally charged experience; a symptom of post-traumatic stress disorder

flight of ideas: a rapid flow of thought with frequent changes of topic

formal thought disorder: a situation in which the flow of thinking and speaking becomes disjointed and confusing

gustatory hallucination: a hallucination in which a taste is perceived, with no real stimulus (no food in the mouth)

hallucination: a perception that occurs in the absence of an external stimulus, such as hearing a voice when no one is there (auditory hallucinations)

hypomania: a mild form of mania

ideas of reference: false ideas that events or statements refer specifically to oneself when they actually do not

inappropriate affect: situations in which one's facial expression and outward emotion are mismatched with one's thoughts

labile affect: rapidly changing external expression of one's inner emotional state

loose associations: a collection of thoughts that are not clearly logically related

mania: a state of euphoria or elation that may be manifested as impaired judgment, excessive spending, a decreased need for sleep, rapid speech, racing thoughts, functional impairment, irritability, and anger

mood: the subjective report of one's inner emotional state

olfactory hallucination: a hallucination in which a smell is perceived with no real stimulus (no odor in the environment)

panic attack: a circumscribed episode of severe anxiety usually lasting 10 to 30 minutes

paranoid delusions: false beliefs that one is being followed, watched, or maliciously pursued

pressured speech: rapid, excessive, and loud speech; a sign of mania

sign: an objective observation indicating that something is out of the ordinary or that a disease process might be present

symptom: a subjective experience that may not necessarily be observed by an onlooker, but is a clue that a disease process might be present

syndrome: a cluster of signs and symptoms that form a specific disease state

tactile hallucination: a perception of touch that occurs in the absence of an external stimulus

tangential: a thought pattern that departs from the topic of conversation, wanders farther and farther from the topic, and never returns to the initial topic

tardive dyskinesia: a serious and long-lasting side effect caused by the long-term use of certain psychiatric medications, consisting of facial movements, lip puckering or smacking, eye blinking, or writhing finger movements

thought blocking: a break in the train of thought

thought content: what the person is thinking about

thought process: how the thoughts are put together

visual hallucinations: seeing things when nothing is really there

word salad: an extreme form of incomprehensible speech, where one word has no relation to the next

Questions for Review and Discussion

1. Why is it important for an officer to be able to recognize the common signs and symptoms of mental illnesses?
2. Which type of delusion is demonstrated by an individual who expresses to a law enforcement officer that he is being tracked by aliens through a metal chip inserted in his brain?
3. Auditory hallucinations are common symptoms of which mental illnesses?
4. What types of behavior do individuals with mental illnesses demonstrate that could appear to be aggressive toward law enforcement officers?

Resources

American Psychiatric Association. *Diagnostic and statistical manual of mental disorders* (4th ed.). Washington, DC: American Psychiatric Association, 2000.

Arizona Peace Officer Standards and Training Board. Recognizing mental illness and developmental disabilities: a proactive approach. 2005. www.azpost.state.az.us/Telecourse/2005/Mental%20Illness%20Jan%202005/mental%20illness%20studentguide.pdf.

Canadian Mental Health Association. (2005). Police Project. Retrieved January 3, 2006, from http://www.cmha.bc.ca/advocacy/police/bcmhapp#factsheets.

Healy G, Hirschon J. (2002). Police pocket guide: responding to youths with mental health needs. Retrieved January 3, 2006, from http://www.ppal.net/downloads/PPG_6-10-2002.doc

Illinois Department of Human Services, Division of Mental Health, Homeless Action Committee. Engaging people who are homeless with a mental illness. Retrieved January 3, 2006, from http://www.nrchmi.samhsa.gov/pdfs/Day%202—October%2027/900am-1030am/Engagement%20Skills%20for%20Mental%20Health%20and%20Homeless%20Service%20Providers-Handout.pdf.

Rayel MG. First aid to mental illness. Clarenville, NF: Soar Dime, 2002.

Sadock BJ, Sadock VA. Clinical manifestations of psychiatric disorders. In: Sadock B, Sadock V. *Kaplan and Sadock's comprehensive textbook of psychiatry* (8th ed). Baltimore, MD: Lippincott Williams & Wilkins, 2005.

Schizophrenia and Related Disorders

Case Vignette: Sam

Sam is a 20-year-old African American male who lives at home with his mother. She called 9-1-1 for emergency assistance due to "threatening and violent behavior" at home. Sam's mother reports that he had kicked six holes in the walls, "looking for the cameras."

Upon arrival at his home, the officers find Sam to be agitated, pacing, and whispering to himself. His mother reports that he is convinced that "the drug dealers" are recording his every move, because they have a "plot" against him. However, Sam has not been leaving the house, tends to stay in his room. He has low energy and low motivation. He dropped out of high school in his senior year and has never worked. Recently, his mother has heard him in his room pacing and talking to himself, which first began about four months ago. Sam has been neglecting his hygiene and self-care, and he refuses to eat any food unless his mother makes it for him. Because of this paranoia, he has lost at least 15 pounds. He has never been in treatment for a mental illness.

The officers try to discuss the situation with Sam, telling him that the cameras in the walls and the plot of the drug dealers are not real. They approach him in an attempt to try to pat him on the back and calm him down, but he unexpectedly tries to attack one of the officers. He is restrained and taken to jail for assault and battery. After a week in jail, it is obvious that Sam's problems are worsening (e.g., pacing, talking to himself, refusing to eat, disheveled appearance), so he is referred for psychiatric evaluation.

■ Introduction

<u>Schizophrenia</u> is a complex and often very disabling psychiatric disorder that affects approximately 1% of people over the course of a lifetime. While extensive research is being conducted on the causes of schizophrenia and the brain mechanisms that create the signs and symptoms of this illness, researchers have not yet clarified the precise sequence of risk factors leading to illness onset. It is very clear, however, that genetic factors play a substantial role in the emergence of this disease. For example, the risk of developing schizophrenia increases by 10 times, from about 1% to roughly 10%, if one's brother or sister has schizophrenia. Some nongenetic or environmental factors, such as complications at the time of birth, marijuana use in adolescence, and prominent life stressors, may also interact with an underlying genetic tendency to bring about the illness.

> Schizophrenia is a biological brain disease that causes a number of psychological symptoms.

To understand schizophrenia, mental health professionals look at this disease from two perspectives: the diathesis-stress model and the neurodevelopmental model. The term **neurodevelopment** refers to brain development and maturation during infancy, childhood, adolescence, and adulthood. Together, these models suggest that (1) some individuals may be born with a diathesis, or tendency, toward developing the illness; (2) certain stressors or nongenetic risk factors may provoke this underlying tendency; and (3) the illness is related to brain development, beginning early in life with subtle abnormalities in brain development. The signs and symptoms of schizophrenia usually become apparent only in late adolescence or early adulthood, however.

The exact brain disturbances that lead to schizophrenia are a focus of ongoing research. These disturbances include abnormalities in certain neurotransmitter systems in the brain. **Neurotransmitters** are the natural brain chemicals that allow one neuron or nerve cell to communicate with the next.

Schizophrenia is a biological brain disease that causes a number of psychological symptoms. In that respect, it is not unlike Parkinson's disease, which is also a biological brain disease, but with movement symptoms. In addition to schizophrenia, several other closely related disorders such as **schizophreniform disorder**, **schizoaffective disorder**, and **delusional disorder** can result in thinking and feeling problems similar to those found in schizophrenia. Although these related disorders will not be discussed here, they can be considered variants of the broader disorder of schizophrenia, as they cause the same types of signs and symptoms.

■ Common Signs and Symptoms

Of all the psychiatric disorders that usually have an onset in late adolescence and early adulthood, schizophrenia may be the most disabling. Like many other mental illnesses, schizophrenia and related disorders cause a broad variety of signs and symptoms, which can in turn be categorized into several overlapping clusters. Different patients have different groups of signs and symptoms, and the signs and symptoms often vary in the same person over the course of the illness.

Positive Symptoms

<u>Positive symptoms</u> of schizophrenia are experiences that are present, but that should not be present (**Table 7.1**). In other words, the person experiences an excess or distortion of normal mental functioning. These symptoms include **auditory hallucinations**, or hearing voices when no one is there; **delusions**, which are fixed, tenaciously held, false beliefs; suspiciousness and paranoia; ideas of reference, such as the belief that the television or radio newscasters are referring to oneself; and bizarre behaviors.

Table 7.1	Positive and Negative Signs and Symptoms of Schizophrenia and Related Disorders

Positive Signs and Symptoms ("Psychosis")	Negative Signs and Symptoms
Hallucinations, usually auditory	Anhedonia (loss of interest or pleasure)
Delusions (persecutory, grandiose, religious, somatic, delusions of control)	Apathy (not caring about what happens)
Suspiciousness and paranoia	Blunted or flat affect
Ideas of reference	Emotional withdrawal
Bizarre behaviors	Low drive, energy, or motivation
	Poor attention to grooming and hygiene
	Slow or empty thoughts and speech
	Slow movements
	Social isolation

While hallucinations from any of the five senses (sight, hearing, smell, taste, and feel) may be present, auditory hallucinations (hearing sounds, especially voices) are by far the most common in persons with schizophrenia. These hallucinations may consist of voices calling one's name, commenting on one's actions, making derogatory comments, or giving commands. Sometimes individuals who are actively hearing voices are noted to be "responding to internal stimuli," such as talking to oneself, whispering to oneself, or looking around as if responding to an external voice.

Delusions, which commonly begin as misinterpretations of everyday experiences, are often paranoid or persecutory in nature, such as the belief that one is being followed or plotted against. They may also be grandiose (e.g., the belief that one has excessive money), religious (e.g., the belief that one is a biblical figure), or somatic (e.g., the belief that one's body has been disrupted or diseased). Delusions of control occur when the individual believes that his or her thoughts, feelings, or actions are controlled by some external force or person. For example, a person with schizophrenia may firmly hold the belief that someone else is putting thoughts into his or her mind through a hex or curse. Delusions are termed *bizarre* when they are clearly implausible, such as believing that thunderstorms are being activated by a remote control from Moscow.

When any of these positive symptoms are present, they are usually accompanied by a variety of other symptoms. This state of being out of touch with reality is referred to as **psychosis**. Thus an individual who is "psychotic" is experiencing the state of psychosis and has perceptions or thoughts that are not well grounded in reality. In other words, the term "psychosis" means a state in which hallucinations or delusions are present. Although psychosis is a common feature of schizophrenia, other psychiatric disorders—such as bipolar disorder, major depression, delirium, and dementia—may also cause psychosis. These illnesses are discussed in later chapters of this book.

Negative Symptoms

Another cluster of signs and symptoms of schizophrenia is referred to as the **negative symptoms** of schizophrenia; these symptoms consist of experiences that are not present, but should be (Table 7.1). Negative symptoms represent a decrease or loss of normal psychological functions. Examples of negative symptoms include **anhedonia** (loss of interest or pleasure); **apathy** (not caring about what happens); **blunted affect** or **flat affect** (mildly or severely reduced emotional intensity evidenced by diminished facial expression, body language, and vocal inflections); emotional withdrawal; low drive, energy, or motivation; poor attention to grooming and hygiene; slow or empty thinking and speech; slow movements; and social isolation.

While negative symptoms are less obvious than positive symptoms, they can be extremely disabling because they interfere with one's ability to attend school, maintain employment, and engage in relationships. Negative symptoms can sometimes be mistaken for laziness or an attitude problem. This view wrongly blames the patient for serious symptoms that are not under his or her control. Whereas positive symptoms tend to vary between better and worse over time, negative signs and symptoms of schizophrenia are usually longer-lasting and more stable.

Disorganized Symptoms

A person with schizophrenia may also exhibit signs of __disorganization__, which are caused by problems with the flow of thinking (**Table 7.2**). That is, the normal linear flow of thinking and speaking can become disjointed, confusing, and thus "disorganized." Psychiatrists also call this disruption of the thought process a __formal thought disorder__. Three types of disorganization of thoughts, and therefore disorganization of speech, are described here. In all three cases—tangential thinking, loosening of associations, and word salad—the thoughts are disorganized and therefore come across as confused and confusing.

First, __tangential thinking__, or tangentiality, occurs when one idea is connected to the next, but the thoughts become confusing because they go off on a tangent. It might sound like this: "I don't want to go to jail. Jail is for the birds. One time I saw birds flying around in the jail. Birds should be out in the air. The air is dirty in this city. All of these big city buses. I ride the bus to get my groceries. FoodMart is my favorite store." Here, the patient starts talking about one topic, but goes off on a tangent that never returns to the initial point of discussion.

Second, __loosening of associations__ is a type of thought disorganization in which one idea does not match the next in a linear way. It might sound like this: "I don't want to go to jail. FoodMart is not open yet. Last time I got hurt in jail. The birds can't fly out of the cage. It's too tight. April fools! And have a very happy New Year!" Here, ideas shift from one subject to another in a completely unrelated way. The thinking process is thus described as "loose" rather than being linear, logical, and tight.

Third, the term __word salad__ is used to describe an extreme form of incomprehensible speech. An example of word salad is the following: "I don't want to go to jail. Genesis, Revelations. April fools! Birds fly in. FoodMart birds. Take the bus to jail, take the birds to FoodMart." Here, the thoughts and speech cannot be understood at all.

Thought patterns also may become vague, empty, or repetitious, a situation that is termed __poverty of content of speech__. __Thought blocking__ occurs when the person experiences an interruption in the train of thought such that the thoughts cannot be put into words. In this case, the individual may be very slow to respond to questions or may not be able to respond at all.

Disorganized behavior often manifests as an inability to follow through with plans or a bizarre appearance, such as having shoes on the wrong feet or wearing clothes inside-out. These kinds of behaviors may suggest to law enforcement officers that someone is acting defiantly. In reality, if the individual is exhibiting disorganized signs and symptoms of schizophrenia, he or she is showing signs of a mental illness that needs treatment. In fact, differentiating between defiant or aggressive behaviors and signs of serious mental illnesses poses a particular challenge to many law enforcement personnel.

Cognitive Signs and Symptoms

Although people with schizophrenia typically have a relatively normal intelligence or IQ (intelligence quotient), they may have some problems with cognitive ability, or cognitive signs and symptoms (Table 7.2). Such problems that may be associated with schizophrenia include subtle difficulties with abstract thinking, attention and concentration, general intellectual ability, information processing, language, memory, and planning. These difficulties are often related to negative symptoms and formal thought disorder. Although the cognitive signs and symptoms are often challenging to detect, these cognitive deficits of schizophrenia can cause major impairments, often preventing the person from achieving

Table 7.2	Disorganized and Cognitive Signs and Symptoms of Schizophrenia and Related Disorders

Disorganized Signs and Symptoms ("Formal Thought Disorder")	Cognitive Signs and Symptoms
Tangential thinking	Difficulty with abstract thinking
Loosening of associations	Poor attention and concentration
Word salad	Problems with information processing
Thought blocking	Memory impairments
Disorganized behavior	Difficulty with planning

educational and occupational advancement. In this way, cognitive impairments are similar to negative symptoms: Both tend to be fairly stable over time, relatively silent and easy to overlook, and strongly associated with difficulties in functioning.

Other Signs and Symptoms

In addition to the clusters of symptoms mentioned previously—positive symptoms, negative signs and symptoms, disorganization, and cognitive deficits—other problems may occur in people with psychotic disorders such as schizophrenia, albeit less commonly. For example, although schizophrenia is not considered to be a mood disorder, some individuals with schizophrenia do have some depressive or manic symptoms. In fact, one of the disorders related to schizophrenia, schizoaffective disorder, features a combination of symptoms of schizophrenia and depression or mania. Sometimes, schizophrenia may also cause signs of a disturbance in movements. For example, people with schizophrenia who are catatonic may appear frozen due to an inability to move or speak. Furthermore, individuals with schizophrenia and related disorders may appear irritated, agitated, and possibly even threatening as the result of positive symptoms, especially paranoia or paranoid delusions.

Diagnostic and Statistical Manual of Mental Disorders

Given the wide variety of signs and symptoms that may be present in individuals with schizophrenia and related disorders, this group of disorders is classified based on the symptoms that are most prominent. The *Diagnostic and Statistical Manual of Mental Disorders,* fourth edition (*DSM-IV*), provides mental health professionals with a classification of schizophrenia and other psychotic disorders. Different patients have different combinations of symptoms. For example, some patients have mostly positive symptoms, such as delusions and hallucinations; others have mostly negative symptoms, such as withdrawal and isolation. Still others have mostly signs of disorganization. The different subtypes of schizophrenia have been defined in an attempt to account for these variations among the psychotic disorders.

Mental health professionals make diagnoses based on specific criteria provided in the *DSM-IV.* For example, the formal diagnosis of schizophrenia requires that individuals meet several conditions based on both the presence and the timing of specific signs and symptoms. Criteria used to diagnose schizophrenia include the following four parts:

1. Two or more of the following specific symptoms for at least one month: delusions, hallucinations, disorganized speech, grossly disorganized or catatonic behavior, and negative symptoms

2. Impairment in one or more major areas of functioning, such as work, relationships, or self-care

3. Signs of a disturbance lasting for at least six months

4. Symptoms and deterioration in functioning not due to other causes, such as other psychiatric disorders, medical problems (e.g., seizures or a brain tumor), or substances (e.g., PCP, ketamine, LSD, cocaine, or prescription medications)

■ Course

The term <u>course</u> is used to describe the pattern of an illness over the span of a lifetime—when the illness develops, how the signs and symptoms fluctuate, and whether the illness goes away on its own. The course of schizophrenia is variable, but some common tendencies can be identified. The symptoms of schizophrenia usually first appear in a person's late teens to mid-thirties. The onset is often gradual. The usual age of onset for men is somewhat younger (15–25 years) than that for women (25–35 years). Women also show a second—albeit smaller—peak of onset after the age of 40. Compared to men with the illness, women tend to have a somewhat better course and social functioning.

Many people with schizophrenia experience three phases of the illness:

- The <u>prodrome</u>, or prodromal phase, which is the beginning of deterioration with mild, often nonspecific symptoms, such as difficulty sleeping and irritability
- The <u>active phase</u>, when symptoms such as delusions and hallucinations become increasingly apparent as psychosis emerges
- The <u>residual phase</u>, which includes a decrease or resolution of positive symptoms, but with lasting negative and cognitive symptoms

Each phase may last from days to years, and there are often relapses of active-phase positive symptoms.

In some instances, patients with schizophrenia remain relatively stable and mostly symptom free. Recurrence of psychotic (positive) symptoms may be triggered by not taking medications as recommended, stress, and substance abuse. Coping skills, problem-solving techniques, and social support (such as a supportive family environment) may reduce the impact of stress on symptom recurrence.

Disability Caused by Schizophrenia

Unfortunately, schizophrenia is often a very disabling disease. In addition to the symptoms described earlier, individuals with schizophrenia may face significant psychosocial impairment, or difficulties in social functioning in the areas of education, employment, leisure time, parenting, relationships, and self-care. Approximately 60% to 70% of individuals with schizophrenia do not partner, and many have very limited social contacts. Educational progress is often disrupted (especially given the usual age of onset), and persons with schizophrenia are much less likely to be employed than others who do not have the disease. About 70% of people with schizophrenia are unemployed. Contrasted to the general population, individuals with schizophrenia have very high rates of cigarette smoking, alcohol and other drug problems, certain medical illnesses, and victimization.

Despite these many challenges associated with schizophrenia and related disorders, modern research is increasingly focused on early detection and treatment of schizophrenia, with the goal of reducing the overall burden of the disease and improving the lives of people diagnosed with the illness. In fact, some individuals who experience a psychotic episode may recover and never have another episode. Getting treatment as early as possible is very important.

Aggression and Suicide in People with Schizophrenia

In some cases, individuals with schizophrenia may become aggressive or violent. However, violent and criminal behavior that is attributable to schizophrenia accounts for only a very small portion of violent and criminal behavior in society, and most individuals with schizophrenia are not assaultive or violent in any way. In the general population and in people with schizophrenia, the best predictor of future violence is a history of past violence. Other risk factors for violence among those with schizophrenia include male gender, younger age, not taking medication, the presence of acute psychotic symptoms (delusions or hallucinations), and co-occurring substance abuse. The risk of an individual with schizophrenia committing homicide is estimated to be 100 times less than the risk of committing suicide. Approximately 10% of all individuals with schizophrenia commit suicide, and 20% to 50% make at least one suicide attempt at some point during their illness.

> The risk of an individual with schizophrenia committing homicide is estimated to be 100 times less than the risk of committing suicide.

■ Treatment

As is true with most psychiatric illnesses, the treatment of schizophrenia can be divided into **pharmacotherapy** (medications) and **psychosocial treatments** (counseling and other supportive psychological or social treatments). (See **Table 7.3**.) Currently, most mental health professionals would agree that the most important first step in the treatment of schizophrenia is the use of medications called **antipsychotics**. The antipsychotic drugs date back to the mid-1950s. The discovery of chlorpromazine (Thorazine), which was the first antipsychotic medication, revolutionized care for people with schizophrenia. The introduction of antipsychotic medications was also one of the most prominent events that sparked the era of **deinstitutionalization**, in which patients were gradually transitioned from long-term care in state hospitals to treatment in community outpatient settings.

Antipsychotic Medications

Two types of antipsychotic medications are distinguished: the **conventional antipsychotics** (also called *neuroleptics, typicals, or first-generation agents*) and the **atypical antipsychotics** (also called *second-generation agents*). Nowadays, psychiatrists rarely use the older conventional medications as first-choice options. Several medications are available in long-acting, injectable forms that may be given every two to four weeks as a shot. This regimen allows for an ongoing supply of medication without the patient having to take a pill every day. Antipsychotic medications often have major effects on relieving positive symptoms, but only modest effects on negative symptoms and cognitive impairment.

Unfortunately, antipsychotic medications may have a number of undesirable side effects, including constipation, dizziness, dry mouth, sleepiness, tremor, and weight gain. **Tardive dyskinesia** is a movement disorder consisting of abnormal, involuntary movements often in the fingers, face, or trunk. It can result from long-term treatment with antipsychotics, especially the older conventional antipsychotics. Such medication side effects frequently cause individuals to stop taking their antipsychotic medications. Other drugs are sometimes prescribed to control some of these side effects.

In addition to the antipsychotics, psychiatrists sometimes prescribe other types of medications in an effort to treat the symptoms of schizophrenia and other psychotic disorders. These agents may include antidepressants, mood stabilizers, and anxiety medications such as benzodiazepines.

The effectiveness of antipsychotic medications has been established repeatedly by extensive research, and antipsychotic medications are able to reduce symptoms in the majority of

Table 7.3 Treatment Methods for Schizophrenia and Related Disorders	
Conventional and atypical antipsychotic medications	Family therapy
Individual supportive therapy (counseling)	Social skills training
Cognitive-behavioral therapy	Day treatment programs
Psychoeducation	Vocational rehabilitation
Alcohol and drug treatment (for dual diagnosis)	Supported employment
Case management	Supported housing
Family psychoeducation	Assertive Community Treatment

patients with schizophrenia. Although the use of such drugs is now widely accepted by mental health clinicians, patients sometimes refuse to take their medications. Reasons for not taking the medications as prescribed are often complex, but may include side effects, cost, and lack of recognition of a need to take medication for the illness. This lack of recognition, termed **impaired insight**, is a particularly challenging aspect of this disease that is present to a variable extent in most individuals with schizophrenia. Persistent social **stigma** that suggests that people with mental illnesses are bad or in some way responsible for their illnesses likely also prevents individuals from seeking appropriate mental health care. Stigma toward mental illnesses is probably a major factor leading to the high rate of noncompliance—not taking medications and not following up with appointments—observed with schizophrenia.

Psychosocial Treatments

In addition to medications, persons with schizophrenia may receive a variety of other important treatments that are termed psychosocial treatments. Supportive counseling and other forms of individual therapy can be very helpful when used in combination with medication. Family therapy is also helpful. Day treatment, education about the illness, social skills training, supported employment, supported housing, and vocational rehabilitation (job training) are other effective psychosocial treatments. For example, psychoeducation is a program in which people with mental illnesses learn about the symptoms, treatments, and warning signs for relapse of their illness. Vocational rehabilitation is a training program that helps people readjust to employment again.

Mental health clinicians tailor these approaches, in conjunction with any medications prescribed, to match the needs of each individual patient. Because of the very high rates of co-occurring alcohol and drug abuse or dependence among individuals with schizophrenia and other psychotic disorders (a situation referred to as **dual diagnosis**), alcohol and drug treatment programs are often incorporated into individuals' overall treatment plans as well. While medications may be helpful in reducing symptoms, the psychosocial treatments are important for recovery in other domains, such as social adjustment, quality of life, and gainful employment.

When both medication and psychosocial treatments are integrated in the outpatient setting, this strategy is called the **community approach** to the treatment of schizophrenia. The broadest treatment approach, it aims to promote return to a meaningful life in the community and prevent relapses of psychotic symptoms. The intent of the community approach to mental illnesses is to treat patients in the least restrictive way within their own communities, rather than in institutions.

As mentioned previously, the era of deinstitutionalization spanned the mid-1950s through the 1990s. During this time, large state hospitals gradually released patients with schizophrenia and other major mental illnesses back to the community for care outside the hospital. In contemporary times, this approach also has its drawbacks—namely, community services are often inadequate for the treatment of complex and disabling disorders like schizophrenia. Effective community care is complex and expensive because it includes the following components:

- Coordinated services and case management
- Integrated treatment with medication and psychosocial therapies
- Short-term hospitalization or crisis stabilization when needed
- Availability of partial hospitalization or day treatment
- Support programs including transitional residences, supportive housing, vocational training, supported employment, and alcohol and drug treatment
- Assertive Community Treatment to engage individuals in the community who are not able to adhere to appointments in traditional outpatient care settings
- A supportive and informed law enforcement community and criminal justice system

Some localities may not be able to finance and support all of these important services. Consequently, many patients do not have access to a full array of essential coordinated community services.

Traditionally, psychiatrists made decisions for patients who may not have wanted at the time to take medications or work to develop improved social support systems. Now, mental health treatment is more patient-centered. In contemporary recovery models of treatment for schizophrenia and other mental illnesses, patients and clinicians work in concert to develop treatment plans that fit patients' desires. <u>Recovery</u> focuses on maximizing individuals' functioning and quality of life by empowering patients to change their lives. It emphasizes the primary role that patients have in their own treatment process, using psychiatrists and other mental health professionals as consultants for decision making.

Despite the availability of effective treatments for schizophrenia, significant barriers to care often deter patients from seeking mental health care. Fewer than half of all people who need them receive appropriate community mental health services. In fact, in any given year, 40% of all people with schizophrenia receive no treatment at all. At least two factors are primarily responsible for this undertreatment: a shortage of services and poor coordination between services. The inadequacy of these services has many unfortunate consequences. For example, some people with schizophrenia become homeless or are incarcerated, usually for petty crimes and misdemeanor charges such as disorderly conduct, disturbing the peace, subway fare evasion, trespassing, or panhandling. The illness is often untreated or undertreated in detention facilities, although some jails do have mental health units.

> Fewer than half of all people who need them receive appropriate community mental health services. In any given year, 40% of all people with schizophrenia receive no treatment at all.

Despite these very serious problems, proper community care has demonstrated great promise for promoting recovery in the context of schizophrenia. Task forces have been created to find more effective ways for all levels of government to meet the needs of people with such disorders. Another important advance has been the formation of national advocacy groups, such as the National Alliance on Mental Illness and the National Mental Health Association. Crisis intervention team (CIT) training is another important part of community care for people with severe and persistent mental illnesses such as schizophrenia. As more law enforcement officers and other criminal justice professionals are educated and certified in the appropriate response to individuals with mental illnesses, access to effective care is likely to improve.

Case Vignette: Susan

Police officers are called to a local gas station for a disturbance involving an agitated woman. Upon arrival, they encounter Susan, a 42-year-old white female who resides at a personal care home several blocks from the gas station. She is yelling at the station's manager and clerks from outside—ranting about how they have embezzled $25,000 from her.

One of the officers is certified in CIT de-escalation. He also knows Susan from previous calls to the neighborhood. He pulls into the area slowly and gets out of his car with a calm demeanor. He knows Susan well enough to know that she becomes delusional and agitated at times, but that she has never posed a real danger to others. He asks Susan what is making her upset. She responds with delusional comments and states that the voices told her to come and demand to get her money back. The officer says, "Susan, I know that you're feeling upset and angry right now. We can't allow you to disrupt the business here. Rather than going to jail, let's go to the psychiatric ER and see if someone can talk to you

continues

about your anger and stress. They might need to check on your medicines to work on getting rid of those voices that are bothering you."

After a few minutes of discussion, Susan agrees to go with the officers to the psychiatric emergency room for evaluation. Another officer briefly talks to the station manager, letting him know that Susan is not a danger, that she is having a flare-up of her mental illness, and that employees of the gas station should call for a CIT response if she ever returns in an agitated state.

■ Engaging and Assessing Individuals with Schizophrenia and Related Disorders

Sam, in the case vignette at the beginning of the chapter, is a young man who is experiencing his first psychotic episode. He may have an illness such as schizophrenia that is just becoming apparent. He exhibits several signs and symptoms of a psychotic disorder: (1) positive symptoms such as suspiciousness, paranoia, and delusions; (2) negative symptoms including withdrawal and social isolation; and (3) irritability, hostility, and aggression, which likely stem directly from his paranoia. With this symptom profile in mind, the officers may have made several mistakes in their attempt to engage Sam. Unfortunately, the officers in this scenario were not able to effectively de-escalate the situation. Although their efforts were well meaning, challenging the truth of his delusions by stating that the plot of the drug dealers is not real and approaching him to try to comfort him by patting him on the back may have made the situation worse.

First, the officers tried to talk Sam out of his untrue delusional ideas. This strategy is rarely successful, especially in an emergency situation. Delusions, by definition, are fixed, false beliefs that are tightly held even in the face of undeniable evidence to the contrary. Because they are fixed, delusions generally cannot be reshaped in an acute intervention. Because they are false, it would not be appropriate to agree with the delusions—this would be dishonest. It may be helpful, however, to affirm that the belief is important to the individual and to convey a desire to understand. As a general rule, the mental health provider or emergency responder should probably comment on the feelings evoked by delusional ideas rather than refuting or supporting the beliefs themselves. Rather than telling Sam that the cameras in the walls and the plot of the drug dealers are not real, perhaps the officer could have said, "It sounds like that is really scary and stressful—we're here to help you out."

A second mistake may have been attempting to get too close to Sam when he was clearly showing signs of paranoia. Specific paranoid delusions, such as the idea that the drug dealers are recording Sam's activity and plotting against him, are frequently accompanied by more generalized paranoid ideas. This phenomenon may lead to misinterpretations of people's motives. Thus, when the law enforcement officers entered the scene, Sam may have assumed that they were part of the specific plot, viewing the situation from his general paranoid frame of thinking. Respecting Sam's personal space, announcing any movements ("I'm going to walk behind you to turn off my car"), and explaining actions ("I'm going to get my notepad out of my pocket so that I can write down your mother's phone number") may be helpful when confronted with this difficult aspect of psychosis.

> Understanding the illness and developing alternative ways to respond to individuals who are experiencing signs and symptoms of schizophrenia will help officers to direct individuals who need help toward mental healthcare services.

In the second case vignette, Susan is likely experiencing a flare-up of a chronic psychotic disorder such schizophrenia. She shows several signs and symptoms of psychosis, including auditory hallucinations, delusions, and agitation. The officers working with Susan were more familiar with the skills of interacting with individuals with active psychosis. Additionally, they knew Susan and had established some rapport with her in the past. At least one of the officers had previously talked to her about what her life is like, where she lives, and what she likes to do. This officer knew that Susan walked to the gas station every day and that she had never presented a real danger, even when experiencing an episode of her illness. Upon de-escalating the situation, the officers were able to safely transport her to a psychiatric emergency receiving facility for psychiatric evaluation rather than to jail, where she would have had less chance of receiving appropriate care for her mental illness.

Psychotic illnesses such as schizophrenia may result in behaviors and symptoms that are confusing or scary for many officers or first responders. Understanding the illness and developing alternative ways to respond to individuals who are experiencing signs and symptoms of schizophrenia will help officers direct individuals who need help toward mental healthcare services. **Table 7.4** suggests some strategies for dealing with these scenarios.

Table 7.4   Pearls for Engaging and Assessing Individuals with Psychosis

- Ensure the patient's safety.
- Be sincere, truthful, nonthreatening, professional, and empathic.
- Avoid attempts to refute or disconfirm delusions.
- Avoid dishonesty and "going along with" or "buying into" delusional ideas, although it may be helpful to affirm that the belief is important to the individual and to convey a desire to understand.
- Rather than commenting on the actual content of the delusion, try to connect with the individual in terms of the feelings that he or she appears to be experiencing.
- Allow the individual to vent some of his or her frustrations.
- Avoid rapid, unexpected, or unexplained movements that may be misinterpreted owing to paranoia.
- Announce your actions before doing something that the individual might misinterpret.
- Provide enough personal space for an individual with paranoia.
- Keep hands visible (avoid putting them into pockets).
- Try to offer choices (e.g., which side of the car to get into).
- Calm the situation and reduce unnecessary sensory stimuli (e.g., sirens, flashing lights).
- Do not try to assure the individual that the voices "are not real," because persons with hallucinations really do experience them.
- Maintain a calm demeanor, don't argue, and don't demand compliance in an angry way.
- Work to develop rapport with individuals who frequently encounter law enforcement (get to know them).
- Try to be a helper, listener, and facilitator of accessing care rather than solely an enforcer (be a collaborator rather than being "in charge").
- Remember that the family may be stressed about the crisis, too.
- Work with the family to obtain information, seek advice, and provide reassurance.
- Discuss the disposition with the family members.

Chapter Wrap-Up

- Schizophrenia is a biological illness related to brain development. Some individuals may be born with a genetic tendency toward developing this disease. Certain stressors or nongenetic risk factors may then provoke this underlying tendency to turn into the actual illness.

- Signs and symptoms of schizophrenia include positive symptoms (such as delusions and hallucinations), negative symptoms (including apathy and social withdrawal), disorganized thinking, subtle cognitive deficits, and hostility and aggression. Hostility and aggressive behavior, when they occur, are usually directly related to positive symptoms, such as paranoia.

- The symptoms of schizophrenia usually first appear in a person's late teens to mid-thirties, and the onset is often gradual.

- With treatment, some patients with schizophrenia remain relatively stable and mostly symptom free. Recurrence of psychotic (positive) symptoms may be triggered by not taking medications as recommended, stress, or substance abuse. Some individuals who experience a psychotic episode may recover and never have another episode.

- Treatment of schizophrenia includes both pharmacotherapy (medications) and psychosocial treatments (counseling and other supportive psychological or social treatments).

- Medications and psychosocial treatments are integrated in the outpatient setting, with the twin aims of promoting a return to a meaningful life in the community and preventing relapses of psychotic symptoms. Such a community approach to mental illnesses seeks to treat patients in the least restrictive way within their own communities, rather than in institutions. Recovery focuses on maximizing individuals' functioning and quality of life by empowering patients to change their lives. Proper community care has shown great potential for facilitating recovery from schizophrenia.

- Understanding the illness and using appropriate and well-informed methods to respond to individuals who are experiencing signs and symptoms of schizophrenia will help officers direct individuals who need help toward mental healthcare services.

Vital Vocabulary

active phase: the phase of schizophrenia during which symptoms such as delusions and hallucinations become increasingly apparent

anhedonia: loss of interest or pleasure

antipsychotics: medications used to treat psychosis

apathy: not caring about what happens

atypical antipsychotics: the newer type of antipsychotic medications

auditory hallucinations: hearing sounds or voices when no one is there

blunted affect: a reduction of emotional intensity

community approach: the integration of medication and psychosocial treatments for mental illnesses within the outpatient setting

conventional antipsychotics: older types of antipsychotic medications

course: the pattern of an illness over the span of a lifetime

deinstitutionalization: the gradual transitioning of patients from long-term care in state hospitals to treatment in community outpatient settings

delusional disorder: a mental disorder in which the patient has nonbizarre, fixed, false beliefs, which involve situations that could occur in real life, and which do not prominently impair functioning

delusions: fixed, false beliefs

disorganization (formal thought disorder): a psychiatric syndrome in which the normal linear flow of thinking and speaking becomes disjointed, disorganized, and confusing

dual diagnosis: co-occurring diseases, usually referring to the presence of a mental illness and a substance use disorder together

flat affect: severely reduced emotional intensity

impaired insight: a patient's lack of a clear understanding about the nature of his or her mental illness

loosening of associations: a situation in which one idea does not match the next in a linear way; a symptom of a formal thought disorder sometimes seen in schizophrenia

negative symptoms: one of the types of symptoms of schizophrenia; a decrease or loss of normal psychological functions, such as decreased energy, decreased interests, and decreased motivation

neurodevelopment: brain development and maturation during infancy, childhood, adolescence, and adulthood

neurotransmitters: chemicals naturally present in the brain that allow one neuron or nerve cell to communicate with the next

pharmacotherapy: medication

positive symptoms: one of the types of symptoms of schizophrenia; an excess or distortion of normal mental functioning, such as hallucinations and delusions

poverty of content of speech: thought patterns that are vague, empty, or repetitious

prodrome: the beginning of deterioration in an illness that warns of an impending disease state

psychosis: a state of being out of touch with reality; the presence of hallucinations or delusions

psychosocial treatments: counseling and other supportive psychological or social treatments

recovery: maximizing individuals' functioning and quality of life

residual phase: a decrease or resolution of positive symptoms of schizophrenia, but with lasting negative and cognitive symptoms

schizoaffective disorder: an illness characterized by symptoms of depression or mania, along with symptoms of schizophrenia

schizophrenia: a biological brain disease that often causes psychosis

schizophreniform disorder: an illness with similar features to schizophrenia, except that symptoms have been present for less than six months

stigma: negative attitudes and beliefs that cause the general public to fear, reject, avoid, or discriminate against people with mental illnesses

tangential thinking: a symptom of disorganization/formal thought disorder in which one idea is connected to the next, but the thoughts do not stay on track, instead going off on a tangent

tardive dyskinesia: an adverse event caused by the long-term use of certain psychiatric medications, consisting of facial movements, lip puckering or smacking, eye blinking, or writhing finger movements

thought blocking: an interruption in the train of thought such that the thoughts cannot be put into words

word salad: an extreme form of disorganization/formal thought disorder in which the speech is incomprehensible because one word has no relation to the next

Questions for Review and Discussion

1. In what ways do the positive symptoms of schizophrenia (such as hallucinations and delusions) make it difficult to engage someone with this disorder?
2. How should an officer talk to someone who holds a delusion that his or her thoughts are being controlled by a satellite?
3. When does schizophrenia usually first become apparent, and how does this pattern of onset interfere with important milestones in life?
4. What are some examples of long-term difficulties in life that individuals with schizophrenia may encounter?
5. Do people with schizophrenia generally tend to demonstrate violent and criminal behavior?
6. Explain some reasons why people with schizophrenia might not adhere to their treatments.
7. How are law enforcement officers part of the community approach to the treatment of schizophrenia?

Resources

American Psychiatric Association. Schizophrenia and other psychotic disorders. In: *Diagnostic and statistical manual of mental disorders* (4th ed., pp. 297–343). Washington, DC: American Psychiatric Association, 2000.

Bustillo JR, Lauriello J, Horan WP, et al. The psychosocial treatment of schizophrenia: an update. *Am J Psychiatry* 2001;158:163–175.

Castellano-Hoyt DW. *Enhancing police response to persons in mental health crisis: providing strategies, communication techniques, and crisis intervention preparation in overcoming institutional challenges.* Springfield, IL: Charles C Thomas, 2003.

Frangou S, Murray RM. *Schizophrenia* (2nd ed.). London: Martin Dunitz, 2000.

Goldstein AP, Monti PJ, Sardino TJ, Green DJ. *Police crisis intervention.* New York: Pergamon Press, 1979.

Miller R, Mason SE. *Diagnosis schizophrenia: a comprehensive resource for patient, families, and helping professionals.* New York: Columbia University Press, 2002.

Mueser KT, Gingerich S. *Coping with schizophrenia: a guide for families.* Oakland, CA: New Harbinger, 1994.

Mueser KT, McGurk SR. Schizophrenia. *Lancet* 2004;363:2063–2072.

Torrey EF. *Surviving schizophrenia: a manual for families, consumers, and providers* (4th ed.). New York: HarperCollins, 2001.

Walsh E, Buchanan A, Fahy T. Violence and schizophrenia: examining the evidence. *Br J Psychiatry* 2002;180:490–495.

Acknowledgements and Disclosures

Michael Compton has received research grant support from the Emory Medical Care Foundation, the American Institute for Research and Education/GlaxoSmithKline, the American Institute for Research and Education/AstraZeneca, and the National Institute of Mental Health. He has served as a consultant for AstraZeneca Pharmaceuticals, WebMD Health, and Medscape.

Mood Disorders: Major Depression and Bipolar Disorder

Case Vignette: Mary

Police officers are called to a neighborhood elementary school, where one of the teachers has locked a child in the closet. Mary is a 26-year-old second-grade teacher who just returned to work after six weeks of maternity leave. She has been teaching at this elementary school since she finished college at the age of 22. Mary has always received the highest marks on her evaluations, and the children and their parents continually sing her praises. However, since she returned to work, the children have complained that she is ignoring them and acting "weird." A teacher's assistant reports that Mary is often late for class and loses her train of thought while teaching the children. Another teacher says that Mary has been acting oddly—she has been very suspicious of both the children and her colleagues—and she saw Mary in the bathroom crying. The principal notes that Mary has been uncharacteristically delinquent in completing paperwork.

When the officers arrive at the scene, Mary has her head bowed and is sitting in front of the closet with the child locked inside. The officers approach Mary and kneel by her side. After introducing themselves, they let her know that she has to let the child out of the closet. Mary begins to cry and says, "I can't." When asked why, she reports that a voice has told her to kill the child, and she is afraid that if she lets him out of the closet, she will harm him. The officers assure her that they will protect the child and help her to her feet. They escort her from the classroom while the principal frees the child from the closet.

■ Introduction

The term <u>mood disorder</u> is used in the mental health field to describe any abnormality of mood that leads to impaired functioning or quality of life. The two major mood disorders are major depressive disorder (also called major depression) and bipolar disorder (which in the past was called manic-depressive disorder). Both illnesses are quite common. At any given time, nearly 1 in 10 people is experiencing symptoms of major depression. Although bipolar disorder is less common than major depressive disorder, with a U.S. prevalence of 1 to 2 per 100 people, the behavioral symptoms associated with bipolar disorder mean that someone who is experiencing those symptoms is much more likely to encounter law enforcement officials. Mood disorders, in conjunction with other mental illnesses, account for more than 40% of workforce losses each year, making them the second most common disability worldwide.

> Mood disorders, in conjunction with other mental illnesses, account for more than 40% of workforce losses each year, making them the second most common disability worldwide.

This chapter focuses mainly on the diagnosis and treatment of major depressive disorder and bipolar disorder. A small section is devoted to other mood disorders, including dysthymic disorder, cyclothymic disorder, mood disorders due to a general medical condition, and substance-induced mood disorders.

■ Common Signs and Symptoms of Major Depression

As noted earlier, major depressive disorder is a very common illness, affecting nearly 1 in 10 people in the United States. Women are disproportionately affected by this disease, with approximately 1 in 5 women experiencing depression during her lifetime, as compared to 1 in 10 men. This difference may be due to biological factors, may result from different life experiences between men and women, or may be driven by underdiagnosis of depression in men. The symptoms of major depression can be disabling and life-threatening. Nevertheless, with adequate treatment, most people recover fully from major depressive episodes.

<u>Major depression</u> is an episodic illness characterized by sadness; difficulty sleeping and/or sleeping too much; preoccupation with guilty thoughts; decreased energy; decreased enjoyment in those activities that, in the past, brought joy; abnormalities of memory and concentration; isolation from friends and family; hopelessness; and thoughts of suicide (**Table 8.1**). These symptoms must be present for at least two weeks to make a diagnosis of a major depressive episode. Left untreated, a depressive episode can last an entire year or longer. Family and friends will note that a person experiencing depression seems different from his or her usual self. Sadness may be expressed as irritability or anger, contributing further to isolation from loved ones. As many as 15%

Table 8.1 Symptoms of Depression (These symptoms can be easily memorized using the "SIG.E.CAPS" mnemonic.)
Sadness **I**nsomnia: difficulty sleeping (or excessive sleeping) **G**uilty thoughts **E**nergy decreased **C**oncentration and memory difficulties **A**nhedonia: decreased pleasure **P**sychomotor retardation: thinking and movements are slowed down **S**uicidal thoughts

of major depressive episodes include psychotic symptoms, meaning that the person has **delusions** or **hallucinations**. Delusions are typically **mood congruent**, such as believing that one's insides are rotting or that an invisible force is trying to harm oneself. Likewise, hallucinations may consist of a voice commenting on the individual's worthlessness or urging him or her to commit suicide. The longer a depressive episode goes untreated, the more difficult it will be to treat.

Case Vignette: Thomas

Security agents at a local airport are called to respond to complaints that a man had interfered with the safety of a flight by barging into the cockpit and demanding that the pilot allow him to land the plane. Upon their arrival, the officers encounter a man in his early forties who is dressed in a business suit and wearing mirrored sunglasses. He is talking very loudly and making large hand gestures, and he intermittently breaks into laughter for no apparent reason.

The flight crew informs the police officers that the man's name is Thomas. He was traveling alone on the plane, which has just landed in the United States following a 16-hour trans-Atlantic flight. During the flight, they noticed that Thomas never slept, and they periodically had to intervene when other passengers complained that he was talking and laughing too loudly.

Thomas thanks the officers for coming, saying, "I'm glad the President sent you to handle this matter." He reports that he has flown to this country on direct orders from the President and that the pilots interfered with his ability to complete his mission by failing to comply with the instructions he gave them.

The security agents attempt to introduce themselves and explain that Thomas has broken the law by interfering with the flight crew. However, they are unable to get a word in edgewise, and Thomas begins to become agitated. He attempts to run away from the police officers, and they have to chase him in the terminal, bring him to the floor, and handcuff him. They call for police backup to have Thomas arrested and transported for booking.

■ Common Signs and Symptoms of Bipolar Disorder

Bipolar disorder, commonly known as manic depression, is an illness that is characterized by abnormalities of mood along two extremes. The first extreme, known as mania, often leads to involvement of law enforcement agencies. A **manic episode** (**Table 8.2**) is a period of at least one week when a person experiences elevated or irritable mood, rapid speech that is difficult to interrupt (termed **pressured speech**), decreased need for sleep, increased impulsivity, involvement in dangerous activity without regard for consequences, distractibility, elevated sense of self-esteem, and rapid switching from thought to thought (called **flight of ideas**). Manic episodes can be devastating to one's life, because they may lead to sexual promiscuity, drug abuse, and financial demise. Because of the characteristic impulsivity and lack of regard for the consequences of one's actions, some manic episodes may result in criminal activity. As with major depressive episodes, **psychotic symptoms** are common with mania.

The other extreme mood that characterizes bipolar disorder is major depression, which was described earlier in this chapter. During the course of the illness, the mood episodes sometimes—but not always—alternate from mania to depression. In general, depressive episodes are more common than manic episodes in bipolar disorder.

Table 8.2	Symptoms of Mania (These symptoms can be easily memorized using the "DIG FAST" mnemonic.)

Distractibility
Insomnia: decreased need for sleep
Grandiosity: elevated sense of self-esteem
Flight of ideas: thoughts jump from idea to idea
Activity increased
Speech pressured: not easily interrupted
Thoughtlessness: increased impulsivity

■ Other Mood Disorders

While major depression and bipolar disorder are the two major mood disorders, other disorders have associated mood problems as well (**Table 8.3**). Treatments for these illnesses are similar to those for the major mood disorders.

Dysthymic Disorder and Cyclothymic Disorder

While major depressive disorder is generally considered an episodic illness, with periods of wellness interspersed between episodes, <u>dysthymic disorder</u> is a form of depression that is characterized by chronic depressed mood for more days than not for at least two years. Poor appetite or overeating, difficulty sleeping or sleeping too much, low energy, fatigue, low self-esteem, poor concentration or difficulty making decisions, and feelings of hopelessness may also accompany the depressed mood.

Just as dysthymic disorder may be considered a less severe form of major depression, so <u>cyclothymic disorder</u> may be considered a less severe form of bipolar disorder. As in bipolar disorder, "ups" and "downs" are common in cyclothymic disorder. However, the mood swings in cyclothymic disorder are not severe enough to meet diagnostic criteria of major depression or a manic episode.

Mood Disorders Due to a General Medical Condition and Substance-Induced Mood Disorders

The brain, like other organs, is sensitive to illnesses that affect other parts of the human body. Much like the heart signals distress by causing chest pain and the stomach by causing nausea and vomiting, the brain can signal distress by causing symptoms of depression or mania. Many illnesses that affect the body—for example, cancer, which releases abnormal chemicals into the bloodstream, and lung disease, which prevents adequate oxygenation to the brain—can produce symptoms resembling mood disorders. The illnesses that are most widely recognized as causing mood symptoms are hypothyroidism, cancer, and stroke. When a mood disorder is caused by a physical illness, it is termed mood disorder due to a general medical condition. The treatment for such conditions is to treat the underlying illness as well as the mood disorder.

Table 8.3	Other Mood Disorders (In addition to major depressive disorder and bipolar disorder)

Dysthymic disorder
Cyclothymic disorder
Premenstrual dysphoric disorder
Mood disorder due to a general medical condition
Substance-induced mood disorder

Just as hypothyroidism, cancer, or stroke can cause mood symptoms, abuse of substances may similarly cause abnormalities of mood. Research studies have shown that at least 50% of those persons diagnosed with mental disorders also have substance use disorders. If a person has abused substances in the past month and also has symptoms of mania or depression, it can be very difficult to determine whether the individual has major depression, bipolar disorder, or **substance-induced mood disorder**, which is a mood disorder that is present because of the drug abuse. Given the frequency of **substance abuse** in those suffering mood disorders, it is important for mental health professionals to evaluate everyone with mood symptoms for the potential use of drugs, and to provide treatment if abuse is discovered.

■ Biopsychosocial Treatment of Mood Disorders

Mood disorders, like other psychiatric illnesses, have biological, psychological, and social components. Biological contributors include genetic factors (i.e., inherited genes) and acquired factors, such as medical illness. Psychological contributors are associated with a person's childhood and adulthood experiences, and the ways in which those experiences shape one's view of the world. Social contributors are the stressors that are currently occurring in the person's life. They may include work, marriage, children, and illnesses, among other things. Effective treatment plans for mood disorders take into consideration all of the biological, psychological, and social factors that contribute to the illness and, therefore, are termed biopsychosocial treatment plans.

Biological Treatments

Biological treatments of mood disorders are classified into two categories: pharmacotherapy (medications) and electroconvulsive therapy.

Most physicians agree that the first-line medications for depressive episodes are **antidepressants**. The newest and most widely prescribed group of antidepressants is named based on the way these agents work in the brain: **serotonin reuptake inhibitors** (SRIs). **Serotonin** is a chemical found in the brain that has been shown to be important for mood regulation. By decreasing the reuptake of serotonin, this class of antidepressants increases the amount of serotonin available to the brain. Although SRIs take an average of four to eight weeks to exert their maximal therapeutic effect, approximately 70% of patients suffering from a major depressive episode will get complete relief using an SRI. Other newer-generation antidepressants have similar effects on the chemical systems in the brain. Older antidepressants include tricyclic antidepressants (TCAs) and monoamine oxidase inhibitors; they are also effective at treating depression, but may be associated with more side effects.

The pharmacologic treatment of bipolar disorder is a bit more complicated. Most psychiatrists prescribe medications called **mood stabilizers** for these patients. Commonly used mood stabilizers include lithium and medications that are also effective at treating seizure disorders. When a patient is in the manic phase of bipolar disorder, mood stabilizers are often combined with **antipsychotics** for both relief of psychotic symptoms and behavior control. Depressive episodes in bipolar disorder are often treated with a combination of mood stabilizers and antidepressants.

Electroconvulsive therapy (ECT), commonly referred to as "electro-shock therapy," is effective for both mania and major depression. Because of the stigma attached to this therapy and the complexity of this treatment method, ECT is generally reserved for the most severe, treatment-resistant cases. During ECT, a patient is placed under general anesthesia and given an electric stimulus that causes a brain seizure. Because the muscles are paralyzed, the patient does not have a full-body seizure. After six to eight treatments, usually given as a series of three treatments per week, as many as 85% of patients will have resolution of mood symptoms. ECT may be the first-line treatment in individuals who have responded to ECT in the past, who have a life-threatening illness that requires immediate treatment, or who are pregnant and do not want to expose the developing fetus to medication. Other biologic treatments for mood disorders like Vagus Nerve Stimulation and Deep Brain Stimulation require surgery, but may produce effective results in specific individuals.

Psychological and Social Treatments

Psychological treatments of mood disorders aim to address a person's experiences and manner of thinking that may contribute to mood abnormalities. Psychological treatments are generally divided into short-term and long-term psychotherapies.

Short-term psychotherapies that have been shown to be effective in treating mood disorders include **cognitive behavioral therapy** (CBT) and **interpersonal psychotherapy** (IPT). CBT aims to highlight the connection between thoughts, feelings, and behaviors. IPT focuses on interpersonal relationships and their contributions to mood abnormalities. Both types of therapy generally take place weekly over a period of 12 to 20 weeks.

The most commonly used long-term therapies are **supportive psychotherapy** and **psychodynamically oriented psychotherapy**. In supportive psychotherapy, the therapist encourages healthy defense mechanisms, or coping strategies, that help the person deal with symptoms, while discouraging defense mechanisms that are maladaptive or contribute to the continuance of symptoms. Psychodynamically oriented psychotherapy concentrates on the childhood and adulthood events that shaped the way a person experiences and responds to life. The theory underlying this therapy is that by understanding why certain feelings and behaviors arise, one is able to better control them.

Social treatments for mood disorders address the social stressors that may be contributing to the abnormality of the patient's mood (**Table 8.4**). For example, because productivity has been linked to improved mood, social intervention may include vocational rehabilitation and job placement. Likewise, financial stress has been associated with poor mood, so a corresponding social intervention may be case management involving securing disability income, supported housing, or government assistance.

The most important social intervention, however, may be **psychoeducation**. To maximize the success of biological and psychological treatments, the person experiencing the mood abnormality—as well as the friends, family, and law enforcement officials who make up that person's social support system—need to be educated on the symptoms, course, and treatment of the illness. Through education, the stigma associated with having a mental illness can be reduced and adherence to treatment can be increased.

Table 8.4 Treatment Methods for Mood Disorders		
Biological Treatments	**Psychological Treatments**	**Social Treatments**
Antidepressants	Cognitive-behavioral therapy	Psychoeducation
Mood stabilizers	Interpersonal psychotherapy	Case management
Conventional and atypical antipsychotics	Insight-oriented psychotherapy	Family psychoeducation
Electroconvulsive therapy	Individual supportive psychotherapy	Vocational rehabilitation
Vagus nerve stimulation	Alcohol and drug treatment	Supported housing
Deep brain stimulation	Family therapy	Social skills training
		Day treatment programs
		Supported employment
		Assertive Community Treatment

■ Engaging and Assessing Individuals with Mood Disorders

The most important aspect of interacting with someone who has a mental illness is remembering that, like everyone, he or she has thoughts and feelings that affect behavior. For example, consider the first vignette describing Mary's dilemma. Upon first hearing the call that a teacher had locked a child in the closet, the officers may have felt angry and intolerant. When they arrived on the scene, Mary was sitting in front of the closet and ignored their requests to move. Mary could sense their anger and, coupled with her recognition of their uniforms, it convinced her that she would be arrested and incarcerated. Furthermore, one of the symptoms of depression—excessive guilty thoughts—supported her idea that she deserved to be punished. Mary was afraid to look the officers in the eye and instead averted her gaze. The officers might have interpreted her behavior as obstinate and uncooperative, thereby increasing their anger and decreasing their patience for dealing with the situation. If they were instead able to view her behavior in the context of a severe, psychotic depressive episode, they might have understood her fright, empathized with her, and found out that she did not want to release the child because she was afraid she would hurt him.

Likewise, the vignette about Thomas illustrates how a mood disorder can affect interactions with law enforcement officials. Initially, Thomas was collegial and cooperative because he believed the officers were sent from the President to support him. As soon as he began to perceive they were not his allies, he attempted to escape and had to be restrained. This example emphasizes the importance of presenting oneself as an ally rather than an enemy. By voicing potential thoughts, such as "I know it must be scary to be surrounded by policemen" or "We are not here to punish you," officers may be able to defuse situations that might otherwise escalate.

■ Conclusion

Mood disorders are very common, affecting as much as 10% of the U.S. population. It is important to be knowledgeable of mood disorders, because their symptoms will influence the way a person responds to and interacts with public safety officers. Most importantly, law enforcement officers can be instrumental in making treatment accessible to people with mood disorders who are in crisis.

Chapter Wrap-Up

- Mood disorders are very common, affecting nearly 10% of the U.S. population.
- In general, the longer a mood disorder goes untreated, the more difficult it will be to treat.
- As many as 15% of major depressive episodes include psychotic symptoms.
- Impulsivity and lack of appreciation for the consequences of their actions often place individuals experiencing manic episodes at high risk for becoming involved in criminal activity.
- Many illnesses that affect the body can cause symptoms of mood disorders.
- All medical and psychiatric illnesses have biological, psychological, and social contributors. A biopsychosocial treatment plan attempts to intervene in all three areas.
- Law enforcement officers can be instrumental in increasing the accessibility of treatment to people with mood disorders.

Vital Vocabulary

antidepressant: medication for depressive symptoms

antipsychotic: medication for psychotic symptoms

bipolar disorder: an illness characterized by abnormalities of mood along two extremes, depression and mania

cognitive behavioral therapy: psychotherapy that aims to highlight the connection between thoughts, feelings, and behaviors

cyclothymic disorder: a less severe form of bipolar disorder, in which the mood swings are not severe enough to meet the diagnostic criteria for major depression or a manic episode

delusion: a fixed, false belief

dysthymic disorder: a form of depression that is characterized by chronic depressed mood lasting for at least two years

electroconvulsive therapy: a treatment modality generally reserved for the most severe, treatment-resistant cases of mania and major depression; it involves an electric stimulus, administered under general anesthesia, which causes a brain seizure

flight of ideas: rapid switching of ideas, from one thought to another

hallucination: a perception that occurs in the absence of an external stimulus, such as hearing a voice when no one is there (auditory hallucinations)

interpersonal psychotherapy: psychotherapy that focuses on interpersonal relationships and their contributions to mood abnormalities

major depression: a psychiatric disorder that includes symptoms such as excessive sadness, difficulty sleeping and/or sleeping too much, preoccupation with guilty thoughts, decreased energy, decreased enjoyment in pleasurable activities, poor memory and concentration, isolation from friends and family, hopelessness, and thoughts of suicide

manic episode: a period of at least one week when a person experiences a state of euphoria or elation that may be manifested as impaired judgment, excessive spending, decreased need for sleep, rapid speech, racing thoughts, functional impairment, and irritability and anger

mood congruent: thoughts or perceptions aligned with the subjective report of one's inner emotional state

mood disorder: an abnormality of mood that leads to impaired functioning or quality of life

mood stabilizers: medication used in treatment of bipolar disorder

pressured speech: rapid speech that is difficult to interrupt

psychodynamically oriented psychotherapy: psychotherapy that concentrates on the childhood and adulthood events that shaped the way a person experiences and responds to life

psychoeducation: education about the symptoms, course, and treatment of mental illness

psychotic symptoms: symptoms such as hallucinations or delusions that indicate an impairment in reality testing

serotonin: a chemical found in the brain that is important for mood regulation

serotonin reuptake inhibitors: the most commonly used group of antidepressant medications

social treatments: treatments aimed at addressing social stressors that may contribute to or result from psychiatric illnesses

substance abuse: a maladaptive pattern of substance use that causes repeated problems

substance-induced mood disorder: an abnormality of mood leading to impaired functioning or quality of life that is due to a substance use disorder

supportive psychotherapy: psychotherapy in which the therapist encourages healthy coping strategies that help the person deal with symptoms, while discouraging defense mechanisms that are maladaptive or contribute to symptoms

Questions for Review and Discussion

1. What signs and symptoms might an officer observe in a person who is suffering from psychotic depression?
2. How might law enforcement officers best approach an individual who is demonstrating signs and symptoms of psychotic depression?
3. Explain why individuals experiencing a manic episode regularly come into contact with law enforcement officers.
4. How might a law enforcement officer successfully defuse a situation that involves an individual who is demonstrating signs associated with a manic episode?
5. What role can law enforcement officers play regarding treatment for people with mood disorders?

Resources

American Psychiatric Association. Mood disorders. In: *Diagnostic and statistical manual of mental disorders* (4th ed., pp. 345–428). Washington, DC: American Psychiatric Association, 2000.

Burns D. *The feeling good handbook.* New York, NY: Plume, 1999.

Ghaemi N. *Mood disorders: a practical guide.* Baltimore, MD: Lippincott Williams & Wilkins, 2003.

Lamb HR, Weinberger LE, DeCuir WJ. The police and mental health. *Psychiatr Serv* 2002;53(10):1266–1271.

Sadock B, Sadock V. *Kaplan & Sadock's comprehensive textbook of psychiatry* (7th ed.). Baltimore, MD: Lippincott Williams & Wilkins, 2000.

Substance Abuse and Dependence

Case Vignette: William

William is a 45-year-old man with a history of drinking alcohol that began when he was 15 years old. He went to a treatment center 2 years ago to get help for alcoholism, because his wife threatened to leave him if he did not stop drinking. Ultimately, William stayed at the rehabilitation facility for only 6 of the 28 recommended days. He left against the advice of the staff after receiving medication for detoxification. He assured his wife that as a result of being "dried out" through his detoxification, he felt able to stop drinking. After leaving treatment, William attended only a couple of 12-step meetings with Alcoholics Anonymous, although it was recommended that he attend at least one meeting per day for 90 days ("90 in 90"). One Friday after work, his coworker convinced William that he deserved to have a beer. From this point forward, which occurred within a month of leaving the treatment facility, William resumed drinking daily. He subsequently lost his job after his employer smelled alcohol on his breath one day when William returned late from lunch.

A week later, William went to his physician for an appointment related to the treatment of his high blood pressure. There, he filled out a questionnaire and reported drinking "a beer or two" after work "a couple of times a week." The truth was that since losing his job, William had been drinking an average of eight beers per day during the week and even more on weekends. William's doctor adjusted his medicine for high blood pressure. During the appointment, William complained to his doctor about feeling nervous since he lost his job. His doctor, unaware of his addictive tendency, prescribed alprazolam (Xanax) for the anxiety symptoms that William had described.

That weekend, William attended a gathering at his former coworker's house to play cards and "unwind." The police were called when a fight broke out between William and a man who he claimed cheated him during the poker game. William appeared to be intoxicated and belligerent, and he attempted to hit one of the officers responding to the call. During the arrest, some blue pills were found in William's pocket. William was taken to jail. The next day, while in detention, he had a seizure.

■ Introduction

Substance use is a major public health problem that affects people in all occupations and from all walks of life. In this chapter, **substances** or **drugs** are defined to include alcohol, illicit drugs, and misused addictive prescription medicines. Oftentimes, people who abuse substances are thought of as criminals or as people who are immoral or lacking willpower. Research has revealed that addiction should actually be considered a brain disease that is often chronic and relapsing. While there is no cure, the disease of addiction is treatable.

The fact that a person makes the initial choice to use drugs or alcohol makes it difficult for many to conceive of addiction as a disease. Most people who experiment with drinking or using drugs will not become dependent on these substances. While it is true that a person makes a conscious decision to initially use drugs, when he or she actually becomes addicted to drugs, that individual suffers from uncontrollable and compulsive drug seeking, even in the face of adverse health and social consequences. This behavior is the hallmark of addiction. For most persons with addiction, treatment is necessary to break the cycle of this compulsion to use substances.

Substances of abuse clearly affect the brain; indeed, a large body of scientific evidence supports the idea that substances interfere with normal brain functioning. With prolonged usage, a person becomes impaired in his or her ability to choose to use or not use the drug. This disability is largely a result of the effects of prolonged drug use on brain functioning and, therefore, on behavior. For example, when a person uses cocaine, the cocaine travels to the brain by way of the bloodstream. Once reaching the brain, the drug activates a pathway that results in euphoria. This pathway—called the reward pathway—involves several brain regions and is activated by a rewarding stimulus such as food, sex, gambling, or drugs.

Information is relayed in the brain through a process called **neurotransmission**, which involves chemicals in the brain known as **neurotransmitters**. One such neurotransmitter, dopamine, is released by brain cells (i.e., neurons) during normal communication of information. The dopamine then binds with a receptor on the neighboring cell, thereby sending a signal to that cell and initiating a cascade effect. Drugs of abuse affect neurotransmission in the brain's reward pathway. In particular, repeated use of a drug alters the functioning of the brain. This long-term alteration may then result in substance dependence or abuse.

The *Diagnostic and Statistical Manual of Mental Disorders*, fourth edition (*DSM-IV*) does not use the term "addiction," but instead refers to "substance dependence" and "substance abuse." The essential feature of **substance dependence**, which is roughly equivalent to what is commonly thought of as addiction, is a cluster of cognitive, behavioral, and physiological symptoms indicating that the individual continues to use substances despite significant substance-related consequences.

According to the *DSM-IV*, a person warrants a diagnosis of substance dependence if, over the course of a year, he or she exhibits three or more specific criteria, which may include tolerance and withdrawal. **Tolerance** is defined by either the need for increased amounts of the substance to achieve the desired effect or a decreased effect when the same amount of the substance is used. **Withdrawal** is a physiological and/or psychological syndrome that occurs when someone who has been regularly using a drug stops abruptly. As discussed later in this chapter, the various substances of abuse have clearly defined patterns of withdrawal symptoms. Sometimes people will consume the substance (or a substance similar to it) in an effort to relieve or avoid withdrawal symptoms. For example, in the chapter-opening vignette, some of William's alcohol withdrawal symptoms may have been masked by his use of Xanax, because alcohol and drugs like Xanax (which belong to a class of medicines called benzodiazepines) have some similar actions in the brain.

> Oftentimes, people who abuse substances are thought of as criminals or as people who are immoral or lacking willpower. Research has revealed that addiction should actually be considered a brain disease that is often chronic and relapsing. While there is no cure, the disease of addiction is treatable.

> Withdrawal is a physiological and/or psychological syndrome that occurs when someone who has been regularly using a drug stops abruptly. The various substances of abuse have clearly defined patterns of withdrawal symptoms.

The *DSM-IV* distinguishes substance dependence from __substance abuse__; and the latter can be thought of as a milder form of addiction or problematic use of a substance that has not yet crossed the threshold to dependence. The essential feature of substance abuse is a maladaptive pattern of substance use manifested by recurrent and significant adverse consequences related to the repeated use of the substance. It is not synonymous with substance use because the person who meets the criteria for substance abuse has actually begun to develop problems related to substance use. These problems may include failure to fulfill role obligations at home, school, or work; using the substance under physically hazardous conditions (such as driving while intoxicated); recurrent legal problems (e.g., arrests for public intoxication); and continued use of the substance despite having social or interpersonal problems related to the substance.

Substance use disorders are quite prevalent in our society. The __lifetime prevalence__ (i.e., the probability that a person will develop the condition during his or her lifetime) of alcohol abuse or dependence is estimated to be 13% in the United States. The lifetime prevalence of drug abuse or dependence (excluding nicotine) is approximately 6%. Substance abuse and dependence cost the United States approximately $484 billion per year. In comparison, diabetes costs approximately $131 billion and cancer costs approximately $171 billion annually. The costs of substance use include healthcare expenses, lost wages, and expenditures related to crime and accidents. The National Highway Traffic Safety Administration reports that substances are involved in an estimated 10% to 22% of all motor vehicle crashes. In addition, a large proportion of the people arrested for serious crimes—including homicide, assault, and theft—are under the influence of substances. Likewise, many adults in federal prisons are there for drug-related crimes. Clearly, substance abuse and dependence are major public health and societal problems.

> Providing treatment to people with substance use disorders can reduce criminal behavior, the spread of infectious diseases, and overall costs to society, and it can prolong lives.

While there is no cure for addiction, effective treatments do exist. During treatment, people who are addicted to substances learn how to deal with the craving for the drug. Just as the consequences of substance abuse can have a tremendous impact on people other than the individual who is addicted, so can treatment. Providing treatment to people with substance use disorders can reduce criminal behavior, the spread of infectious diseases, and overall costs to society, and it can prolong lives.

■ An Overview of Specific Substances of Abuse

Alcohol

In the United States, the use of alcohol is common and, in most circles, considered acceptable. Approximately 90% of U.S. residents have consumed alcohol at least once, and about half of American adults currently drink alcohol. An estimated 5.6% (12 million people) drink "heavily," defined as consuming five or more drinks on one occasion. Some 30% to 45% of people in the United States have had at least one alcohol-related problem (e.g., driving while impaired, alcohol-related absence from school or work). Driving while under the influence of alcohol continues to be a major public health and safety problem. Approximately 20% of males who drove in the past year were on at least one occasion intoxicated to the point of being in trouble with the law if stopped. In 2001, 35% of fatal car accidents were associated with a blood alcohol level of at least 0.08%.

Alcohol intoxication can be a serious condition. Indeed, in severe cases, it can lead to coma and death. The effects of alcohol intoxication are roughly correlated with the blood concentration of alcohol, which in turn reflects the alcohol concentration in the brain. At a blood alcohol concentration of 0.03%, a person experiences euphoria. Mild impairment of coordination occurs at 0.05%. More severe problems with coordination occur at 0.1%. Confusion is noted at a level of roughly 0.2%. At levels greater than 0.3%, coma and even death may occur. Of course, there is some variability in these levels, because of differences in tolerance from one person to the next. Medical complications of alcohol intoxication also include falls that can result in brain injury and trauma that occurs during fights while impaired. People often abuse more than one substance, as exemplified by the vignette about William, who was drinking alcohol in addition to using Xanax—behavior that put him at increased risk for complications during both intoxication and withdrawal.

Just as intoxication with alcohol can be dangerous, so can the withdrawal syndrome that occurs when a regular drinker abruptly stops or drastically cuts down on his or her consumption of alcohol. For some, alcohol withdrawal syndromes can even be fatal when untreated. Chronic heavy drinkers who stop drinking suddenly or who significantly reduce their alcohol intake may begin to experience alcohol withdrawal symptoms within 4 to 12 hours. The signs and symptoms of alcohol withdrawal vary but will often begin with tremors, heart palpitations, and sweating. Tremors and sweating, or "the shakes and sweats," often begin 6 to 8 hours after the last drink. Some heavy drinkers will experience seizures within 12 to 48 hours after the last drink.

Those who experience alcohol withdrawal symptoms should be observed, usually in a medical setting, to prevent progression to **alcohol withdrawal delirium**, also known as **delirium tremens** (DTs), which is the most severe—and potentially fatal—form of alcohol withdrawal. DTs may occur within a week after a person who drinks heavily stops or reduces the amount of alcohol consumed. People who experience DTs have a disturbance of consciousness that may include disorientation (such as not knowing the date or place), problems with attention, restlessness, and sleepiness. Other symptoms may include anxiety, fever, increased blood pressure and heart rate, insomnia, sweating, and hallucinations. People in DTs may pose a danger to themselves or others, as they tend to have unpredictable behavior. For example, they may act on delusional thoughts or hallucinations. If medical treatment is not provided, DTs have a mortality rate of 15% to 20%.

> Those who experience alcohol withdrawal symptoms should be observed, usually in a medical setting, to prevent progression to alcohol withdrawal delirium, also known as delirium tremens (DTs), which is the most severe—and potentially fatal—form of alcohol withdrawal.

Amphetamines and Amphetamine-Like Substances

The category of amphetamines and amphetamine-like substances includes drugs such as dextroamphetamine (Dexedrine), methylphenidate (Ritalin), and methamphetamine. The last substance is also referred to as ice, meth, and crystal, and it can be taken orally, smoked, snorted, or injected intravenously. According to the National Institute on Drug Abuse, methamphetamine abuse continues to spread across the United States and among different population groups. In recent years, there has been alarming growth in the number of small laboratories producing methamphetamine across the country, especially in rural areas. The abuse and manufacturing of methamphetamine have continued at high levels in Hawaii and the West Coast areas as well. The percentage of arrested adult males who tested positive for methamphetamine increased in many regions throughout the United States between 2000 and 2002.

Amphetamines are rapidly absorbed and usually have an onset of action within an hour of being taken orally. If used on an intravenous (IV) basis, the effects are felt almost immediately. Amphetamine intoxication may lead to some of the following signs and symptoms: abnormal heart rhythms, agitation, anger and aggression, anxiety, chest pain, dilated pupils, euphoria, impaired judgment, increased or decreased blood pressure and/or heart rate, nausea and vomiting, repetitive behaviors, and sweating. After coming off amphetamines, a period of withdrawal—that is, a "crash"—can occur. Symptoms of amphetamine withdrawal may include agitation, fatigue, increased appetite, and sleep disturbances. Just as in cocaine withdrawal, people who are coming off amphetamines can become very depressed and even suicidal. These suicidal thoughts should be taken seriously, and measures should be implemented to ensure the person's safety. People who use amphetamines can also become **manic** or **psychotic**. If psychosis occurs, it is usually manifested as paranoia. People who are psychotic because of amphetamines therefore need to be evaluated by a mental health professional for consideration of short-term use of an antipsychotic medicine.

Cannabis

The hemp plant, *Cannabis sativa,* is an herb whose active substances are referred to as cannabis. It is commonly referred to as marijuana, dro, ganga, grass, herb, Mary Jane, pot, or weed. Delta-9-tetrahydrocannabinoid (THC) is the chemical in marijuana that is responsible for its mind-altering effects. Cannabis is the most commonly used illicit substance in the United States, with a 5% lifetime rate of cannabis abuse or dependence. Recent trends indicate that the lifetime use of marijuana by high school students is increasing. Another cause for concern is the fact that the potency of marijuana has increased in comparison to the marijuana available in the 1960s and 1970s.

After smoking marijuana, the effects begin within minutes and then peak in about 30 minutes, with effects typically lasting from 1 to 3 hours. When marijuana is eaten, the onset of action is slower (about 1 hour) and the effects last for as long as 4 hours. The level of THC in the blood is higher when marijuana is smoked. Some motor and cognitive effects of marijuana may last 5 to 12 hours, which makes it dangerous to operate heavy machinery and automobiles after marijuana use. Marijuana can also affect coordination. Studies show that 6% to 11% of victims of fatal car crashes test positive for THC. In fact, research by the National Highway Traffic Safety Administration has shown that even a moderate amount of marijuana impairs driving performance. Additionally, the effects of a small amount of marijuana when combined with alcohol are significantly greater than the effects of either marijuana or alcohol alone. To reach these conclusions, such studies assess reaction time, the capacity to analyze and respond to changes in the speed of other cars, and the checking of side streets before crossing.

Once THC reaches the brain, the individual will feel high or euphoric as the drug acts on the reward pathway in the brain. Signs and symptoms of marijuana intoxication include dry mouth, increased appetite, increased heart rate, and reddening of the eyes. After smoking marijuana, an individual may be euphoric or anxious. Some people who use cannabis have the sensation that time is moving slowly and that colors are more intense. Marijuana can sometimes cause serious psychological symptoms including **hallucinations**, **delusions**, and a sense of fear or paranoia. After the sensation of being high wears off, the person may feel sleepy or depressed. Some individuals may feel paranoid or anxious when their THC levels drop. The previously mentioned effects of intoxication and the withdrawal symptoms that can occur when a person has stopped using cannabis may be different if the individual had mixed the marijuana with another substance, such as cocaine or phencyclidine (PCP).

Contrary to popular belief, marijuana is not harmless. Not only can it be addictive, but smoking it can also cause lung damage. Other adverse consequences include distorted perceptions, impaired judgment, low motivation, and short-term memory problems.

Cocaine

Cocaine is a derivative of the *Erythroxylon* coca bush. It is sometimes referred to as blow, coke, powder, or snow. Cocaine may be snorted, smoked, injected, and, on rare occasion, eaten. Cocaine was first derived in the 1800s and initially used for medicinal purposes. Although it is still used as a local anesthetic, it is classified by the Food and Drug Administration as a Schedule II drug, which means that it is highly addictive but has some recognized medicinal purposes. Crack is a form of cocaine that has been processed. Crack is sold in small quantities, often referred to as "rocks," that are ready to be smoked. Nationally, in 2002, the Drug Enforcement Agency seized more than 61,000 kilograms of cocaine—this amount was 3.6% higher than that seized in 2001 and 35.9% more than that seized in 1995.

The effects of cocaine on the central nervous system may lead to a feeling of euphoria and increased alertness. In addition, the individual's appetite and need for sleep may decrease. In addition, a person under the influence of cocaine may experience anger, anxiety, or tension. He or she may also have abnormal heart rhythms, abnormal movements, chest pain, dilated pupils, increased or decreased blood pressure and/or heart rate, nausea and vomiting, seizures, sweating, and weight loss. Sometimes, people who use cocaine develop **paranoid delusions** and hallucinations. Psychosis is most commonly seen among those using the drug on an IV or those smoking the drug as crack. Hallucinations may be auditory, visual, or tactile (such as the sensation that bugs are crawling underneath the skin). The use of cocaine can be fatal, and the risk of toxicity is intensified when mixed with alcohol.

The withdrawal phenomenon associated with the use of cocaine, also known as the "crash," may include depression, fatigue, inability to sleep or increased sleep, increased appetite, and nightmares. In severe cases, some people experience suicidal thoughts. Attempts should be made to protect people with suicidal thoughts from self-injurious behavior. In addition, people who experience withdrawal from cocaine may sometimes use other substances such as alcohol or sedatives in an attempt to alleviate the symptoms of withdrawal. As discussed elsewhere in this chapter, withdrawal from alcohol and sedatives can be life-threatening if left untreated.

Hallucinogens

A hallucinogen is a "producer of hallucinations." This class of drugs includes several different substances, such as lysergic acid diethylamide (LSD), mescaline, MDMA (3,4-methylenedioxymethamphetamine), psilocybin, and dimethyltryptamine. Although both PCP and cannabis can also have hallucinogenic properties, they are described separately in the *DSM-IV* (as they are in this chapter) because of some differences in the psychological and behavioral effects they cause.

The use of LSD, a synthetic hallucinogen also referred to as acid, decreased from the mid-1970s through the 1980s, though this trend appeared to be reversing in the 1990s. Although the drug is classified as a hallucinogen, people who use LSD do not commonly experience overt hallucinations. Instead, they typically experience a misperception of an actual stimulus, which is called an **illusion**. LSD is highly potent, and changes in behavior can occur even with low doses of this drug. Its high potency allows LSD to be applied to the backs of stamps or on paper blotters. The onset of psychological and behavioral changes occurs about an hour after oral ingestion of LSD, and the effects last for approximately 10 to 12 hours. The first few hours are sometimes called the "trip." Effects of LSD can include alterations in vision and hearing, an altered sense of time, dizziness, tingling, and tremors. **Synesthesia**, which is the blending of various senses (for example, "seeing" different sounds or "smelling" various colors) may also occur with the use of LSD.

Mescaline occurs naturally in the peyote cactus, which is found in the southwestern United States. This drug is less potent than LSD. The effects of mescaline last 6 to 10 hours. Psilocybin is found naturally in some mushrooms. The effects of this substance last about 2 hours.

Several amphetamine-like substances have properties similar to those of hallucinogens, but are chemically related to amphetamines. These substances produce effects that resemble those of both amphetamines and hallucinogens. Although this category includes several other drugs, MDMA (also called ecstasy, XTC, or Adam) is the most thoroughly researched and probably the most widely used. The effects of ecstasy occur within about an hour of taking the drug. The person may experience a sense of diminished anxiety, increased empathy toward others, and excessive well-being. Agitation, blurred vision, involuntary clenching of the teeth, muscle cramps, nausea, and sweating may also occur. A person taking ecstasy may have sustained physical activity, which can lead to increased body temperature that requires emergency medical attention. An overdose of ecstasy can cause increased blood pressure, loss of consciousness, and seizures.

In general, when a person has an adverse reaction to a hallucinogen, that individual must be protected from hurting himself or herself or others. The anxiety can be managed by support and reassurance. The person should be placed in a quiet room with avoidance of physical intrusion until he or she is experiencing less anxiety. Some individuals may remain agitated and need medication.

Inhalants

The inhalants include a variety of substances such as spray paint, glue, gasoline, paint thinners, correction fluid, and spray-can propellants. Because inhalants are cheap and readily available, they are the substances of abuse often used by young people. Some reports estimate that as many as 18% of high school seniors have used inhalants at least once.

Inhalants are abused for their psychoactive effects. These substances may be sprayed directly into the mouth or nose. When a person practices "bagging," the substance is placed in a bag from which it is inhaled. The most common route of administration is "huffing," which entails putting a substance on a rag that is then placed over the mouth and nose. Because some users may try to heat the substances, inhalant use poses a fire or explosion hazard. Clues that an individual may be abusing inhalants include an odor of paint or chemicals on the breath or clothes or irritation of the mouth and nose. The use of inhalants can cause permanent damage to the nervous system, liver, and kidneys. In addition, death may result from an abnormal heart rhythm and insufficient delivery of oxygen to the body's organs.

When a person is intoxicated with an inhalant, he or she may manifest behavioral or psychological changes such as apathy, belligerence, or impaired judgment. Other effects include blurred or double vision, dizziness, euphoria, lethargy, muscle weakness, poor coordination, slowed movements, slurred speech, tremor, unsteady gait, or even coma. People who have been using inhalants may develop hallucinations or delusions and can be very confused, which can lead to injury. A clinically significant withdrawal phenomenon associated with inhalants has not been identified, however.

Opiates

Opiates, also termed narcotics, have been used for thousands of years. Examples of opiates include heroin, codeine, morphine, methadone, hydrocodone (Lortab, Lorcet, Vicodin), hydromorphone (Dilaudid), meperidine (Demerol), oxycodone (Oxycontin, Percocet), and propoxyphene (Darvon). The first of these substances, heroin, is illicit; the others can be prescribed by physicians. Because a heroin habit can become quite costly, people addicted to this drug will often resort to criminal activities to support their habit. If they engage in prostitution and use unclean needles, people addicted to heroin are at risk for infectious diseases such as those caused by human immunodeficiency virus (HIV), hepatitis B virus, and hepatitis C virus.

When under the influence of opiates, a person may initially be euphoric. When intoxicated with opiates, the individual may also experience constriction of the pupils (pinpoint pupils), drowsiness, problems with attention and memory, slurred speech, or even coma. The withdrawal symptoms experienced by someone who has abruptly stopped or cut down on the use of opiates can be very uncomfortable. A person withdrawing from an opiate may have dilated pupils; excessive yawning; fever; goose bumps; joint pain; muscle aches; nausea, vomiting, or diarrhea; increased blood pressure and heart rate; insomnia; runny nose; sweating; and watery eyes. Although these symptoms of opiate withdrawal are often quite uncomfortable, individuals rarely die from opiate withdrawal unless they have a severe physical illness such as major heart disease. Conversely, an overdose on opiates can be deadly. A person who has overdosed on opiates is often unresponsive, has a decreased rate of breathing, and often has constricted pupils.

The onset and duration of withdrawal symptoms depend on the type of opiate being abused. For example, heroin is relatively short acting, and its withdrawal symptoms usually start within 8 hours of the last use of the drug. These withdrawal symptoms, however, can last up to a week. By contrast, methadone is long acting. Therefore, when a person is coming off methadone, the withdrawal begins later than it does with heroin—usually 1 to 3 days after the last dose of methadone—and ends in 10 to 14 days. Although withdrawal from opiates is seldom fatal, if a woman is pregnant, the withdrawal syndrome can cause harm to the fetus and may lead to miscarriage. Pregnant women who are using opiates should be evaluated by medical personnel.

Case Vignette: Rob

Rob is a 32-year-old male who was arrested for burglary. Upon arrest, he begged the officer to take him to the hospital, because he felt "sick." The officer told him that after he was booked, he could request to see the doctor on call at the jail. Fearing additional repercussions, Rob did not inform the police officer that he uses heroin daily and that he had planned to use the stolen money to get a "fix" because of withdrawal symptoms.

After being at the jail for a couple of hours, Rob asked for blankets and some medicine for nausea. Later that night, he reported that he needed to see the doctor for diarrhea. He was told that he could see the doctor in the morning. Feeling very irritable and unable to sleep, Rob again requested to see the doctor because he felt like he was "going to die." Due to his sweating and vomiting, he was taken to the local emergency room. The physician there noticed track marks on Rob's arms, at which point Rob admitted that he had been injecting heroin for several years. He was reassured that he was not going to die, given some medication to help control the symptoms of withdrawal, and discharged back into the custody of the officers.

Phencyclidine and Related Substances

PCP, also known as angel dust, was used initially as an anesthetic in humans. Because of its adverse effects, which include hallucinations, it is no longer used in medical settings. A similar compound, ketamine (sometimes called special K), is also an anesthetic that is a drug of abuse.

PCP is sometimes added to marijuana. The use of PCP can be fatal. Because PCP is made illegally, it may contain contaminants. When a person is "high" or intoxicated on PCP, he or she may be belligerent, combative, impulsive, or agitated, and may exhibit impaired judgment. In addition, those abusing PCP may have abnormally acute hearing, decreased response to pain, difficulty coordinating their movements and speech, increased blood pressure or heart rate, muscle rigidity, vertical or horizontal movement of the eyes (called **nystagmus**), seizures, and even coma. Notably, some individuals will experience delusions and hallucinations as a result of taking PCP. Someone who is intoxicated on PCP and demonstrating psychotic symptoms may need medications to control the agitation and psychosis. Physical withdrawal symptoms from PCP are rare, however.

Sedatives, Hypnotics, and Anxiolytics

Drugs in this class include barbiturates (such as phenobarbital), barbiturate-like substances (including Quaaludes), and benzodiazepines (such as Ativan, Valium, and Xanax). The latter are **hypnotic** and **anxiolytic** medications, which means they can be prescribed by a physician for the treatment of insomnia or anxiety, respectively. Sedatives decrease feelings of tension, hypnotics induce sleep, and anxiolytics reduce anxiety. However, these definitions are not clear cut—for instance, anxiolytics can lead to sleepiness in addition to reducing anxiety.

Users of sedatives, hypnotics, and anxiolytics can develop a tolerance to these agents. In addition, a serious withdrawal phenomenon is associated with these drugs, and the substances are cross-tolerant with alcohol. For example, when a person is suffering from alcohol withdrawal, benzodiazepines are commonly used in medical settings to prevent seizures or DTs. However, when benzodiazepines are abused with alcohol, the additive effects can be deadly. Some people abuse only the drugs in this class and no others. Other people take these drugs to "come down" or to alleviate withdrawal symptoms from their use of amphetamines or cocaine.

Barbiturates have not been prescribed by many doctors since the advent of benzodiazepines, although they can still be found on the street. Nicknames for barbiturates include yellow jackets, red devils, seggies, reds, tooies, and reds and blues. One of the most popular barbiturate-like agents is methaqualone (Quaaludes, also called ludes). Barbiturates are more deadly in overdose than benzodiazepines.

Benzodiazepines are prescribed for many different purposes, including the treatment of anxiety, insomnia, alcohol withdrawal, and seizures. Flunitrazepam, one of the "date rape drugs," is a type of benzodiazepine, albeit one that is not prescribed in the United States. A person who is intoxicated on sedatives, hypnotics, or anxiolytics resembles an individual who is intoxicated on alcohol. Symptoms include mood instability, poor judgment, slurred speech, poor coordination, unsteady gait, problems with attention and memory, stupor, or even coma.

Also similar to alcohol in terms of their withdrawal symptoms, benzodiazepines, when abruptly discontinued or decreased, can result in agitation, anxiety, difficulty sleeping, hallucinations (which may be auditory, tactile, or visual), increased heart rate or blood pressure, sweating, tremors, and seizures. Withdrawal from this class of drugs, as with alcohol, can be fatal if left untreated.

■ Treatment of Substance Abuse and Dependence

There is no single treatment prototype that is appropriate for everyone with a substance abuse problem. In addition to addressing the substance use, effective drug treatment must consider associated legal, occupational, psychological, and medical problems. Detoxification from drugs and alcohol, while necessary for some people, does not constitute comprehensive treatment. Without follow-up in a recovery program, detox itself does not contribute to long-lasting behavioral changes.

In addition to being used for detoxification of alcohol, opiates, and sedatives/hypnotics/anxiolytics, medications may be prescribed as a part of treatment for substance abuse. For example, many individuals who have abused opiates are encouraged to take methadone as part of their long-term maintenance treatment. Some people with alcohol dependence may use medications, such as acamprosate (Campral), which decreases cravings, or disulfiram (Antabuse), which causes a toxic reaction should the person consume alcohol.

> While medications are sometimes helpful in the treatment of alcohol and drug abuse and dependence, psychosocial treatments are of critical importance. These treatments may range from residential recovery programs to outpatient programs and 12-step programs.

While medications are sometimes helpful in the treatment of alcohol and drug abuse and dependence, psychosocial treatments are of critical importance. These types of treatments may range from residential recovery programs, where patients may live on-site for several months, to outpatient programs and 12-step programs including Alcoholics Anonymous and Narcotics Anonymous.

Decreased drug use due to treatment leads to decreased crime rates and decreased risk of infectious diseases. Treatment for drug use is less expensive than treating some of the consequences of substance use. For example, for every $1 spent on addiction treatment, there is a return of $4 to $7 in decreased crime and court costs. That ratio is even higher when one includes the savings related to health care.

■ Comorbidity and Dual Diagnosis

A critical issue in the area of substance abuse relates to providing treatment services for people with both a mental illness and an alcohol or drug use disorder. The presence of both types of disorders is referred to as <u>comorbidity</u> or <u>dual diagnosis</u>. Public health research indicates that the majority of people with a drug use disorder and nearly half of all people with an alcohol use disorder also have at least one psychiatric disorder. Unfortunately, when a person has co-occurring disorders, his or her prognosis is typically poorer. Symptoms of depression, anxiety, mania, and psychosis often are magnified by substance use. Likewise, the risk of accidental death and homicide is increased by the use of substances. In addition, studies have shown that there is an increased risk of suicide among people who abuse substances.

> The preferred mode of treatment for individuals with a dual diagnosis is to provide integrated care. With this approach, the mental illness and the substance use disorder are treated at the same time by clinicians who are trained to understand both mental illnesses and substance use disorders.

Historically, the challenges faced by people with a dual diagnosis were addressed either sequentially or simultaneously—but always separately. More specifically, in sequential treatment, the person would receive treatment for either the substance use disorder or the mental illness first. Then, after the completion of that treatment, he or she would receive treatment for the other disorder. In the simultaneous or parallel treatment model, the patient would receive treatment for the mental illness and for the substance use disorder at the same time, but the two treatments would be provided by different programs. It is now recognized that the preferred mode of treatment for individuals with a dual diagnosis is to provide integrated care. With this approach, the mental illness and the substance use disorder are treated at the same time by clinicians who are trained to understand both mental illnesses and substance use disorders. This strategy helps the patient to receive comprehensive services.

Chapter Wrap-Up

- Intoxication with any substance can be fatal because of either the direct effects of the substance or the user's self-injurious behavior. A person who states that he or she is suicidal, when intoxicated or when experiencing withdrawal symptoms, should be evaluated by a mental health professional.

- Withdrawal from two classes of substances—alcohol and sedatives/hypnotics/anxiolytics—can be life-threatening. While very uncomfortable, withdrawal from opiates, such as heroin, is rarely fatal.

- The rates of alcohol and drug abuse and dependence are particularly high among individuals with serious mental illnesses, a condition referred to as comorbidity or dual diagnosis. Specialized integrated treatment programs are recommended for such individuals.

- While there is no cure, treatment can be effective for people with substance use disorders, and treatment has a positive effect on society as a whole.

Vital Vocabulary

alcohol withdrawal delirium (delirium tremens): the most severe, and potentially fatal, form of alcohol withdrawal

anxiolytic: medication prescribed by a physician for the treatment of anxiety

comorbidity (dual diagnosis): two or more disorders occurring together in the same person at the same time

delusions: fixed, false beliefs

formal thought disorder: the disruption of the thought process

hallucination: a perception that occurs in the absence of an external stimulus, such as hearing a voice when no one is there (auditory hallucinations)

hypnotic: medication prescribed by a physician for the treatment of insomnia

illusion: a misperception of an actual stimulus

lifetime prevalence: the probability that one will develop a particular condition during his or her lifetime

manic: being in an abnormal state of euphoria, elation, or irritability

neurotransmission: the process by which information is relayed in the brain

neurotransmitters: natural brain chemicals that allow one neuron or nerve cell to communicate with the next

nystagmus: involuntary vertical or horizontal movement of the eyes

paranoid delusions: false beliefs that one is being followed, watched, or maliciously pursued

psychotic: having symptoms such as hallucinations or delusions that indicate an impairment in reality testing

substance abuse: a maladaptive pattern of substance use that causes repeated problems

substance dependence: recurrent and significant adverse consequences related to the repeated use of the substance; often accompanied by tolerance for the substance of abuse and withdrawal when the substance is withheld

substances (drugs): alcohol, illicit drugs, and misused addictive prescription medications

synesthesia: the blending of various senses

tolerance: the need for increased amounts of the substance to achieve the desired effect or a decreased effect when the same amount of the substance is used

withdrawal: a physiological and/or psychological syndrome that occurs when someone who has been regularly using a drug stops abruptly; different addictive substances are associated with different withdrawal syndromes

Questions for Review and Discussion

1. Which signs and symptoms should make a law enforcement officer suspect that a person in custody, who is known to be abusing drugs, needs medical attention?
2. Why should suicidal thoughts, when expressed by individuals who are known to be abusing drugs, be taken extremely seriously by law enforcement officers?
3. Why are individuals who abuse intravenous heroin particularly at risk for diseases such as HIV, hepatitis B virus, and hepatitis C virus infection?
4. How should a person who is experiencing withdrawal symptoms, and who states that he or she is suicidal, be treated by law enforcement officers?

Resources

Books and Articles

American Psychiatric Association. Substance-related disorders. In: *Diagnostic and statistical manual of mental disorders* (4th ed., pp. 191–295). Washington, DC: American Psychiatric Association, 2000.

Frances R, Miller S, Mack A. Clinical textbook of addictive disorders (3rd ed.). New York, NY: The Guildford Press, 2005.

Galanter M, Kleber H. *Textbook of substance abuse treatment* (3rd ed.). Arlington, VA: American Psychiatric Publishing, 2004.

Graham A, Schultz T, Mayo-Smith M, Ries R, Wilford B. *Principles of addiction medicine* (3rd ed.). Chevy Chase, MD: American Society of Addiction Medicine, 2003.

Inaba D, Cohen, W. *Uppers, downers, all arounders* (4th ed.). Ashland, OR: CNS Publications, 2000.

Lowinson J, Ruiz P, Millman R, Langrod J. *Substance abuse: a comprehensive textbook* (4th ed.). Philadelphia, PA: Lippincott Williams and Wilkins, 2005.

Sadock B, Sadock V. *Kaplan and Sadock's synopsis of psychiatry: behavioral sciences/ clinical psychiatry* (9th ed., pp. 380–470). Philadelphia, PA: Lippincott Williams & Wilkins, 2003.

Websites

- National Institute on Drug Abuse: http://www.nida.nih.gov
- National Highway Traffic Safety Administration: http://www.nhtsa.dot.gov
- Monitoring the Future: http://www.monitoringthefuture.org
- Chudler E: http://faculty.washington.edu/chudler/amp.html

CHAPTER 10

Delirium and Dementia

■ Introduction

This chapter focuses on delirium, an acute state of confusion, and dementia, a progressive dysfunction of memory. Even though some aspects of these cognitive disorders may seem similar, these illnesses are two very different conditions, and their treatments are likewise very different. The two are considered together here because both cause confusion and disorientation (such as being unsure of the date or the place). First responders may encounter individuals who appear to be lost, confused, or even irritable or aggressive as a result of these disorders. Therefore, public safety personnel must always consider the possibility that delirium or dementia may be the real culprit underlying behavior problems, public disturbances, or other emergency situations.

Case Vignette: George

Shopping mall security agents were called by one of the mall's retailers to help control an agitated man in front of a store. When the security agents arrived, they encountered George, who appeared to be approximately 60 years old. He seemed upset, anxious, and somewhat agitated. When the security agents asked George what was wrong, he reported that ever since he entered the mall, people had been watching him and making fun of him. George also complained of seeing bugs everywhere and said that they were crawling on his skin and would not go away. Security agents tried to convince George that there were neither bugs nor spies in the mall, but their arguments failed to convince him. George became more defensive and irritated, and he eventually started to yell and curse. The situation escalated until a shopper called 9-1-1. When the city police came to the mall to provide assistance, George was arrested and taken to the police station for disorderly conduct.

Details from George's friend, who had been visiting him from out of town for the last two days, revealed that George is a single, unmarried man who lives alone in a nearby apartment complex. He had never exhibited this kind of behavior before, and he had no criminal charges on his record except for a remote history of driving under the influence of alcohol. He continues to drink alcohol regularly. George's friend said that he accompanied George to an Alcoholics Anonymous meeting the day before this incident, and that he had been encouraging his friend to quit drinking since he arrived. George's medical history included no major medical problems except for episodes of blackouts due to drinking.

After less than a day in jail, George became increasingly anxious and agitated. He began sweating profusely, started to tremble, was unable to calm down or rest, and became even more paranoid and confused. Finally, George's speech became incoherent and he became disoriented, unable to state the month, the year, or even the name of the building in which he was confined. As a result of these symptoms, he was taken to the local hospital, where he was diagnosed with probable alcohol withdrawal delirium and admitted for stabilization and further treatment.

■ What Is Delirium?

The term <u>delirium</u> describes a disturbance of consciousness, attention, cognition, and perception. This disturbance usually develops over a short period of time (hours to days) and tends to fluctuate over the course of the day. Delirium is not a disease *per se*, but rather a syndrome that results in the state of acute confusion, attention problems, misperceptions or hallucinations, and problems with thinking. Potential causes of delirium include some medical conditions, drug or alcohol intoxication, and drug or alcohol withdrawal. Sometimes there is more than one cause of delirium, and sometimes the cause cannot be determined.

Delirium is also called by various other names, including acute confusional state, acute brain syndrome, and acute toxic psychosis. As these names suggest, delirium usually occurs quickly, involves odd behaviors and thoughts, and is often related to substances, medical illnesses, or chemicals affecting the brain. Indeed, the word "delirium" is derived from the Latin term *delinare,* meaning "off the track."

Researchers suggest that the prevalence of delirium in the general population is 0.4% for people between the ages of 18 and 55 years, and 1.1% for people aged 55 years and older. Advanced age is a major risk factor for the development of delirium, in part because the innate mechanisms that maintain balance or homeostasis within the body are less able to tolerate significant extremes in older persons. As many as 30% to 40% of hospitalized patients older than age 65 years have an episode of delirium during their hospitalizations, caused in many cases by hospital infections, new medications, or even changes in sleep patterns in the new environment. As many as 60% of nursing home residents older than age 75 have recurring episodes of delirium. Other populations at increased risk for delirium include people with cancer, acquired immune deficiency syndrome; those who had recent surgery (especially heart surgery, hip surgery, and organ transplants); and patients with burns, dialysis, or strokes. This syndrome is also common in individuals with terminal illnesses, often occurring just before death.

The emergence of delirium highlights the mind–body connection. Just as depression can result in many physical symptoms including generalized pain and cardiovascular problems, physical insults such as alcohol intoxication or infection can cause problems with the mind. For this reason, taking a holistic point of view that acknowledges the linkage between how one's body works and how one thinks and acts is essential in understanding mental and medical illnesses.

Unlike patients with mental illnesses such as schizophrenia or bipolar disorder, someone who develops delirium is not necessarily born with a genetic predisposition to delirium. Moreover, delirium is not long-lasting, because it usually resolves once the underlying physical or chemical problem is fixed. Clinicians therefore think about delirium in terms of risk factors, which increase the likelihood of delirium developing, but by themselves do not necessarily cause the illness. Major risk factors for delirium fall into two categories:

- Things that directly affect one's brain, such as drug intoxication, alcohol abuse, medications (especially <u>polypharmacy</u>—taking multiple medications that interact with one another), dehydration with resultant electrolyte imbalances, multiple medical illnesses, and infections
- Variables that render one's brain more vulnerable to these insults, such as advanced age, prior brain damage, a preexisting cognitive impairment (e.g., dementia), sensory problems (e.g., difficulty hearing or seeing), or environmental stimuli that lead to confusion (e.g., not having access to a clock or calendar)

Treating delirium involves both removing the underlying insult (such as treating an infection) and bolstering the individual's resiliency (such as keeping the mind sharp and clear, and ensuring access to adequate sleep and nutrition).

> Delirium is a disturbance of consciousness, attention, cognition, and perception. The disturbance usually develops over a short period of time and tends to fluctuate over the course of the day.

> Taking a holistic point of view that acknowledges the linkage between how one's body works and how one thinks and acts is essential in understanding mental and medical illnesses, including delirium.

Delirium Due to a Medical Condition

As mentioned earlier, delirium can be associated with numerous medical conditions. A medical examination and laboratory results may help pinpoint the cause of the delirium. In the field, first responders may ask the patient if he or she has any known medical problems; they may also observe the environment for any signs of medical problems. Drug paraphernalia, empty alcoholic beverage containers, insulin needles, or even antibiotic bottles may provide valuable insight into the cause of delirium. **Table 10.1** lists common medical causes of delirium.

Delirium Related to Substance Use

Delirium frequently occurs due to substance use or withdrawal. Delirium due to substance intoxication may arise within minutes to hours after ingestion of high doses of drugs such as cocaine or hallucinogens, whereas substances such as alcohol or phenobarbital (a seizure medicine) may cause delirium after intoxication is sustained for several days. Usually delirium resolves as the intoxication ends or within hours to days thereafter. By contrast, delirium associated with substance withdrawal may develop as the body's concentration of the substance decreases. Once it emerges, substance-withdrawal delirium may continue for only a few hours or it may persist for as long as two to four weeks. Although relatively rare, alcohol withdrawal can cause delirium, known as *delirium tremens*, which usually begins 24 to 72 hours after cessation or reduction of alcohol use. Delirium tremens can be fatal if not recognized and treated (see Chapter 9 for a discussion of substance withdrawal signs and symptoms).

■ Common Signs and Symptoms of Delirium

The behavior of people with delirium can vary, but generally resembles the behavior of a person who is becoming increasingly intoxicated. Symptoms tend to fluctuate during the course of the day and are likely to worsen late in the day (a phenomenon called **sundowning**). People

Table 10.1	Medical Conditions Associated with Delirium
System	**Disorder**
Central nervous system	Head trauma
	Infection (meningitis, encephalitis, HIV, neurosyphilis)
	Seizures and post-seizure confusion
	Vascular disorders (stroke, bleeding after head injury)
	Degenerative disease (dementia)
Metabolic causes	Kidney failure
	Liver failure
	Anemia
	Low blood sugar
	Dehydration
	Vitamin deficiency such as B_{12}, folate, or thiamine deficiency
	Electrolyte imbalance
Cardiac and respiratory system	Myocardial infarction (heart attack)
	Congestive heart failure (heart failure)
	Cardiac arrhythmia (irregular heart rhythm)
	Shock
	Respiratory failure
	Decreased oxygenation
Systemic illness	Infections (urinary tract infection, pneumonia)
	Postoperative state
	Tumor (cancer)
	Severe trauma (fractures)
	Temperature dysregulation (hypothermia/heat stroke)
	Sleep deprivation

with delirium may have reduced awareness of their surroundings and may have trouble focusing on an activity or conversation. During the worst periods, delirium may induce delusions, hallucinations, aggressive and agitated behavior, and even death.

People who are delirious have difficulty focusing on the task at hand. They may have problems with attention, memory, language, or perceptions. When talking to an individual with delirium, questions must be repeated because the person's attention wanders and the person may stick with an answer to a prior question rather than correctly shifting attention to the new question being asked. Such an individual is easily distracted by unrelated environmental stimuli.

Taking these attention problems into consideration is of paramount importance when first responders encounter someone who is delirious. Questions must be asked slowly and repeated frequently. Surrounding stimuli need to be minimized. Directions must be clear, simple, and direct. Interacting with someone who is delirious is similar to working with an individual who is intoxicated or cognitively disabled, except that a delirious person may be experiencing these symptoms for the first time.

People with delirium often have problems with thinking and memory. Typically, recent memory is affected more dramatically than long-term memory. While a person with delirium might be able to tell you all about his or her elementary school experiences, he or she may not be able to repeat the question you asked one minute ago. Persons with delirium also have trouble processing new information. These cognitive difficulties have obvious implications for first responders who encounter delirious people in the community. If their cognition and memories are so impaired, delirious people may appear as though they are acting out of resistance or aggression. In reality, delirious people may not be aware of their behaviors or even able to think clearly enough to change them.

Delirious people may also have problems with orientation and perception. Disorientation is frequently seen in delirium, and it typically occurs with respect to time. For example, a delirious person may think that it is morning in the middle of the night, or he or she might not know the day of the week, the month, or even the year. Disorientation may be the first symptom to appear in mild delirium. Indeed, one easy way to check whether someone might be delirious is to assess whether he or she is oriented to person (who he or she is), place (where), time (when), and situation (what is going on). If the individual answers any of these orientation questions incorrectly, delirium might be present. When first responders or public safety personnel encounter a disoriented person in the community who has other signs of intoxication or illnesses, they should consider taking the person to an emergency medical facility for evaluation.

Language disturbances are also possible in delirium. Affected individuals may have slurred speech due to an inability to articulate, difficulty naming objects, difficulty writing, and possibly an inability to understand speech or writing. Not being able to communicate with someone may be a result of delirium-related language difficulties and not defiance. In such situations, it is helpful to obtain information from other informants, particularly family members or friends. Collecting information from family or friends is very important during an encounter with a delirious person, because thinking, perception, and communication problems associated with delirium can prevent an individual from telling you what is going on.

> Collecting information from family or friends is very important during an encounter with a delirious person, because thinking, perception, and communication problems associated with delirium can prevent an individual from telling you what is going on.

■ Course of Delirium

The course of delirium can be quite variable, depending on both the underlying cause and the care received. This condition can last for hours, days, or even longer. If the cause of delirium is not quickly identified and treated, the person gradually may become drowsy and unresponsive. Ultimately, a delirious person can become stuporous, which may lead to coma or even death. In fact, people who become delirious in the hospital or other facilities have higher overall death rates than those who become delirious in other settings. Recognizing delirium is of paramount importance because it may be the first sign of a serious underlying disorder, especially in older people.

■ Treatment of Delirium

The primary goal in the management of delirium is to treat the underlying cause. Other important objectives are to provide physical, psychosocial, and environmental interventions so as to reduce the severity of the symptoms and to facilitate recovery.

The initial step in the evaluation of delirium is to identify the signs and symptoms of delirium and to distinguish it from psychiatric syndromes that can cause confusion, such as dementia, depression, schizophrenia, and mania. Once delirium is suspected, taking a detailed history to determine the person's underlying medical condition, medication history, drug and alcohol use, or exposure to any other toxin often helps to pinpoint the underlying cause of the delirium. In addition, appropriate physical examination and laboratory studies may help to uncover the underlying cause. First responders who witness the conditions in affected individuals' homes and talk with families and friends of someone who is acting oddly may provide essential information to healthcare providers.

> First responders who witness the conditions in affected individuals' homes and talk with families and friends of someone who is acting oddly may provide essential information to healthcare providers.

The majority of individuals with delirium require medication to overcome their distressing symptoms. Agitation, confusion, sleep disturbances, hallucinations, and bizarre behaviors associated with delirium may be lessened or relieved with these medicines. Providers treating delirious people usually prescribe antipsychotic agents, sedatives such as benzodiazepines, vitamin supplements, and pain medications to treat these symptoms. The risk of precipitous declines in delirious people necessitates close monitoring, usually as a hospital inpatient.

People with delirium are usually frightened by their symptoms and problems remembering recent events. Symptoms of disorientation, suspiciousness, and hallucinations cause significant distress and can create enormous anxiety in the patient. Everyone who comes in contact with individuals with delirium should offer reassurance and help orient them by reminding them of where they are; the day, date, and time; and what is happening to them. Allowing family members to stay with the patient also can prove helpful, especially during transportation to a medical facility. Perhaps most importantly, first responders must remember that delirious people are sick and not purposefully oppositional. Recalling this fact can significantly change one's approach to someone who is delirious.

When engaging people with delirium, focus on safety, respect, and comfort. Foremost, ensure that there are no objects, people, or situations (e.g., oncoming traffic) that could cause injury or death. In the chapter-opening vignette, security guards could have escorted George out of the general mall area and into a quieter room for further questioning and for the safety of himself and others. Extend the same respect to delirious persons that you would to anyone else. Call the individual by name, say things slowly but without sounding condescending, and offer such comforts as a glass of water, a soft place to sit or lie, and even the person's hearing aids or eyeglasses if appropriate. Remind delirious people where they are, what is going on, and that you are present to help. Collect as much information from the community as possible, and talk with family members or friends who might provide helpful details illuminating why the person might be delirious. When it is clear that a person's delirium is due to a medical condition, quickly and safely arrange for transportation to an emergency medical facility for assessment and treatment.

Case Vignette: John

A woman driving to work observed an elderly man walking in the middle of the road. Quite concerned, she stopped her car and tried to ascertain whether the elderly gentleman needed any help. He appeared lost and had difficulty providing basic information. The woman was worried for the man's safety, so she called 9-1-1 for help.

Police officers arrived on the scene and tried to talk to the elderly gentleman. He appeared somewhat confused, defiant, and unwilling to provide information. Except for identifying himself as "John," he did not respond to the officers' questions. Wondering if John had hearing problems, the police officers repeated the questions loudly. John started to get irritated and angry at the officers. When an officer tried to search his pockets to find identification such as a driver's license, John became very upset from this perceived invasion of his privacy and tried to push away the officer. Due to his disoriented and agitated behavior, officers were unable to obtain any further information.

Communication with the precinct revealed that a person fitting the man's description had been reported as missing. The man was determined to indeed be the missing person, and information from his daughter revealed that John had memory problems and had wandered away from his home.

According to his daughter, John appears to get intimidated when faced with new people and situations. As a result of his fear, he may become defiant and refuse to answer questions. Lately he appears to have experienced changes in his personality, which have been both challenging and confusing for his family. Once this information was learned, John was taken to the local hospital for psychiatric evaluation.

■ Dementia

Dementia refers to a progressive dysfunction of the brain that results in gradual decreases in intellectual function, memory, and other cognitive skills. Almost everyone has days or situations in which it is difficult to remember things. These times are not like dementia, however, in that they are transient. While inconvenient, these memory problems do not cause interference in one's ability to perform daily functions. Dementia, by contrast, impedes daily functioning and makes independent self-care challenging.

The word "dementia" translates literally from Latin as "irrationality." Persons with dementia often become confused, are disoriented, and act irrationally. They may exhibit agitated behavior and may not recognize family members and friends. Unlike delirium, which is most often acute and usually reversible with treatment of the underlying problem, dementia is a progressive, chronic **neurodegenerative disorder**. Delirium and dementia differ in several other significant ways as well. **Table 10.2** compares and contrasts these two conditions.

Dementia usually occurs in elderly people. It affects more than 15% of people older than 65 years, and as many as 40% of people older than 80 years. More than half of all nursing home admissions in the United States are believed to occur because of dementia-related problems. While memory ability is known to decrease slightly with age in most everyone, dementia causes more prominent problems with memory as well as other cognitive functions. People with dementia face significant declines in functioning.

> Unlike delirium, which is most often acute and usually reversible with treatment of the underlying problem, dementia is a progressive, chronic neurodegenerative disorder.

Table 10.2 Delirium Versus Dementia

Feature	Delirium	Dementia
Onset	Develops suddenly	Develops slowly
Course	Fluctuating; most cases resolve with correction of the underlying medical condition	Chronic and progressive
Duration	Days to weeks	Months to years
Cause	Frequently caused by medical illness and drugs	Usually caused by Alzheimer's disease or other neurodegenerative diseases
Level of consciousness	Fluctuating levels of consciousness with decreased attention	Normal until late stages
Distinguishing feature	Predominantly affects attention	Predominantly affects memory
Memory	Trouble processing new information and inability to recall recent events	Gradual loss of recent memory in mild to moderate stages. Eventual loss of remote memory in severe stage
Language	Slow and often incoherent	Difficulty in finding the right word
Sleep	Reversed sleep-wake cycle	May have insomnia
Other associated symptoms	Disorientation, visual hallucinations, agitation, apathy, withdrawal	Disorientation, agitation
Treatment and outcome	Involves immediate workup and treatment of underlying medical condition; potentially reversible	Involves non-emergent medical workup and treatment; not reversible

■ Alzheimer's and Non-Alzheimer's Types of Dementia

Several causes of dementia are distinguished, which traditionally have been classified into two groups: Alzheimer's disease and non-Alzheimer's-type dementias.

Alzheimer's disease, the most common cause of dementia, is caused by loss of nerve cells in the areas of the brain dealing with cognitive functions, such as memory. A buildup of abnormal proteins in some brain cells is seen in the Alzheimer's type of dementia. Alzheimer's disease affects mostly the elderly population, but it is also reported in younger individuals, albeit rarely. The exact causes for this disease are not completely understood; however, researchers are actively working to better understand this disease and to develop effective treatments for it. Having others with Alzheimer's disease in one's family and advanced age are the most common risk factors identified for Alzheimer's disease.

Other non-Alzheimer's types of dementia include vascular dementia, Lewy body dementia, and dementia caused due to neurological diseases such as Parkinson's disease and Huntington's disease. <u>Vascular dementia</u> (which is estimated to account for 15% to 25% of dementia cases) is caused by minor strokes that accumulate over a long period of time and eventually affect blood flow to the areas of the brain related to memory and thinking. High blood pressure and other cardiovascular illnesses contribute to the development of vascular dementia. When blood flow or blood pressure is the origin of dementia, often people report that they lose their memories or abilities to think in discrete episodes. This presentation of vascular dementia can be very frightening for family members and friends who witness abrupt changes in memory and personality.

Less common causes of dementia include Parkinson's disease; Huntington's disease; vitamin B_{12} deficiency; infections due to human immunodeficiency virus, tuberculosis, or syphilis; meningitis; and encephalitis. Unlike Alzheimer's dementia and vascular dementia, some of these rather uncommon causes of dementia can be reversible if they are detected and treated in a timely manner. In most cases, however, dementia is progressive and not reversible.

> Dementia is most common in the elderly population; it is also seen in younger people, albeit rarely. Dementia is usually progressive and not reversible.

■ Common Signs and Symptoms of Dementia

The onset of Alzheimer's disease is gradual, which often makes it difficult to detect. One of the first symptoms may be mild forgetfulness, which can easily be mistaken for age-related memory change. In the early stages of Alzheimer's disease, people may exhibit trouble remembering recent activities, names of familiar things or people, the way to return home, or the reason why they went to the store. These difficulties may be bothersome but are not too serious. Such minor or moderate symptoms are often dismissed as simple aging or lack of concentration. Consequently, few individuals with early Alzheimer's disease seek evaluation or treatment from a healthcare provider.

As Alzheimer's disease progresses, symptoms are more easily noticed. Moderate or severe symptoms are quite readily recognized by families and loved ones, which prompts seeking medical attention. In contrast, people with dementia often remain unaware of their limitations and deny having any problems. People in the middle stages of the disease develop short-term memory difficulties, language disturbances, and problems with daily activities. These individuals may have trouble finding the right words, resulting in lapses in speech, and they may forget how to do simple tasks such as brushing their teeth and combing their hair.

Eventually people with Alzheimer's disease become unable to care for their own hygiene or to remember where they live or how to care for themselves. During later stages of the disease, individuals may not be safe alone, because they can wander off and not recall where they live. They may lose control over their bowel and bladder functions, and they may lose touch with reality. People at this severe stage of Alzheimer's dementia frequently require nursing home care or intensive help in an assisted living facility.

Dementia is a family illness that necessitates care and support for all family members, not just the person with dementia. **Table 10.3** outlines the specific signs and symptoms of dementia as the disease progresses.

> Dementia is a family illness that necessitates care and support for all family members, not just the person with dementia.

■ Course of Dementia

The typical course of dementia has an onset between 50 to 60 years of age, with a gradual decline occurring over a period of 5 to 10 years. The rate of progression of dementia varies widely and depends on its cause. Survival ranges from 2 to 20 years after diagnosis, with

Table 10.3 Common Signs and Symptoms of Dementia		
Mild Symptoms	**Moderate Symptoms**	**Severe Symptoms**
■ Memory lapses ■ Inability to perform everyday tasks ■ Confusion and disorientation in familiar surroundings	■ Language disturbances ■ Needs help with bathing, grooming, and hygiene ■ Inability to recognize family and friends ■ Disturbing behavior (aggression)	■ Slowed or incomprehensible speech ■ Loss of bladder/ bowel control ■ Increased/total dependence on caregiver

an average of about 8 years. Factors that mediate the rate of decline in one's cognition and functioning include an individual's level of education, intelligence, and social support system. In general, the more someone used his or her mind before developing dementia, the longer he or she will be able to maintain cognitive and functional abilities with the disease. As in most other illnesses, the more social support someone has, the more likely functionality will be preserved for longer periods of time.

Once dementia is suspected, individuals must undergo a complete medical and neurological workup, because 10% to 15% of all patients with dementia have a potentially reversible condition such as a brain infection or vitamin B_{12} deficiency. Timely identification and prompt medical intervention to treat these conditions may prevent permanent brain damage and stop the progression of dementia.

In advanced stages of dementia, safety concerns become extremely important. Individuals with severe dementia may be totally unaware of their surroundings. A person with advanced dementia can wander onto a street and be run over by oncoming traffic, or forget to turn off a stove and start a house fire that places others at risk for injury or death.

■ Treatment of Dementia

Currently, there are no treatments that can prevent or cure dementia. For some people in the early and middle stages of the disease, certain medications may delay worsening of signs and symptoms. Other medications such as antianxiety agents and antidepressants may help control associated symptoms, such as insomnia, irritability, anxiety, and depression. Treatment of these symptoms can help an individual with dementia feel more comfortable and allow for easier care.

> Currently, there are no treatments that can prevent or cure dementia. For some people in the early and middle stages of the disease, certain medications may delay worsening of signs and symptoms.

Some environmental and social factors also may facilitate care for people with dementia. People with dementia should be housed in rooms that are bright and contain sensory stimuli such as a television and radio. These stimuli help individuals with dementia to remain alert and focus attention. The environment should be safe (no stoves, sharp objects, cigarettes, or other potentially dangerous objects) and should have monitoring systems to avoid wandering. Activities that may lead to anxiety and confusion should be avoided. With simplification of daily routines, consistent support, and cognitive and physical engagement in activities, people with dementia may be able to maintain reasonable quality of life.

■ Engaging and Assessing Individuals with Dementia

In the case vignette presented earlier, John is an elderly gentleman with dementia. As first responders attempt to engage someone with dementia, it may be impossible to determine details such as the individual's name, address, and phone number due to loss of memory and disorientation. If you encounter an elderly person who seems disoriented or forgetful in the community, do not press him or her to provide information. Rather, ensure the individual's safety and attempt to collect additional information from others to determine who the person is and where he or she is from. Demanding information from someone with dementia may exacerbate the anxiety and confusion the individual feels. Such heightening confusion and irritability can be misinterpreted as aggression.

John appeared confused and became agitated when the officer searched his pockets in an attempt to find a form of identification. Sometimes people with memory problems may have engraved identification bracelets, a necklace, or clothing labels indicating their addresses and other identifying information. These identification tools, which are available from the Alzheimer's Association, are most helpful to first responders who may find someone with dementia in the community. Search for signs to help identify people with dementia instead of pressing them to tell you directly.

Learning to recognize certain signs and symptoms of dementia (loss of memory, disorientation, and agitation) will help officers develop alternative ways to deal with people experiencing dementia. Observing the scene for additional information (dementia medications, identification necklaces or bracelets) and gathering collateral information from others may prove extremely helpful in clarifying the situation when a first responder interacts with someone with dementia. If you have any uncertainty about the situation, it is always best to secure a medical evaluation for someone who is disoriented and agitated, because a treatable delirium may be present or a medical evaluation may help create a treatment plan for someone with dementia.

> If you have any uncertainty about the situation, it is always best to secure a medical evaluation for someone who is disoriented and agitated.

Chapter Wrap-Up

Chapter Highlights

- Delirium is an acute state of confusion that develops over a short period of time and is associated with a fluctuating level of consciousness and impaired ability to pay attention. It is also associated with problems with recent memory, disorientation, language disturbance, and misperceptions such as illusions and hallucinations. Emotional disturbances, personality changes, and disturbances in the sleep-wake cycle may be part of delirium as well.

- Older adults are particularly at risk for developing delirium. They are also particularly vulnerable to negative consequences of delirium, including medical complications, impaired cognitive function, functional decline, and even a greater risk of institutional placement (such as in a nursing home).

- Recognizing the signs and symptoms of delirium and gathering additional information from the surroundings, family members, or friends may help first responders seek timely medical care to treat the underlying cause of delirium. The more quickly delirium is treated, the better the outcome.

- During an encounter with any confused person, ensure that the individual is using his or her eyeglasses and hearing aids. Bringing trusted family or friends into the situation as much as possible also decreases anxiety in the situation. Finally, first responders who have few demands, offer reassurance and respect, and contain their own frustrations have the best interactions with confused individuals.

- Dementia is a progressive dysfunction of the brain that results in a chronic deterioration of intellectual function and other cognitive skills including memory.

- The symptoms of the dementia usually appear gradually and include loss of memory, inability to perform daily activities, confusion and disorientation in familiar surroundings, and difficulty remembering common words and names.

- Currently, there is no cure for dementia. Some medications can decrease the progression of symptoms or treat underlying depression and anxiety. Environmental, social, and cognitive interventions are useful to maintain quality of life for people with dementia.

Vital Vocabulary

delirium: a disturbance of consciousness, attention, cognition, and perception that usually develops rapidly over the course of hours to days

dementia: a progressive dysfunction of the brain that results in gradual decreases in intellectual function, memory, and other cognitive skills over the course of months to years

homeostasis: the balance one's body and mind attempts to keep in the face of environmental or physiological changes

neurodegenerative disorder: a disorder that leads to an irreversible loss of neurons within the brain

polypharmacy: the use of multiple medications that may interact with one another

sundowning: a phenomenon in which symptoms tend to fluctuate during the course of the day and are likely to worsen in the evening or at night

vascular dementia: a form of dementia caused by minor strokes that accumulate over a long period of time and eventually affect blood flow to the areas of the brain related to memory and thinking

Questions for Review and Discussion

1. What are some reasons why individuals become delirious?
2. What clues at the scene might suggest that a person behaving inappropriately may be either delirious or demented?
3. What types of support would the family of someone with dementia require or appreciate?
4. In what ways do delirium and dementia differ? How are they similar?

Resources

American Psychiatric Association. Delirium, dementia, and amnestic and other cognitive disorders. In: *Diagnostic and statistical manual of mental disorders* (4th ed., text revision, pp. 135–180). Washington, DC: American Psychiatric Association, 2000.

Cheston R, Bender M. *Understanding dementia: the man with the worried eyes.* London, UK: Jessica Kingsley Publishers, 1999.

Coffey CE, Cummings JL. Delirium. In: *The American Psychiatric Press textbook of geriatric neuropsychiatry* (2nd ed., pp. 441–452). Washington, DC: American Psychiatric Publishing, 2000.

Henry M. Descending into delirium. *Am J Nursing* 2002;102(3):49–56.

Killick J. *Communication and the care of people with dementia.* Buckingham, UK: Open University Press, 2001.

Leentjens AFG, Van der Mast RC. Delirium in elderly people: an update. *Curr Opin Psychiatry* 2005;18(3):325–330.

Rabins PV. Delirium. *Maryland Med J* 1994;43(2):145–147.

Sadock BJ, Sadock VA. *Kaplan and Sadock's synopsis of psychiatry: behavioral sciences/clinical psychiatry* (9th ed., pp. 329–344). Philadelphia, PA: Lippincott Williams & Wilkins, 2002.

Responding to Children and Adolescents with Emotional and Behavioral Disorders

Case Vignette: *Zachary*

Zachary is a 15-year-old Caucasian male who lives at home with his mother and his 9-year-old younger brother. Zachary's mother called 9-1-1 for emergency assistance because of his aggressive and threatening behavior.

Upon arrival to their home, the responding officers see Zachary standing in the middle of the living room holding a baseball bat while yelling at his mother. Parts of the sofa are charred, there are holes in the wall, and broken glass is scattered on the floor. His mother states that Zachary has been completely out of control during the last hour, and that she has been unable to calm him down. She reports that over the last several months, Zachary has become increasingly more aggressive, initially making verbal threats, but now actually hitting her and destroying items in their home. Zachary's mother also suspects that he has been using drugs because his eyes are often red, he is quite irritable, and the friends he has been hanging out with lately are known to use drugs. Today Zachary has been swinging the bat at both his brother and his mother, and threatening to kill them. While the officers are attempting to intervene and initiate a conversation with Zachary, he begins cursing loudly and screaming, "Back up! Back up!" His eyes are red, and a faint odor of marijuana can be detected.

■ Introduction

The 2003 National Health Interview Survey estimated that 5% of American youth (2.7 million children) suffer from severe emotional and behavioral disorders. Given this staggering statistic, it is likely that many adult mental illnesses have their onsets in childhood, underscoring the great need for early diagnosis and effective treatment of youth with mental illnesses. Working with youth with severe emotional and behavioral disorders is fraught with challenges, however. The difficulties in dealing with this population include a fragmented system of mental health services, limited resources, the need to collaborate with caregivers in the provision of treatment, and the role that development and environment play in a child's ability to relate to others and function in his or her environment. In short, treating children and adolescents with mental illnesses can be both exciting and frustrating.

Undoubtedly, one of the biggest obstacles to caring for youth with severe emotional and behavioral disorders is the paucity of resources directed toward this group. Both outpatient and inpatient services are limited. The national shortage of child psychiatrists, particularly in rural areas, often results in a significant delay between the time when a caregiver seeks help and the point at which the child is first seen. Services for children with special needs are even more limited. Youth with developmental disorders, mental retardation, or substance abuse may not have access to any specialized treatment programs at all. Even if programs exist for children with mental illnesses, when children are hospitalized, their hospital stays are often brief. Short stays in psychiatric care facilities provide little time to address the unique and complex needs of children and adolescents. Funding issues frame this shortage of services, because neither public nor private systems have provided the financial backing required to meet the needs of youth with mental illnesses.

> One of the biggest obstacles to caring for youth with severe emotional and behavioral disorders is the paucity of resources directed toward this group.

■ Engaging Caregivers in Children's Mental Health Treatment

Because adult caregivers are responsible for the welfare of children, engaging caregivers is a very important and necessary task in ensuring that children receive appropriate mental health treatment. Typically, the caregiver is a parent. Clinicians must first develop rapport with and engage the primary caregiver because, without those elements, the caregiver may choose to forgo treatment. The caregiver provides additional clinical history that can be incredibly useful in understanding the child's difficulties. He or she is also responsible for transporting the child to treatment, consenting to medications, and ensuring that the child adheres to the treatment plan.

When caregivers are not involved in treating a child with a mental illness, the process can be much more difficult. Imagine the challenges that arise when the parent is not the primary caregiver and the child is instead in the custody of child protective services due to abuse or neglect. The caseworker may not know the child well and will not be able to comment on that child's particular difficulties. The support that might otherwise be offered by family members is lacking, leaving the child with few other adults on whom to rely. Consent for care may be difficult to obtain, and the child may not have the resources to be able to attend appointments or follow through with therapies. Children's mental illnesses affect their entire community, because involvement of a child's caregivers, teachers, friends, and siblings may be crucial to the success of a comprehensive treatment plan.

Communication also may pose challenges when treating children with mental illnesses. For example, a three-year-old child cannot describe his or her emotions, which makes it much more difficult to diagnose the cause of symptoms. While a six-year-old has some idea about feelings, his or her ability to communicate those thoughts and feelings and reliably connect them to life events is limited. Caregivers play essential roles in relaying observed behaviors and piecing together children's feelings so as to communicate concerns to mental health clinicians.

■ Developmental Milestones

Developmental milestones are important childhood physical, emotional, and cognitive developmental targets. Development in these various domains occurs at varying rates. Normal development in any of these areas may be impaired.

Deficits in physical development can occur, for example, if a child's mother did not receive appropriate prenatal care, if the mother used drugs or alcohol during pregnancy, or if the child's basic needs were not met as a result of neglect. Impaired physical development can result in stunted growth, poor coordination, or even recurrent illnesses.

Deficits in emotional development are seen when youth have been physically and/or sexually abused or neglected by their caregivers. Stunted emotional development may result in immature behaviors, poor self-esteem, failure to form a stable self identity, and difficulty forming attachments to others.

A variety of deficits can arise when normal cognitive development is impaired. Learning disabilities, attention and concentration problems, mental retardation, or even pervasive developmental disorders such as autism may appear if cognitive development does not appropriately progress.

When evaluating youth, it is important to keep in mind their developmental levels. Developmental levels can be described as the combination of a person's chronological or true age and his or her developmental age. Ideally, these two ages match. Sometimes, however, the developmental age may lag behind the true age. A youth who is 17 years old but appears to have global difficulties comprehending information may have the developmental age of a 5-year-old child. This youth may have mental retardation, defined by low intelligence—an intelligence quotient less than 70—and deficits in adaptive functioning (the inability to carry out activities of daily living such as grooming and caring for hygiene, or appropriately using community resources such as the bus without assistance). Responding to this youth will be quite different from responding to a 17-year-old youth without a developmental lag who has normal intelligence. Children with developmental delays are at higher risk for having a psychiatric disorder, and many present with symptoms of impulsivity, hyperactivity, and irritability. Treatment interventions for developmentally delayed youth will be different as well.

■ Self-injurious Behavior and Suicidal Ideation in Children

Over the past few years, suicidal behavior in children and adolescents has drawn significant attention and has been identified as a major public health concern. According to the 2004 Youth Risk Behavior Survey conducted by the Centers for Disease Control and Prevention (CDC), 16.9% of youth in the United States have seriously contemplated attempting suicide, 16.5% made a plan to attempt suicide, and 8.5% actually attempted suicide. These startling numbers emphasize the need to take suicidal behavior seriously regardless of the age of the child or a child's socioeconomic background.

Suicidal behavior is often an impulsive act, although some youth are preoccupied with thoughts of death and carefully plan their actions. A child's intention to die from suicidal behavior is not always clear. Many children who make suicidal gestures wish to be removed from a situation rather than to permanently end their lives. A thorough suicide evaluation requires assessment of a child's intent to truly die as well as the lethality of the stated suicide plan.

Similarly, a suicidal child's age and developmental level need to be considered during a suicide evaluation. Younger children are cognitively unable to appreciate the finality of death. A younger child may also not grasp that he or she will never be able to see his or her parents again after a completed suicide. Very young children may not have the cognitive capacity to understand the implications of a suicide attempt, even if the child intends to die.

By contrast, older youth may consider making a suicide attempt for completely different reasons. Consider an older adolescent who is angry with a parent and takes extra pain pills to make the parent feel guilty for imposing consequences. In this case, the act is potentially lethal, but the intent is not to die but rather to communicate something to the parents. Clearly, motivations, methods, and results of suicidal behavior differ according to children's **developmental stages.**

Adolescent girls and boys also differ in their rates and means of suicide attempts and completed suicide. Young men tend to use more lethal means to attempt suicide, such as firearms. Boys' means of suicide attempts increase the risk of a completed act. While girls attempt suicide more frequently than do boys, they do so using less lethal means, such as intentional overdose or **cutting**.

Suicidal behavior almost always suggests significant psychiatric distress and an underlying psychiatric diagnosis. Common psychiatric diagnoses leading to suicidal behavior in children and adolescents include **mood disorders** and **substance use disorders**, particularly in boys. Signs of depression in youth can differ from those observed in adults. Depressed children tend to be more irritable than sad, and they typically exhibit physical problems such as failure to gain expected weight during growth phases. They may also withdraw and isolate themselves from family and peers. Additionally, depressed youth may experience a decline in their academic performance as well as changes in their sleep, appetite, energy, and concentration. Caregivers, teachers, peers, and law enforcement officers should be observant for these signs and symptoms of depression, as depressed youth do not necessarily communicate their feelings with words.

Other risk factors for suicidal behavior in children and adolescents include the following: **nonadherence** with mental health treatment, social isolation, family history of suicide, abuse and/or neglect, medical illness in the child, and parental mental illness. Adolescents, in particular, may contemplate suicide as a result of social losses or embarrassments. Losing a boyfriend or girlfriend, being cut from a sports team, experiencing legal and academic stressors, facing family discord, and having incurred recent punishment can all precede suicidal behavior. Table 11.1 summarizes risk factors for suicide in children.

Professionals must take suicidal statements or acts very seriously, even in situations in which one believes the child's or adolescent's goal is not truly to die. As with suicidal adults, ensuring the safety of children with suicidal behavior is the paramount concern. Often suicidal children need emergency psychiatric evaluation to determine whether hospitalization is necessary. Determining whether a child needs hospitalization or can be managed as an outpatient can be a difficult decision. Factors to keep in mind in making that decision include the severity of the suicidal behavior (intent and lethality), the prevalence of recent stressors, any previous attempt history, information about whether the child is currently receiving and adherent with mental health treatment, and the family's ability to monitor the child. If a mental health professional has concerns about any of these factors, it may be best to hospitalize the suicidal youth.

Table 11.1   Risk Factors for Suicidal Behavior in Children
Previous suicide attempts Family history of suicide attempts or completed suicide Substance use Family dysfunction Nonadherence with psychiatric treatment

Once in treatment, it is important to address the underlying mental illness, because suicidal behavior almost always suggests significant psychological distress and an underlying psychiatric diagnosis. Children and adolescents with suicidal behavior may be treated with individual or family therapy, **psychoeducation**, medications, substance abuse treatment, or some combination of treatment approaches.

> Suicidal behavior almost always suggests significant psychological distress and an underlying psychiatric diagnosis.

■ Aggressive and Disruptive Behavior in Children

Aggression itself is not classified as a mental illness, but rather is a behavior that sometimes can be observed in youth with mental illnesses. Disruptive behavior disorders, which include **attention-deficit/hyperactivity disorder** (ADHD), **oppositional defiant disorder**, and **conduct disorder**, can all feature aggressive behavior. The hallmark symptoms of ADHD include inattention, impulsivity, and hyperactivity. Children who are diagnosed with oppositional defiant disorder may disobey rules and come across as argumentative and hostile, but they do not seriously violate others' rights. In contrast, youth with conduct disorder may commit serious violations of rights. For example, they may be aggressive to people or animals, destroy property, run away from home frequently, be truant from school, and be calculating or purposely deceptive. Children diagnosed with conduct disorder may typically develop into adults who have extensive legal problems, or criminal histories, and antisocial personality disorder.

The causes of aggressive behavior in youth remain unclear, but are likely to be combinations of biological, psychological, and social factors. Abnormalities in the **serotonin** (**neurotransmitter**) system in a child's brain, much like the abnormalities seen in mood disorders, have been implicated as one cause of aggression in children. Youth who witness violence or who are victims of violence (child abuse)—particularly at a young age—are at increased risk of displaying aggressive behavior. Youth who abuse alcohol or drugs may also display aggression. Some researchers suggest that normalization of violence through children's exposure to violence on television or in video games may lead to increased aggression in real life. Caregivers must therefore closely monitor what children observe in the media or from adults, because children may later mimic these observed violent behaviors. **Table 11.2** summarizes the risk factors for childhood aggression.

> Youth who witness violence or are victims of violence (child abuse)—particularly at a young age—are at increased risk of displaying aggressive behavior.

Treatment of aggressive behavior in children can be difficult, because many adults tend to mirror aggression when they respond to aggressive children. Some caregivers spank children or have the urge to physically punish youth who act aggressively. Aggressive responses to children rarely decrease children's aggressive behaviors. Rather, exploration of aggressive children's underlying psychiatric disorders and nonviolent treatment strategies are more likely to decrease their aggressive behaviors. Education of parents and other caregivers that includes development of a behavioral management plan can be very helpful. A **behavioral plan** is a predetermined set of rules with explicit consequences for aggressive behaviors. In addition to behavioral plans, effective nonviolent ways to treat childhood aggression include medications that tar-

Table 11.2   Risk Factors for Aggressive Behaviors in Children
History of violent threats or violent behavior
History of early victimization such as child abuse
History of neurologic insult such as a serious head injury or seizure disorder
Substance use
Violence "normalization" through witnessed behaviors or the media
Access to weapons

get impulse control and attention difficulties; therapies including group, family, and individual psychotherapy; and ensuring social support at home and school.

Like suicidal behavior, aggression in children must be addressed quickly and deliberately, emphasizing the safety of both the aggressive child and other parties. The appropriate intervention hinges on the level of aggression, the access to weapons, the history of violence, and the family's ability to contain the aggression. If any of these factors is somehow compromised, a psychiatric assessment and likely hospitalization are required for safety.

Case Vignette: Maya

A father calls 9-1-1 because his youngest daughter, Maya, a 13-year-old African American female, cut her wrist and forearm. Upon arrival to their home, the emergency medical personnel talk with Maya's father, who states that he came home from work and found Maya locked in the bathroom. When he first called Maya's name, she did not respond. When he found the bathroom locked, her father called her name multiple times. This time Maya responded, "Leave me alone!" Maya's father then forced the door open and found her sitting on the bathroom floor with multiple lacerations on her right wrist and forearm and a knife at her side. She was crying. Recently, Maya and her father had engaged in an argument because she had been skipping school, and Maya had been grounded.

The first responders at the scene notice multiple bruises on Maya's arms and legs as well as what appears to be a cigarette burn on her hand. She also appears quite thin and small for her age.

■ Childhood Abuse and Neglect

<u>Child maltreatment</u> includes physical abuse, sexual abuse, emotional abuse, and neglect. According to the U.S. Department of Health and Human Services' Children's Bureau, the incidence of child maltreatment in 2003 was 12.4 per 1,000 children in the United States. Of these cases, 60% involved neglect, 20% involved physical abuse, 10% involved sexual abuse, and 5% involved emotional abuse. A child can be a victim of more than one type of maltreatment. In most cases (about 80% of the time), the perpetrator is a parent, but other relatives and unmarried partners of a parent are also frequently the source of the maltreatment. In 2003, some 1,500 children died as a result of maltreatment, and 75% of these victims were younger than 4 years of age.

All states have laws that require professionals who suspect childhood abuse or neglect to report it to child protective services, although definitions of abuse and neglect, and specific reporting requirements, vary from state to state. Mandated reporting does not require confirmed abuse—just suspicion of childhood abuse or neglect. Mandated reporters include physicians, educators, social workers, and law enforcement officers. There are legal consequences for professionals who suspect but fail to report childhood abuse or neglect.

> Mandated reporting does not require confirmed abuse—just suspicion of childhood abuse or neglect.

<u>Physical abuse</u> is defined as injury or risk of injury to a child younger than age 18 years resulting from being hit, kicked, shaken, thrown, burned, stabbed, or choked by a parent or caregiver. Signs of physical abuse (**Table 11.3**) include multiple injuries in various stages of healing, bruises in the pattern of fingers or other weapons, "belt burns," burns seen from cigarettes, immersion burns, head and eye injuries, and certain types of fractures such as fractures of the skull, ribs, or face. Oftentimes the explanation of the injuries provided by the caregiver does not fit with the observed injury.

Table 11.3 Signs of Childhood Abuse and Neglect		
Physical Abuse	**Sexual Abuse**	**Neglect**
Multiple bruises	Abrasions or bruises of	Failure to meet expected
Bruises that form regular	the external genitalia	weight gains
patterns resembling the	Sexually transmitted diseases	Disheveled appearance
shape of the object used	Pregnancy	Lack of appropriate supervision
to inflict the injury	Sexual acting out	
Cigarette or	or promiscuity	
immersion burns		
Skull, rib, and		
facial fractures		
Multiple fractures		
Head and eye injuries		

A variety of risk factors for physical abuse of children have been identified. A caregiver with a mental illness or substance use is at increased risk of perpetrating child abuse or neglect. Children who are very young and require a great deal of ongoing care and attention, and adolescents with difficult temperaments or developmental delays, are also at increased risk of abuse or neglect. Any of these factors combined with poverty and lack of social supports produce a volatile environment in which physical abuse or neglect is more likely to occur. Nevertheless, physical abuse and other forms of childhood maltreatment occur in all social classes.

<u>Childhood sexual abuse</u> is defined as the experience of a sexual act involving penetration, molestation with genital contact but without penetration, and other sexual acts such as genital fondling or exposure, in children younger than 18 years. Sexual abuse also includes inadequate or inappropriate supervision of sexual activities. An estimated 1.6 per 1,000 youth were sexually abused in the United States in 1998, though this incidence is probably an underestimate because much abuse likely occurs covertly.

Physical findings of childhood sexual abuse can include abrasions or bruises of the external genitalia, the presence of sexually transmitted diseases in children, and pregnancy (Table 11.3). Sexually abused children are at increased risk of experiencing symptoms of poor self-esteem, anxiety, fear, depression, suicidal behavior, running away, and substance abuse. Sexually abused children or adolescents may also become sexually active or promiscuous early in life.

Girls are more commonly the victims of sexual abuse, and perpetrators are typically male and know the victim. Sexual abuse of boys is less frequently reported but continues to occur. Gay men and women are no more likely to sexually abuse children than heterosexual adults.

<u>Childhood neglect</u> refers to failure of a caregiver to provide for a child's basic needs, which include medical care, appropriate supervision, nutrition, housing, clothing, education, and emotional support. Neglect is the most common form of maltreatment of children, but it is often ignored or overlooked. Signs of neglect are more subtle than those of abuse, and professionals may be reluctant to express concern for a child's well-being based on such signs (Table 11.3).

Child maltreatment is an emergency situation and requires immediate action. Practically speaking, this means having a high index of suspicion and reporting those suspicions to child protective services. A report of child abuse or neglect to child protective services prompts an investigation, followed by removal of the child from the home if evidence of abuse or neglect is found. Whether or not an abused or neglected child has been diagnosed with a mental illness, any victim of abuse or neglect requires psychiatric assessment because of the increased risk of psychiatric disorders associated with maltreatment. Treatment focused on issues surrounding abuse or neglect is enormously important and can reduce the severity of illness or even prevent mental illness from developing after the abuse or neglect has been addressed.

■ Substance Use Disorders in Adolescents

Adolescence is a critical period of experimentation, and this behavior often includes experimentation with alcohol and drugs. Substance use among adolescents ranges from casual use to abuse and dependence. While the criteria for diagnosing substance use disorders in youth are the same as those for adults, some clear differences are noted between youth and adults who abuse substances.

Developmentally, adolescents may have difficulty delaying gratification and planning for their futures, which might contribute to substance abuse. They may also be more likely to use multiple drugs compared to adults. Adolescents typically move from trying tobacco to alcohol to marijuana, followed by use of other illicit drugs such as cocaine and methamphetamine. Younger users are also more likely than their adult counterparts who abuse substances to use inhalants such as Freon, glue, or gasoline, and club drugs such as ecstasy, ketamine, and gamma hydroxybutyrate. Additionally, adolescents may use over-the-counter cold medicines to get a high from dextromethorphan, the main ingredient in some of these medicines. Adults with substance use disorders generally have easier times obtaining substances such as alcohol, tobacco, and even marijuana compared to adolescents. As a result, adolescent substance users have developed ways to abuse common, legal substances.

Many youth who abuse substances also have psychiatric disorders such as ADHD, conduct disorder, learning disorders, or mood or **anxiety disorders**. Multiple risk factors are associated with adolescent substance abuse, including a family history of substance use, physical or sexual abuse, family conflict, a negative peer group, academic difficulties, and disordered parenting. Children known to have psychiatric problems or histories of abuse or neglect should be closely observed for concomitant substance abuse.

The potential **morbidity** from adolescent substance use is high. Youth are more likely to engage in impulsive and dangerous behavior when they are intoxicated. In particular, intoxication may lead them to engage in indiscriminate sexual activity and reckless driving. Suicidal behavior increases in frequency when adolescents are under the influence of substances, as does accidental medication or substance overdose. The impairment in judgment that accompanies intoxication exacerbates the typical impulsivity and lack of long-term thinking that characterize adolescence. Poor academic performance, sporadic school attendance, family discord, and association with a negative, substance-abusing peer group may result from substance abuse during adolescence.

> The impairment in judgment that accompanies intoxication exacerbates the typical impulsivity and lack of long-term thinking that characterize adolescence.

Comprehensive and successful treatment of substance use disorders in adolescence includes many components: education of the child and the family about substance abuse; participation in individual, family, or group therapy; identification and treatment of co-occurring mental illnesses; development of a recovery plan; and prevention of relapse. The 12-step approach to substance abuse recovery advocated by groups such as Alcoholics Anonymous has been adapted for adolescent substance abuse treatment with good success. Relapse is very common, however, so it should be viewed as an expected occurrence in substance abuse treatment for adolescents. Relapse is *not* a reason to end treatment.

■ Conclusion

The process of engaging youth in mental health care can be challenging, especially given the variability of children's developmental stages and the role of caregivers in association with this population. Children may have difficulty conveying all that is going on inside them, though they may be able to communicate internal emotions such as depression and anxiety, even if their choice of words may be different. Caregivers are needed to describe a child's behaviors such as aggression and impulsivity, which the child likely could not report on his or her own. Younger children may be reluctant to share their feelings and may regress and act younger than their chronological age when they are anxious. These challenges make diagnosing and treating mental illnesses in children quite complicated.

Fortunately, specific techniques have proven effective for engaging children in mental health care. First, it usually helps to physically place oneself on the child's level. Sitting on a low chair or even on the floor with a child may help the child feel calm and willing to talk. Authority figures can be frightening for children, and demonstration of equality through sitting like a child may ease that fear. Asking direct and concrete questions that are developmentally appropriate often helps to get answers to questions. When working with children, it also helps to ask one question at a time rather than throwing out a barrage of questions that may leave the child feeling overwhelmed and more anxious. Beginning a conversation with nonthreatening topics also can facilitate rapport. Keep your tone firm and respectful, without yelling or labeling.

These recommendations, which are summarized in **Table 11.4**, are designed to prevent escalation of the situation when working with a child or adolescent in the community. Always remember that these youth are not just "bad kids," but rather kids in crisis dealing with multiple stressors. They often feel that adults do not care about or understand their difficulties. Treating youth with compassion, respect, and understanding will greatly improve the chances that youth will remain safe and be able to obtain the treatment and support they require.

Table 11.4   Techniques Professionals May Use to Engage Youth
Physically placing oneself at the child's level
Using developmentally appropriate and direct questions
Beginning with nonthreatening topics first
Remembering that the child is in crisis—not assuming that he or she is just a "bad kid"

Chapter Wrap-Up

Chapter Highlights

- Many adult mental illnesses have their onsets in childhood, underscoring the need for early identification and treatment of children with severe emotional and behavioral disorders.

- Children mature along expected developmental pathways. Any deficits in these developmental pathways may impair a child's ability to interact with his or her environment.

- Child maltreatment is an emergency situation that requires immediate action, including reporting suspicions to child protective services.

- According to the 2004 Youth Risk Behavior Survey conducted by the CDC, 16.9% of youth seriously contemplated attempting suicide, 16.5% made a plan to attempt suicide, and 8.5% attempted suicide. These startling numbers emphasize the need to take suicidal behavior seriously, regardless of the age of the child.

- Specific techniques have been developed that can be useful for diffusing volatile situations and engaging children in mental health care. Treating youth with compassion, respect, and understanding will greatly improve the chances that youth will remain safe and be able to obtain the treatment and support they require.

Vital Vocabulary

adaptive functioning: the ability to carry out activities of daily living such as grooming, and caring for hygiene, or appropriately using community resources such as the bus without assistance

anxiety disorders: a group of conditions in which there is extreme or pathological anxiety that is manifested by disturbances in mood or emotions and changes in the body, such as rapid breathing and rapid heart rate

attention-deficit/hyperactivity disorder: a disorder characterized by poor concentration, distractibility, hyperactivity, and impulsiveness that is inappropriate for the individual's age or developmental level

behavioral plan: a predetermined set of rules with explicit consequences for negative behaviors

child maltreatment: behaviors that include physical abuse, sexual abuse, emotional abuse, and neglect

childhood neglect: failure of a caregiver to provide for a child's basic needs

childhood sexual abuse: a sexual act involving penetration, molestation with genital contact but without penetration, and other sexual acts such as genital fondling or exposure, in children younger than 18 years

conduct disorder: a disorder in which children may express aggression to people or animals, destroy property, run away from home frequently, be truant from school, and be calculating or purposely deceptive

cutting: making intentional superficial cuts with a blade, razor, or sharp object on one's skin

developmental delays: situations in which the development of an infant or child is slower than normal

developmental milestones: important childhood physical, emotional, and cognitive developmental targets

developmental stages: a series of changes that an individual undergoes throughout the life cycle

global difficulties: trouble experienced in many spheres of life

hyperactivity: excessively active behavior

impulsivity: acting out on impulse without consideration of the consequences

mental retardation: an IQ (intelligence quotient) less than 70 that is accompanied by impairments in adaptive functioning

mood disorders: abnormalities of mood that lead to impaired functioning or quality of life

morbidity: the severity of a disease

neurotransmitters: natural brain chemicals that allow one neuron or nerve cell to communicate with the next

nonadherence: not agreeing with or following treatment recommendations

oppositional defiant disorder: a disorder in which children may disobey rules and come across as argumentative and hostile, but do not seriously violate others' rights

physical abuse: injury or risk of injury to a child younger than age 18 years resulting from being hit, kicked, shaken, thrown, burned, stabbed, or choked by a parent or caregiver

psychiatric disorder: a mental illness

psychoeducation: education about the symptoms, course, and treatment of a mental illness

serotonin: a neurotransmitter in the brain that is important for mood regulation

substance use disorder: disorders related to the misuse of alcohol, addictive prescription medications, or illicit drugs, which cause meaningful impairment in functioning; these disorders include abuse and the more severe dependence

Questions for Review and Discussion

1. Depressed youths do not necessarily communicate their feelings in words. Law enforcement officers should be observant for which signs and symptoms of depression in this group?
2. What are some visible signs of physical abuse that should raise a law enforcement officer's suspicion that the child is being abused?
3. What should law enforcement officers do when they see signs and symptoms that lead them to believe that a child is being sexually abused?
4. Explain techniques useful for engaging children that are designed to prevent escalation of a situation.

Resources

American Psychiatric Association. Disorders usually first diagnosed in infancy, child-hood, or adolescence. In: *Diagnostic and statistical manual of mental disorders* (4th ed., pp. 39–124). Washington, DC: American Psychiatric Association, 2000.

Dulcan M, Martini DR, Lake M. *Concise guide to child and adolescent psychiatry* (3rd ed.). Washington, DC: American Psychiatrist Publishing, 2003.

Lewis M. *Child and adolescent psychiatry: A comprehensive textbook* (3rd ed.). Philadelphia, PA: Lippincott Williams & Wilkins, 2002.

Wilens T. *Straight talk about psychiatric medications for kids.* New York: Guilford Press, 2004.

Responding to Individuals with Developmental Disabilities

Case Vignette: Agnes

In the quiet of the night, a woman clothed in a torn dress sat on the curb. She wore neither shoes nor a coat, even though the temperature was in the mid-forties. In the shadows, she seemed lost and confused. She held herself and rocked while singing quietly.

At first, Officers Townley and Bazner approached slowly, expecting another junkie strung out on the latest cheap street drug, but there was something different about this woman. She said a name loudly and with slurred speech the minute they approached: "Agnes!" She handed them an identification card, even though the officers did not ask for one yet. It was not a driver's license or picture ID, but rather an ID card that was printed in what looked like a first grader's handwriting. The ID card had the name Agnes Myers and an address about a mile away, but it included no phone number or other identifying information.

Once she handed over this card, the woman grabbed Officer Bazner's hand and looked intently into his eyes. She did not let go. She did not answer questions or offer any information about what was going on or why she was sitting on the curb at 2:47 A.M. She did not tell the officers where she came from or where she lived. She just kept repeating the word "Agnes," holding on, and rocking. When Officer Townley reached for his notepad, she let go of Officer Bazner, winced, and held her arm up to protect herself.

Despite their previous experience on the force, Officers Bazner and Townley did not know exactly what to do. Sure, the woman was vagrant and appeared disoriented, but was this a case of substance abuse, or was there something else going on? Although this was their beat, they did not recognize her as a regular offender. Was she safe to transport without cuffs? Was she "Agnes"? Was "Agnes" in trouble? Had a crime been committed? The streets were empty and all of the bars had closed a few hours ago. The officers decided that their best option was to call for backup and take the woman to the hospital. As the ambulance and backup arrived, "Agnes" began to cry and rock faster. Instinctively, Officer Bazner patted her hand, just like he would his granddaughter, and told her to relax. The woman seemed younger than her age. She also seemed so vulnerable.

After an examination, the ER doctor reported that the woman, who was assigned the name "Agnes Doe" until they could confirm her real identity, appeared to have mental retardation and had been raped, probably that evening. She had considerable bruising on her legs and thighs and required minor sedation during the examination. Very little physical evidence was obtained, however. At this point, it was difficult to determine whether there would be enough evidence to get a decent DNA sample or to begin to identify any perpetrators. All toxicology screens came out clean. The woman did not appear to have any other medical concerns. The doctor hypothesized that the trauma of rape probably had led to a decrease in her already vulnerable communication system. He hoped that she would be able to talk a bit more once she awoke from the sedation, but he was not sure of her level of functioning. This situation hit both officers hard. What kind of creep would harm such a person? They wanted to find the creep and get justice, but would Agnes be able to help them? Only time would tell.

continues

Agnes's story raises important questions for first responders. These well-intentioned, hard-working officers were unprepared to assist Agnes. Many signs indicated that she was a person with a developmental disability and that she would require specialized care and communication strategies. For example, Agnes did not rely on words to communicate her message to the officers. She handed them a homemade ID card without a picture. She seemed to need help, but the officers could not establish a line of communication with her. The fact that Agnes winced and cowered in response to Officer Townley's movements suggested that she was the victim of violence. Finally, what evidence was lost in the important moments after the assault? Would these officers have been more successful had they been prepared to communicate with a person with a developmental disability? They appeared to have taken a good course of action in that they recognized a potential psychiatric illness or developmental disability requiring medical evaluation and did not mistreat, ignore, or arrest Agnes.

■ Introduction

Sadly, Agnes's story is not unique. In fact, persons with developmental disabilities are 10 times more likely than others to be victims of a sexual assault, and 12 times more likely than others to be victims of a robbery. Some authors have referred to the incidence of violence and exploitation against persons with developmental disabilities as an epidemic. One way to combat such an epidemic is to increase first responders' awareness of such vulnerabilities and to inform them about helpful responses to persons with developmental disabilities. As first responders, police, fire, and rescue personnel are on the frontlines of serving such individuals during the most traumatic times. The best way for first responders to protect persons with developmental disabilities is to know and understand the characteristics of these individuals and to be skilled in communicating with such persons. In Agnes's case, had the officers been better prepared to assist her at the scene, they would have been able to begin collecting evidence immediately. Given the fact that they were hours from the crime and miles from the scene when they recognized that Agnes was a victim, their ability to collect evidence was seriously hampered.

> Persons with developmental disabilities are 10 times more likely than others to be victims of a sexual assault and 12 times more likely than others to be victims of a robbery.

This chapter describes developmental disabilities and their characteristics. It also provides helpful tips about ways to increase communication between first responders and persons with developmental disabilities. As part of this effort, it is essential to increase awareness of the needs of persons with developmental disabilities throughout the first response system. Finally, first responders need to increase their understanding of how persons with developmental disabilities may respond to traumatic incidents.

■ What Are Developmental Disabilities?

<u>Developmental disabilities</u> represent a cluster of many disabilities that affect a person's abilities to think, communicate, interact with others, remember facts and details, and take care of oneself. This cluster of disabilities includes intellectual disabilities such as mental retardation, physical and motor disabilities such as cerebral palsy, and communication disabilities such as autism. For the purposes of this chapter, we will focus on mental retardation and autism-spectrum disorders.

All developmental disabilities appear before the age of 18 years and remain with the person throughout his or her life. Most such disabilities remain constant, although persons

Developmental disabilities represent a cluster of many disabilities that affect a person's abilities to think, communicate, interact with others, remember facts and details, and take care of oneself. This cluster of disabilities includes intellectual disabilities such as mental retardation, physical and motor disabilities such as cerebral palsy, and communication disabilities such as autism.

with such disabilities usually can learn new skills and grow as people throughout their lives. Developmental disabilities have a number of causes—for example, the person's genetic make-up, exposure to toxic substances (such as drugs, alcohol, or dangerous chemicals) during gestation (before birth), brain injury during birth or early childhood, and unknown and untreated medical conditions that can cause brain damage (e.g., overexposure to lead, seizures, or severe allergies to certain foods). **Table 12.1** lists types of mental retardation and autism-spectrum disorders and provides a brief description of their effects.

Most persons with developmental disabilities can be fully included in all aspects of society with varying degrees of support. Some may require help from paid disability service workers for most or all of the day. Many individuals, however, are able to live independently, work in the community, and manage their own homes. In fact, since the 1970s, people with developmental disabilities have been shattering long-held beliefs about their supposed need for constant supervision by working in community-based jobs, living independent lives, marrying, and taking care of their family affairs just as any other person in society would. To paraphrase a popular bumper sticker in the disability community, people with developmental disabilities are "boldly going where everyone else has already been!"

Table 12.1 Developmental Disabilities and Their Major Characteristics	
Mental retardation	**Major Characteristics** ■ Below-average intelligence as measured by an intelligence test. ■ Difficulty with basic skills such as adding, subtracting, and counting money. ■ Communication abilities range from relatively unimpaired (the person can talk and engage in simple conversation) to severely impaired (the person is not able to talk at all and relies on sign language or pictures to communicate). ■ Wide range of abilities to interact with others. ■ Memory for facts and details is usually poor. ■ Difficulty taking care of oneself. ■ The more severe the disability, the more support the person will need in the community.
Autism-spectrum disorders	■ Intelligence can range from below average to well above average. ■ Basic abilities vary depending on intelligence. ■ Communication is impaired in varying degrees, ranging from not using words to using words but with difficulty communicating effectively. ■ Interaction with others is significantly impaired—some individuals appear disinterested, others do not seem to understand how to respond. ■ Memory for facts and details tends to be very specific and very good. While most persons with autism-spectrum disorders have excellent memories, they may not be able to communicate what they have heard or seen. ■ Care for self varies based on the severity of the disability. ■ The more severe the disability, the more support the person will need in the community. ■ Such persons do not respond well to changes in their routines, and they may reject first responders' attempts to help due to fear of different people or situations. ■ May sometimes have tantrums when changes in routine occur.
Multiple developmental disabilities	■ A person may potentially have more than one of the previously mentioned developmental disabilities at the same time.

In short, people with developmental disabilities are U.S. citizens, just like the rest of us. They share the same hopes, dreams, fears, stresses, rights, and responsibilities as individuals without such disabilities. Nevertheless, their disabilities may sometimes affect these persons' ability to achieve their dreams, and they may make them more vulnerable to victimization. One goal of the law enforcement community should be to do our part to eliminate that criminal element, or, when necessary, assist the person in seeking justice.

All service personnel—including first responders—must recognize and adhere to a code of conduct when dealing with persons with developmental disabilities. First, all people—even those with developmental disabilities—deserve their dignity. Part of dignity is the right to try, and perhaps fail at, new tasks. Persons with developmental disabilities do not desire pity or praise for living regular lives. They deserve the right to take the same risks that all of us assume when going about our day-to-day business. We should never question an adult citizen's right to attempt tasks, even if we think that person will likely fail. Our responsibility is to prohibit activities that will put others at risk. Balancing both the rights and the responsibilities of citizens is an important goal for all law enforcement personnel, and one that people with developmental disabilities deserve to have applied to them.

Second, people with developmental disabilities are people first. They are more like us than they are different. Consequently, it is essential to call people by their names and to show respect for them, rather than to label them. For example, it is both incorrect and highly offensive to say "the *retard*, Agnes." When talking about Agnes, remember her name. Then describe her by her physical characteristics, such as her hair color or her height. When absolutely necessary in a professional document or report, you can refer to the individual as a "person with mental retardation." Notice that you always begin such a phrase with the term "person with" followed by the name of the disability. This practice is called "person-first language." **Table 12.2** demonstrates other incorrect and correct terminology when referring to people with disabilities.

Finally, even though it may be difficult to communicate effectively with individuals with developmental disabilities, always try to talk directly with them. Do not talk down to or use infantile speech when speaking with people with developmental disabilities. Also, when referring to adults, use the same form of name as you would for any other adults. For example, if you would call another adult by a formal name (e.g., George), then call the person with a developmental disability by the same formal name. Avoid asking other people about the individual with a developmental disability while in that person's presence. No one likes to be talked about, whether the person is present or not. Likewise, when working with a person with a developmental disability, always talk to that person, directly and clearly. If the consumer has a support person with him or her, and you do not understand what the consumer said, turn to the support person and ask for help—but only after you have asked the consumer for clarification.

> People with developmental disabilities share the same hopes, dreams, fears, stresses, rights, and responsibilities as individuals without such disabilities. Nevertheless, their disabilities may sometimes affect these persons' ability to achieve their dreams, and they may make them more vulnerable to victimization.

Table 12.2 Incorrect and Correct Ways to Refer to Persons with Developmental Disabilities	
Incorrect	**Correct**
Retardate, retarded, slow, mental, moron, idiot, imbecile, retard, special Eddie, special, a tard, Mongoloid, etc.	Person with mental retardation, woman with intellectual disabilities, individual with cognitive impairments
The autistic person, idiot savant, "Rainman," etc.	Person with autism, individual with an autism-spectrum disorder, young man with a pervasive developmental disorder

■ Mental Retardation

Mental retardation is a disability that consists of lower-than-average intellectual functioning combined with difficulties in life skills such as communication, self-care, home life, social skills, school functioning, work, or safety. The Centers for Disease Control and Prevention (CDC) estimates that 1% of children between the ages of 3 and 10 years have mental retardation. A 1993 study showed that approximately 1.5 million Americans between the ages of 6 and 64 years had mental retardation (CDC, 2005).

Mild mental retardation occurs three times more often than moderate or severe forms of the disability. People who have this disability typically have difficulty reading, writing, and performing math problems. They tend to interpret words literally and misunderstand sarcasm or subtle turns of phrase. They have poor short-term memories, can get stuck on phrases, and have extreme difficulty with abstract concepts such as money or time. Finally, people with mental retardation do not fully understand the motives of others. Consequently, they are more prone to be manipulated out of their desire to please others, and they usually do not fully appreciate the consequences of their actions.

These characteristics result in a person who is vulnerable to suggestions and not able to evaluate the motives of others. Such characteristics render the individual more vulnerable to victimization. Additionally, crimes committed against people with mental retardation are frequently labeled as "abuse" or "neglect" rather than rape, assault, or murder.

People with mental retardation are also over-represented in the prison population, constituting between 4% and 10% of the incarcerated population, even though they represent only 1% of the total U.S. population. In fact, there have been numerous cases in which persons with developmental disabilities were coerced into confessing to crimes that they did not commit, simply to please their interrogators. One of the most infamous cases involved Earl Washington, Jr., who confessed to the rape and murder of a woman in Virginia in 1982. After spending 18 years in prison based on a confession that got many of the facts wrong, Washington was cleared by DNA evidence in 2000 and released in 2001. Writers investigating the case have suggested that Washington answered questions so that he could "go home" without understanding to what he was admitting (Clines, 2000).

The desire to please others is common in people with mental retardation, who may not fully understand the consequences of confessing to crimes under typical interrogation techniques. This same desire to please may also make these persons reluctant to accuse caretakers who assault or rape people with disabilities. Many individuals with developmental disabilities fear disappointing or speaking out against someone who "takes care" of them, so they may hesitate to report a crime at the hand of a caretaker. Thus, as first responders, it is critical to collect careful evidence when there is suspicion that a crime has occurred involving a person with mental retardation.

Case Vignette: Jamie

One day, during the heat of the summer, an Amber Alert was called for a 14-year-old youth with autism. The boy was reported to be an African American, 5 feet 6 inches tall, with a medium build, wavy brown hair, and brown eyes. He answered to the name Jamie. Most importantly, the Amber Alert said that Jamie did not talk and might try to hurt anyone who came near him.

When Marc Baskins of the EMS squad saw a youth matching that description near the reservoir, he really did not know what to do. It was a hot day, and Marc watched as the

continues

---

young man stripped naked and walked into the water. He called, "Jamie," but the youth did not turn his head or look at Marc. Marc used his cell phone to call 9-1-1, but knew that he had to get to this youth quickly so that he did not lose sight of him; otherwise, Jamie—if it was, indeed, Jamie—might drown. Marc ran to the shore of the reservoir and called again. The youth began to make humming noises and repeat the same phrase repeatedly—"You are okay, you are okay, you are okay, you are okay"—as he struggled to dog paddle away from the shore. Marc called out, "Jamie, stay there. I'll help you." Jamie did not look at Marc or move toward him. He began humming loudly and continued to swim.

Marc thought about going into the water to get Jamie, but realized that it was too dangerous. Jamie might grab onto him and drown both of them. Finally, Marc decided to remain on the shore of the reservoir and say calm, reassuring things to Jamie. That seemed to do the trick! The calmer Marc was, the closer Jamie came to him. Finally, Marc remembered that he had a bottle of water with him in his fanny pack. He held out his hand and offered it to Jamie. Jamie came out of the water and took the bottle from Marc. Marc patted the grass and said, "Sit with me." Jamie slowly but surely cooperated. Marc offered his hand to Jamie and held it for a few moments while sitting quietly with Jamie. Then Marc reached, while sitting, for Jamie's clothes. He handed the pieces of clothes to Jamie one at a time and told him to put on each item of clothing. When Jamie was dressed, Marc said, "Walk with me," and stood up. Jamie rocked for a few seconds, said, "You are okay, you are okay, you are okay," and stood up as well. Slowly, Marc walked with Jamie toward the street from where he had first spotted Jamie.

Shortly, the squad car and ambulance arrived, sirens blaring and lights flashing. Jamie froze and held tight to Marc. Marc quietly whispered, "You are okay, you are okay, you are okay," and waited while Jamie stood still. He waved at the guys in the squad car and ambulance. One of his buddies from EMS ran near. Marc signaled him to stop and told him to kill the lights and sirens. Little by little, Marc moved with Jamie to the ambulance. He stayed with Jamie, hand in hand, while the crew transported him to the hospital.

■ Autism

<u>Autism</u> and several related disorders are characterized by impaired development in social interactions and communication, as well as a restricted scope of interests. The CDC estimates the prevalence of autism-spectrum disorders to be 2 to 6 per 1,000 individuals. This prevalence, which is much higher than originally thought, translates to between 1 in 500 people and 1 in 166 people (CDC, 2006).

Autism-spectrum disorders do not always include intellectual disabilities. That is, people with autism and related disorders display the entire range of human intellectual abilities. In fact, some individuals have above-average intellectual abilities, but very little understanding of how to effectively communicate or interact with other people. In other words, the disability is primarily related to communication, social skills, and interpreting sensory information.

People with autism fail to use or understand nonverbal means of communicating messages. They frequently have difficulty making eye-to-eye contact and resist encouragement to do so. They have extreme difficulty with complex tasks that require many steps and do best with simple, one-step directions. Individuals with autism tend to get lost in long conversations and do not follow abstract concepts. They have trouble answering open-ended questions (e.g., "What sorts of things do you enjoy doing?"), tend to talk in robotic or monotone speech patterns, and sometimes repeat phrases over and over again. Many people with autism confuse pronouns and will say "you" when they really mean "I," as in "You are going to the store," when they really mean "I am going to the store."

Many people with autism talk to themselves. While this behavior may sound similar to the description of <u>schizophrenia</u>, a person with autism is frequently repeating dialogue from a favorite television show or movie, whereas the person with schizophrenia may be responding to an auditory hallucination.

Finally, a small percentage of people with autism or related disorders do not speak at all, but instead rely on pulling people around by the hand to get their needs met. People with autism will not necessarily ask for means to satisfy even simple and basic wants and needs. It is important to offer the person access to water, food, or the bathroom if you notice that the person has not eaten, had a drink, or used the bathroom in some time.

Currently, most people with autism-spectrum disorders are treated in school-based settings. But it is possible—even likely—that some adults with autism have never been diagnosed, despite demonstrating all of the characteristics of the disorder.

A person with autism, like a person with mental retardation, is very vulnerable to suggestions from other people. In general, people with developmental disabilities are more vulnerable to being victimized by perpetrators and less able to get help for themselves. Consequently, it is essential for first responders to receive training in recognizing and helping people with developmental disabilities in high-risk situations. The next sections provide a number of tips and suggestions that will assist first responders in recognizing and interacting with persons with developmental disabilities.

■ How to Identify People with Developmental Disabilities in Emergencies

The following list describes some simple ways first responders can determine whether a person has a developmental disability.

- *Ask for identification.* People with developmental disabilities often do not drive, so having a driver's license may help to rule out mental retardation. These individuals may, however, have other forms of identification. In addition, people with mental retardation sometimes wear medical alert bracelets or necklaces. Look for such informational tools.

- *Ask if the person has a disability.* While asking this question may help you find out that the person has a disability, it is also possible that the person does not want you to know about his or her disability. If you get a negative response but still have suspicions, you should maintain the possibility that the person has a developmental disability.

- *Ask the person to read a paragraph in the newspaper.* Some people with mental retardation can read, but many cannot. If the person has difficulty reading a paragraph from the newspaper, he or she may have mental retardation.

- *Ask the person to count change.* Persons with developmental disabilities may have difficulty completing a simple task, such as counting change.

- *Ask the person to read a clock.* If the person does not seem to understand time, or if the individual has difficulty with the task, he or she may have mental retardation.

- *Observe the way in which the person responds to you.* People with autism and related disorders tend to avoid eye-to-eye contact, and they frequently appear to talk at rather than with others. Finally, people with autism may repeat words and phrases to themselves.

■ Communicating with People with Developmental Disabilities

These tips may help you when communicating with a person with a developmental disability.

- Try to calm the person down if the individual is upset. Keep your own calm demeanor as well.
- Use simple sentences and basic words. Avoid words that have double meanings. Avoid using sarcasm, jargon, or idioms.
- Give requests and ideas one at a time. Avoid asking more than one question at a time. Break concepts and requests down into their smallest parts. If you want a person to come to the squad car or ambulance, say "Stand up." Wait for the person to respond, and then say "Come here."
- Ask "what" or "who" questions and avoid "when" or "why" questions.
- Avoid questions with only yes or no answers.
- Allow extra time for the person to answer questions and respond to requests.
- Ask important questions in different ways at different times to confirm that the person understood you and that you understood him/her.

When interrogating suspects with developmental disabilities, it is important to remember that the person may try to cover up his or her disability so as to better fit into society. These individuals may not understand their rights, even if they say they do. Always check in multiple ways to make sure they understand what you are saying. For some people, having police officers near them may be upsetting and they may attempt to run away. They will not understand commands that are shouted quickly while they are running. They are prone to repeating what they just heard, or saying what they think others want to hear. These suspects are likely to be the first to leave the scene of a crime and the first to be caught. They will have difficulty describing the details or facts of an event. Finally, they may be confused about who is responsible for an event and "confess" to a crime even though they are innocent.

When an individual with a developmental disability is the victim of a crime, keep in mind that the person may not know that what happened is a crime. These victims may think that the perpetrator is a friend. They may not know how serious the situation is or how badly injured they are. They may have very few ways to reach safety and consequently are likely to be victimized again. Finally, and sadly, they may think that the way they were treated in this situation was expected or normal. As a result, they may not know that they need help.

When a first responder is called to assist in finding or providing emergency medical care to a person with a developmental disability who is confused, disoriented, or hurt, the following tips may be helpful.

- Make sure the person is not armed, even with everyday objects such as books or sticks, before getting too close. The confusion of feeling hurt or lost and having a stranger come close may trigger a fight-or-flight response.
- Talk calmly and softly to the person. Offer short requests one at a time and allow time for the person to respond.
- Carry simple pictures that illustrate the common requests you frequently make to help the person understand what you want him or her to do. For example, carrying a picture of someone calmly entering an ambulance may be one of the best ways to show a person with a developmental disability to do the same thing.
- Use slow and calm gestures. Avoid rapid movements and arm waving, because they may upset the person.
- Model calm body language. Also, show the person what you want him or her to do. Offer calming objects, such as soft blankets.

- Do not interpret a failure to respond quickly as noncompliance and a signal for more force. Give the person extra time to respond.
- Do not try to stop the person from engaging in rocking or other repetitive movements. These movements sometimes help people with developmental disabilities to calm themselves.
- If possible, turn off the lights and sirens, and turn the sound down on communication radios. These noises and other sensory stimuli may be overstimulating and hence may exacerbate the person's fight-or-flight response.

Because of their vulnerabilities, people with developmental disabilities require special treatment at the hands of law enforcement officers, public safety officials, and criminal justice professionals. Effective skills for supporting people with developmental disabilities and an ability to communicate effectively can mean the difference between a repeated cycle of violence and the beginning of healing and wellness.

Chapter Wrap-Up

- When dealing with people with disabilities, always refer to them by their names or their physical characteristics. Avoid talking about someone in the third person when that person is present. Avoid slang, jargon, sarcasm, or name calling. Always use "person-first language."

- Assess the abilities of a person before you make any assumptions. Remember, someone who appears to be under the influence of drugs or alcohol may actually have a disability. Ask the person to read, count change, or tell the time before you make an incorrect assumption.

- When giving directions to or making requests of a person with a disability, break larger tasks into small tasks. Give the person time to think and respond before you talk again.

- When interrogating persons with developmental disabilities, remember that these individuals may have difficulty remembering or communicating facts. They are vulnerable to suggestion and may confess to crimes they did not commit just to please you. Finally, they may be reluctant to "tell on" a person they think of as a friend.

- People with developmental disabilities may be eager to please others, hide their disabilities, or say they understand something when they really don't. Always confirm that the person understood you by restating the question or command in another way or by presenting a specific scenario to check the person's comprehension.

- When approaching a frightened or traumatized person who has a disability, remain calm and try to limit loud sounds, bright lights, or bold and fast body movements and gestures. Do not put your hands on a frightened or traumatized person unless you assess that it is safe and you have told the person first.

- People with disabilities may forget or not be able to request that their basic needs be met. Offer food, drinks, and bathroom access if the person has not asked for such items and basic needs.

Vital Vocabulary

autism: a disorder consisting of impaired development in social interactions and communication, as well as a restricted scope of interests

developmental disabilities: mental impairments that affect a person's abilities to think, communicate, interact with others, remember facts and details, and take care of oneself; all developmental disabilities, such as mental retardation and autistic disorder, appear before the age of 18 years and remain with the person throughout his or her life

mental retardation: a disability that consists of lower-than-average intellectual functioning combined with difficulties in life skills such as communication, self-care, home life, social skills, school functioning, work, and safety

schizophrenia: a mental illness that often causes psychosis (e.g., hallucinations or delusions)

Questions for Review and Discussion

1. Reread the scenario in which Marc finds a young man with autism swimming in the reservoir. Do you think Marc took appropriate actions given the situation? What do you think he did well? What do you think he did not do well? What would you have done differently?

2. What kind of materials would help you better communicate with a person with a disability? Make a list of pictures, written instructions, or other tools that you think would assist you in better protecting and defending persons with disabilities. Discuss ways you could get these materials for your unit, division, or squad.
3. Have you had any interactions with people with disabilities while on duty? Discuss how your interactions went. What did you do well? What would you have done differently? What do you wish you would have done?

Resources

Books and Articles

American Psychiatric Association. Developmental disabilities. In: *Diagnostic and statistical manual of mental disorders* (4th ed., pp. 41–49, 69–84). Washington, DC: American Psychiatric Association, 2000.

Clines FX. Virginia man is pardoned in murder; DNA is cited. *The Washington Post*, October 2000.

Davis B, Schunick WG. *Dangerous encounters: Avoiding perilous situations with autism*. Philadelphia, PA: Jessica Kingsley Publishers, 2002.

Davis LA. *People with intellectual disabilities in the criminal justice system: Victims and suspects*. Silver Spring, MD: ARC, 2005.

Debbaudt D. *Autism, advocates, and law enforcement professionals: Recognizing and reducing risk situations for people with autism spectrum disorders*. Philadelphia, PA: Jessica Kingsley Publishers, 2001.

Debbaudt D. *Autism and law enforcement: Roll call briefing video*. Port St. Lucie, FL: Debbaudt Legacy Productions, 2005.

Federal Emergency Management Agency. *Orientation manual for first responders on the evacuation of people with disabilities*. Washington, DC, 2002.

Sobsey D. *Violence and abuse in the lives of people with disabilities: The end of silent acceptance?* Baltimore, MD: Paul H. Brookes Publishing, 1994.

Tyiska C. Working with victims of crime with disabilities (OVC bulletin). Washington, DC: U.S. Department of Justice, 1998.

Wilson C, Powell M. *Guide to interviewing children: Essential skills for counselors, police, lawyers and social workers*. New York: Routledge, 2001.

Websites

Centers for Disease Control and Prevention. (2005). Mental retardation: How common is mental retardation? Retrieved March 27, 2006, from http://www.cdc.gov/ncbddd/dd/mr3.htm.

Centers for Disease Control and Prevention. (2006). How common are autism spectrum disorders? Retrieved March 27, 2006, from http://www.cdc.gov/ncbddd/autism/asd_common.htm.

Acknowledgements and Disclosures

As director of the Virginia Autism Resource Center, Carol Schall receives grants from the Virginia Department of Mental Health, Mental Retardation and Substance Abuse Services, and the Virginia Board for People with Disabilities.

Anxiety Disorders

Case Vignette: Lisa

Lisa is a 32-year-old female who has a history of depression and alcohol abuse. At the age of 18, she married an emotionally and physically abusive man named Jim. Over the course of their marriage, Lisa was severely beaten on numerous occasions, and she was admitted to the hospital twice for life-threatening injuries that Jim inflicted on her.

After four years, Lisa escaped to a battered women's shelter, relocated, and attempted to put the past behind her. She met and married Steven, who she described as "the opposite of Jim—supportive, caring, and not at all abusive." Although Lisa continued to struggle with some difficulty sleeping, irritability, mild depression, and occasional nightmares, life was generally much better for her than it had been while she was married to Jim.

One day, after a verbal argument with Steven, Lisa called 9-1-1 in a panic, stating, "Jim's going to kill me." When the officers arrived at the scene, there were no signs of a physical altercation, but Lisa appeared jumpy and irritable. Police noticed that she seemed nervous and fearful. She also appeared to be distracted, and she avoided interacting with the police, other than to state, "All of a sudden, I saw my ex-husband Jim, and it was just like all those times before when he hit me."

■ Introduction

As a group, anxiety disorders are the most common of all psychiatric illnesses. Recent studies have estimated that in any given year, 16.4% of the U.S. population has an anxiety disorder; in comparison, 7.1% of the population has a mood disorder such as depression or bipolar disorder. Most anxiety disorders co-occur with other illnesses, including mood disorders, substance use disorders, and medical conditions. Mental health professionals evaluate and treat a number of disorders that are classified into this category, all of which are characterized by some form of excessive anxiety.

Anxiety is a normal human emotion. It serves as a warning sign, alerting the person to an unknown but impending threat. For the majority of people, this response is helpful because it prepares the mind and body for potentially stressful situations. For example, when a person is told that he or she must give a public speech, the individual usually experiences feelings of worry and fear. Preparing thoroughly for the speech minimizes the anxiety leading up to the event. In this circumstance, anxiety is helpful. Anxiety becomes problematic, however, when it is prevalent even when there is no impending threat. Also, it can become so excessive that it interferes with a person's ability to function.

The causes of anxiety disorders are largely unknown. Current theories suggest that some degree of family inheritance may render certain people genetically vulnerable to developing anxiety disorders. Exposure to stressful and traumatic experiences at an early age also may increase the likelihood of developing an anxiety disorder. Furthermore, abnormal regulation of several neurotransmitters (i.e., chemical messengers in the brain) appears to play a major role in the development of anxiety disorders. Medications that target these neurotransmitters often bring about significant improvement in symptoms.

■ Common Signs and Symptoms

All anxiety disorders are characterized by an increased level of anxiety; however, different disorders manifest these symptoms uniquely (Table 13.1). Each anxiety disorder consists of a discrete collection of signs and symptoms that form a specific diagnosis. The major anxiety disorders are panic disorder, social anxiety disorder, obsessive-compulsive disorder, generalized anxiety disorder, and post-traumatic stress disorder.

Panic Disorder

Panic disorder is characterized by a brief (less than 15 minutes), but intense feeling of fear or impending doom (Table 13.2). Initially, such attacks are not triggered by any particular event, but instead come without warning. Many times, people with panic attacks will seek treatment in emergency rooms, because their symptoms may appear very

Table 13.1 Anxiety Disorders and Their Primary Symptoms	
Anxiety Disorder	**Symptoms**
Post-traumatic stress disorder	Persistent re-experiencing, avoidance, and arousal after exposure to a traumatic event
Panic disorder	Recurrent, unexpected panic attacks
Obsessive-compulsive disorder	Recurrent, intrusive thoughts and/or repetitive behaviors
Social phobia/social anxiety disorder	Excessive fear of social/performance situations involving unfamiliar people or scrutiny by others
Generalized anxiety disorder	Excessive worry (apprehensive expectation) and anxiety

Table 13.2	Symptoms of a Panic Attack	
Palpitations, pounding heart, or accelerated heart rate	Nausea or abdominal distress
Sweating	Feeling dizzy, unsteady, lightheaded, or faint
Trembling or shaking	Feelings of unreality
Shortness of breath or smothering feeling	Feeling detached from oneself
Choking sensation	Fear of losing control or going crazy
Chest pain or discomfort	Fear of dying
Chills or hot flushes	Numbness or tingling sensations

similar to symptoms of a heart attack, stroke, or other major medical condition. Often, medical problems must be ruled out before a diagnosis of panic disorder can be made.

Over time, some people with panic disorder may develop increasing worry about having a panic attack in a public situation or place. This condition is called **agoraphobia**, a term that means "abnormal fear of open or public places." In extreme cases, people with agoraphobia are afraid to leave their homes for fear of having a panic attack in public.

Social Anxiety Disorder

Phobias are excessive, irrational fears about certain situations, activities, or subjects. **Social phobia**, now more commonly known as **social anxiety disorder**, is characterized by an excessive and irrational fear of humiliation in social situations. People with social anxiety disorder tend to avoid social situations because of these intense fears. In severe cases, social anxiety disorder can be extremely disabling, causing impairments in role functioning in school, on the job, or in relationships.

Obsessive-Compulsive Disorder

Obsessive-compulsive disorder (OCD) is a relatively common psychiatric disorder, with its associated disabilities ranging from mild to severe. This disorder has become more widely recognized in recent years because of media exposure. Movies and television shows such as *The Aviator, As Good as It Gets, Dirty Filthy Love*, and *Monk* have provided viewers with diverse pictures of individuals with OCD.

OCD is characterized by **obsessions**—recurrent, intrusive thoughts—and **compulsions**—conscious, recurring patterns of behavior (**Table 13.3**). People with OCD tend to have a cycle of anxiety, in which obsessions lead to a heightened sense of tension, and compulsions then serve to reduce this tension. If a person with OCD does not spend time performing a specific compulsion, his or her anxiety tends to increase dramatically.

Individuals with OCD can become disabled by their disorder owing to the amount of time they spend thinking about obsessions and carrying out compulsive behaviors. For example, if a person has an obsessive thought that he or she will be contaminated by germs, bodily waste, or secretions, that person may engage in compulsive hand washing, bathing, or grooming. This may become excessive, taking up several hours each day. By contrast, the obsession

Table 13.3	Symptoms of Obsessive-Compulsive Disorder	
Obsessions	**Compulsions**
Contamination	Washing
Pathological doubt	Checking
Need for symmetry, order, exactness	Need to ask or confess
Aggressive thoughts	Symmetry and precision
Sexual thoughts	Counting
Intrusive sounds, words, music	Hoarding and collecting
	Repeating

known as **pathological doubt** is characterized by an intense fear of danger related to having forgotten something. Checking compulsions are associated with pathological doubt. Examples include checking door locks multiple times and checking the stove over and over to ensure that it is off before leaving the house. In addition to causing undue tension, these checking behaviors can negatively affect the lives of people with OCD in that these individuals may spend many hours each day on these activities rather than engaging in other, more productive tasks.

Generalized Anxiety Disorder

Generalized anxiety disorder is characterized by long-standing, excessive worry about many different issues in life. People with generalized anxiety disorder report symptoms of restlessness, muscle tension, fatigue, irritability, sleeplessness, and concentration problems. Everyday concerns go through their minds over and over again, making it difficult to focus. At times, people with generalized anxiety frequent primary care doctors and specialists due to recurrent symptoms of pain and discomfort that are directly associated with anxiety symptoms.

Post-traumatic Stress Disorder

Post-traumatic stress disorder (PTSD) refers to a cluster of symptoms that develops in an individual after exposure to a traumatic event. While most people have a common response of anxiety and fear after experiencing a life-threatening trauma, people who develop PTSD do not experience the characteristic improvement of symptoms that occurs over time. Instead, they continue to have problems in functioning over a period of months to years.

Many people associate PTSD with veterans who have been exposed to combat. Although this group is certainly at high risk for developing PTSD, many other members of society are also at risk. An overwhelming majority of people living in inner cities have been exposed to significant trauma, especially violent crimes such as battery and rape. Many people in the vicinity of the World Trade Center in New York City who feared repeated terrorist attacks or lost loved ones in the September 11, 2001 tragedies developed PTSD. Other types of traumatic events that could lead to PTSD include natural disasters such as hurricanes, tornados, and earthquakes.

In the chapter-opening vignette, Lisa appears to be suffering from PTSD. People with PTSD develop a state of increased arousal, characterized by difficulty sleeping, an easy startle response, irritability, and anger (**Table 13.4**). In addition, they avoid thoughts, feelings, activities, or people associated with the traumatic event. They can have feelings of numbness and detachment from others. Furthermore, people with PTSD often re-experience thoughts of the trauma, including flashbacks, hallucinations, or nightmares about the traumatic event. At times, these experiences of reliving the initial event can cause people with PTSD to seem out of touch with reality.

Table 13.4   Symptoms of Post-traumatic Stress Disorder

- Recurrent and intrusive memories of the event, including images, thoughts, or perceptions
- Recurrent frightening dreams or nightmares of the event
- Acting or feeling as if the event were happening again (illusions, hallucinations, flashback episodes)
- Intense anxiety on exposure to reminders of the trauma
- Physical symptoms on exposure to reminders of the trauma
- Efforts to avoid thoughts, feelings, conversations, activities, places, or people reminiscent of the trauma
- Difficulty remembering parts of the traumatic experience
- Decreased interest or participation in regular activities
- Feeling of detachment or estrangement from others
- Insomnia
- Irritability or outbursts of anger
- Poor concentration
- Heightened sense of fear

■ Course of Anxiety Disorders

Anxiety disorders have a variable course, age of onset, and **prognosis**. The severity and the disability associated with anxiety disorders also vary widely. Fortunately, most anxiety disorders respond to currently available treatments. Although these disorders are often thought to be less debilitating than other mental illnesses such as schizophrenia, bipolar disorder, substance use disorders, and major depressive disorder, they cause significant impairment to individuals affected by them. Anxiety disorders cost the United States more than $42 billion each year in healthcare expenditures, accounting for one-third of the total costs for the entire field of mental health.

Panic disorder can develop at any age, though it often begins in late adolescence. Whereas many people have experienced a **panic attack**, a recurrent pattern of panic attacks is apparent in panic disorder. It is more common in women than in men. Many people with panic disorder have additional psychiatric illnesses such as **major depressive disorder**, other anxiety disorders, **personality disorders**, and **substance use disorders**. Symptoms generally tend to get better over time, although there is considerable variation among individuals with panic disorder.

Social anxiety disorder has a largely unknown course. The onset of phobic symptoms usually begins in childhood or early adolescence. These symptoms can be associated with a traumatic event, or they may not have obvious origins. Social phobia typically is longstanding; in fact, adults with this disorder were usually shy as children. Symptoms are often continuous, but they tend to improve with avoidance of anxiety-provoking symptoms.

OCD often presents with a sudden onset, and many times it emerges after a stressful life event. While women and men are equally likely to develop OCD, adolescent boys are more commonly affected than adolescent girls. The symptoms of OCD often become apparent when a person is in his or her early twenties. While many people experience constant symptoms throughout their lifetime, others have a fluctuating course, which means that their symptoms come and go over time. Many people with OCD are embarrassed to share their symptoms with other people, which may prevent them from seeking help. The majority of people who do receive treatment respond in some part to medications and therapy, but a significant percentage of people with OCD (20% to 40%) do not get better and sometimes get worse. Because many people with OCD have coexisting symptoms of depression, these individuals have a risk of suicide.

> "Many people with OCD are embarrassed to share their symptoms with other people, which may prevent them from seeking help."

Generalized anxiety disorder is often a chronic, lifelong condition. It occurs in conjunction with other psychiatric conditions more commonly than any of the other anxiety disorders. In this way, it follows a course similar to that of panic disorder and major depressive disorder. Unlike other disorders, however, generalized anxiety disorder has less of a chance of spontaneously remitting. People with generalized anxiety disorder tend to seek treatment for their symptoms from primary care doctors and other medical specialists.

Symptoms of PTSD may emerge immediately after exposure to a trauma, or they may take months or years to develop. Symptoms can be constant, or they can come and go in times of stress. The majority of people who develop PTSD continue to have significant problems associated with the illness over time. The people who are most susceptible to developing PTSD include the very young and the very old. Because PTSD is so closely associated with substance abuse and depression, many individuals with this disorder have a high risk of suicide. People without adequate social support are at the greatest risk for having long-term complications from PTSD.

> "Symptoms of PTSD may emerge immediately after exposure to a trauma, or they may take months or years to develop."

■ Treatment of Anxiety Disorders

Because the symptoms and courses of the individual anxiety disorders are so diverse, many options exist for their treatment. As with most psychiatric illnesses, the treatment of all anxiety disorders follows certain general principles. The combination of the right medication, therapy, and social support can often lead to recovery.

Many medications are available to treat people who have anxiety disorders. For example, the drug class called **selective serotonin reuptake inhibitors** includes citalopram (Celexa), escitalopram (Lexapro), fluoxetine (Prozac), fluvoxamine (Luvox), paroxetine (Paxil), and sertraline (Zoloft). These medicines can be very effective in treating anxiety disorders. In particular, PTSD and OCD often respond well to these medications. These medications are generally well tolerated and have no risk of abuse or dependence, making them safe for long-term use. Because many anxiety disorders are associated with depressive disorders, selective serotonin reuptake inhibitors and other antidepressant medications can serve to treat multiple conditions at once.

Other medications that can greatly decrease the symptoms associated with most anxiety disorders include the **benzodiazepines**. Benzodiazepines are classified as sedative-hypnotics, because they reduce anxiety, cause drowsiness, and induce sleep. These medications have a rapid onset of action, and many patients experience improvement of their symptoms within minutes to hours of taking benzodiazepines. As a result, benzodiazepines can be very effective for illnesses such as panic disorder and generalized anxiety disorder. In addition, people with social phobia may take benzodiazepines prior to exposure to a feared event. Unfortunately, these medications are associated with a high risk for abuse and addiction. Because addiction can occur after long-term use, benzodiazepines are best used on a short-term basis, particularly when symptoms are extremely severe or until a long-acting, less-addictive medication has had time to work. Withdrawal can be associated with life-threatening seizures, changes in blood pressure, changes in heart rate, and other serious symptoms. Due to their rapid onset and potential for addiction, benzodiazepine medications—which include alprazolam (Xanax), clonazepam (Klonopin), and diazepam (Valium)—may have a high street value as illicit drugs.

As with all psychiatric disorders, medications represent only one component of an effective treatment plan for anxiety disorders. Most people with anxiety disorders show the greatest improvement in their symptoms when they receive a combination of **psychotherapy** and medications. Many different types of psychotherapy have proven helpful in treating anxiety disorders. For example, by learning techniques of deep muscle relaxation and deep breathing, patients can often gain control of the symptoms of generalized anxiety disorder and panic disorder.

Cognitive-behavioral therapy, a type of psychotherapy, helps train people to change the thoughts that lead to fear and anxiety. When people are committed to recovery, this therapy can be extremely effective in treating anxiety disorders such as OCD and panic disorder. Because people tend to avoid situations that lead to increased anxiety, a particular type of cognitive-behavioral therapy known as **exposure therapy** can be very effective in treating OCD and PTSD. Exposure therapy slowly introduces a person to the situation or event that produces stress and guides the person with relaxation techniques. Over time, the situation becomes more familiar, and the individual's stress response and anxiety level is decreased.

For many anxiety disorders, family and group therapies are extremely effective treatments. Therapy can help enhance support systems for people who may feel isolated and detached from others. Engaging the family in a therapeutic setting can serve to educate and strengthen relationships between all members of

> Cognitive-behavioral therapy helps train people to change the thoughts that lead to fear and anxiety.

the family. Support groups for people with anxiety disorders also exist to build relationships through common experiences. The focus of these groups ranges from trauma groups, which include people with PTSD who have experienced similar traumatic events, to organizations such as Toastmasters, which provide exposure in a support-group format to people with social anxiety disorder.

Case Vignette: Sarah

Sarah is a 26-year-old woman with a history of anxiety problems. Security was called when Sarah insisted that the driver stop the subway car in which she was riding. Sarah yelled that she needed to get off the subway, pulled the emergency alarm, and banged on the doors. Subway security officers found Sarah struggling to catch her breath, sweating, trembling, and complaining of chest pain. She kept repeating to herself over and over, "I'm going to die, I'm going to die."

The officers who arrived on the scene had received crisis intervention team training, and they recognized that Sarah's high level of anxiety might be consistent with a panic attack. They properly asked Sarah if she had any medical problems, such as heart or breathing problems, as well as if she had experienced problems like her current difficulty before. Sarah responded that she had no medical problems and that these attacks, while terrifying, had recently begun occurring quite frequently.

Security helped to improve the situation by escorting Sarah off the subway car and leading her to a more secluded, less active area; encouraging her to take slow, deep breaths; and assuring her that her symptoms would most likely improve shortly. After 15 minutes, Sarah was feeling significantly better. She was able to report that she had started to have symptoms while on the subway, and felt the overwhelming need to escape the situation. At the suggestion of the officers, Sarah agreed to seek psychiatric treatment as soon as possible to prevent such symptoms from recurring.

■ Engaging and Assessing Individuals with Anxiety Disorders

In the chapter-opening vignette, Lisa appears to be suffering from PTSD. She has multiple active symptoms, including a high state of arousal and re-experiencing of past events (in the form of nightmares and flashbacks). It appears that her verbal argument with Steven triggered a flashback of a violent encounter with her ex-husband, Jim.

Police officers and first responders can best interact with an individual with PTSD by approaching the person in a nonthreatening way, removing the person from the situation if it serves as a reminder of the past trauma. Also, it is helpful to allow the person to openly discuss the trauma, should he or she choose to do so, while being careful not to force someone to talk. Because police officers are often present during the initial traumatic event, it is essential to provide trauma victims and witnesses with appropriate resources for support, which may prevent the development of PTSD. It is also helpful to stress to trauma victims and witnesses that they should keep contact numbers for future reference, because many symptoms may not emerge until months after the traumatic experience occurs. Many people with PTSD may be anxious and scared around police officers, so it is important to be available and supportive without being confrontational.

> Many people with PTSD may be anxious and scared around police officers, so it is important to be available and supportive without being confrontational.

Sarah, the woman in the second vignette, is also suffering from an anxiety disorder, yet her symptoms are very different from Lisa's symptoms. Sarah appears to have had a panic attack while on the subway. Security officers who responded to the scene were sensitive to the issues involved, and they responded appropriately to the complications of the situation.

First, the officers assessed the possibility that Sarah had panic disorder versus a medical emergency such as a heart attack or stroke. If Sarah has experienced multiple episodes like her current problem in the past and has no medical conditions, there is a greater probability that her symptoms reflect panic disorder. However, if there is any doubt about the cause of the symptoms or no improvement over time, further evaluation in an emergency room would be needed.

Second, the police officers helped Sarah cope with her panic attack by taking her to a place with less stimulation, encouraging relaxation techniques, and providing reassurance. They were able to de-escalate the situation and decrease the overall levels of stress, both for Sarah and other riders on the subway.

In general, it is best to approach a person with an anxiety disorder in a non-threatening way that communicates concern and reassurance. People with anxiety disorders may have a need to describe their current symptoms and problems in detail, or they might be avoidant and anxious around others. Police officers who are familiar with the broad range of behaviors in people with anxiety disorders can be better prepared to respond and offer appropriate assistance.

> Police officers who are familiar with the broad range of behaviors in people with anxiety disorders can be better prepared to respond and offer appropriate assistance.

Chapter Wrap-Up

- Anxiety disorders are the most common psychiatric illnesses. Often, they occur in conjunction with other psychiatric disorders, including mood disorders, substance use disorders, and medical illness.

- All anxiety disorders are characterized by an increased level of arousal, but people with distinct anxiety disorders manifest these symptoms differently.

- Important anxiety disorders include panic disorder, social anxiety disorder, OCD, generalized anxiety disorder, and PTSD. These anxiety disorders have differing courses.

- Anxiety disorders can be treated with medications, therapy, or a combination of the two. Treatments for anxiety disorders can be very effective if individuals have adequate access to care.

- Police officers and first responders should recognize that people with anxiety disorders may interact with them in very different ways. The most helpful strategy is to approach someone with a suspected anxiety disorder in a calm, reassuring, and nonthreatening way, and to be available for interaction should the person wish to talk about the situation. Note that forcing victims to discuss the trauma event can worsen symptoms and prolong the course of the illnesses.

Vital Vocabulary

agoraphobia: an abnormal fear of open or public places

anxiety: an unpleasant emotion that is experienced in anticipation of a usually ill-defined event; nervousness

benzodiazepines: medications with a high risk for abuse and addiction that are used to treat anxiety or insomnia

cognitive-behavioral therapy: psychotherapy that aims to highlight the connection between thoughts, feelings, and behaviors

compulsions: conscious, recurring patterns of behavior

exposure therapy: a type of cognitive-behavioral therapy that slowly introduces a person to the situation or event that produces anxiety; by guiding the person with relaxation techniques, the anxiety level decreases over time as the stressful situation becomes more familiar and an individual's stress response decreases

generalized anxiety disorder: a disorder that causes long-standing, excessive worry about many different issues in life

major depressive disorder: a psychiatric disorder that includes symptoms such as excessive sadness, difficulty sleeping or sleeping too much, preoccupation with guilty thoughts, decreased energy, decreased enjoyment in pleasurable activities, poor memory and concentration, isolation from friends and family, hopelessness, and thoughts of suicide

neurotransmitters: natural brain chemicals that allow one neuron or nerve cell to communicate with the next

obsessions: recurrent, intrusive thoughts

obsessive-compulsive disorder: a disorder characterized by a cycle of anxiety, in which obsessions lead to a heightened sense of tension, and compulsions serve to reduce this tension

panic attack: an episode of severe anxiety characterized by a brief (often less than 15 minutes), but intense feeling of fear or impending doom, often accompanied by physical symptoms

panic disorder: an anxiety disorder characterized by a recurrent pattern of panic attacks

pathological doubt: a type of obsession that is characterized by an intense fear of danger related to having forgotten something

personality disorders: long-standing disorders consisting of an enduring pattern of impairment in relationships, occupation, and other areas of functioning, in many different situations

phobias: excessive, irrational fears about certain situations, activities, or subjects

post-traumatic stress disorder: a mental illness characterized by symptoms that develop after exposure to a traumatic event

prognosis: the severity of the future disability associated with a disorder

psychotherapy: a type of treatment for mental and emotional disorders that uses psychological interventions rather than medications

selective serotonin reuptake inhibitors: a class of medications used to treat depression or anxiety disorders

social phobia (social anxiety disorder): a mental illness characterized by excessive and irrational fear of humiliation in social situations

substance use disorders: also called addictive diseases; disorders characterized by psychosocial impairment due to abuse of or dependence on addictive substances (e.g., alcohol or drugs)

Questions for Review and Discussion

1. What signs could officers responding to a scene look for to help them recognize that the person responsible for a disturbance was demonstrating a high level of anxiety that might be consistent with a panic attack?
2. What would be the best way to approach and effectively deal with someone who is experiencing a panic attack?
3. Explain how an individual suffering from post-traumatic stress disorder might act toward a law enforcement officer.
4. Describe the best way for officers and first responders to interact with individuals with post-traumatic stress disorder.
5. How can law enforcement officers assist in preventing the development of post-traumatic stress disorder in individuals who have witnessed or experienced a traumatic event?

Resources

American Psychiatric Association. Anxiety disorders. In: *Diagnostic and statistical manual of mental disorders* (4th ed., pp. 429–484). Washington, DC: American Psychiatric Association, 2000.

Barlow DH. *Anxiety and its disorders: The nature and treatment of anxiety and panic* (2nd ed.). New York: Guilford Press, 2002.

Burns D. *The feeling good handbook.* New York: Plume, 1999.

Sadock B, Sadock, V. *Kaplan and Sadock's comprehensive textbook of psychiatry* (7th ed.). Philadelphia: Lippincott Williams & Wilkins, 2000.

Sadock B, Sadock V. *Kaplan and Sadock's pocket handbook of psychiatric drug treatment* (3rd ed.). Philadelphia: Lippincott Williams & Wilkins, 2001.

Maladaptive Coping Skills, Personality Disorders, and Malingering

Case Vignette: Maria

Maria is a 23-year-old Hispanic female who is well known in her neighborhood for both her temper tantrums and her numerous boyfriends. Maria lives in an apartment with her new boyfriend of six weeks, and she supports him financially. At her job at the local grocery store, she often arrives late; she has also been warned by her supervisor several times to stop being rude to customers. Maria often feels alone and has no lasting friendships. She gets along well with her father, whom she sees several times a year, but she hates her mother. As a teenager, Maria frequently ran away from home, only to be found at a neighbor's house down the street. Now Maria refuses to speak to her mother, saying that she is a drunk who never cared about her.

Recently, Maria got into a fight with her boyfriend, after she found out that he was cheating on her. She hit him and threw him out of her apartment. After he left, Maria began sobbing uncontrollably and thinking about suicide. She had attempted suicide on numerous occasions in the past, often by overdosing on pills or making cuts on her wrists. When her boyfriend returned to get his belongings, she screamed at him, "I'm going to kill myself!" She grabbed some scissors and locked herself in the bathroom, where she slowly began to cut lightly on her wrists. In response, her boyfriend called the police.

The officers knew Maria very well because they had responded to her suicide attempts several times previously as well as to calls from neighbors who had complained about her screaming during arguments. After talking with Maria for a while through the bathroom door and becoming increasingly frustrated, one of the officers said, "Maria, you need to stop this right now and unlock the door—we all know that you aren't really trying to kill yourself." With that, Maria opened the window and jumped from her second-story apartment, breaking a leg and an arm.

■ Introduction

All people have stress in their lives and have to cope with difficult situations and difficult feelings. No one likes to be dumped by a girlfriend or boyfriend, but many people have had to face that experience. Some people deny that the relationship meant anything. They tell themselves that the other person was no good anyway, and they act as if they were never dumped at all. Others talk to everyone they know and enlist all the support they can get. Still others feel that they are bad people and withdraw socially.

To cope with all sorts of potentially stressful situations, people develop strategies to help themselves avoid overwhelming feelings such as grief, terror, or rage, or avoid a blow to their self-esteem. These means for dealing with life are collectively called **coping skills** or **coping strategies**. People often turn to a particular set of coping skills that eventually become habitual, thus giving rise to one's **personality**. Personality, in psychological terms, is a repeated and predictable set of thoughts, feelings, and behaviors, and a predictable set of coping skills that one employs to master and adapt to one's environment. For example, a person who continually uses humor to avoid feeling embarrassed or nervous becomes known as the class clown. He or she is recognized by the classmates for this predictable use of humor. Being the class clown is, in a way, this individual's personality.

Personalities are shaped by many different factors. Research suggests that part of one's personality is genetic. We can even see this idea play out in babies. For example, some babies are very anxious and difficult to console, whereas others are almost always calm and require very little comforting. Another factor is the way a parent interacts with his or her child. Some parents are very patient and tolerate their children's emotional development; others are very nervous and always try to control their children. A great deal of someone's personality comes from identifying with his or her parents. Another factor that shapes personality is stressful life events—for example, the divorce of one's parents or the experience of child abuse. Still other factors shaping personality include early friendships, one's choice of life partners, or one's career choice. A personality is something that develops over a long period of time. While it can change, this evolution is very slow, and an individual's personality tends to become more firmly fixed as he or she matures.

Sometimes coping strategies are maladaptive and create problems. For example, someone might attempt to cope with stress in a marriage by drinking. While this is one way to deal with the pain of marital difficulty, it can create problems with the person's career and lead to health problems. Usually someone with maladaptive coping strategies is trying to deal with stress in life, but needs to learn new coping skills. If the person has a longstanding pattern of maladaptive behavior, then a **personality disorder** may be present. A personality disorder is an enduring pattern of impairment in relationships, occupation, and other area of functioning, in many different situations, and it can be traced far into the individual's past. Of course, when people face stress, we all can behave in ways that are harmful to us and to those we love. A mental health professional will diagnose someone with a personality disorder only if there is an enduring pattern of maladaptive behavior.

Although there are 10 specific personality disorder diagnoses, this chapter discusses only two in depth: borderline personality disorder and antisocial personality disorder. Many of the other personality disorders, such as schizoid personality disorder and avoidant personality disorder, are rarely encountered by public safety and criminal justice professionals because they typically do not lead to "externalizing" behaviors that require urgent responses or criminal proceedings.

> All people learn coping skills—strategies to help themselves avoid overwhelming feelings such as grief, terror, or rage, or avoid a blow to their self-esteem. People often turn to a particular set of coping skills that eventually become habitual, thus giving rise to one's personality.

■ Borderline Personality Disorder

Law enforcement officers will sometimes encounter borderline personality disorder, because individuals with this personality disorder account for 1% to 2% of the U.S. population. People diagnosed with this disorder are twice as likely to be female as to be male. These unpredictable individuals often lead chaotic lives that are punctuated by frequent crises. Because their emotions and thoughts—their inner lives—are chaotic, these people find it difficult to calm themselves down. They become overwhelmed with their feelings and often revert to self-destructive behavior, such as suicide attempts. In short, people with this disorder are highly impulsive and rarely take the time to consider the consequences of their actions.

People with borderline personality disorder often lead painful lives because they feel so empty at times and have great difficulty establishing stable and enduring relationships. What they crave most—stable relationships—is what they are least likely to have in their lives, owing to their dysfunctional coping strategies. Individuals with borderline personality disorder often despise being alone, so they accept a new person as a friend or a lover too quickly, often with ensuing bad consequences.

When they feel abandoned by others, people with borderline personality disorder are at their most vulnerable and are at greatest risk for suicide. While they may have a genuine wish to kill themselves, they sometimes use their plans to commit suicide as a way to threaten and manipulate others into rescuing them. This behavior may allow them to get the attention they so deeply desire. For people with borderline personality disorder, suicidal behaviors are matters of survival and the only way they know to cope with overwhelming and unbearable situations. Fortunately, they often survive their suicide attempts or suicide "gestures," which frequently are not serious, such as making multiple superficial cuts on the wrists. Nevertheless, people with borderline personality disorder are just as likely to die from suicide as are people with major depressive disorder. The rate of death by suicide for people diagnosed with borderline personality disorder is approximately 15%.

> " The rate of death by suicide for people diagnosed with borderline personality disorder is approximately 15%. "

People with borderline personality disorder often use a maladaptive coping strategy that mental health professionals term **splitting**. That is, individuals with borderline personality disorder may see people as either all good or all bad. For example, one coworker may be seen as nurturing, kind, and even perfect at everything she does, while the boss is perceived as mean, hateful, and wanting to torture others. This coping strategy can lead to major problems in a contained environment, such as an office, a jail, or a hospital. The people who are on the "good side" of a split feel positively about that person and may demonstrate some loyalty to him or her. Those who are hated by the person with borderline personality disorder (i.e., on the "bad side" of the split) feel annoyed and angry. This can lead to heated conflict when a team of people must work with a person with borderline personality disorder. The alliances of the person with borderline personality disorder can flip rapidly, however, so that suddenly the person once perceived as all good is seen as all bad. Many therapists have experienced having a patient with borderline personality disorder heap praise on them in one session, only to tell them that they are horrible in the next session.

Just as people with borderline personality disorder split others, so they also have an unstable view of themselves. For example, one minute they may see themselves as innocent victims of a horribly mean boss, and the next minute they may feel disgusted with themselves and believe that they are unlovable.

Unfortunately, the prognosis is rather poor and treatments are somewhat limited for people with borderline personality disorder. Personalities change very little over time, although some evidence suggests that as they mature through adulthood, people with borderline personality disorder can learn to control their emotions more effectively and be less impulsive. These individuals often have __comorbid__ substance abuse, major depression, or eating disorders. If these co-occurring illnesses are treated, the prognosis may improve. Persons with borderline personality disorder often have trouble with major life stages, including maintaining an intimate and lasting relationship, raising children, and choosing a stable and rewarding career. They occasionally get into legal trouble, usually for minor offenses, though they may commit more serious offenses such as domestic violence. They almost always show remorse for their actions, however, and they usually judge their own actions harshly.

Some help is available for individuals who have borderline personality disorder. While medication rarely cures them of their emotional instability and emptiness, research shows that patients are more emotionally stable when they take medications such as antidepressants, antipsychotics, or mood stabilizers. Psychotherapy can be very helpful as well. Patients can learn new coping skills, such as being able to stop and think before acting on their impulses. A long-term relationship with a psychotherapist can prove very valuable to these people, especially in a time of crisis. People with borderline personality disorder have much lower rates of suicide and hospitalization when they are in stable treatment. A good therapist can help calm a patient down and help him or her rethink bad decisions such as attempting suicide or doing something dangerous or illegal.

> People with borderline personality disorder have much lower rates of suicide and hospitalization when they are in stable treatment. A good therapist can help calm a patient down and help him or her rethink bad decisions such as attempting suicide or doing something dangerous or illegal.

■ Antisocial Personality Disorder

Antisocial personality disorder is encountered by law enforcement officers even more often than it is seen by most mental health professionals, because people with this personality disorder rarely seek treatment. As much as 75% of the prison population may have diagnosable antisocial personality disorder, and part of the very definition of the disorder is that the individual may repeatedly engage in actions that lead to arrest. Unlike borderline personality disorder, the rate of antisocial personality disorder in men is three times higher than the rate in women, and men with this disorder account for 3% of the total U.S. male population. If a man has this disorder, he is five times more likely to have a brother or a father with this disorder compared to a man in the general population. Thus genetics likely plays a role in the development of antisocial personality disorder, as does one's early-life family environment.

Typically, people with antisocial personality disorder come from chaotic and over-indulgent families. Often the father is violent, mean, and abusive to the child and the mother provides little or no structure for the child. The overindulgent mother quickly gives in to any demands by the child, leaving the child with no way to understand his or her emotions and no meaningful interaction with his or her mother. For example, the child may be upset that the father will not be home for Christmas, so the child grows increasingly demanding, asking for more presents. The over-indulgent mother gives the child more and more presents, but the child never gets to talk about missing the father and never receives any emotional comfort. Thus the child lives in a world with no real emotional connection to the parents, one of whom is abusive and the other is absent emotionally in many ways. With no understanding of emotional attachment to others, the child may quickly come to see other people as things to be manipulated and used to show power. This quest to demonstrate power over others is the primary motivation for a person with antisocial personality disorder. A hallmark of people with antisocial personality disorder is a lack of remorse for violating the rights of others.

> A hallmark of people with antisocial personality disorder is a lack of remorse for violating the rights of others.

In many ways, people with antisocial personality disorder have no conscience, sense of remorse, or guilt. They may express regret that they were caught for committing a crime, but they typically show no sincere sense of guilt for what they have done to others. These individuals have great difficulty caring about others. This is not to say that these persons don't care what others think of them. Indeed, they want to impress others with their power and gain respect for their clout. They get a certain joy out of knowing that they have "pulled one over" on someone else. People with this personality disorder can be very charming and initially may seem to be very likable. In addition, they can be very envious of others, though they would never own up to this feeling because that would be tantamount to admitting weakness.

The course of this disorder is poor, often with a poor social prognosis. In particular, people with antisocial personality disorder often have high rates of substance abuse and depressive disorders. They often end up in prison and have difficulty maintaining long-term relationships. They try to cheat their way through jobs and are often caught, so they don't have long careers. If they are clever and do not get caught, they can be highly successful people with impressive jobs. In fact, some people with this disorder actually become model citizens as they age. It is thought that when they grapple with the limits of old age, these individuals learn to accept their limitations and have less of a need to prove their power over others.

Treatments for people with antisocial personality disorder are limited. The impulsivity commonly associated with this disorder can be helped with a medication such as a mood stabilizer, and depressive episodes can be treated with an antidepressant. If individuals have a substance abuse problem, treating this problem may decrease their violent and impulsive behaviors. In a jail or prison setting, they may do well in individual or group therapy in which the therapist sets firm limits. Therapy may help individuals with antisocial personality disorder become more aware of their emotions and less likely to act on them. It may also help people with this disorder understand the consequences of their actions, such as failed marriages and lost jobs, and increase their motivation for changing these patterns of behaviors.

■ Malingering

The term **malingering** refers to the deliberate production and reporting of physical or psychological problems for the purpose of avoiding a difficult or dangerous situation, responsibility, or punishment. People who engage in malingering are fully aware of their deceptions. Although not a specific personality disorder, this behavior is a maladaptive attempt to cope with a difficult situation. People who malinger often have antisocial personality disorder, and most of them are men. Common scenarios in which people resort to malingering include getting out of the military, avoiding a financial difficulty, avoiding prison, avoiding capture by the police or gang members, or just finding shelter in a warm hospital on a cold night.

In a case of malingering, the person's symptoms are often vague, and he or she may not be able to provide a consistent history of recent events. Such a person typically complains about symptoms that are difficult to test objectively, such as headaches, dizziness, amnesia, and hallucinations. A lack of cooperation with the assessment and failure to comply with medical treatment may be other indicators of malingering.

> It can be very difficult for a mental health professional (or a law enforcement/criminal justice professional) to tell whether or not a person is malingering, or intentionally feigning, a symptom.

In assessing and treating someone who may be malingering, one needs to be very careful. Some people have other motives in claiming illness and are not deliberately making up symptoms. For instance, a person may become paralyzed temporarily in a situation involving severe psychological stress. There is no neurological reason for the individual to be paralyzed, but he or she is not behaving in this way purposefully. Instead, the person's mind is paralyzing the body, without the person knowing it. Another important consideration is that the individual may really have an illness and truly need treatment. An inmate who claims to hear voices may actually be psychotic and quite ill. It can be very difficult for a mental health professional (or a law enforcement/criminal justice professional) to tell whether or not a person is malingering, or intentionally feigning, a symptom. Frequently, long periods of observation can sort out the diagnosis. While a person might easily deceive a professional during an initial interview, it is very hard to keep up the charade for days or weeks at a time.

> ### Case Vignette: Jake
>
> *Jake was a financial officer for a major corporation. He lived with his wife of three years and their two children in a home located next to that of a young woman and her successful husband. The young woman would occasionally stop and say hello to Jake and ask him about his children. On one such occasion, she invited Jake in for coffee. After accepting her offer, he raped and strangled her.*
>
> *The woman and her husband were a prominent couple in the community, so the murder was featured on all of the major news networks. Reporters interviewed several of the neighbors—including Jake—before it became known who perpetrated the crime. Jake's interview on television was moving, and he expressed his shock and dismay in such a convincing way that his interview was featured prominently on the local news.*
>
> *When another neighbor reported that he had seen Jake entering the house just before the victim was killed, Jake was brought in for questioning. One of the interrogating officers demanded that Jake confess to the rape and murder. Jake remained calm, however, and even appeared to be amused by the whole process.*

■ Engaging and Assessing Individuals with Personality Disorders

Engaging Jake, like engaging any person with antisocial personality disorder, may be quite difficult. Several things must be kept in mind. First, for Jake to cooperate and work with an officer, he must respect the officer's authority. He will do so only if the officer is strong and respectful to Jake. This means not saying demeaning things to Jake or being abusive, yet setting clear limits and not being flexible about those limits. Any bending of the rules will be seen as a sign of weakness—and an indication that the officer can be manipulated. Jake derived satisfaction from gaining power over others. Withholding a confession became an important way for Jake to enjoy power over the officer. Jake also received pleasure from fooling the community by giving a television interview, appearing as if he were a concerned neighbor and a bystander in this crime. Many good interrogators know that if they remain calm and even stoic, deliberate, methodical, and respectful, the criminal will eventually confess to the crime. Often, there is a need for criminals to claim their violations as a matter of pride.

Jake is a good example of how difficult it can be to spot people with antisocial personality disorder. These individuals can be charming and often come across as quite likable. They are talented at lying and may have made it their goal to be a good con artist. Like Jake, about half of all people with antisocial personality disorder have no significant arrest record. Nevertheless, nearly half of all people with antisocial personality disorder do have criminal histories. Of course, not everyone who is a murderer, rapist, or thief has antisocial personality disorder. For example, some criminals may have committed their crimes while high on drugs, or they may be so dependent on drugs that they will steal and lie to get the next fix. Some people who are incarcerated have other personality disorders and can show genuine concern for others and remorse for their crimes.

Recognizing Maria from the chapter-opening vignette or someone like her as having borderline personality disorder is easier because these people do not hide their difficulties. In fact, they seem to want everyone to notice their distress. Maria exhibited many borderline personality disorder features, including a history of chaotic relationships. For example, she had ended contact with her mother and had taken up with numerous boyfriends. She also exhibited impulsive, self-destructive behavior such as the history of cutting herself. Unfortunately, her impulsivity in hitting her boyfriend and her numerous suicide attempts are common behaviors in persons with borderline personality disorder. Although these individuals' attempts at self-injury are often not life-threatening, they still need to be taken seriously. Living with her boyfriend of six weeks also shows how quickly Maria becomes attached to someone—yet another sign of her borderline personality. Her suicide attempt occurred in reaction to breaking up with her boyfriend. In people with borderline personality disorder, suicide attempts often occur in the context of a significant loss, such as when an important relationship ends.

Engaging someone with borderline personality disorder requires much patience and skill. Such people are highly sensitive to criticism and often feel rejected by others, even when they perceive the most subtle of slights. At the same time, they will demand more from others than can possibly be given. For example, people with borderline pathology sometimes express a wish to move into their therapists' offices and may follow them home. Like anyone who interacts with people with borderline personalities, law enforcement officers need to express interest and concern, but set limits on destructive behavior. If a person with borderline personality starts screaming because of his or her hurt feelings, an officer might say, "I hear that you are in pain, but screaming will not make it easier for me to help you." This statement may need to be repeated several times before the person calms down. Notice how this statement focuses on the individual's emotional pain, not on the officer's experience. If the officer were to focus on himself or herself, the person would perceive it as rejecting, which could make the situation worse. Notice also how the officer gives a reason for setting a limit on this individual's behavior in a way that he or she can accept it. This statement is far more effective than something like "You need to stop screaming—now!"

Occasionally, but only as a last resort, an officer may need to set a limit on the behaviors of someone who has borderline personality disorder with physical force. If the person with borderline personality disorder is doing something that is imminently dangerous, this may be the necessary course of action.

The responding officer's actions in the scenario featuring Maria may have been improved with these suggested engagement strategies. Perhaps the officer should not have expressed his frustration aloud or dismissed Maria's feelings so quickly. This reaction caused Maria to feel rejected and may have increased her need to show everyone how serious her painful feelings really were. Jumping out of the window became a way for Maria to demonstrate her hurt feelings to others and a means to stop her inner emotional turmoil. As mentioned earlier, people with borderline personality disorder have very high death rates from suicide.

Working with people who have borderline personality disorder can be difficult even for well-intentioned professionals. Anyone who works with these individuals may occasionally become frustrated with them and lose his or her composure. In such situations, it is best to acknowledge the frustration, apologize, and quickly move the focus back to the person who needs understanding and help.

Chapter Wrap-Up

Chapter Highlights

- Coping skills are ways to deal with the overwhelming emotions that may occur in reaction to stressful situations. Some people use maladaptive coping strategies, which can make things worse for them. If there is a lasting pattern of maladaptive coping, a person may have a personality disorder.

- People with borderline personality disorder lead chaotic lives and have unstable emotions. They are self-destructive and may attempt suicide multiple times. They are just as likely to die of suicide as are people with major depression.

- Many people in prison have antisocial personality disorder. The hallmark of this disorder is a lack of remorse for violating the rights of others. Individuals with this personality disorder enjoy manipulating others, and encounters with people who have this disorder can feel more like a game rather than a genuine interaction.

- Malingering is the deliberate production of symptoms for the purpose of getting out of responsibility, danger, or punishment. Mental health professionals can have great difficulty spotting someone who is malingering, as can law enforcement/criminal justice professionals.

- People with antisocial personality disorder need to respect authority, so when law enforcement officers engage them, they need to be strong (i.e., not bend rules) and respectful (i.e., not say demeaning things to them). Not all criminals have antisocial personality disorder.

- Engaging people with borderline personality disorder requires that law enforcement officers be understanding of the person's emotions, but set firm limits on behavior. When working with individuals with borderline personality disorder, it is often helpful to focus on their emotions.

Vital Vocabulary

comorbid: the simultaneous presence of two different disorders

coping skills (coping strategies): strategies to help individuals avoid overwhelming feelings such as grief, terror, or rage, or avoid a blow to their self-esteem

malingering: the deliberate production and reporting of physical or psychological problems for the purpose of avoiding a difficult or dangerous situation, responsibility, or punishment

personality: a repeated and predictable set of thoughts, feelings, and behaviors, and a predictable set of coping skills that one employs to master and adapt to one's environment

personality disorder: a long-standing and enduring pattern of impairment in relationships, occupation, and other areas of functioning, in many different situations

splitting: a maladaptive coping strategy in which one tends to see people as either all good or all bad

Questions for Review and Discussion

1. Which features might make a law enforcement officer suspect that a person has borderline personality disorder?
2. How might first responders best approach people who appear to have borderline personality disorder?
3. What might make law enforcement officers suspect that a person is malingering?
4. What are the hallmark features of antisocial personality disorder?
5. What should law enforcement officers keep in mind when engaging a person with antisocial personality disorder?

Resources

American Psychiatric Association. Personality disorders. In: *Diagnostic and statistical manual of mental disorders* (4th ed., pp. 685–729). Washington, DC: American Psychiatric Association, 2000.

Kaysen S. *Girl interrupted.* New York: Random House, 1993.

Mason PJ, Kreger R. *Stop walking on eggshells: Coping when someone you care about has borderline personality disorder.* Oakland, CA: New Harbinger Publications, 1998.

McWilliams N. *Psychoanalytic diagnosis.* New York: Guilford Publications, 1994.

Stout M. *The sociopath next door.* New York: Random House, 2005.

Responding with Enhanced Knowledge and Skills

15 **De-escalation Techniques**
Kevin J. Richards, Ph.D.

16 **Responding to Special Populations**
Raymond J. Kotwicki, M.D., M.P.H.

17 **A View of Law Enforcement–Consumer Interactions Through the Lens of Psychosis**
Frederick J. Frese III, Ph.D.
Milt Greek

18 **Emergency Receiving Facilities and Other Emergency Resources**
Barbara D'Orio, M.D., M.P.A.
Denise Garrett, M.S.W.

19 **Mental Health Resources and Levels of Care**
David W. Covington, N.C.C., L.P.C., M.B.A.

De-escalation Techniques

Case Vignette: Jack

Officers responded to a call concerning an individual creating a disturbance at a local community health facility. Upon arriving at the facility, the officers encountered Jack, a 43-year-old male. The health center staff members do not know Jack very well, because he has only recently moved to the community. The individual who made the call stated that Jack came to the center that morning to have his medications checked and to have his food stamp benefits renewed. Jack became belligerent with her almost immediately and began accusing her of stealing from him and wanting to hurt him.

The officers found Jack in a waiting area, which had been cleared of other consumers. Jack was pacing rapidly back and forth and talking to himself in a low voice. He appeared dirty and disheveled. Occasionally he moved his arms as if he was swatting at something in the air. Jack did not appear to notice the staff members or the officers who had entered the waiting area with him.

Introduction

It has been said that in the crisis intervention team (CIT) model of training for law enforcement officers, "All roads lead to de-escalation." Gaining an understanding of the signs and symptoms of various mental disorders, becoming aware of community resources, and learning what having a brain disorder is like from the perspective of consumers (i.e., mental health patients) and family members are all important components of the foundation that supports first responders who have specialized knowledge about crises involving mental illnesses. De-escalation, however, is what officers actually do when they put such specialized knowledge to use in the field. First responders' de-escalation skills often have a profound effect on the outcome of a crisis situation.

What, exactly, is meant by "crisis"? No matter how it is defined, a crisis involves a change. Of course, not all changes are crises, and the reasons why a change becomes a crisis can differ dramatically from one individual to the next.

In the early 1970s, psychologists Albert Ellis and Robert Harper proposed a simple formula to explain how people can have different reactions to the same situation. The formula "A + B = C" states that an event (A) plus the individual person's judgment, interpretation, or perception of the event (B) determines the type of reaction (C) the person will have (Ellis & Harper, 1973; as cited in Castellano-Hoyt, 2003). The reaction will consist of not only the emotional response experienced by the individual, but also his or her resulting behavior.

In Ellis and Harper's equation, events are neutral and the variable that determines the individual's reaction to the event is the way the event is *perceived*. Thus whether an event becomes a crisis depends largely on a person's perception of the incident. Many factors can affect this perception, which explains why people can have such a range of reactions to the same event. For example, the symptoms of a brain disorder may exert a powerful influence on the perception of events. Severe symptoms, such as **psychotic symptoms** (**hallucinations** and **delusions**), will have obvious effects on the way one perceives an event. In addition, more subtle experiences such as changes in mood or the presence of anxiety can have a surprisingly strong effect on one's perception of an event. Recent use of alcohol or drugs also can influence a person's perceptions of events, as can longstanding developmental disabilities such as mental retardation.

Nevertheless, the simple presence of a brain disorder—whether a **psychiatric illness**, a **substance use disorder**, or a **developmental disability**—does not mean that a crisis will arise whenever a potentially stressful event occurs. Individuals with mental illnesses are no different from other people in that they possess certain **coping skills** or **coping strategies** that enhance their capacity to deal with stressful events. Like all people, individuals with brain disorders are more likely to experience a crisis when their abilities to cope effectively are exceeded by the number and intensity of the demands they perceive in the event. For the purposes of this chapter, a **crisis** is defined as a situation in which a person experiences a negative change in thinking and behavior because his or her capacity to cope effectively has been exceeded by the perceived environmental demands.

> Whether an event becomes a crisis depends largely on a person's perception of the incident.

De-escalation is an intervention directed at the "B" element in Ellis and Harper's equation. It entails moving a situation from a state of high tension to a reduced state of tension. De-escalation is a specialized form of communication. Like any communication, it involves the transmission of information from one person to another. However, de-escalation is rarely as simple as just passing along information. Think about the game "Gossip," in which a statement is passed through a group of people by each person whispering the message to the next person. Remember what usually happens by the time the message reaches the last person in the group? Generally, it bears little resemblance to the original message. Why does this transformation happen? The answer is that communication is not always a smooth and perfect flow of information. It is a two-way street, so to speak, and its effectiveness can be influenced by both the sender and the receiver of the message.

Brain disorders can interfere with both ends of the communication chain—sending and receiving. A person with a psychiatric illness may be trying to communicate something that is not being understood, or he or she may be misinterpreting what is being said. For example, commands given by law enforcement officers such as "Drop the knife" or "Get down on the ground" might seem to be straightforward and easy to understand. When dealing with people who live with mental illnesses, however, officers need to take into account the types of barriers to effective communication that the brain disorder might create.

Think about Jack from the chapter-opening vignette for a moment. He is talking to himself and appears to be swatting at objects he sees or hears around him. He also has expressed a belief that staff at the center mean to do him harm. For Jack, the commands an officer gives him might represent only one of the many voices that he hears. Having the commands delivered in an aggressive manner from an authority figure might cause Jack to feel more afraid and to become more upset because of his belief that others want to harm him. Jack's perception of the situation is that it is very frightening and dangerous—probably more so than would be perceived by someone without a mental illness. Jack is in a crisis, so communication with him may no longer follow the everyday rules of conversation. Officers who are willing to learn new ways of communicating with individuals in crisis have the best chance of intervening with them effectively, thereby achieving positive outcomes and reducing injuries to officers and consumers alike.

Are officers with outstanding communication skills born or made? The answer to this question is probably "both," though officers who are successful at de-escalation tend to share certain characteristics, which are summarized in **Table 15.1**.

First, these officers are team players. Within the CIT model, the training that officers receive is designed to develop crisis intervention *teams* rather than intervening individuals. Anyone who has ever played team sports likely realizes that winning or losing usually relates to team performance rather than the performance of a solitary hero. In this same way, successful de-escalation pivots on effective coordination with other responders in an effort to resolve potentially dangerous situations.

Good listening skills are similarly essential for de-escalation. Active listening and some specific listening and responding skills that are used in de-escalation are reviewed later in this chapter. However, these skills will not be effective unless a strong willingness to listen already exists.

In addition, officers who can successfully de-escalate crisis situations are able to have and show **empathy**. When one has empathy or is empathic, the individual makes an attempt to truly understand the perspective and feelings of another person. Empathy is sometimes confused with sympathy. Sympathy implies pitying or feeling sorry for someone as opposed to making a genuine connection with someone and seeing things from another perspective.

Table 15.1 Characteristics of Officers Who Are Successful at De-escalation
Team player
Good listening skills
Empathy
Good problem-solving skills
Ability to think quickly and flexibly
Assertiveness
Capacity to remain calm, patient, and in control

Officers who effectively de-escalate potential crises also tend to have good problem-solving skills. The ability to think quickly and flexibly, sometimes under great pressure, is another requirement for a successful de-escalator. The ability to be assertive is likewise a characteristic shared by people who are successful at de-escalation. A person who is assertive is able to be forceful and direct without being aggressive or threatening.

Finally, officers who prove successful at de-escalating crises share a capacity to remain calm, patient, and in control. De-escalation can be a long and arduous process, and officers who are effective at de-escalation are willing to allow this process to run its course without rushing or becoming unduly frustrated.

■ Cochran and Dupont's Continuum of Escalation

To effectively de-escalate a crisis, it is helpful to have a framework for understanding how the intensity of a crisis increases or decreases. It is also helpful to have a framework for assessing the complexity of a crisis to decide which resources officers will need to manage the crisis situation effectively. Major Sam Cochran and Dr. Randolph Dupont, developers of the Memphis CIT program, utilize a continuum of escalation in their training model, which has been adopted by training programs across the country. This model includes nine stages of escalation, each with its own specific characteristics and each presenting a different set of demands for the CIT officer. For each stage, there are both goals to be accomplished and issues to avoid, which are described briefly here.

Uncertainty

In this stage, the subject may appear oblivious to the presence of the officer or behave in a way that suggests that he or she is unsure of the reason why the officer is present. Eye contact and body movements will be minimal in this stage. The subject may or may not engage in verbal exchange. If there is a dialogue, it will generally consist of one-word statements. In the uncertainty stage, the officer should try to begin providing structure. One simple way to do so is to introduce oneself and to state the reason for being there. This initial structure begins the tasks of focusing the consumer and building rapport. Remaining completely passive or becoming impatient with the subject during this stage would be counterproductive and could lead to crisis escalation.

Questioning

In the questioning stage, the consumer becomes more engaged with the officer. Eye contact and motor movements may increase. The consumer's verbal statements will consist primarily of questions, some of which will be relevant (e.g., "Who are you?" or "Why are you here?") and some of which will likely be irrelevant (e.g., "Why is your badge that color?" or "Where did you get that watch?"). During this stage, the subject may be moving toward a more confrontational and challenging stance. Officers need to answer relevant questions with short, direct answers and try to avoid becoming defensive when peppered with irrelevant questions. This is especially true if the consumer asks questions that are of a personal nature or are insulting to the responding officer.

Refusal

During this stage, the subject may attempt to cut off the interaction with the officer. Eye contact may be deliberately avoided, and motor movements may become more intense and dramatic. The consumer's verbal statements will likely focus on trying to avoid talking to the officer or insisting that he or she doesn't need or want any help. Officers dealing with a subject in this stage should work on settling the situation by making simpler requests. During the refusal stage, there is a danger of getting into a power struggle with the consumer. Officers need to keep their composure and continue using their de-escalation skills to keep the interaction moving in a positive direction.

The stages of uncertainty, questioning, and refusal are those during which the officer has the greatest chance for a positive verbal interaction with the subject. They are also the stages the officer is most likely to encounter when first arriving at the site of the crisis. In the stages that follow, officers must attend more diligently to safety issues and evaluate whether continuing with de-escalation is likely to produce the desired outcome.

Demanding

Although officer safety is always an issue in de-escalation, in the demanding stage, it becomes an even more significant concern. During this stage, the consumer may engage in significant verbal escalation. He or she may shout at the officer, and physical movements may become much more agitated and potentially threatening. A consumer in this stage may attempt to close the distance between himself or herself and the officer in an effort to intimidate the officer or possibly as a precursor to a physical attack. Although an officer working with a subject in this stage of escalation needs to attend to safety as a primary concern, he or she need not abandon the de-escalation process. The officer can take a step back to maintain a safety zone or "back off" verbally. Sometimes creating this safety zone and backing away a bit may allow the consumer in crisis some time to "vent" or even wear himself or herself out. Officers who find themselves confronted with a consumer in this stage need to be careful not to intervene too quickly or try too hard to control the interaction by interrupting or talking over the consumer.

Generalized Acting Out

During this stage, the consumer will engage in potentially dangerous behaviors that are not directed at a specific target. Examples include turning over furniture, throwing objects to the ground, or breaking something in the immediate vicinity. Obviously, officer safety is a significant concern during this stage, but—as in the demanding stage—it does not necessarily signal an automatic end to the de-escalation process. So long as safety issues are managed, an officer can wait until the consumer calms down with time or let him or her blow off steam. Of course, it is crucial that officers ensure that no one—including the officer, the consumer, and any other people who are present—faces excessive risk for injury during this stage. Officers' gut feelings about whether there is a possibility of bringing the situation back under control without physical intervention should not be ignored, although these feelings should be balanced against the officers' specialized de-escalation training and CIT experience.

Specific Acting Out

In this stage, the consumer has escalated to a point where he or she is engaging in potentially dangerous behaviors that are directed at a specific target. This target can be an object, but is more often a person. Officers working with a consumer who has escalated to this point may need to abandon the de-escalation process in the interest of safety. The same instincts described in the generalized acting out stage will come into play during this stage, and it will be up to the officer to make the call about whether to abandon de-escalation or to continue the effort. Officers can use limit-setting movements and statements in an attempt to counter the acting out. Nevertheless, sometimes de-escalation will not be successful in resolving crises, so officers need to maintain constant awareness for any danger signals that may arise during the de-escalation attempt.

Recovery

During the recovery stage, the consumer often begins to settle down both physically and verbally. Perhaps he or she runs out of steam, or perhaps the consumer begins to "come around" in response to the officer's de-escalation skills. In any event, the primary objective in this stage is to maintain the calm environment that has been established. Reinforcing the consumer's calm behavior and projecting a calm demeanor will serve to counter possible re-escalation.

Rapport

At this point, the consumer has not only calmed down, but has also initiated a relatively reasonable dialogue with the CIT officer. The officer can then express empathy and show support to the consumer while continuing to reinforce calm verbal and physical behaviors. Sometimes, rapport is attained only after a long and arduous de-escalation process. It is important for officers to put that process behind them and not rehash it or make blaming or guilt-inducing statements to the consumer. When crises produce significant emotional reactions in responding officers (which they often do), these appropriate feelings must be expressed in other contexts in which the consumer is not present, such as in officer debriefings.

Cooperation

The cooperation stage represents the ultimate goal of the de-escalation process. During this stage, the consumer has calmed down, has engaged in a reasonable dialogue, and is likely ready to proceed to a resolution of the crisis. At this point the officer can make behavioral requests directed at bringing the crisis to a resolution. Nevertheless, officers need to keep in mind that making excessive or complicated behavioral demands during this stage may lead to re-escalation.

> To effectively de-escalate a crisis, it is helpful to have a framework for understanding how the intensity of a crisis increases or decreases.

This model developed by Cochran and Dupont (and summarized in **Table 15.2**) is intended to be a tool that aids in understanding how crises develop and change. Clearly, the escalation cycle does not always follow this orderly progression. Although officers are most likely to reach the scene of a crisis at one of the first three stages in this model, it is possible for them to arrive at any stage. Similarly, consumers may not escalate or de-escalate the situation in the order in which the stages are listed. For example, consumers often skip the acting out stages and go straight to recovery or cooperation. Obviously, this pattern is consistent with the goal of de-escalation, because the process is designed to decrease dangerous behaviors and avoid unnecessary injuries to both officers and consumers.

Table 15.2	Stages of Escalation of a Crisis	
Stage	**Try to . . .**	**Avoid . . .**
Uncertainty	Provide structure Introduce yourself	Passivity Impatience
Questioning	Address relevant questions	Defensiveness
Refusal	Make simpler statements and requests	Power struggles
Demanding	Maintain safety zone Back off verbally and nonverbally	Intervening too quickly
Generalized acting out	Be patient Wait and let the consumer blow off steam	Putting oneself at risk
Specific acting out	Use verbal and nonverbal limit setting Be careful	Ignoring danger signals
Recovery	Reinforce calm behavior Maintain calm demeanor	Re-escalating the situation
Rapport	Show support Acknowledge progress	Rehashing past comments or behaviors Blaming
Cooperation	Make specific behavior requests	Excessive or unduly complicated demands

Source: Crisis Intervention Team (CIT) Model of Cochran and Dupont, Memphis Police Department

■ Levels of Crisis Complexity

In addition to progressing through different stages, crises may vary in terms of their complexity. For the purposes of this chapter, the complexity of a crisis is determined by the number and severity of factors with which the officer is confronted during a crisis situation. Factors that contribute to the complexity of a crisis situation include the physical setting, stage of escalation, number of available officers, number of additional people present (especially if they are also consumers), and number and complexity of the outcome goals. The responding officer must take into account the complexity of the crisis situation and determine which resources will be needed to manage the crisis effectively.

To conceptualize the level of complexity in a manageable way, a crisis can be categorized into one of three types: low, moderate, or high complexity (**Table 15.3**).

Low-Complexity Crisis

At this level of complexity, there is generally only one consumer and no other involved individuals. The level of escalation is generally minimal; the potential for further escalation is similarly low. One or two responders may be present at the scene, and there is generally a single, fairly straightforward outcome goal.

The vignette that began this chapter is an example of a low-complexity crisis. In that scenario, Jack is the only consumer, the level of escalation is not creating apparent danger, no other individuals are involved in the crisis, and the most likely outcome goal would be to help Jack regain control and see a mental health professional to have his condition evaluated.

Moderate-Complexity Crisis

This type of crisis situation may include the presence of other individuals, a higher potential for continued escalation, a more challenging physical location, and outcome goals that are more complex or poorly defined. A two-officer team will likely be needed in these types of situations, and backup officers may become involved as well.

An example of this type of crisis would be a scenario in which officers respond to the residence of an individual who has a consumer living in the home. The situation has a greater number of potential challenges, and the ones that are encountered are likely to be

Table 15.3	Levels of Complexity of Crisis Situations		
	Low Complexity	**Moderate Complexity**	**High Complexity**
Consumers	One	One or few	One or more
Other individuals	Generally few	Family members, other nonconsumers	Other consumers, crowds, fellow officers
Physical setting	Simple	Some challenges	Difficult, complicated
Other officers	None or one backup	One backup and possibly other officers	Backup generally needed
Stage of escalation	Low; verbal intervention likely to succeed	Moderate; may be some behavioral acting out	Generally involves some level of behavioral acting out
Potential for further escalation	Low	Moderate	High
Outcome goals	Simple; generally one	Maybe more than one or one with increased complexity	Multiple; generally includes at least one complex goal

more complicated. For example, the person who called law enforcement may be very upset when officers arrive at the home, the consumer may be in another part of the house, or there may be increased potential for continued escalation. The consumer may have already engaged in behavior indicating an advanced level of escalation, such as demanding, refusal, or even generalized acting out. In this situation, officer safety issues are of great concern, and the outcome goals are more numerous and not as clearly defined as they are in a low-complexity crisis.

High-Complexity Crisis

This type of crisis presents the greatest challenge to responding officers. High-complexity crises involve a multitude of factors, such as multiple consumers, crowds, complicated physical settings, multiple officers (some of whom may be trained in de-escalation techniques, whereas others may not be), and the potential for significant escalation. High-complexity crises generally require a two-officer primary team, plus identified trained backup officers to manage additional de-escalation needs that may arise with secondary consumers, bystanders, and family members. In addition, backup officers who are not necessarily trained in de-escalation techniques may be needed to handle such issues as crowds and traffic.

An example of a high-complexity crisis is an incident in which an agitated consumer is creating a disturbance on a crowded street, where multiple onlookers are present. The consumer may be in an advanced stage of escalation when the officers reach the scene, and people in the crowd may be provoking the consumer further. Supervisors may urge the de-escalation officers to hurry and bring the situation to a close. Other officers who are not trained in de-escalation or who do not see the virtue of de-escalation, and who might be more inclined to simply make an arrest without further discussion, may also be present.

High-complexity crises can involve significant officer safety issues and multiple potential outcome goals. At this level of complexity, officers generally need to prioritize the goals in terms of those requiring the most immediate attention, such as safety, and those that can be attained only after the crisis is significantly de-escalated, such as taking the consumer to an emergency receiving facility for evaluation.

Clearly, crisis de-escalation does not occur in a vacuum, but rather in complex contexts. Each situation presents a different set of challenges for the officer, and he or she must be ready to evaluate the scenario in terms of the stage of escalation and the complexity of the crisis. Using these assessment tools, officers can work to ensure that the necessary resources are available on scene to increase the likelihood of success in de-escalation and to decrease the possibility of injury to officers, consumers, and any other individuals who are involved.

■ How to De-escalate a Crisis Situation

De-escalation of a crisis involves a series of verbal and nonverbal behaviors. More than 90% of communication is nonverbal. As such, the first impression you make upon a consumer in crisis may significantly influence the progression of the subsequent interaction.

The first step in the process is simply to introduce yourself. This introduction begins to create a relationship with the consumer, even if he or she initially resists or refuses to engage. The introduction should provide information that will begin to create structure. Identify yourself and your departmental affiliation, and state that you are there to help. Try to maintain a relaxed, nonthreatening body posture and keep your voice tone calm and respectful. During the introduction, you can continue your assessment of the situation by observing the consumer's nonverbal behaviors and,

> If you are given a choice between listening and talking during de-escalation, it is almost always better to listen.

most importantly, by listening. If you are given a choice between listening and talking during de-escalation, it is almost always better to listen.

Listening

In de-escalation, listening is an active process. **Active listening** means being able to truly hear what someone is saying as well as the ability to communicate back to that person that he or she has been heard. It consists of four steps:

1. You must *control the physical environment* by eliminating, to the extent possible, distractions that may take away from the ability to listen.

2. You must *physically attend* to the situation. While maintaining officer safety, lean in slightly, keep still, and make eye contact to demonstrate to the person that you are paying attention. Be careful to avoid staring when making eye contact, because this behavior might be perceived as aggressive or threatening.

3. You must *mentally attend* to the situation. That is, to actively listen to someone, you cannot be thinking about what you are going to say next, daydreaming, or otherwise allowing your mind to wander.

4. You must *listen for the whole meaning of the statement.* Pay attention not only to what the person says but also to how they are saying it. Work to understand the entire message the consumer is giving you.

Active listening can accomplish several objectives during de-escalation. Namely, it builds rapport between officer and consumer, it focuses the consumer on the officer as opposed to other things going on in the environment, it helps the officer refine the assessment of the crisis, and it provides information that lays the groundwork for an eventual resolution of the crisis.

Of course, eventually you will need to respond to what the consumer is telling you. A natural tendency might be to begin asking questions of the subject. However, this is generally not a good idea, especially early in the interaction. Asking many questions can begin to sound like an interrogation and may alienate the consumer or cause further escalation. In de-escalation, encouraging the consumer to continue talking is more effective than asking a lot of questions. Also, if you are thinking about which questions you are going to ask, that energy would be better spent on listening at this point in the interaction. At least initially, your responses should demonstrate to the consumer that you are listening and trying to understand. This approach will help continue the dialogue and will provide the consumer with additional opportunities to give information that will help to resolve the crisis.

> In de-escalation, encouraging the consumer to continue talking is more effective than asking a lot of questions.

Five specific responsive techniques are typically used in de-escalation to accomplish the objective of furthering dialogue, building rapport, and gathering information: minimal encouragers, reflecting/mirroring, restating or paraphrasing, emotional labeling, and "I" statements. These techniques are discussed briefly next.

Minimal Encouragers

Minimal encouragers are brief statements that can be either nonverbal, such as a positive nod of the head, or simple verbal responses, such as "Okay," "Uh-huh," "I see," or "I am listening." Minimal encouragers demonstrate to the consumer that you are listening and paying attention, without stalling the dialogue or creating an undue interruption. Especially early in the encounter, consumers need these types of encouragers to feel that the officer is really attending to them and listening to what they are saying.

Reflecting/Mirroring

Whereas minimal encouragers provide initial confirmation that you are listening, reflecting or mirroring adds another dimension to the communication. Here, you provide the consumer with evidence that you are listening by actually repeating what he or she has said. Often the reflecting/mirroring response will simply consist of the last few words the consumer says. These statements should be brief and used in such a way as not to interrupt the consumer.

Restating or Paraphrasing

Restating or paraphrasing is similar to mirroring except that now you begin to communicate that you are trying to understand the consumer's entire message by putting what the consumer has said into your own words. This should be done with a calm voice tone and in an effort to avoid what might sound like mocking or insulting the consumer. Often such statements will begin with something like "What I hear you saying is . . . ," "If I am hearing you right . . . ," or "Let me see if I understand what you are saying . . . ." These types of statements also summarize what has been said in the communication.

Emotional Labeling

In emotional labeling, you again take active listening to a higher level by trying to help the consumer identify feelings. This is different from "telling" the consumer what he or she is feeling because your statement is based on what the consumer has been communicating through his or her words and behaviors. If you have used your active listening skills well, it will often be rather easy to provide an emotional label to assist the consumer. Examples of emotional labeling statements include "You seem to be . . . ," "It seems to me like you feel . . . ," or "If I were in your situation, I think I'd feel . . . ." In addition to demonstrating that you have listened to the consumer intently, emotional labeling represents a good example of the sophisticated connection between feelings and behaviors that may assist in consumers' recoveries.

"I" Statements

When attempting to de-escalate a situation, try to begin many of your statements with "I" as opposed to "you" or even "we." Beginning a statement with "I" rather than "you" avoids putting the consumer on the defensive or making it seem as if you are blaming the consumer for creating the crisis. Moreover, one of the goals of de-escalation is to have the consumer focus on you so that you can communicate that you are listening. Beginning a statement with "we" depersonalizes this process and can make the de-escalation officer seem less like an individual trying to render aid and more like a representative of a group or establishment about which the consumer may be frightened or angry. In other words, "we" can refer to "they," and "they" (i.e., law enforcement, family members, hospital staff) may be what the consumer sees as creating the problem in the first place.

You can use "I" statements at many points during the de-escalation. For example, "I see" and "I am listening" are examples that combine minimal encouragers and "I" statements. Using "I" statements also can be very useful later in de-escalation, once you are ready to begin working toward a solution. A statement such as "I would like to help," when made after establishing some level of rapport with the consumer, can help open the door to problem solving and eventual resolution of the crisis.

If the active listening process and responsive techniques outlined above have been effective, there will come a time when it is appropriate to begin working toward a resolution of the crisis. This transition will require switching from active listening and developing rapport to actually directing the consumer to do something. One of the most effective methods for making this transition is the three-step assertive intervention (**Table 15.4**):

1. The *empathy statement* is similar to the dialogue in which the consumer is already engaged. This statement reinforces the notion that the consumer is being listened to and that the officer is trying to understand what the consumer is experiencing.

2. The *conflict statement* is intended to communicate to the consumer that, while you are trying to understand where he or she is coming from, there exists a situation that needs to be addressed. In this statement, the officer has an opportunity to present his or her view of the situation to the consumer and to explain why something now needs to be done.

3. The *action statement* is the officer's specific recommendation or request of the consumer.

The chapter-opening vignette involving Jack provides an excellent example of a situation that may have been resolved using a three-step assertive intervention. The assertive intervention might have sounded something like this:

> Jack, I understand that you are upset and that you feel like no one is listening to you or doing enough to help you. But you and I need to let these people get back to work here, so we are going to have to get out of this waiting room. I'd like you to let me take you down to the ER so you can see a doctor right away and get your medications looked at to see if something can be done to help you feel better.

Of course, the three-step assertive intervention can be used to achieve other intermediate goals in the de-escalation process, such as having the consumer give up a potentially dangerous object or weapon or moving the consumer to a safer location (e.g., out of the street) where the officer can continue the interaction more safely. The main benefit of this intervention is that it allows the officer to direct the consumer's behavior without giving authoritative commands, which might hinder the de-escalation process.

■ Putting It All Together

The following vignette about Daisy summarizes the stages of escalation involved in a crisis, the complexity levels of a crisis, specific challenges faced by the responding officers, and the goals for the de-escalation.

Table 15.4   Three-Step Assertive Intervention

Step 1
Empathy statement: A statement that lets the consumer know that you understand where he or she is coming from and how he or she likely feels.

Step 2
Conflict statement: A statement that describes to the consumer that you have a conflict that needs to be addressed.

Step 3
Action statement: A statement that lets the consumer know what you want him or her to do. This statement can be in the form of a request.

Examples
- "Jack, I understand that you are upset and that you feel like no one is listening to you or doing enough to help you. But you and I need to let these people get back to work here, so we are going to have to get out of this waiting room. I'd like you to let me take you down to the ER so you can see a doctor right away and get your medications looked at to see if something can be done to help you feel better."

- "It looks to me like you're pretty upset, and I'm here to help you. But I'm afraid someone is going to get hurt by those pennies. So I'd like you to stop tossing them and step up here on the curb so I can talk to you and try to understand what is going on with you today."

Daisy has already engaged in generalized acting out by tossing pennies at passing cars, so the crisis is already in an advanced stage of escalation when the officers arrive on the scene. These officers will need to develop both immediate and longer-term goals for the de-escalation. Because Daisy appears to have a mental illness, the ultimate goal of the de-escalation will be to transport her to an emergency facility for evaluation and treatment. Several intermediate steps must be covered, however, before that goal can be realized. In this case, it does not appear as though the de-escalation can proceed safely before officers address some of the complicating factors.

This vignette is a good illustration of how crises do not necessarily follow a steady progression and how de-escalation skills must be used flexibly to address the multitude of issues present in these circumstances. Obviously, Daisy's situation represents a high-complexity crisis. Numerous complicating factors are present, including a large, busy, and potentially dangerous physical location; a crowd; a potentially unsympathetic fellow officer who is not familiar with the principles of de-escalation; the presence of a potentially dangerous object (the pennies and whatever else may be in Daisy's bag); and a high potential for further escalation.

Backup officers will likely be needed to reroute traffic and provide support for crowd control at a minimum. Also, the first officer on the scene must be willing to turn the call over to an officer trained in de-escalation (such as a CIT-certified officer), because his current demeanor is likely to cause the situation to deteriorate further. This issue can be tricky, especially if rank or seniority plays a role or if the fellow officer is especially upset or agitated. As a way to avoid this dilemma, some departments have made it a matter of policy that once a CIT or similarly trained officer arrives on the scene, he or she becomes the primary responder.

If multiple CIT officers are on the scene, a decision must also be made about who will begin as the primary leader and who will serve as the backup. Keep in mind that the consumer may not cooperate with this arrangement and could insist on talking to the officer identified as the backup. In such an instance, officers need to be willing to shift roles without ending up in a power struggle, because this strife would be detrimental to the de-escalation.

As mentioned earlier, CIT officers are entering this situation after Daisy has already engaged in generalized acting out. Additionally, because Daisy has been stepping in and out of the street at a busy intersection, safety issues need to be addressed immediately. Even though it is early in the de-escalation process, the lead officer can use a three-step assertive intervention to give Daisy directions about her location and the penny tossing, while remaining calm and supportive and beginning to build rapport. This can even be incorporated into the officer's introduction, which might sound like this:

> Hi. I am Officer Johnson with the county police department, and I am a crisis intervention team officer. It looks to me like you're pretty upset, and I'm here to help you. But I'm afraid someone is going to get hurt by those pennies. So I'd like you to stop tossing them and step up here on the curb so I can talk to you and try to understand what is going on with you today.

From this point, the de-escalation of Daisy's crisis could proceed in a number of different directions. De-escalation is less like a recipe or formula and more like a flexible set of options. No two consumers or crises will ever be exactly alike. The skills outlined in this chapter should serve as guidelines, but they must always be applied to match the demands of the individual consumer and the unique crisis.

■ Conclusion

By the end of this chapter, some officers will be left asking how they can become effective at de-escalation without "letting down their guard," giving up control, or sacrificing their position of authority. In his 2005 article "The Art of De-escalation," Lt. Michael Woody (retired), of the Akron (Ohio) Police Department, addressed this concern very succinctly with these words of advice: "It is the wise officer who can, at times, conceal [his or her] combat-ready status." Once officers become trained in de-escalation, they do not simply abandon all of the training and experience that came before it. Both officer and consumer safety always remain paramount concerns in a crisis involving a person with a mental illness. De-escalation is another tool that officers have at their disposal to be judiciously applied in controlling a potentially volatile situation, rather than serving as a substitute for sound judgment and attentiveness to safety.

Chapter Wrap-Up

- What constitutes a crisis varies from person to person and depends largely on the individual's ability to deal effectively with the demands being placed on him or her. The symptoms of brain disorders—including mental illnesses, substance use disorders, and developmental disabilities—often significantly influence this capacity.

- Escalation during a crisis can be broken down into nine stages. Each stage is characterized by a set of goals to accomplish and problems to avoid. In reality, crises do not always proceed in an orderly fashion, so these stages may occur in a different order or even be skipped altogether.

- Crises vary in terms of their complexity. The level of complexity that characterizes any given crisis will depend on the number and intensity of the factors facing the officers who respond.

- Active listening is a crucial part of the de-escalation process. Listening is often more effective than talking when working with consumers in crisis.

- Responsive techniques used in de-escalation include minimal encouragers, mirroring/reflecting, restating or paraphrasing, emotional labeling, and "I" statements. Once rapport is established, a three-step assertive intervention can be used to begin directing the consumer toward resolution of the crisis.

- De-escalation training does not replace the other knowledge and experience officers bring to a crisis situation. Rather, it is meant to be an additional tool that enhances officers' abilities to deal with consumers in crisis. Issues of officer and consumer safety are always a paramount concern during any de-escalation episode.

Vital Vocabulary

active listening: being able to truly hear what someone is saying and to communicate back to that person that he or she has been heard

coping skills (coping strategies): strategies to help individuals avoid overwhelming feelings such as grief, terror, or rage, or avoid a blow to their self-esteem

crisis: a situation in which a person experiences a negative change in thinking and behavior because his or her capacity to cope effectively has been exceeded by the perceived environmental demands

de-escalation: a specialized form of communication aimed at moving a situation from a state of high tension to a reduced state of tension

delusions: fixed, false beliefs

developmental disability: a mental impairment that affects a person's abilities to think, communicate, interact with others, remember facts and details, and take care of oneself; all developmental disabilities, such as mental retardation and autistic disorder, appear before the age of 18 and remain with the person throughout his or her life

empathy: an attempt to truly understand the perspective and feelings of another person

hallucinations: perceptions that occur in the absence of an external stimulus, such as hearing a voice when no one is there (auditory hallucinations)

psychiatric illness: a mental illness

psychotic symptoms: symptoms such as hallucinations or delusions that indicate an impairment in reality testing

substance use disorder: a maladaptive pattern of substance use manifested by recurrent problems related to the repeated use of an addictive substance

Questions for Review and Discussion

1. Which special characteristics do law enforcement officers who are particularly successful at de-escalation possess?
2. At what point of escalation do officers working with a consumer need to abandon the de-escalation process in the interest of their own safety and the safety of others?
3. Active listening means being able to truly hear what someone has said and to communicate back to that person that he or she has been heard. What are the four steps of active listening?
4. Explain the three-step assertive intervention that is used by law enforcement officers in the de-escalation process to accomplish the objective of furthering dialogue, building rapport, and gathering information.
5. How does an officer effectively achieve the transition from active listening to directing the consumer to do what the law enforcement officer wishes to achieve?

Resources

Books and Articles

Castellano-Hoyt DW. *Enhancing police response to persons in mental health crisis: Providing strategies, communication techniques and crisis intervention preparation in overcoming institutional challenges.* Springfield, IL: Charles C Thomas, 2003.

Ellis A., Harper R. *A guide to rational living.* North Hollywood: Wilshire Book Company, 1973.

Goldstein AP, Monti PJ, Sardino TJ, Green DJ. *Police crisis intervention.* New York: Pergamon Press, 1979.

Romano AT. *Taking charge: Crisis intervention in criminal justice.* Westport, CT: Greenwood Press, 1990.

Westbrook C. De-escalation techniques. Presentation as part of the Georgia Crisis Intervention Team Training Program, Cherokee County Georgia Sheriff's Department, 2006.

Websites

Woody MS. The art of de-escalation. 2005. http://www.neoucom.edu/CJCCOE/DeEscalationSummer20052.pdf. (Retrieved October 20, 2006).

Memphis Police Department, Crisis Intervention http://www.memphispolice.org/Crisis%20Intervention.htm. (Retrieved October 20, 2006).

Responding to Special Populations

CHAPTER 16

Case Vignette: James

A familiar man whom people in the neighborhood nicknamed "Snowsuit Man" lived outside a downtown church for five years. He told no one his actual name and rarely spoke to others. Snowsuit Man always wore a bright orange snowmobile suit, even in the middle of summer. He had poor hygiene and sometimes talked out loud when no one else was there. Although he did not cause specific problems in the neighborhood, sometimes Snowsuit Man would panhandle or urinate in public, prompting well-intentioned citizens to call 9-1-1. Most of the responding officers knew Snowsuit Man, so they tried to redirect his behavior without arresting him or harassing him.

One day a rookie officer responded to an emergency call from someone reporting that Snowsuit Man had scared a tourist in the area when he persistently asked for money to buy something to eat. The tourist from the rural Midwest had never seen a homeless person before, and she began screaming when she was approached by Snowsuit Man. Her screaming confused Snowsuit Man, who began waving his hands in the air and shouting, "I am Jesus! Help Jesus!" When the responding officer arrived at the incident, she witnessed this disheveled man dressed inappropriately in a snowmobile suit in July, acting bizarrely and apparently aggressively. Despite her efforts to rationalize with Snowsuit Man, the officer was not able to comfort the tourist or calm Snowsuit Man. Because the man lurched at the tourist, the officer had to "take down" Snowsuit Man, handcuff him, and bring him to the detention center where he awaited trial for panhandling, loitering, and public assault.

■ Introduction

While general de-escalation tactics are useful for law enforcement officials to know, some individuals may present special circumstances that require specific considerations. Just as different cultures throughout the world have unique traditions in dress, food, language, and societal rules, unique groups of people in the United States have histories and circumstances that shape their lives and responses to others, including mental health professionals and members of the law enforcement community. This chapter explores the characteristics of three **special populations**: homeless individuals, people thinking about suicide, and paranoid people who may act aggressively based on their assumption that others mean to hurt them. While reviewing the information in this chapter, you are encouraged to monitor your own biases toward people who are part of these groups and consider the ways in which personal stereotypes may influence interactions with individuals from these "special populations."

■ Responding to Homeless Persons with Mental Illnesses

Snowsuit Man is one of the 2.3 to 3.5 million Americans who find themselves without stable housing during a calendar year. Snowsuit Man, whose real name is James, is a 45-year-old African American man who has a Ph.D. in philosophy from Harvard University. James was evicted from his housing after the symptoms of schizophrenia caused him to lose his teaching job, his Boston apartment, and his significant relationships at age 25. Since then, James has moved south to a warmer climate, where he has lived in yards, under bridges, and in makeshift dugouts in the earth known as "cat holes." James has no income except for the money he receives from panhandling. Similarly, he has no health insurance or general assistance such as food stamps or Section 8 housing vouchers, so James has never had medical or psychiatric care for his illness. James's situation is becoming increasingly more common as housing costs and unemployment rates rise. His unique life and experiences significantly shape his behaviors and interactions with other people.

Of the 13.5 million Americans who have been homeless at some point during their lifetimes, an estimated 25% to 40% have some mental illness, and nearly half struggle with current and/or past alcohol or other substance abuse problems. Consequently, in addition to facing limited resources, many homeless persons must deal with cravings for drugs, hallucinations, paranoia, and other symptoms of addictions and mental illnesses. Imagine how difficult it must be to apply for housing, wait in lines for meals and toilet use, and navigate other social service systems while hearing voices that others cannot hear or while suspecting that others are spying on you and plotting to kill you. Yet, homeless individuals somehow survive in our country's cumbersome and bureaucratic social service system. Homeless men, women, and children develop tremendous resiliency and capacity to cope with extraordinary circumstances that many others could not withstand. While many of the skills and coping strategies that homeless persons develop to survive on the streets are functional given their circumstances, people who do not lack homes—including mental health and law enforcement professionals—may misinterpret those adaptations as senseless or aggressive. It is therefore extremely important for informed professionals to understand unique aspects of homeless individuals.

> Homeless men, women, and children develop tremendous resiliency and capacity to cope with extraordinary circumstances that many others could not withstand.

Several examples might be helpful in illustrating how adaptive behaviors of homeless people might be misinterpreted by others. First, the ways in which homeless people dress may seem bizarre to other people. Homeless people typically have no place to store their possessions. Either items are sold or stolen, or individuals without stable housing carry everything with them throughout the day. Because it may become too tiring to carry bags filled with clothes around all day, sometimes homeless individuals wear as many clothes as possible to decrease the work of carrying their possessions. Police patrols and tourists may observe homeless individuals wearing several hats, scarves, shirts, and pants, and suspect that they have a mental illness or are unstable. In fact, that way of dressing is quite reasonable when one understands that it may be functional for people who have nowhere to live.

Dressing in a snowmobile suit or a heavy coat in warm months as Snowsuit Man does may also make sense, given how important it is to remain insulated and temperature controlled while sleeping under a bridge. Even in summer months, nighttime temperatures may fall below 50 degrees—cool enough to die from hypothermia if one's body does not retain heat. It is likely that Snowsuit Man developed an innovative way to keep warm while sleeping in the church yard rather than purposefully or unknowingly standing out by dressing in his snowmobile suit.

Another example of how a functional behavior for someone who is homeless may be misinterpreted as inappropriate or defiant behavior centers on medication adherence. Many psychiatric medications are quite sedating for hours, which is why they are often given at bedtime. Homeless individuals staying in shelters or in a private yard or a public park frequently must wake up before 5:30 A.M. to clear out of the shelter or avoid being arrested for trespassing . Furthermore, sleeping too soundly in a crowded shelter may render an individual more vulnerable to robbery, rape, or assault. Considering these particular aspects of being homeless, one can understand why some homeless individuals choose not to take their medications. Mental health professionals may refer to such a choice as **noncompliance** or "resistance," but to a homeless person, the decision not to take sedating psychiatric medications may make good sense.

Understanding homeless persons' unique experiences may also assist law enforcement officers in working more effectively with homeless individuals. Homeless individuals often have many encounters with law enforcers or paramedics that influence their future willingness to engage with emergency professionals. One Canadian study found that 61% of all 160 shelter tenants surveyed had at least one interaction with the police in the previous year (Zakrison, Hamel, & Hwang, 2004). Many of those interactions were negative, because 9% of the respondents reported that a police officer assaulted them in that year. Even if these numbers do not accurately reflect law enforcement encounters, the perspective of homeless persons—that police officers are out to make their lives difficult—automatically lends a confrontational tone to subsequent interactions.

> Considering the particular aspects of being homeless, one can understand why some homeless individuals choose not to take their medications. Mental health professionals may refer to such a choice as "noncompliance" or "resistance," but to a homeless person, the decision not to take sedating psychiatric medications may make good sense.

Homeless people who use illegal substances face the potential for even greater conflict with law enforcement personnel. A drug bust in the homeless community may drive substance use into more obscure locations as a way to prevent its discovery. Whereas individuals who have housing could use illegal substances in the privacy of their homes, homeless individuals cannot. Out of necessity, homeless people who have drug addictions may feel forced to use drugs in unsafe but remote locations such as rural fields, basements of clubs, or even restaurant bathrooms. These locations predispose homeless drug users to unsafe outcomes and limit harm reduction practices such as using sterilized needles to inject drugs and prevent infections and the transmission of infectious diseases such as human immunodeficiency virus and hepatitis (Cooper et al., 2005). Homeless drug users therefore have a greater likelihood of being sick or injured than housed counterparts. In fact, homeless persons in general face higher rates of illnesses and death than their housed counterparts.

Their historic mistrust of police, doctors, and other people who are part of "the establishment" frames homeless individuals' expectations of how they will be treated by these professionals in the future. Unfortunately, these expectations are often self-fulfilling prophecies. The cycle of expected abuse and misunderstanding that leads to actual disrespect of homeless persons can undermine law enforcers' effectiveness at de-escalating volatile situations involving homeless people.

Just as many homeless individuals have expectations of being mistreated by law enforcement professionals, many law enforcement professionals hold biases about homeless individuals. Some believe that homeless persons are dumb or lazy, or that they chose to be homeless. Snowsuit Man, like many other homeless individuals, is smart, innovative, and ended up without permanent housing not because of choice, but because of illness and economic factors. Accepting the notion that homeless people have the capabilities to do amazing and complex things may change officers' approaches to homeless persons during crises.

An important ethical issue arises while considering law enforcement professionals' potential interactions with homeless people. Homeless people who are doing their best to secure housing, income, and a sense of self-worth require **autonomy**—the right to make one's own decisions—to be able to make progress in their lives. However, autonomy that results in behaviors that put homeless persons or the public in danger cannot be accepted. For example, if a homeless person chooses to stay in an abandoned lot where she feels safe and can pursue better quality of life, it may be reasonable to respect her autonomous decision to stay there. If the property is privately held or located near a toxic dump that could cause cancer in the homeless woman, however, perhaps her autonomy should not be accepted for health, public safety, and legal reasons.

> The potential conflict between autonomy and public safety can complicate decision making for members of law enforcement.

This potential conflict between autonomy and public safety can complicate decision making for members of law enforcement. If a law enforcement professional knows that it is a misdemeanor for a homeless person to urinate outside and a homeless person could be arrested for that behavior, should observed urination always result in arrest when there are no public restrooms for homeless people to use? Homeless persons might make autonomous decisions that are functional but challenge public laws. Individual law enforcers have to decide where the ethical boundaries separate autonomy from anarchy.

> Identifying your personal stereotypes and biases toward homeless people or any other people who have major differences from yourself, and choosing to reject those biases, is crucial to establishing competent and useful community interactions.

When considering the unique challenges faced by homeless people in general and by homeless people with mental illnesses or substance abuse issues in particular, it becomes crucial for law enforcement officers to develop specific strategies for responding to crisis calls involving homeless individuals. Remember that people who are homeless are people foremost, just like the rest of us. If they are dressed oddly or dirty, or if they exhibit symptoms of untreated mental or medical illnesses, recall that some of those behaviors are actually adaptive for homeless people. Also, remember that homeless people are often just as intelligent and motivated to succeed as anyone else. Showing immediate respect for homeless people and treating them kindly may help to counter the historic mistrust some homeless individuals have for law enforcers. Perhaps most importantly, identifying your personal stereotypes and biases toward homeless people or any other people who have major differences from yourself, and choosing to reject those biases, is crucial to establishing competent and useful community interactions.

Case Vignette: Miguel

Miguel is a 42-year-old Latino man who worked for a local automobile manufacturing company until he was laid off last month. Miguel has a history of bipolar disorder that was well controlled with lithium until he lost his employer-sponsored health insurance owing to his layoff. Miguel began feeling depressed a month ago, and his condition has worsened to this point. Now Miguel feels like he might be becoming manic, as he is agitated, impulsive,

continues

not sleeping, and quite distractible. He started contemplating suicide yesterday and decides to leave a suicide note for his partner as he walks downstairs to get his loaded gun.

Miguel's partner stumbles across the note while cleaning and hears Miguel unlocking the gun cabinet. The partner calls 9-1-1, reporting that Miguel appears to be suicidal, and a local police officer is dispatched to the couple's home. When the officer arrives at the house, she has no idea what to say or do in the situation. Although he was unable to get to the gun, Miguel begins taunting the officer, who becomes angry and even considers aggressive take-down strategies to end the standoff.

■ Responding to People with Suicidal Thinking or Behavior

Suicide is a major public health concern. Suicide is the eighth leading cause of death for males in America, and the third leading cause of death for youth younger than age 24 years. In fact, suicide accounts for more deaths in the United States annually than do diseases such as breast cancer. Despite its high incidence, it is often ignored as a public health issue. As potential first responders to possible suicides, law enforcers play an important role in preventing completed suicides.

While it is impossible to predict with certainty who will kill himself or herself, certain risk factors increase the chances that someone will make a suicide attempt. **Risk factors** are traits or characteristics that do not determine that someone will try killing himself or herself, but that are associated with an increased risk of suicide. Risk factors for suicide include a previous history of a suicide attempt; a mental illness (particularly bipolar disorder, major depressive disorder, and schizophrenia); alcohol or other substance abuse; male gender; a limited social support system; gay, lesbian, bisexual, or transgendered sexual identity; easy access to weapons; and certain chronic physical illnesses. In the United States, the subgroup with the highest risk of suicide in 2005 was white, elderly men. Often people who are at risk for suicide do not seek appropriate treatment due to the stigma associated with mental illnesses or a lack of knowledge of how to get help.

Protective factors shield people from acting on suicidal thoughts. One of the most important protective factors for suicide is securing appropriate mental health and substance abuse treatment. Criminal justice professionals play key roles in diverting people who are considering suicide toward appropriate mental health care. Other protective factors include sufficient social supports, skills in problem solving and dispute resolution, and limited access to handguns.

Firearms account for the majority of completed suicides. Although women attempt suicide roughly three times more often than do men, men typically employ more lethal means when making a suicide gesture. Adults who successfully commit suicide use firearms more than 70% of the time. Gun locks can be useful in preventing children from using a gun to kill themselves if there are firearms in the home. Policies limiting firearm possession have also been shown to decrease both suicide attempts and homicides in localities. Public policies such as firearm ordinances shape both public health and social ideals.

Individuals with suicidal thoughts often feel desperate to get out of what seems like an impossible situation. This desperation may be manifested as aggression, antagonism, or defiance. Law enforcement personnel who are working with someone who is suicidal should keep in mind that the person may be antagonizing the officer as a way to get the officer to act on the individual's suicide wishes. Furthermore, people who feel that they have "nothing to lose" and who are suicidal may not take into consideration how their behaviors could affect others. Protecting the public as an officer attempts to prevent a suicide can be quite challenging.

Strategies that keep the person talking and encouraging the consideration of options besides suicide may be the most useful responses to people contemplating suicide. Reacting to impulsivity or antagonism through either aggressive words ("You'll go to hell if you kill yourself") or aggressive deeds (shooting the suicidal individual) rarely help. From a prevention standpoint, bolstering social support systems in communities and limiting firearm access may be important mechanisms for decreasing suicide rates. Suicidal people who are incarcerated rather than treated through mental health and medical programs remain at risk for suicide while in jail. People who are suicidal and who have a plan and the intent to carry out that plan need to be closely monitored to ensure their safety. Suicide is an emergency just like having a heart attack or a stroke; timely and informed care needs to be accessed to prevent death.

Case Vignette: Barbara

Barbara is a 23-year-old Syrian woman who emigrated to the United States to study law after she fell in love and married her American boyfriend. During her first year of law school, Barbara performed extremely well on the tests and made excellent grades. Eventually, however, she began worrying that her classmates were copying her work and reading her papers. She became preoccupied with her privacy and maintaining distance from others whom she suspected of copying. This suspicion worsened to the degree that Barbara believed that people had planted cameras in her apartment to monitor her every move, and that the government had tapped her phone to make sure she was not a terrorist. Her social and academic functioning declined over the course of the semester, and Barbara became increasingly withdrawn and isolated, while experiencing decreased energy and difficulty concentrating. Ultimately, one of Barbara's professors called the university health service's psychiatrist for a consultation.

The psychiatrist diagnosed Barbara with schizophrenia, paranoid type, and recommended that she start an antipsychotic medication. Barbara declined, stating that "The pills contain mind-altering poison to make it possible for others to read my mind." Barbara became so fixated on the notion that others were out to get her that she dropped out of law school and within several months became homeless. She prefers living in isolation under a highway bridge: "I don't have to worry about people spying on me there."

Other homeless individuals in the area know Barbara and call her "Osama" because of her Middle Eastern ethnicity. People who live in her area try to avoid "Osama" at all costs; when they are forced to see her, they either ignore her completely or attempt to scare her by spitting on her or shouting at her. One kind stranger asked if Barbara wanted to stay at a local homeless shelter where there was a bed, food, and people to help her connect with local resources. Barbara simply ran away, returning to her safe haven under the bridge.

■ Engaging and Assessing Individuals Who Are Paranoid or Aggressive

People with paranoid delusions (i.e., fixed false beliefs that others are out to harm them) tend to isolate themselves and refuse services that are offered to them. Barbara exemplifies a paranoid person who has above-average intelligence, but for whom a mental illness has substantially affected her life. Individuals with paranoia—who may be diagnosed with schizophrenia, major depressive disorder with psychotic features, bipolar disorder with psychotic features, delirium, or dementia—suspect that people are conspiring against them. This paranoia influences their views toward law enforcement personnel as well. Individuals who are paranoid typically prefer to remain alone and disconnected from people and social service agencies to protect their confidentiality and personal integrity. Even though Barbara may have benefited from staying at a shelter where she could be connected with social services and entitlement programs, the prospect of living with other people and sharing personal information in applications or databases overshadowed the potential benefits she could have received. Individuals who are paranoid pose a particular challenge to law enforcement officers who are attempting to work with them.

Because paranoid individuals are suspicious of almost everyone, engaging such individuals in their recovery processes is difficult. Paranoid people tend to be skeptical of everyone, whether the skepticism is well founded or not. If paranoid people experience actual trauma such as assault, rape, or robbery (which can be common among homeless persons), their paranoia is reinforced and strengthened. As a result, many people who are paranoid decline altruistic assistance, believing that the safest option is to remain alone.

> Many people who are paranoid decline altruistic assistance, believing that the safest option is to remain alone.

Working with paranoid persons in the community requires showing respect for the delusional paranoia without colluding with the individual's beliefs. Engaging Barbara in new behaviors or treatment, for example, necessitates an understanding of her world perspective. Living under a bridge or on the streets may actually represent the safest place for someone like Barbara. On her own, Barbara is able to come and go as she pleases, escaping any situation that seems confining. Moreover, living without rules under a bridge may feel liberating and create a sense of autonomy for someone who is paranoid. Expecting paranoid individuals to accept assistance and move into a stable living environment dismisses such delusional thinking and renders kind offers useless. Nevertheless, it is dangerous for authorities to agree with someone's paranoid ideas, because such reinforcement might perpetuate other paranoia.

Law enforcement officials who are attempting to change paranoid persons' behaviors need to imagine what it must be like to believe the world is conspiring against them. Watching activities or monitoring behaviors reinforces the paranoia. Demanding action plays into the idea that officials are trying to control the person. Sometimes consistently visiting paranoid people where they feel safe—under the bridge for Barbara—and respectfully offering assistance without requiring its acceptance may be the best way to interact with paranoid people. Oftentimes, paternalistic demands cause paranoid individuals to flee or act out in other ways.

> Oftentimes, paternalistic demands cause paranoid individuals to flee or act out in other ways.

Sometimes paranoia results in aggression. According to Surgeon General Satcher's 1999 report, people with mental illnesses are no more dangerous to others than anyone else; nevertheless, paranoia may lead to attempts to protect oneself that appear aggressive to outsiders. If paranoid people believe that cameras and microphones are buried within the walls of a shelter, it is no wonder that some will kick or punch through drywall in an effort to remove the surveillance equipment. If a paranoid person assumes that a police officer is a government spy out to capture him, it is no wonder that the individual might try to run away despite clear directions from the officer. If a paranoid person thinks it safest to live outside away from others, it is no wonder that she will decline housing or other social services. Safety among others, housing, and engagement with services may not be seen as helpful among people who are paranoid.

> The 1999 Surgeon General's Report notes that people with mental illnesses are no more dangerous to others than anyone else.

In fact, paranoia or other symptoms of mental illnesses may prove to be more dangerous to the person with the illness than to others. As mentioned earlier, suicide attempts are quite common among individuals with serious mental illnesses such as schizophrenia, bipolar disorder, or depression. Research data suggest that more than 90% of all people who commit suicide have mental illnesses. In fact, nearly 40% of all people with schizophrenia will make at least one suicide attempt during their lifetime. Clearly, people with serious mental illnesses who have limited support or inadequate treatment alternatives are more dangerous to themselves than to others.

Paranoid individuals fear many things that most of us assume are helpful. Other individuals who are not overtly paranoid or psychotic may also have important emotional responses to interactions with security guards, police officers, and other authority figures. Fear, anxiety, or dread may activate the **amygdala**, a primitive part of the brain that prompts a person to fight or flee a potentially dangerous encounter. Once the amygdala has been activated, it becomes nearly impossible for a person to rationalize or think in complex ways. Instead, the amygdala, in essence, overrides the cortex (the part of the human brain responsible for planning and cognition). Anyone who has been in a fight with a significant other knows that once a person feels angry or scared, it becomes nearly impossible to listen to one's partner or truly understand his or her point of view. That is the amygdala working, sending a reminder in no uncertain terms to either fight or leave the confrontation.

Individuals in the community who reach a similar emotional state have the same amygdala-driven urges to fight or flee. Therefore, attempting to rationalize with such individuals or asking them to reconsider the situation may be impossible. Survival has imprinted the desire to act rather than to think onto humans' brains, making it unreasonable to expect emotional individuals to be able to think through crises.

Given the low likelihood that emotional people in crises can succeed in rationalizing alternatives, law enforcement responses to emotional people in volatile situations cannot rely on convincing people by making a rational proposal to think differently. Rather, responders need to create a stable and respectful environment within which emotional individuals can take solace and rest. Arguing with a paranoid or aggressive person is futile. Ensuring that such an individual does not hurt himself or herself or anyone else, coupled with offering respectful but clear instructions, is essential. Emotional individuals who are fighting or fleeing may injure themselves through careless behaviors, such as running across a busy freeway to escape police who are thought to be stalking them, or by making rash decisions, such as responding to directions aggressively in an effort to be safe. Preventing injuries due to such behaviors and working to contain the volatile situation become a law enforcer's primary objective when managing emotional individuals.

■ Conclusion

Understanding and appreciating the unique perspectives of people who are from "special populations" will make one a better law enforcement official and a good public service agent. It is short-sighted to expect all people to have the same backgrounds or experiences. Working in the community necessitates that we "meet people where they are," both physically (under bridges, in shelters, away from the precinct) and philosophically (distrusting all officials, suspecting that no one intends to help, feeling desperate and impulsive). This chapter highlights unique aspects of certain individuals' experiences, but its descriptions do not apply to all homeless, suicidal, or paranoid and aggressive individuals. Sociologists suggest that there is just as much variability within any group as there is between different groups. With this caveat in mind, we must open our minds to individual situations rather than group stereotypes. Attempting to truly understand an individual's situation and resulting behaviors is much more important than recognizing patterns of behaviors within specific socioeconomic

> People with serious mental illnesses who have limited support or inadequate treatment alternatives are more dangerous to themselves than to others.

> Survival has imprinted the desire to act rather than to think onto humans' brains, making it unreasonable to expect emotional individuals to be able to think through crises.

> Working in the community necessitates that we "meet people where they are," both physically and philosophically.

groups. The officer responding to a crisis should always ask "What peculiar feelings, thoughts, or behaviors shape this person?" before becoming involved in the situation.

Assuming a professional role in mental health or law enforcement necessarily requires becoming involved in other aspects of a community. Homelessness is a political, economic, and even racial issue (64% of all homeless people treated through the organization Health Care for the Homeless were African American during one year, a disproportionate share relative to the U.S. population). If one's role as a law enforcement officer or peacekeeper involves interactions with homeless people, dealing with the factors affecting homelessness may also be part of one's responsibilities. Similarly, if one deals with suicidal people, perhaps it would be prudent to advocate for suicide prevention programs or improved access to mental health care. Researchers have shown that simply learning about different populations is of limited value; rather, the best way to develop true understanding is to increase direct exposure and involvement in new groups. Advocacy and immersion in the communities one serves are crucial, given the important roles played by law enforcement professionals.

> Knowing that responsible, caring, and informed law enforcement professionals and other community leaders have prepared for positive interactions with homeless, suicidal, and paranoid and aggressive individuals may be paramount considerations if people from these "special populations" are to engage in their own recovery processes.

Individuals who are members of "special populations" often face daily ridicule or ostracism from others who may be ignorant or malicious. Knowing that responsible, caring, and informed law enforcement professionals and other community leaders have prepared for positive interactions with homeless, suicidal, and paranoid and aggressive individuals may be paramount considerations if people from these "special populations" are to engage in their own recovery processes.

Chapter Wrap-Up

- Appreciating the unique backgrounds and circumstances of individuals is essential in responding to people with mental illnesses in the community.
- People may become homeless as a result of mental illnesses, lack of affordable housing, loss of social supports, and economic problems. Homelessness does not reflect the fact that these individuals are lazy, stupid, or chose homelessness.
- Suicide is a primary public health concern characterized by high mortality rates, especially in older white men, African American youth, and subgroups such as gay/lesbian/bisexual/transgendered teenagers, people with chronic physical illnesses, and individuals with mental illnesses or substance use disorders.
- While no one can predict who will kill himself or herself, certain risk and protective factors influence the likelihood that a person will make a suicide attempt.
- In highly emotional situations during which the amygdala is activated in the brain, it becomes nearly impossible to rationalize or carry out complicated thinking.
- Paranoia and impulsivity are two factors that require particular attention when de-escalating a situation.
- "Special populations" include individuals who have just as many differences between themselves as members of different groups have from one another. Respect for these differences is a good predictor for successfully stabilizing a volatile situation.

Vital Vocabulary

amygdala: a part of the brain that prompts a person to fight or flee a potentially dangerous encounter due to fear, anxiety, or dread

autonomy: the right to make one's own decisions

noncompliance: choosing not to take one's medication; also called nonadherence

protective factors: characteristics that protect a person against an illness or adverse outcome

risk factors: traits or characteristics that are associated with an increased risk for illness or adverse outcome

special populations: homeless individuals, people thinking about suicide, and paranoid people who may act aggressively based on their assumption that others are out to hurt them

Questions for Review and Discussion

1. How might a homeless person's actions that appear criminal actually be clever survival-related choices?
2. In what ways are social policies related to insurance coverage, employment, housing laws, and firearms availability associated with mental illnesses and homelessness?
3. Describe a situation in which your amygdala kicked in during an emotional situation and you behaved or spoke in a way that you later regretted. How would you have acted if you had your reasoning intact and more time to plan your response?

4. What information would be useful to know about someone to have a good idea of who the person truly is or how the individual thinks? How could a law enforcement officer learn that information?
5. In what ways might first responders and other law enforcement officers influence social policy to help their own professions as well as the individuals within the community whom they serve?

Resources

Books and Articles

Cooper H, Moore L, et al. The impact of a police drug crackdown on drug injectors' ability to practice harm reduction: A qualitative study. *Social Sci Med* 2005; 61(3):673–684.

Lamb HR, Weinberger LE. Persons with severe mental illness in jails and prisons: A review. *Psychiatr Serv* 1998;49(4):483–492.

Tolomiczenko GS, Goering PN, Durbin JF. Educating the public about mental illness and homelessness: A cautionary note. *Can J Psychiatry* 2001;46(3):253–257.

Vostanis P, Tischler V, et al. Mental health problems and social supports among homeless mothers and children victims of domestic and community violence. *Int J Soc Psychiatry* 2001;47(4):30–40.

Wilson EF, Davis JH, et al. Homicide or suicide: The killing of suicidal persons by law enforcement officers. *J Forensic Sci* 1998;43(1):46–52.

Zakrison TL, Hamel PA, Hwang SW. Homeless people's trust and interactions with police and paramedics. *J Urban Health* 2004;81(4):596–605.

Websites

America Foundation for Suicide Prevention: www.afsp.org

Centers for Disease Control and Prevention: www.cdc.gov/ncipc/factsheets/suifacts.htm

Mental Health: A Report of the Surgeon General: www.surgeongeneral.gov/library/mentalhealth/home.html

National Health Care for the Homeless: www.nhchc.org

Police Pocket Guide, Responding to Youth with Mental Health Needs: https://ppal.net/dowloads/PPG_6-10-2002.doc

Acknowledgements and Disclosures

Raymond J. Kotwicki has received grant support from the American Psychiatric Institute for Research and Education (APIRE/GlaxoSmithKline Research Award in Severe Mental Illness), the United Way of Metropolitan Atlanta, and the Woodruff Foundation. He also served as a consultant for Pfizer Pharmaceutical Company in 2005, and is a member of the Speakers' Bureau for AstraZeneca Pharmaceuticals, Pfizer Pharmaceuticals, and Janssen Pharmaceutical Company. Dr. Kotwicki is President of the Board of Directors for Positive Impact, Inc., an HIV and AIDS prevention and mental health services organization, and has provided consulting to the Atlanta Regional Commission on Homelessness. Dr. Kotwicki is Co-director of the Emory University School of Medicine's Post-doctoral Fellowship in Community Psychiatry and Public Health along with Dr. Michael Compton.

17

A View of Law Enforcement–Consumer Interactions Through the Lens of Psychosis

■ Introduction

This chapter presents views of interactions between public safety/criminal justice professionals and consumers, from the perspectives of two people who have been living with a mental illness for some time. Both authors of this chapter have been diagnosed with **paranoid schizophrenia** and have been under treatment for this condition for many years. Both also have been frequent presenters at crisis intervention team training courses for law enforcement officers as well as related sessions and conferences in different regions of Ohio during the past few years. In that the authors have been very open about their conditions, they are obviously not as concerned about confidentiality issues as are many persons with this and similar disorders.

Although the authors believe that law enforcement officers and other first responders should be exposed to the views of persons who have actually experienced serious mental illnesses, we are very aware that people with such illnesses often will differ regarding what they think is most important for officers to know. Nevertheless, we believe that first responders should have some experience with the views and opinions of persons who have been the recipients of interventions from both police officers and mental health providers. In that both of the authors of this chapter have been diagnosed with schizophrenia, the views herein are necessarily skewed toward the experiences of persons with this form of mental illness. Of course, many of the thoughts shared also may be applicable to persons with other mental illnesses, particularly other forms of **psychosis**, such as **schizoaffective disorder** and some types of **bipolar disorder**.

The first part of this chapter takes the viewpoint of a person who has lived with a serious mental illness for approximately 40 years. At the age of 25, Fred Frese was a U.S. Marine Corps security officer who was hospitalized and diagnosed with paranoid schizophrenia. During the ensuing 10 years, Fred was repeatedly rehospitalized and discharged—usually involuntarily—in various military, veteran, state, county, and private psychiatric hospitals in different regions of the United States. Despite these difficulties, he has been able to recover to the extent that he completed a doctoral degree in psychology and has functioned as a licensed, practicing psychologist and mental health administrator during the past 30 years. Details of his experiences with his frequent hospitalizations and his journey of recovery have been published previously. What follows are a few of Fred's thoughts concerning how law enforcement officers may benefit from knowing about mental illnesses.

■ Cultural Competence

In the era of globalization, Americans are increasingly finding ourselves confronted with missives and media messages imploring us to recognize our societal diversity and to become more aware of our multicultural society. These messages are inevitably accompanied by demands that we all become more culturally, and even linguistically, competent.

As I write this, I notice that the first of Muharram (January 30) and Ashura (February 8) are now mentioned on my desk calendar as notable dates. I confess that I have little understanding of whatever cultures may be celebrating these dates. I also see that my desk almanac lists Hindi, Bengali, and Telugu, along with several varieties of Chinese, as being among the most commonly spoken languages in the world. Not only do I know almost nothing about these languages, but I also realize that I still cannot understand most of what I encounter on the local Spanish-language television station, even though I have taken many semester-hours of college-level Spanish. Put bluntly, as a native speaker of American English, I am finding the continuous call for cultural and linguistic competence a bit perplexing—even overwhelming.

Despite my consternation in the face of the barrage of calls for multiculturalism, I must admit that I was very pleased with what I found a few years ago while delivering a presentation at California's Patton State Hospital. For some time that storied facility has celebrated an annual multicultural day, where all-day training focuses on differences among the members of the various ethnic and racial groups residing in the hospital.

The year that I visited, however, Patton State had chosen to focus its training activities on the culture of people with mental illnesses. For those who serve these individuals, viewing us as members of another culture makes sense. Indeed, I have previously suggested that there is some advantage in having our "normal" friends view us as though we come from another culture, or even another planet. The point being made here is that those of us with mental illnesses can be quite different from most people in the "normal" world in which we live. Given this reality, it becomes important for those interacting with us to know as much as possible about these differences.

> Those of us with mental illnesses can be quite different from most people in the "normal" world in which we live. Given this reality, it becomes important for those interacting with us to know as much as possible about these differences.

■ How Are We Different?

Before discussing differences between individuals with mental illnesses and those without such disorders, it is important to keep in mind the basic fact that people with mental illnesses are first of all people—people who think, care, love, desire, and aspire. However, the brains of persons with serious mental illnesses do not function like most other people's brains. To some extent, we are "wired differently." For this reason, when a police officer has an encounter with one of us, he or she should have an understanding of how we are different and how the officer can most effectively act so that the encounter is maximally satisfactory to the officer, to the person with the mental illness, and to society. All people are different, of course. Nevertheless, people living with mental illnesses can be very different from our more "normal" neighbors. We also can be very different from one another. We can differ in many ways, and we can differ in different ways at different times.

When a law enforcement officer encounters a person with a mental illness, ideally that officer should already know as much as possible about mental illnesses. Learning about mental illnesses in a classroom or from a book can be helpful, but first-hand, direct experience is particularly valuable when it comes to dealing with those of us with mental illnesses.

The more experience the officer has with people with mental illnesses in general, the better prepared he or she will be when answering a call involving one of us. Also, it is usually an advantage when the officer knows, and knows about, the specific person he or she is encountering. Ideally, the officer will have been able to develop a reasonably trusting relationship with the person over time. The opportunity for such experience and relationship building comes not just when responding to calls, but also from visiting community mental health centers, shelters, drop-in centers, and other facilities frequented by people with serious mental illnesses.

As the law enforcement professional is gaining such experience, it is wise to keep in mind some of the most important aspects of mental illnesses that make us different from others in the general population. Some of these aspects of our conditions—including delusions, hallucinations, heightened sensitivity, sensitivity to drugs, and cognitive difficulties—are discussed next.

Delusions

One way in which a person with mental illnesses experiences thinking that is different from others' thinking is in **delusions**. By definition, a delusion is a fixed, false or erroneous belief. The person who is experiencing a delusion, however, does not know that this belief is false. If the person understood that his or her belief was false, then obviously he or she would not continue to hold the belief. It therefore follows that the person experiencing a delusion does not, and cannot, know that his or her thinking is delusional. This circular logic is a "Catch-22" aspect of this symptom.

For this reason, people with mental illnesses who are encountered by police officers frequently do not and cannot understand or accept that they are affected by a mental illness. If the police officer asks about the presence of current or past mental illnesses, such a person will usually deny having a history. Indeed, the affected person may claim that another person nearby—perhaps a relative—is actually the one who is experiencing a mental illness. Sometimes this denial creates a difficult situation for the officer.

For instance, suppose a police officer encounters a person who happens to hold a delusional belief that the members of the "green gang" are conspiring against and threatening him. The person with this delusion may believe that "green gang" members can be identified by a green article of clothing or jewelry—perhaps socks, a necktie, or a gemstone in a ring. If the officer is not wearing anything green and does not happen to talk about anything green, on the surface, that person may appear fairly normal and controlled as the officer interacts with him. How should the officer act in such a situation?

In such a circumstance, it is best to remain as calm and respectful as possible. If more than one person is present at the scene, talk to others. In the event that two persons are present and both claim that the other party is affected by a mental illness, talk to each individual separately, if possible. Try to find out why one is saying that the other has an illness. Ask each if he or she knows whether the other person is seeing a psychiatrist or another type of mental health professional. The officer might also carefully ask if the person has ever been in a mental health facility and whether the person is taking—or has been prescribed—medication for a mental illness.

Also ask if the person has any strange or unusual beliefs. If the two people know each other well, one will usually know something about the delusional beliefs of the other. By obtaining information about a person's psychiatric treatment, medications, beliefs, and other history, an officer can usually determine which person is experiencing delusional thinking, even though the person with such experiences may not realize that he or she has a mental illness.

> "A person who is experiencing delusional thoughts cannot give up these thoughts easily, and may become quite disturbed and agitated when someone even suggests that his or her beliefs are not rational."

Once the officer has identified which person has the mental illness, how should the officer proceed? At one time, mental health workers were advised "not to buy into the person's delusional system." Too often, this advice was interpreted to mean that the person should be told that he or she was "not thinking right" or was "mentally ill," "crazy," or other comments to that effect. Unfortunately, a person who is experiencing delusional thoughts cannot give up these thoughts easily, and may become quite disturbed and agitated when someone even suggests that his or her beliefs are not rational.

So what does the officer do when the person states that members of the "green gang" are threatening and plan to kill him or her? Once again, it is strongly recommended that the officer not directly contradict the person with the mental illness. Do not attempt a "frontal assault" on the person with the delusion. That is, to use an old Marine Corps expression, do not try to go "hi diddle-diddle, right up the middle." Persons with delusions are frequently fearful. They are usually willing, and often eager, to share those fears with others who express a willingness to listen. At the same time, they are likely to become defensive if their beliefs are challenged. For this reason, if the person starts talking about what the "green gang" is up to, the officer should say something similar to "How very interesting—tell me more about the green gang and what they are doing."

By making a statement of this type, the officer is not specifically agreeing with the delusional person and is not saying that the green gang really exists. Rather, the officer is establishing himself or herself as a fellow human being who is willing to listen and one who is at least trying to understand what the person with the mental illness is experiencing.

Frequently, when a delusional person speaks, what is said may sound quite ridiculous. In fact, his or her statements may be so ridiculous that it is difficult for others to keep from laughing. Try to resist this tendency, as best as you can, when dealing with someone with a mental illness. Laughing is disrespectful, and it may escalate the situation or bring communication to an end. As is true for everyone else, persons affected by mental illnesses resent being belittled or being seen as the object of jokes or laughter.

By taking a maximally respectful posture, the officer can often defuse what might otherwise turn into a trying—and possibly even explosive—situation. By showing a willingness to listen and understand, the officer may come to be viewed as an ally by the person with a mental illness, who is then much more likely to cooperate with the officer's requests.

Many persons with mental illnesses who have delusions may live their entire lives without understanding or accepting that they experience delusions. However, during the past few decades—particularly with the advent of modern psychiatric medications—people with such illnesses have been increasingly recovering, at least for some periods of time. As we experience periods of recovery, many of us begin to understand that our minds fool us when we experience episodes of the mental illness. As persons with mental illness begin to have more experience with their conditions, they often can begin to understand that the delusions are not real, even though the beliefs may be just as compelling as when they first experienced them. Nevertheless, too many people with mental illnesses are forced by their own conditions to live their lives in constant denial of their disorders.

Hallucinations

In addition to having delusions, many persons in a state of psychosis experience **hallucinations**. Hallucinations occur when a person is sensing (hearing, seeing, feeling, tasting, or smelling) something that is not there—at least, not apparent to other people. The most common hallucination is hearing something that others do not hear, usually in the form of voices of known or unknown persons. These voices can be particularly problematic when they begin to demand that the person hearing these voices engage in particular behaviors. When such **command hallucinations** order a person to harm someone or engage in some other dangerous act, they can be the cause of seriously dangerous behavior. Fortunately, command hallucinations are fairly unusual. More frequently, the voices are not demanding. Sometimes they can be friendly and even comforting. Whatever form the voices may be taking, for the person who is hearing them, these voices are real.

For the first responder who encounters a person who is experiencing hallucinations, it is important to understand that even though the officer may not hear or see what the person is experiencing, for that person these "imaginary" voices or

> Persons with delusions are frequently fearful. They are usually willing, and often eager, to share those fears with others who express a willingness to listen. At the same time, they are likely to become defensive if their beliefs are challenged.

> By showing a willingness to listen and understand, the officer may come to be viewed as an ally by the person with a mental illness, who is then much more likely to cooperate with the officer's requests.

> For the first responder who encounters a person who is experiencing hallucinations, it is important to understand that even though the officer may not hear or see what the person is experiencing, for that person these "imaginary" voices or visions are real—they are not imagined, they are truly experienced.

visions are real—they are not imagined, they are truly experienced. The officer may want to ask about what the person is hearing or seeing; in doing so, remember to be respectful of what the person is experiencing.

Heightened Sensitivity

Persons with schizophrenia typically exhibit a heightened or "exquisite" sensitivity to stimuli in their environment. This tendency may manifest itself as the person being particularly easily startled by sudden noises, or being overly reactive to sudden changes in lighting or quick movements by persons or objects in his or her surroundings. For this reason, it is recommended that when an officer first encounters a person with a mental illness, the environment should be altered to reduce stimulation. For example, the loud nearby radio or television set may be politely turned down or off, and flashing lights and sirens likewise should be minimized.

Another important aspect of this heightened sensitivity relates to the concept of **expressed emotion**. Expressed emotion refers to excessive hostility and criticism that may be difficult for the person with a mental illness to handle. In other words, people with schizophrenia and related disorders may have a heightened sensitivity to these negative expressions of emotion, including statements of resentment or disapproval, or speaking with a critical tone, pitch, rhythm, or intensity. Persons with schizophrenia are particularly vulnerable to insults, innuendo, and disparaging remarks. When faced with these reactions, the person may appear to be deeply hurt, beyond the degree that might normally be expected. This reaction may even extend to the degree that the person becomes temporarily unable to respond to questions and comments in the usual manner. Hostile remarks, criticism, and other forms of expressed emotion may lead to inordinate stress and potentially worsen the symptoms of the illness.

Conversely, warmth, expressed in terms of positive comments and voice tone, appears to give the person some form of added protection from symptoms of the mental illness. An officer who takes care to avoid being overly critical, threatening, or demeaning will frequently find that such precautions can pay significant dividends.

Good Drugs and Bad Drugs

The discovery of antipsychotic medicines a half century ago dramatically improved the ability of people with mental illnesses to live and work in the community. It is estimated that more than 90% of those of us who were, or would have been, placed in psychiatric institutions 50 years ago are now out in the community, free to live our lives. Fifteen years ago, the effectiveness of these drugs improved substantively with the introduction of the **atypical antipsychotic medicines**. Currently, six of these "second-generation" antipsychotic medicines are available in the United States.

Regarding the value of these medications, I think of myself, in essence, as having a "broken brain." If my leg were broken, I might need a crutch to walk. As I see it, my broken brain also needs a crutch. Because the "break" in my brain is in the neurochemical system, I view the medications that I take as a sort of chemical crutch. With these medications, I can function fairly well most of the time. For police officers who may encounter people with mental illnesses, it is important that they have some familiarity with these medications.

While these prescribed antipsychotic medications act in such a way as to assist my brain to function, certain other chemicals could further impair my brain's functioning. Because of my condition, my brain is more vulnerable to the effects of such chemicals than are the brains of most people. The chemicals I am referring to are street drugs. Evidence continues to mount indicating that persons who are vulnerable to mental illnesses are made even more vulnerable when they take alcohol, barbiturates, cocaine, marijuana, methamphetamine, and similar psychoactive substances. Furthermore, persons with mental illnesses who use drugs are much more likely to engage in dangerous activities when they take these substances. It is obviously important for officers to recognize the heightened seriousness of the effects of street drugs for people with mental illnesses. In summary, ingesting these substances not only makes it increasingly likely that the person will become symptomatic, but these substances also heighten the likelihood that dangerous acts might occur.

Cognitive Difficulties

In recent years, researchers have discovered that although the "positive" symptoms of schizophrenia, including delusions and hallucinations, tend to be the more obvious symptoms of this disorder, persons with schizophrenia actually tend to be more impaired by difficulties in cognitive functioning. The National Institute of Mental Health and the Food and Drug Administration are now co-sponsoring a major scientific project called Measurement and Treatment Research to Improve Cognition in Schizophrenia (MATRICS) that is focusing on the development of new medications intended to enhance the cognitive functioning of persons with schizophrenia. For the past several years, I have had the privilege of being a member of the group that is working on this project. Through this project, researchers have identified seven specific dimensions of cognitive functions as being impaired in many persons with schizophrenia: attention/vigilance, reasoning and problem solving, social cognition, speed of processing, verbal learning, visual learning, and working memory.

The search for appropriate new medicines to treat these domains is currently underway, and we are hopeful that some will become available within the next few years. However, as we wait for the possible development of these new medicines, the cognitive impairments identified by the MATRICS project suggest some points to be kept in mind when interacting with people with major mental illnesses.

One strong message that has emerged from this research is that persons with mental illnesses often can be expected to process information slowly and to have difficulty remembering things. This includes understanding and remembering instructions given by a police officer. An implication of these findings is that police officers should not assume that the person with a mental illness has understood and remembered what has been said.

Another important finding is that impairment in social functioning is associated with major mental illnesses. Among other things, the person with a mental illness may not understand the social implications of what he or she is saying or doing. This person also may not understand or appreciate commonly accepted social signals of approval and disapproval that are readily understood by others. For example, facial expressions may be particularly difficult for a person with a mental illness to read.

These findings suggest that when law enforcement officers interact with an individual with a mental illness, they can expect better results if they slow things down, and in general exercise much more patience than they would when dealing with persons without such illnesses.

■ A Second Perspective on Dealing with a Person with Schizophrenia in Crisis

While attending college in the 1980s, the second author of this chapter, Milt Greek, developed paranoid schizophrenia. At first resistant and hostile to medical treatment, he recognized his need for medication in the Spring of 1987. Once stabilized, Milt was able to finish degrees in psychology and sociology. However, because his instability cast a shadow over his college performance, he was unable to find work until he retrained in computer programming.

In 1996, Milt began a relationship with his current wife. With her support and understanding, he has been able to understand the relations between the delusions he experienced and his actual reality. In addition to his everyday activities, Milt founded a schizophrenia peer-support group and volunteered to work with a couple of other people with schizophrenia in acute psychosis, to try to return the tremendous kindness and generosity of spirit that has made his new life possible. What follows are some of Milt's suggestions for law enforcement officers based on his experiences as another person who is in recovery from schizophrenia.

The hallmark of schizophrenia is a chemical imbalance in the brain that has an effect similar to that of secretly being given small amounts of lysergic acid diethylamide each day. Over a period of months and years, the person with this mental illness experiences increasing levels of hallucinations and delusions that are misunderstood as actual reality. Sometimes included in these experiences are intuitive and coincidental events that seem to support the possibility of a mystical and magical universe where anything is possible.

As schizophrenia progresses, the person may become concerned about horrendous events occurring, such as the end of the world (the rapture), or personal nightmares, such as death and being condemned to hell. These beliefs cause the person with schizophrenia to become deeply worried and sometimes agitated. Believing in a magical world, the person begins to look for magical means to solve both real and imaginary problems. These magical solutions are often minor rituals that go unnoticed. Sometimes, however, they involve wild behaviors that can result in a crisis.

When a person with schizophrenia experiences a crisis, one of the most important points to remember is that people with this illness act as emotional sponges. As a consequence, being calm will calm the person with schizophrenia. An example of this effect occurred when I saw a counselor talking to a patient with schizophrenia who was very angry. The patient was yelling at the counselor standing outside his house, telling the counselor to leave him alone. The counselor responded by casually folding his arms, leaning against the wall of the house, and looking away momentarily as if distracted or bored. The counselor then replied to the patient calmly and simply. Within a minute, the man with schizophrenia was leaning against the house, much calmer and cooler. He continued to calm down and eventually agreed to meet with the counselor again.

A second point to remember when dealing with people with serious mental illnesses who are in crisis is to never mention medication. That topic is best left to mental healthcare providers after the person has calmed down. In many situations, the crisis is actually an attempt by the person with the illness to magically solve a real or imagined dilemma; mentioning medication may appear to that person to be an attempt to thwart the magical solution. After all, if the person with schizophrenia can be convinced to give up the magical ritual because "such ideas are unrealistic," the possibility of a miraculous change for the better is lost.

A more involved way to work with a person with schizophrenia who is in crisis is to see the good seed in the problem. Because crises often follow from attempts to symbolically solve a problem, the person will see interference with extreme or magical solutions as a sign that the intervening person is responsible for worsening of the problem. For example, if a man with schizophrenia is causing a disruption by trying to enter a radio station and broadcast a warning in code that the end of the world is approaching, people who attempt to stop him will be viewed as wanting the world to end.

To counteract this possibility, the intervening law enforcement officer should recognize the perceived problem and express sympathy and a willingness to listen and help. Do not try to talk the person with psychosis out of the delusions or minimize either perceived or real problems. Instead, express concern for the well-being of the individual and the world. In the example of the person with schizophrenia at the radio station, first responders should attempt to establish a dialogue to understand what the man thinks is going on and what others are trying to do to him. Responders should engage the psychotic individual in a way that suggests that what he is saying may be plausible, explaining that they want the world to be okay and all of this information is new to them. Say things like "It must be very hard on you to be dealing with this all alone" and "This is new to me; it would help me if I could understand what you see going on." Remaining calm and attentive helps the person with schizophrenia feel safe and believe that the responders are allies. Despite the fact that they often do not trust those around them, people with schizophrenia are looking for others to be their allies and to share their understanding of the world.

If the responder understands the point of view of the person with schizophrenia, it is helpful to step inside the delusional framework of that person with "if" statements, such as "If what you say is true . . . ." For example, I once met with a patient in a crisis who told me that everyone was God except for him and that God wanted him to kill himself. The patient had cut himself slightly and was saying that he had to kill himself. I responded that if everyone was God, then I was part of God and I could tell him that God loved him and wanted him to live and be happy. After working with this man for about an hour or so, he calmed enough to agree to meet with mental health workers and consider going to a three-day inpatient facility. A few days later, he had a breakthrough in which he decided to reject his hallucinatory voices and commit to taking medication.

> If the responder understands the point of view of the person with schizophrenia, it is helpful to step inside the delusional framework of that person with "if" statements, such as "If what you say is true . . . ."

If a person with schizophrenia shows paranoia toward the intervening responder, such as being frightened or hostile toward a police officer, the best response is to deal with the problem on the individual level. Instead of saying that the person should trust police in general, respond with statements such as "I'm a good guy who wants to help." This reassurance, along with a calm demeanor and interest in what the person is saying, helps him or her feel safer.

Finally, it is important to be aware of the calm after the storm. Crises involving people with schizophrenia seem to be caused by a slow buildup of adrenalin-like chemicals prior to the crisis. This buildup is expended in the crisis, so that after the crisis has passed, the person is often more suggestible and willing to work with others. At that point, it may be helpful to have friends and family whom the person likes and trusts to visit the patient and express their concerns and hopefulness. This caring strategy may help the person with schizophrenia to become more cooperative with mental health workers.

Chapter Wrap-Up

Chapter Highlights

- In the era of globalization, Americans are increasingly confronted with messages imploring us to recognize our societal diversity. For people with mental illnesses, who are viewed as persons who are different, it becomes important for law enforcement personnel interacting with them to know as much as possible about these differences.

- It is recommended that the officer not attempt a "frontal assault" on a person who is experiencing delusions or hallucinations. Instead, take a maximally respectful posture. People with this illness act as emotional sponges. As a consequence, being calm will calm the person down. By showing a willingness to listen and understand, the officer may come to be viewed as an ally by the person with a mental illness, who is then much more likely to cooperate with the officer's requests.

- The discovery of antipsychotic medicines dramatically improved the ability of people with mental illnesses to live and work in the community. An estimated 90% of those persons who were, or would have been, placed in psychiatric institutions 50 years ago are now out in the community, free to live their lives.

- Persons who are vulnerable to mental illnesses are made even more vulnerable when they use alcohol, barbiturates, cocaine, marijuana, methamphetamine, and similar psychoactive substances. Persons with mental illnesses who use drugs are also much more likely to engage in dangerous activities when they take these substances.

- Persons with mental illnesses often can be expected to process information slowly and to have difficulty remembering things. Law enforcement officers, when interacting with an individual with a mental illness, can expect better results if they slow things down, and in general exercise much more patience than they would for persons without such illnesses.

Vital Vocabulary

atypical antipsychotic medicines: the newer type of medications used to treat psychosis

bipolar disorder: an illness characterized by abnormalities of mood along two extremes, depression and mania

command hallucinations: auditory hallucinations that instruct a person to do something

delusions: fixed, false beliefs

expressed emotion: excessive hostility and criticism that may be difficult for the person with a mental illness to handle

hallucination: perceptions that occur in the absence of an external stimulus, such as hearing a voice when no one is there (auditory hallucinations)

paranoid schizophrenia: a subtype of schizophrenia in which the individual often has false beliefs that he or she is being followed, watched, or maliciously pursued

psychosis: state of being out of touch with reality; the presence of hallucinations or delusions

schizoaffective disorder: an illness characterized by symptoms of depression or mania, along with symptoms of schizophrenia

Questions for Review and Discussion

1. How should a law enforcement officer approach an individual who appears to be expressing delusional beliefs?
2. What are the dangers that arise when law enforcement officers express hostile remarks, criticism, and other forms of expressed emotion toward people who have a psychotic disorder?
3. What would be the best response in a situation in which a person with schizophrenia demonstrates signs of paranoia toward the intervening responder?
4. Persons with mental illnesses often process information slowly and have difficulty remembering things. How do these tendencies affect the way in which law enforcement officers should interact with individuals with mental illnesses?

Resources

Brown GW, Rutter M. The measurement of family activities and relationships: A methodological study. *Human Relations* 1966;19:241–263.

Frese FJ. *Cruising the cosmos—part three*. Psychosis and hospitalization: A consumer's recollection. Surviving mental illness: stress, coping and adaptation. New York: Guilford Press, 1993.

Frese FJ. A calling. *Second Opinion* 1994;19(3):11–25.

Frese FJ. *Twelve aspects of coping for persons with serious and persistent mental illness. Psychological and social aspects of psychiatric disability.* Boston: Boston University Press, 1997.

Frese FJ. *Advocacy, recovery, and the challenges of consumerism for schizophrenia.* Psychiatric Clinics of North America. Philadelphia: W. B. Saunders, 1998.

Frese FJ. Psychology practitioners and schizophrenia. A view from both sides. *Journal of Clinical Psychology/In Session* 2000;56(11):1413–1426.

Frese FJ. *Inside "insight"—a personal perspective on insight in psychosis. Insight and psychosis* (2nd ed.). London: Oxford University Press, 2004.

Green MF, Nuechterlein KH, Gold JM, Barch D, Cohen J, Essock S, et al. Approaching a consensus cognitive battery for clinical trials in schizophrenia: The NIMH-MATRICS conference to select cognitive domains and test criteria. *Biological Psychiatry* 2004;56(5):301–307.

Lehman AF, Kreyenbuhl J, Buchanan RW, Dickerson FB, Dixon LB, Goldberg R, et al. The schizophrenia Patient Outcomes Research Team (PORT): Updated treatment recommendations 2003. *Schizophrenia Bulletin* 2004;30(2):193–217.

Marom S, Munitz H, Jones PB, Weizman A, Hermesh H. Familial expressed emotion: Outcome and course of Israeli patients with schizophrenia. *Schizophrenia Bulletin* 2002;28(4):731–743.

Swanson JW, Swartz MS, Essock SM, Osher FC, Wagner HR, Goodman LA, Rosenberg SD, Meador KG. The social–environmental context of violent behavior in persons treated for severe mental illness. *American Journal of Public Health* 2002;92(9):1523–1531.

Tengstrom A, Hodgins S, Kullgren G. Men with schizophrenia who behave violently: The usefulness of an early- versus late-start offender typology. *Schizophrenia Bulletin* 2001;27(2):205–218.

CHAPTER 18

Emergency Receiving Facilities and Other Emergency Resources

Case Vignette: David

Officers respond to the home of David, an 82-year-old man whose daughter called 9-1-1 because she was alarmed by his violent and aggressive behavior. The officers observe a trash can overflowing with liquor bottles in the garage as they approach the residence door. Upon entering the home, they find David running around the house and striking furniture with a baseball bat. He appears to be very confused. His home is in complete disarray, with broken furniture and glass scattered about, dishes piled up in the kitchen sink, and the water left running.

David's daughter tells the officers that she dropped by to check up on her father and found him in his current condition. She further states that he does not remember her visiting him the day before; when she asked him about this event, he became very agitated and claimed that he had not seen her in ages. The daughter has been concerned about her father due to a recent illness in which he had a fever. She also tells the officers that after the death of his wife, David was diagnosed with major depression and began drinking heavily, but that he had recently stopped this behavior. In addition, she reports that David has been really angry with her since she filed for legal guardianship of him and suggested that he might be better off in a nursing home.

David is cooperative when talking to the officers. When one of the officers asks his name, he responds, "David," even as he continues to swing the bat at a spot on the sofa, with no intention to hit anyone. The officer then asks him if he knows where he is, and David responds, "I'm chasing rats out of the submarine."

■ Introduction

Most law enforcement officers are familiar with having to decide whether to bring an individual with a mental illness to a receiving facility for an emergency psychiatric evaluation. While options for mental health evaluation vary considerably across jurisdictions, they share some similarities in terms of how best to negotiate the system. This chapter reviews types of **emergency receiving facilities**, alternative options for obtaining a mental health evaluation, issues that arise when law enforcement officers interact with mental health professionals, and ways that officers might best decide where to take individuals in need of a mental health assessment.

Before discussing issues regarding options for obtaining emergent evaluations, we must emphasize the need to establish communication between care providers and law enforcement officers. At a minimum, having a basic knowledge of each other's procedures can help avoid unnecessary frustration and improve safety for all concerned. Solid communication lines can also allow mental health providers to serve as bridges that link law enforcement officers with alternative mental health resources and advocacy groups. Establishing partnerships is vital to effectively providing people in need with appropriate services, and to making work experiences more gratifying for both law enforcement and mental health professionals.

Solid communication lines can also allow mental health providers to serve as bridges that link law enforcement officers with alternative mental health resources and advocacy groups. Establishing partnerships is vital to effectively providing people in need with appropriate services, and to making work experiences more gratifying for both law enforcement and mental health professionals.

■ Options to Obtain a Mental Health Assessment

Jurisdictions typically offer several options through which an emergency mental health assessment can be quickly obtained. These options are briefly described in this section. Individual cities or localities may also provide other ways in which officers might connect individuals who are experiencing signs and symptoms of mental illnesses with appropriate, timely evaluations and treatment; however, regional variations in funding, politics, and resources determine the availability of and access to these unique programs.

Emergency Receiving Facilities

It is of utmost importance for officers to know which types of healthcare facilities are found in their localities. In general, an officer may transport someone in need of a mental health evaluation to three types of facilities: a general hospital with a psychiatric emergency clinic, a general hospital without a psychiatric emergency clinic, and a mental healthcare facility that has no onsite medical backup. Because mental healthcare facilities are not equipped to manage medical emergencies, determination of medical stability becomes an important first step in deciding where to take a person in need of care.

When approaching a person with a possible mental illness such as David, it is important to quickly and accurately assess whether the person might have a medical condition that requires immediate medical attention. Officers trained as first responders recognize the importance of the initial assessment of an individual's medical stability, thereby ensuring that people who need it receive appropriate medical intervention. Even when a person has a mental illness, the individual's immediate, potentially life-threatening medical emergency—if present—takes precedence. When officers determine that emergency medical treatment is needed, it is recommended that they request an ambulance for immediate transfer to a general hospital, either with or without a psychiatric emergency clinic. If the degree of medical illness is uncertain, emergency medical service personnel can help determine whether an urgent medical need exists.

The importance of determining the need for emergency medical treatment cannot be overemphasized, because bringing such persons to mental health facilities instead of general

It is of utmost importance for officers to know which types of healthcare facilities are found in their localities. In general, an officer may transport someone in need of a mental health evaluation to three types of facilities: a general hospital with a psychiatric emergency clinic, a general hospital without a psychiatric emergency clinic, and a mental healthcare facility that has no onsite medical backup.

medical facilities could delay potentially life-saving treatment. Regardless of which type of facility to which the officer takes the person, he or she needs to follow safety procedures. Individuals with serious mental illnesses whose liberties are being restricted can sometimes become quite agitated and display aggressive behaviors just like anyone else, even if they initially appear calm.

Other Options

If the person is medically stable and the need for an emergency mental health evaluation is not clear, the officer may contact a **mobile crisis team** that is trained to assess the level of care the person might need. In less urgent situations, the officer may be able to facilitate the person in engaging with his or her current mental healthcare provider, after which the individual may not require transport to a receiving facility. Other options in such situations include having the person speak with a counselor from a mental health hotline or the local mental health treatment center. Given that resources may vary widely from one community to the next, every officer must know which resources are available in his or her area. When in doubt, officers should err on the side of safety and either transport the person to a healthcare facility or engage other emergency medical services.

> Given that resources may vary widely from one community to the next, every officer must know which resources are available in his or her area. When in doubt, officers should err on the side of safety and either transport the person to a healthcare facility or engage other emergency medical services.

In some situations, the officer may feel that he or she cannot transport the person against the individual's will, even though the person may be causing significant distress for family members or others in the area. In this scenario, the officer might discuss with the family the option of petitioning a probate court to obtain a court-ordered evaluation through which a mental health evaluation would be legally required. If one is available, a mobile crisis team might also come to the home should the situation fail to improve. The officer might even provide information on the **National Alliance on Mental Illness** so that the family can learn more about mental illnesses and obtain further support. Mental health staff at the local emergency receiving facility may be helpful in providing other referral information to caregivers and officers alike.

■ The Law Enforcement–Mental Health Interface

Differing goals between law enforcement officers and healthcare providers may cause friction during emergency mental health evaluations. While law enforcers are charged with maintaining community peace and control, healthcare providers aim to ensure the individual's safety and appropriate treatment. Often, these intentions conjoin; when they do not, the potential for strained communication and interactions arises.

This section describes strategies through which law enforcement officers and healthcare providers might interact in an effort to assist each other as well as the individual in crisis. As mentioned earlier, officers should have a basic knowledge of the procedures of receiving facilities in their area. This awareness lays the groundwork for a positive interaction with healthcare providers. Likewise, it is important for healthcare providers to be sensitive to the needs of officers.

One example of using communication to avoid misunderstandings is to have a **no-refusal drop-off policy**, in which all individuals brought by officers to emergency receiving facilities are unconditionally accepted for evaluation. Research suggests that a no-refusal policy both maximizes treatment efficiency and reduces potential conflict between law enforcement officers and healthcare providers. Another helpful approach is for emergency receiving facilities to highly prioritize acceptance and evaluation of individuals transported by police officers, so that emergency clinicians can quickly and safely deliver the person being transported into the care of mental health experts.

Another strategy that facilitates interactions between officers and healthcare providers focuses on information sharing. Obviously, the officer plays a vital role in conveying important information to care providers. In almost every case, the officer has access to critical information that can affect patient evaluation and treatment decisions. The officer needs to be aware that the person has the legal right to not allow care providers to contact family members or other providers. This issue becomes incredibly problematic when the person undergoing evaluation is too confused or paranoid to provide a relevant history. In such a case, the healthcare provider may find it difficult to make an accurate diagnosis, which could in turn affect treatment planning. Also, the care provider may be forced to order unnecessary and expensive tests to evaluate the person for a possible medical cause of the inappropriate behavior if he or she is unable to verify prior psychiatric history or recent events. Information that officers observe or learn in the field becomes crucial to care providers in such circumstances.

For example, if the person is extremely paranoid and psychotic, healthcare providers may find it problematic to determine whether the person is paranoid due to a medical condition, a psychiatric condition, or a substance use disorder. The officer on the scene may have access to valuable information that can legally be shared with the healthcare provider. Witnessing the presence of drug paraphernalia or seeing full bottles of unused antipsychotic medications around the individual may aid understanding and treatment of the person displaying paranoia.

Given that the patient may or may not give contact information to the healthcare provider, the officer may be the only source of personal information such as the person's address and phone number, as well as the names and phone numbers of family members, friends, the individual's therapist, a payee, or a legal guardian who may be identified at the emergency scene or during transport. Another basic piece of information that is helpful to care providers is the name and phone number of the officer who responded and/or transported the individual so that collateral information may be obtained at a later time if necessary.

Describing the circumstances in the community in which the person was found can greatly assist care providers. Where and with whom does the person live? Was the home in complete disarray with trash piled up? Was there hoarding of food, clothes, paper, or other items? Were the utilities turned off? Did the officer observe stove burners left turned on or water left running? Was there any food in the home? Were there any pill bottles and, if so, what did the labels say? Was there any evidence of alcohol or drug use? Was there evidence of physical injury to others or damage to property? Were there any weapons in the home? If there were weapons, were they removed? These essential details enable healthcare providers to accurately diagnose and treat people brought to emergency receiving facilities in addition to helping ensure public safety.

> Describing the circumstances in the community in which the person was found can greatly assist care providers.

Gathering information from individuals who are familiar with the person's recent behaviors is also important. Have they noticed any significant changes in the person's condition or behavior recently? How long has the person's behavior been different? Has he or she been in mental health treatment before? If so, when did he or she stop taking any prescribed medicine? Is the family able and willing to come to the healthcare facility with the person? When individuals are ill and out of touch with reality, healthcare providers must gather others' information rather than solely relying on self-reported information.

Information about how the person was secured and any incidents that occurred during transport is also useful to clinicians. Did the person put up much resistance to coming in for evaluation? Were extra officers needed to control the person? Was the person thoroughly searched prior to transport? Were any weapons or drug paraphernalia found? Did the person try to kick out the windows of the patrol car? By describing the scene and conveying history from informants, the law enforcement officer serves as a vital link in the healthcare process when information could have life-saving implications.

Healthcare providers recognize that officers may become frustrated with this one-way flow of information to the care provider, because the officer might feel that information about the person's mental health history might be interesting or help the officer better manage future interactions with the individual. Unless the patient signs a release of information to allow transfer of information to the officer, however, federal and state laws expressly forbid care providers from sharing personal health information with others. Protecting patients' privacy is very important in most healthcare settings, but especially in mental health situations in which patients are subject to stigma or judgment. Exceptions to this protection of personal health information include situations in which a person has threatened to kill someone, or when the person is unable to give consent and the information could prove vital to his or her safety. These laws vary by state, so it is important for officers to become familiar with their state's privacy laws.

Yet another strategy for assisting law enforcement officials and emergency healthcare providers to work as partners centers on appreciating the impact that a person in uniform has on individuals in the community. Generally speaking, when people with mental illnesses are dealing with uniformed officers, they tend to contain their aggressive impulses. This is true not only because officers may be trained in ways to manage and contain aggressive behavior, but also because the very presence of an officer in uniform can have a calming effect on someone in crisis. Although they may sometimes provoke fear and defensiveness in individuals with paranoia, police uniforms have been credited with inducing feelings of safety, increasing people's cooperativeness with officers' requests, and limiting illegal behavior. Both on the scene and in the emergency department, the presence of a uniformed officer creates a sense of greater safety for all concerned.

Law enforcement officers are often able to gain a person's cooperation with simple requests and—in some cases—the mere presence of a uniformed officer deters violent, aggressive, threatening, or deviant behaviors. Consequently, the officer's role as an authority figure is another important way through which law enforcement officers may assist care providers. Officers who bring in a person who has displayed aggressive or threatening behavior at the emergency scene or during transport can assist healthcare providers by staying with the person until he or she can be appropriately managed by staff at an emergency receiving facility.

■ Management of Agitation in the Emergency Department

The goal for both law enforcement officers and healthcare personnel should be to secure potentially violent situations with calm, therapeutic means. Nevertheless, if a person interacting with law enforcement officers in the community or at the emergency receiving facility becomes agitated and violent, the strategies used to maintain safety differ between law enforcement officers and healthcare providers. Many containment measures used by officers in routine police work are expressly forbidden by healthcare regulations. In addition, using force within an emergency health facility may scare other patients and undermine the therapeutic alliance care providers aim to forge with patients.

As mentioned earlier, an officer's presence often facilitates containment of aggressive behavior. Yet, once the person is in the hospital or healthcare facility, medical personnel must assume the lead in the care and treatment of the patient, including the management of agitation. Clear agreements between healthcare providers and officers when dealing with violent behavior in the healthcare facility are best made before a crisis situation occurs, rather than in the middle of an acute crisis. The following sections detail several issues about which emergency healthcare providers and law enforcement officers need to make proactive decisions.

Weapons in Secure Areas

Most mental health facilities do not allow officers to carry weapons in secure areas where patients are being evaluated and treated. Given the mayhem that may occur on an acute psychiatric unit because of limited insight into patients, possible involuntary treatment, and psychotic symptoms, it is safer for all concerned if weapons are not allowed in these areas. Mental health facilities have different rules regarding how weapons are to be handled, but a lockbox is one common means of securing weapons. Becoming aware of an emergency receiving facility's policies on weapons may prevent potentially dangerous situations from occurring.

Arrests in the Emergency Department

On occasion, after arriving at the treatment facility, an individual "acts out," or communicates feelings through aggressive behaviors, such as attacking staff or other patients, or destroying hospital property. In these cases, every effort needs to be made to ensure the safety of the aggressive individual, other patients, and staff. Strategies involving verbal de-escalation techniques typically assuage these kinds of situations. When such tactics do not work, more overtly forceful actions may be required. For example, a team of staff members may need to confront the aggressive individual together as a "show of force" to demonstrate their authority. Sedatives or antipsychotic medications may also need to be administered involuntarily to treat acute aggression that could pose a danger to the patient or to others.

Mental health providers often prefer not to bring charges against individuals who act inappropriately in emergency receiving facilities. If someone must be arrested as a consequence of "acting out" in a healthcare facility due to reasons unrelated to his or her mental illness, however, the mental health provider should make any necessary treatment recommendations at the time of arrest.

Case Vignette: Kathy

Officers are called to the apartment of Kathy, a 23-year-old woman who called 9-1-1 because she has suicidal thoughts. When the officers arrive, Kathy is tearful, saying that she cannot go on without her boyfriend. She says her boyfriend of two months broke up with her that day because she was "depressed all of the time" and because she relapsed on cocaine the day before. Although Kathy says that she cut her wrist, there is no evidence of injury beyond a faint red mark on her left wrist. Kathy reports that she is thinking of overdosing on two over-the-counter cold medicines, an act that she believes will make her "go to sleep and never wake up."

According to Kathy, she is in treatment with an outpatient therapist at a local mental health center, but missed her last two scheduled appointments. She had been attending Narcotics Anonymous meetings and says that she had a sponsor, but stopped attending when she became involved with her boyfriend. She says that the boyfriend told her that she didn't need counseling or meetings. Kathy reports a history of making multiple suicide attempts that have not required medical attention.

■ Determining How Best to Obtain a Mental Health Assessment

Various ways of obtaining mental health screenings or assessments were discussed earlier in this chapter, including bringing the person to an emergency receiving facility, contacting a mobile crisis team, or having the person speak with a mental health clinician via telephone. This section includes suggestions about how a law enforcement officer might best decide which option to use. In most states, individuals can be involuntarily detained for a psychiatric assessment based on suicidality, dangerousness to others, or inability to care for themselves. Problems that can lead to severely impaired self-care include confusion, disorganization, disorientation, memory impairment, agitation, destruction of property, and not eating or drinking.

Dangerousness to Self or Others

Individuals who report thoughts of harming themselves or others must be evaluated by a mental health provider. A law enforcement officer must decide whether the person needs to be transported immediately to an emergency receiving facility or whether an assessment can occur at the scene. While different jurisdictions will have rules that dictate how officers manage these situations, there are some guidelines that an officer can use to assist with decision making within the framework of local rules. For example, does the person have a plan to harm himself or herself, or to hurt someone else? Is the person intent on carrying out the plan? Does the person have the means or ability to carry out the plan? Is the person receiving mental health treatment?

Table 18.1 provides some example situations and identifies how an officer can approach individuals who are voicing suicidal or homicidal thoughts. Of course, any local jurisdictional rules for managing these situations override these generalized suggestions.

Inability to Care for Oneself

The criteria used to define inability to care for oneself can be quite nonspecific. Included in these criteria are considerations of the person's current level of functioning and the risk of rapid medical or psychiatric decline. Level of functioning is considered in this section.

The essential question in assessing the level of functioning is this: Can this person function safely in society? Is the person so agitated or paranoid that he or she could easily end up in an altercation? Is the person beginning to act on delusions or respond to hallucinations? Is the person's behavior destructive (e.g., breaking out windows) or bizarre (e.g., putting clothes on the bushes because God said to do so)? Is the person too impaired to find his or her way home? Is the person unable to manage basic activities of daily living, such as eating, walking, bathing, dressing, grooming, and toilet use? For a person living alone, is he or she able to perform "instrumental activities of daily living," such as the ability to manage housekeeping, meal preparation, obtaining food, taking medication, and monetary budgeting? If not, does the person have assistance to manage the basic or instrumental activities of daily living?

Table 18.2 details examples of the inability to care for oneself and suggests potential management options.

Table 18.1 Management of the Suicidal or Homicidal Individual	
Situation	**Management**
Thoughts, plan, means, and intent	Bring to emergency receiving facility
Thoughts, no plan or intent, but appears anxious, emotionally or physically agitated, very impulsive	
Thoughts with plan and intent, but no means to carry plan out	Consider mobile crisis or telephone assessment
Thoughts without plan or intent	
Low-lethality suicide attempt not requiring emergency medical treatment	

Table 18.2	Assessment of the Individual Who May Be Unable to Provide Self-Care

Examples	Management
Severe Impairment Significant property destruction Very poor hygiene Incoherent speech Not eating or drinking	Bring to emergency receiving facility
Moderate Impairment Left stove burners turned on Tangential thoughts Not eating, with a normal weight Acting on hallucinations and delusions, but not in a potentially dangerous manner	Consider mobile crisis or telephone assessment
Mild Impairment Mild depressive symptoms with no suicidal thoughts Delusions and hallucinations but not acting on them, and currently engaged in mental health treatment	Suggest an outpatient mental health evaluation in the community

■ Challenges and Frustrations

Law enforcement officers can at times become frustrated when individuals are back out on the streets not long after the officers brought them to the emergency receiving facility. An emergency mental health assessment that determines whether an individual meets the criteria for hospitalization can differ from the assessment of what an individual needs while in the community. An officer's expectation that a person should be admitted to the hospital because of observed behavior outside an emergency receiving facility may prove unrealistic because of local mental health statutes that limit how long someone can be committed against his or her will for treatment. In such cases, the frustrated officers may conclude that they would be better off arresting a person instead of taking him or her to a healthcare facility for mental health treatment.

Having knowledge of local statutory limitations and treatment options can help reduce such frustrations. More assertive **community treatment**, social work interventions, use of **long-acting psychiatric medications**, outpatient commitment, referral to a **partial hospitalization program**, or even the appointment of a legal guardian may be appropriate in certain cases in which individuals frequently exhibit behavioral problems that arise from a mental illness. A law enforcement officer can be assured that mental health providers share their frustration toward individuals who cycle in and out of mental health services because treatment is declined or resources are not sufficient to meet their needs. It is important to recognize that care providers and officers have similar goals—namely, to stabilize the person who is suffering from an untreated mental illness so that he or she can enjoy life and function within and contribute to society.

■ Conclusion

Clearly, law enforcement officers need strategies to help them properly determine when individuals who are exhibiting signs or symptoms of mental illnesses in the community should preferentially be diverted away from the criminal justice system and into the mental healthcare system. Several concerns are paramount when making this decision: ensuring overall public safety, assessing medical stability prior to transport, understanding local mental health laws and systems, and attempting to share information with healthcare providers. While local availability and rules frame the work of emergency receiving healthcare facilities, positive interactions between law enforcement/criminal justice professionals and healthcare providers are critical for integrating officers' and care providers' priorities.

Consistent communication between providers and law enforcement officers represents a useful tool that can reduce frustration and provide officers with information about community-based options to assist persons in need. Chapter 19 reviews in greater detail those community-based resources that an officer can access as alternatives to escorting someone to an emergency receiving healthcare facility.

Chapter Wrap-Up

- Establishing partnerships is vital to effectively provide the appropriate services to people in need, and to make work experiences more gratifying for both law enforcement and mental health professionals.

- When in doubt, officers should err on the side of safety; that is, they should either transport the person to a healthcare facility or engage other emergency medical services.

- Details concerning an individual's living situation, primary supports, and behaviors in the community are extremely important for healthcare providers so that they can accurately diagnose and treat people brought to emergency receiving facilities while ensuring public safety.

- Officers who bring in a person who has displayed aggressive or threatening behavior at the emergency scene or during transport can assist healthcare providers by staying with the person until he or she can be appropriately managed by staff at an emergency receiving facility.

- When a person with a mental illness who is acting out in the community is brought to a hospital or healthcare facility, medical personnel assume the lead in the care and treatment of the patient, including the management of agitation.

- Individuals who are suicidal, homicidal, or gravely disabled and in danger of not being able to fend for themselves may be taken involuntarily to an emergency receiving facility for a psychiatric evaluation in some jurisdictions. Laws governing this option vary between states.

- Healthcare providers and the officers have similar goals—namely, to stabilize a person who is suffering from an untreated mental illness so that he or she can enjoy life and function within and contribute to society. Hospitalization may be one way in through which these goals are pursued. More intense community care, outpatient treatment commitments, appointment of a legal guardian, and even partial hospitalization programs may be effective alternatives to inpatient hospitalization in working toward such goals.

Vital Vocabulary

community treatment: treatment of mental illness in a community outpatient setting

emergency receiving facility: a psychiatric emergency clinic that may receive referrals from public safety personnel

long-acting psychiatric medications: medication for mental illness that continue to work over the course of two to four weeks

mobile crisis team: a specialized mental health response team—often including a psychiatric social worker or psychiatric nurse—that serves as a "psychiatric ambulance" to go to the site of a crisis and assess the level of care the person might need

National Alliance on Mental Illness (NAMI): the nation's largest grassroots mental health organization dedicated to improving the lives of persons living with serious mental illness and their families through advocacy, research, support, and education. There are NAMI organizations in every state and in over 1,100 local communities across the country

no-refusal drop-off policy: a policy under which all individuals brought by officers to emergency receiving facilities are unconditionally accepted for evaluation

partial hospitalization program: a treatment setting that serves as a step-down from inpatient care or an intensive program to prevent traditional hospitalization

Questions for Review and Discussion

1. Explain why establishing communication between healthcare providers and law enforcement officers in emergency receiving facilities is important.
2. What role does the mobile crisis team play in the community?
3. Which differing goals between law enforcement officers and healthcare providers may cause friction during emergency mental health evaluations?
4. Which criteria allow an individual to be involuntarily detained for a psychiatric assessment in most states?

Resources

Johnson RR. The psychological influence of the police uniform. *FBI Bull* 2000;70:27–32.

Massaro J. *Overview of the mental health service system for criminal justice professionals.* Delmar, NY: GAINS Technical Assistance and Policy Analysis Center for Jail Diversion, 2005.

Price M. Commentary: The challenge of training police officers. *J Am Psychiatr Law* 2005;33:50–54.

Redondo RM, Currier GW. Characteristics of patients referred by police to a psychiatric emergency service. *Psychiatr Serv* 2003;54:804–806.

Reuland M. *A guide to implementing police-based diversion programs for people with mental illness.* Delmar, NY: Technical Assistance and Policy Analysis Center for Jail Diversion, 2004.

Reuland M, Cheney J. *Enhancing success of police-based diversion programs for people with mental illness.* Delmar, NY: GAINS Technical Assistance and Policy Analysis Center for Jail Diversion, 2005.

Steadman HJ, Stainbrook KA, Griffin P, Draine J, Dupont R, Horey C. A specialized crisis response site as a core element of police-based diversion programs. *Psychiatr Serv* 2001;52:291–222.

Strauss G, Glenn M, Reddi P, Afaq I, Podolskaya A, Rybakova T, et al. Psychiatric disposition of patients brought in by crisis intervention team police officers. *Com Mental Health J* 2005;54:804–806.

Acknowledgements and Disclosures

Barbara D'Orio has received research grant support from the Emory Medical Care Foundation and the American Foundation for Suicide Prevention. Denise Garrett has received grant support from the Office of Homeland Security.

Mental Health Resources and Levels of Care

CHAPTER

Case Vignette: Eugene and His Family

A family from New Orleans, Louisiana, was living in an extended-stay hotel in a neighboring state in the aftermath of 2005's Hurricane Katrina. The group occupied several rooms in the hotel, and three adult brothers in the family were looking for work. Their mother had significant medical problems, was using a wheelchair, and required supplemental oxygen. Her 30-year-old son, Eugene, had a previous history of a serious mental illness and had been without medication since the storm evacuation one month earlier. Although he had experienced a long period of stability while in New Orleans, Eugene's condition seemed now to be worsening—he had not eaten for several days and was sleeping throughout much of the day. He also appeared to be hearing voices. He had also been taking Tylenol because he was complaining of a headache, but his mother stopped him from consuming this medication because she was unsure how much he had actually taken in the past few days.

Eugene's mother was unsure who to contact for help, so she called 9-1-1. She was connected to the local crisis and access hotline. A mobile crisis team met Eugene at the hotel. After a face-to-face assessment, the team transported Eugene voluntarily to the local psychiatric emergency room for a more thorough medical and psychiatric evaluation. After any urgent medical problems were ruled out, Eugene was evaluated in a 23-hour temporary observation unit and then spent five days and nights in a crisis stabilization unit. At that point, he was referred to outpatient services and resumed taking his medications. His mother and brother were referred to the National Alliance on Mental Illness (NAMI) for family support and education.

■ Introduction

When Hurricane Katrina struck the Louisiana and Mississippi coastlines in August 2005, it displaced hundreds of thousands of people. Evacuees were dispersed across the United States, though most evacuees were housed initially in shelters, hotels, and private homes in Texas. All of these displaced survivors had many issues to address, including housing, medical needs, and employment. For those with severe mental illnesses or addictions, the situation was complicated further by the need to learn about local behavioral healthcare providers and to connect with services in a new community. Many other individuals who had no prior history of mental health treatment experienced the onset of new symptoms, such as those of post-traumatic stress disorder, and had to access treatment for the first time.

> Knowing the right program for one's particular mental health treatment needs and accessing services successfully can be quite challenging.

Unfortunately, in many areas of the country, it is difficult for local residents—much less displaced evacuees—to understand the local mental health and substance abuse treatment delivery system. Knowing the right program for one's particular mental health needs and accessing services successfully can be quite challenging. The 2003 President's New Freedom Commission on Mental Health reported that the fragmented mental health service delivery system, the stigma attached to mental illnesses, and a lack of culturally competent care are all important factors that keep many people who need mental health treatment from receiving it. Many people with serious mental illnesses feel as though they cannot enjoy life as much as others can and do not believe that mental health care can increase their quality of living. Consequently, some people who might greatly benefit from appropriate mental health services wait until they are in crisis before accessing help, if they seek help at all. Knowledge of the mental health system and ways to access services can be a powerful tool for law enforcement officers and other first responders in supporting timely and appropriate access to mental health services and ultimately the recovery of people with mental illnesses.

A psychiatric crisis frequently can become an opportunity for a person to seek out appropriate and helpful interventions that then lead to recovery. How can an officer provide the advocacy and support that will enable a person to receive help and to navigate the maze of disconnected services that often confronts the individual with a mental illness during a crisis? This chapter describes national-level resources available from the federal government's Substance Abuse and Mental Health Services Administration (SAMHSA) and the Center for Mental Health Services that can assist in mental illness recovery. It also highlights the need for law enforcement officers to make a personal connection to their local crisis and service systems. Finally, it provides a model for understanding the various types of service programs by examining the six levels of care that are common in mental health treatment settings.

■ National-Level Resources

More than 40 years ago, the federal government established funding for a system of community mental health centers across the United States. Although funding streams have changed, many of these mental health programs have been kept alive through a combination of state, county, and local funding. The original federal community mental health center initiative did not evolve as planned, and responsibility for community mental health services now falls on local—rather than federal—authorities. As a consequence, access to services is determined at a local level, and much variation is evident across localities. Because no unified national crisis/access number for mental health and addictive disease services exists, efforts to assist people with these illnesses remain uncoordinated and unmonitored in local jurisdictions. At no point was this fragmentation more apparent than during the aftermath of Hurricane Katrina, which displaced thousands of people from their homes and created severe stressors that often required assistance from mental health professionals.

Although few federally coordinated mental health services exist, the Center for Mental Health Services, which is part of SAMHSA, sponsors the **National Suicide Prevention Lifeline network** of 120 crisis call centers in almost all 50 states. Calls to the toll-free number 1-800-273-TALK are answered by the crisis call center that is geographically closest to the caller. Trained call operators assess the caller for his or her level of need and degree of risk, and provide crisis intervention. When necessary, Lifeline operators enact rescue protocols to dispatch emergency personnel to help callers. These call center operators have expertise in local community mental health resources and know how to best access local programs. The 1-800-273-TALK service operated as a focal point for disaster assistance and crisis outreach following Hurricane Katrina.

SAMHSA also offers information about local mental health and addiction programs through the **National Mental Health Information Clearinghouse** (1-800-789-2647) and the National Clearinghouse on Alcohol and Drug Information. This toll-free service provides prompts to guide callers to local mental health and addictive disease services, and will assist callers in obtaining written materials for follow-up care. Similar tools are also available online through the www.samhsa.gov website and represent important resources for law enforcement officers as well as people with mental illnesses and their friends and family. Click the state or U.S. territory on the website's map or select it from the drop-down menu to find information about local services as well as individualized statistics on mental illnesses and information about suicide prevention programs in any given locality.

In addition to government agencies such as SAMHSA, a discussion of national mental health resources would be incomplete without referencing key **advocacy groups**, especially NAMI and the National Mental Health Association (NMHA). NAMI is a grassroots advocacy organization founded in 1979 that is committed to improving the quality of life for persons with severe mental illnesses. Family members, friends, and others affiliated with NAMI provide the leadership that supports many crisis intervention team (CIT) training programs, which offer certification courses for law enforcement officers in a number of communities. NAMI operates a variety of support and education programs in more than 1,000 local communities and all 50 states. Local NAMI educational programs promote public awareness of mental health issues, and the alliance frequently sponsors ongoing peer education, support groups, and other mental health advocacy initiatives.

NMHA was founded in 1909 by a man with a mental illness, Clifford Beers. The injustices that Beers witnessed during his own psychiatric hospitalizations led to a reform movement that now boasts 340 affiliates across the United States. To symbolize its mission to end the stigma attached to those individuals with mental illnesses, in the 1950s, NMHA collected shackles from mental institutions and melted them down into a mental health "Liberty Bell." Like NAMI, NMHA is dedicated to advocacy, education, and research that promotes mental health. Local affiliates of this national organization sponsor National Depression Screening Day each October as well as other innovative mental health programs specific to local needs.

> Calls to the National Suicide Prevention Lifeline network of 114 crisis call centers in 45 states (1-800-273-TALK) are answered by the crisis call center that is geographically closest to the caller.

> ## Case Vignette: Roshanda and Her Family
>
> *Roshanda initially called the local United Way social services information line and was then transferred to a local crisis call center. During her call, she asked about "a place where I can drop off my kids so I can kill myself." She refused to provide her name or address, and stated that she did not want to be visited by a mobile crisis team or a CIT officer. The crisis call center staff traced Roshanda's phone number and determined that she was using a cell phone.*
>
> *The clinician at the crisis call center was able to engage Roshanda in a dialogue about the stress of raising three young children with little emotional support from her family. Roshanda did not feel understood by her mother or her husband, but she did not want to burden anyone else with her problems. She was separated from her husband and did not have enough money or resources to raise her children alone. Additionally, she was recovering from addiction and was fearful that she might relapse given her current stressors. Roshanda shared with the clinician her feeling that her children would be better off if she were "gone," but she wanted to ensure that they would be safe before she ended her life. She denied having a specific plan for suicide.*
>
> *The clinician spoke at length with Roshanda, attempting to gain her confidence and trust. The two discussed her family and her future, focusing on her children and the need for her presence in their lives. Roshanda eventually agreed to allow the mobile crisis team to visit her for an evaluation. At that time, she agreed to an urgent appointment to be evaluated by a psychiatrist at the local community mental health center, and a walk-in appointment was arranged. The mobile crisis team transported Roshanda to the center, and she agreed to begin a 12-step program that night and follow up in an outpatient mental health program to help her to maintain abstinence from drugs. She thanked the crisis worker for the support and care she received that ended up saving her life.*

■ Local Crisis and Access Service Systems

According to the website of the National Association of State Mental Health Program Directors, the 50 U.S. states annually spend $23 billion on public mental health programs that serve 6.1 million people. Each state organizes and delivers its mental health services in a unique way based on the mandates of that state's mental health authority. For individuals without private insurance, states provide funding for community-based outpatient programs and inpatient psychiatric units. These programs deliver varying levels of care depending on the particular needs of the individual, ranging from the most intensive options (e.g., a locked inpatient psychiatric unit) to the least intensive services (e.g., relapse-prevention support groups). States also must have systems for serving individuals in crisis and helping them access appropriate services after the crisis resolves. These crisis service systems of care are individualized to meet the needs of the particular area, so they may be organized quite differently depending on factors such as whether the services are provided in rural or urban settings. Despite their differences, all of these crisis services are key access points to mental health and addictive disease programs.

An example of a local crisis service system of care is the Crisis Center in Memphis, Tennessee, which operates local hotlines. A goal of this center is to provide the most efficient mental health care in the least restrictive way. When someone in crisis first calls a local hotline, an individualized plan of action can be developed—whether it takes the form of an outpatient appointment with a local community mental health center or a visit by a psychiatric mobile crisis team. This system avoids unnecessary trips to emergency rooms or visits by law enforcement professionals, so that these important resources are reserved for persons with more acute needs. A crisis hotline call also enables individuals to initiate their own care plans, rather than relying on authorities to intervene. This self-report option may be an important factor in engaging people in their own recoveries.

In Georgia, Behavioral Health Link operates a program called the Georgia Crisis & Access Line (GCAL) that incorporates crisis and access services with a mobile crisis response. Professional staff members (including licensed clinical social workers, licensed professional counselors, and registered nurses) provide around-the-clock coverage for callers with routine, urgent, or emergency needs. Callers are paired with the most appropriate service for them. In Atlanta, a caller with more serious needs is visited in their home by a psychiatric mobile crisis team (or on the street if homeless). BHL distributes thousands of wallet cards to law enforcement highlighting the key services of this Single Point of Contact system, the 24/7 toll-free number at 1-800-715-GCAL and the service information website at mygcal.com.

In Durham, North Carolina, the community was concerned about over-utilization of its inpatient state hospital facilities. To deal with this issue, it developed a comprehensive crisis response system to attempt to divert care to less-restrictive, outpatient settings. Durham Center Access provides screening and evaluation as well as crisis service programs including crisis stabilization, detoxification, and crisis residential programs. This assessment and evaluation unit has recliners that a person can stay in under observation for as long as 23 hours. Instead of going to the local emergency room at the hospital, law enforcement officers transport individuals to this access center for initial evaluation.

While these three areas have crisis service systems of care that are designed differently, the core elements are the same. Such programs are essential resources for an officer who is engaging people who are in crisis. As stated earlier, the vast majority of states have crisis call centers that participate in the National Suicide Prevention Lifeline network. An important step in learning about resources in one's local area is to call the National Suicide Prevention Lifeline at 1-800-273-TALK to determine which crisis call centers serve that locality. Although officers frequently transport individuals to local emergency receiving facilities for emergency psychiatric evaluations, sometimes a person in crisis may not meet the criteria for involuntary commitment, yet still need mental health care. Such people may benefit from other referrals that a local crisis call center or mobile crisis response team can readily provide.

> While these three areas have crisis service systems of care that are designed differently, the core elements are the same. Such programs are essential resources for an officer who is engaging people who are in crisis.

Law enforcement officers who serve rural communities often face greater challenges when dealing with individuals with mental illnesses compared to their counterparts who work in metropolitan areas, due to insufficient local resources in the rural localities. Mental health services have endured frequent cutbacks and closures that tend to limit the availability of services, especially in rural settings. Officers who operate in rural communities should work with local mental health professionals to learn about available resources for people with mental illnesses in need of crisis services.

■ Levels of Care

When a person accesses the mental health and substance abuse system in a given locality, whether during a crisis situation or for non-emergency routine needs, he or she will be served by a local agency. Regardless of how state and local services are organized, any service delivery system offers the same basic service levels. It is helpful for law enforcement officers to understand these levels of care. In particular, while officers often interact with people in a psychiatric crisis, the majority of people with serious mental illnesses who are pursuing recovery are doing so through ongoing outpatient "community" services.

The American Association of Community Psychiatrists developed a tool in the 1990s for determining the best level of service for an individual with a mental illness based on his or her needs at a particular time. Mental health professionals use this rating system, which is called the **Level of Care Utilization System** (LOCUS), to make recommendations about the intensity of care most appropriate for consumers (i.e., mental health patients). To determine the appropriate level of care, clinicians must consider co-occurring disorders such as substance addictions, mental retardation, or significant medical complications; stressors and supports in the recovery environment; the patient's past experiences with and success using various treatment interventions; and the ability and willingness of the individual to engage in recovery. Mental health treatment settings can be classified into six LOCUS subtypes (**Table 19.1**), which are discussed below.

Secure Residential Inpatient Care

Secure residential inpatient care is the highest level of intensity of service identified by LOCUS. If an individual poses a danger to himself or herself or to others as a result of a mental illness and its acute symptoms, this may be the appropriate service level. Some patients may be admitted to this level of care involuntarily, based on the state's involuntary commitment criteria. In this treatment setting, such as a hospital psychiatric unit, medical and social services are available around the clock.

Nonsecure Residential Treatment

The second highest level of intensity of service, nonsecure residential treatment, includes active services delivered seven days per week. Nursing services, activity monitoring, and medication administration are available as needed. Crisis group homes and residential rehabilitation programs fall into this service category. Individuals participate in these programs voluntarily.

Intensively Managed Nonresidential Service

Intensively managed nonresidential service is the next most intensive level of service. These services are generally available at least five days per week with three to eight hours of programming, but the participating consumer does not stay overnight in the program. Partial hospitalization, day treatment programs, and Assertive Community Treatment teams are services that would fit this description.

Intensive Outpatient Care

The next level of service intensity, intensive outpatient care, provides services for a minimum of three days per week with two to three hours of service per day. For example, many community mental health centers offer substance abuse intensive outpatient services that are available during the evening for individuals who are employed during regular business hours. People treated in this level of service are typically assessed by a physician about every two weeks, or more often as required.

Table 19.1   Levels of Care in Mental Health Treatment Settings

Most Intensive
    Secure residential inpatient
    Nonsecure residential
    Intensively managed nonresidential
    Intensive outpatient
    Outpatient services
    Recovery maintenance and health management
Least Intensive

Outpatient Care

Outpatient care is the next level of service. In this level of treatment, consumers meet with a counselor, social worker, psychiatric nurse, or other mental health professional roughly every two weeks. Consumers in outpatient mental health service programs usually see a physician (psychiatrist) approximately every two to three months.

Recovery Maintenance and Health Management Services

Recovery maintenance and health management services are the least intense services described in LOCUS. Mental health clinicians and advocates desire for consumers to reach this level of care, as progression to this stage signals that consumers have worked hard to recover from the mental illness. In these settings, consumers focus on aftercare or support groups, and they may visit the agency one or fewer times per month. They may see a physician every three months or less for a check-up, but the focus is on sustaining the recovery that already has been achieved.

The LOCUS description of mental health service intensity helps remind consumers and mental health professionals alike that recovery from mental illnesses occurs in stages and is a lifelong process. While the goal of treatment is to provide appropriate care in the least restrictive environment, individuals with severe and persistent mental illnesses may need more or less intensive services at different times. And unlike a bacterial infection that can be cured with a single course of antibiotics, mental illnesses may require lengthy treatment with continued relapse-prevention strategies once symptoms are controlled.

Chapter Wrap-Up

- In many areas of the United States, it is difficult for healthy citizens—much less those with serious mental illnesses—to understand the local mental health and substance abuse treatment delivery system. Identifying the right program for one's particular mental health treatment needs and accessing services successfully can prove quite challenging. Knowledge of the mental health system and strategies to access those services can be a powerful tool that law enforcement officers can use to support the recovery of people with mental illnesses.

- The federal Center for Mental Health Services sponsors a National Suicide Prevention Lifeline network of 120 crisis call centers in almost all 50 states. Calls to 1-800-273-TALK are answered by the crisis call center that is geographically closest to the caller. Trained call operators provide crisis intervention and assess the caller for the level of need and degree of risk. When necessary, rescue protocols are enacted to dispatch emergency personnel to help. These call centers have expertise in local community mental health resources.

- The National Mental Health Information Clearinghouse offers information about local mental health and addiction programs through its toll-free number (1-800-789-2647).

- The National Alliance on Mental Illness and the National Mental Health Association are two large advocacy organizations that can be extremely helpful for patients and their family members.

- Each state organizes and delivers its mental health services in a unique way based on the mandates of the state's mental health authority and funding constraints. These programs provide varying levels of care, ranging from highly intensive services (e.g., secure residential inpatient facilities) to much less intensive services (e.g., recovery maintenance and health management programs).

- The goal of effective mental health care is to provide the most appropriate services in the least restrictive way, based on the recognition that recovery is a lifelong process.

Vital Vocabulary

advocacy groups: organizations of mental health consumers and their family members and loved ones, who advocate for improvement in treatment services; the two largest mental health advocacy groups in the United States are the National Alliance on Mental Illness (NAMI) and the National Mental Health Association (NMHA)

Level of Care Utilization System: a rating system used by mental health professionals to give recommendations about the most appropriate intensity of care for patients

National Mental Health Information Clearinghouse: a toll-free support system (1-800-789-2647) that provides information about local mental health and addiction programs; it is sponsored by the Substance Abuse and Mental Health Services Administration (SAMHSA)

National Suicide Prevention Lifeline 1-800-273-TALK: a network of more than 120 crisis call centers in almost 50 states, sponsored by the Center for Mental Health Services, an agency of the U.S. federal government

Questions for Review and Discussion

1. Explain what information the National Mental Health Information Clearinghouse provides for the public.
2. Six levels of care are available for individuals suffering from mental illness. Why are these different levels of care necessary?
3. The National Suicide Prevention Lifeline network provides the public with emergency assistance for mental health concerns. How would someone access this system?

Resources

Collins BG, Collins TM. *Crisis and trauma: developmental–ecological intervention.* Boston: Houghton Mifflin, 2005.

New Freedom Commission on Mental Health. *Achieving the promise: transforming mental health care in America—executive summary.* Washington, DC: SAMHSA's National Mental Health Information Center, 2003.

Acknowledgements and Disclosures

David Covington is chief operating officer of Behavioral Health Link, a service of Integrated Health Resources, and Director of the Georgia Crisis & Access Line (1-800-715-GCAL and mygcal.com). These services are funded by the Georgia Department of Human Resources Division of Mental Health, Developmental Disabilities and Addictive Diseases. Behavioral Health Link provides screening, triage and referral services, and a 24/7 crisis hotline statewide as well as mobile crisis teams in Atlanta and Augusta. BHL also serves as the regional Crisis & Access Call Center for the 1-800-273-TALK National Suicide Prevention Lifeline network funded by the Center for Mental Health Services of the Substance Abuse and Mental Health Services Administration.

INDEX

A

Abuse and neglect of children
  case vignette: Maya: cutting and child abuse, 121
  child maltreatment, 121, 125
  childhood neglect, 122, 125
  childhood sexual abuse, 122, 125
  immediate action required, 122–123
  physical abuse, 121–122, 126
  signs of, 122t
Acamprosate, 100
ACT (Assertive Community Treatment), 52
Acting out stage, escalation of a crisis, 164
Action statement, assertive intervention, 170
Active listening, 168, 173
Active phase, schizophrenia, 72, 78
Adaptive functioning, 118, 125
Addictive diseases. *See also* Substance abuse
  and dependence
  defined, 10
  prevalence of in the United States, 5–6, 5t
  types of, 4
Addington v. Texas, 23
ADHD (Attention-deficit/hyperactivity disorder),
  120, 125
Adjudication, 49, 55
Adolescent disorders. *See* Children with emotional
  and behavioral disorders
Advocacy groups, 209, 214
Affect, 60, 64
African Americans, rate of homelessness
  among, 183
Aggression, 62, 181
  in people with schizophrenia, 72–73
Aggressive and disruptive behavior in children
  attention-deficit/hyperactivity disorder (ADHD),
    120, 125
  behavioral plan, 120–121, 125
  causes of, 120
  conduct disorder, 120, 125
  oppositional defiant disorder, 120, 125
  risk factors for, 120t
  Zachary: aggressive and violent behavior, 116
Agoraphobia, 141, 147
Akathisia, 63, 64
Albuquerque, NM, CIT program, 40
Alcohol abuse and dependence
  affect on the brain, 94–95
  alcohol withdrawal delirium, 95, 102, 104
  driving while under the influence, 94

  prevalence of in the United States, 5t
  treatment, 92, 100
Alcoholics Anonymous, 92, 100
  adolescent treatment, 123
Alzheimer's disease, 3, 3t, 110. *See also* Dementia
  signs and symptoms of, 111
American Psychiatric Association (APA), mental
  health care in correctional institutions, 24
Amphetamines and like substances, 95–96
Amygdala, 182, 184
Angel dust, 99
Anhedonia, 69, 78, 83t
Antabuse, 100
Antidepressants
  monoamine oxidase inhibitors, 86
  selective serotonin reuptake inhibitors (SSRIs),
    86, 90
  tricyclate, 86
Antipsychotic medications, 73–74, 73t, 86
Antisocial personality disorder, 26, 30
  causes of, 152
  course of, 153
  lack of conscience, sense of remorse, or guilt,
    152–153
  rate of, men *vs.* women, 152
  treatment, 153
Anxiety disorders, 3, 3t, 4, 139–148
  adolescent, 123, 125
  agoraphobia, 141, 147
  anxiety defined, 61, 64, 147
  case vignette
    Lisa: post-traumatic stress disorder (PTSD),
      139, 142, 145
    Sarah: panic attack on a subway car,
      145, 146
  causes of, 140
  course of, 143
  described, 140, 147
  engaging and assessing individuals with,
    145–146
  generalized anxiety disorder
    course of, 143
    signs and symptoms, 142, 147
  major depressive disorder with, 143
  obsessive-compulsive disorder (OCD)
    course of, 143
    signs and symptoms, 141–142, 141t, 147
      compulsions, 141, 147
      obsessions, 141, 147
      pathological doubt, 142, 148

panic disorder
  course of, 143
  signs and symptoms, 140–141, 141t, 148
percentage of people with, 140
personality disorders, 143
phobias, 141, 148
post-traumatic stress disorder (PTSD)
  course of, 143
  reacting to individuals with, 145
  signs and symptoms, 142, 142t, 148
resources, 148
social anxiety disorder
  course of, 143
  signs and symptoms, 141, 148
social phobia, 141, 148
substance use disorders, 143
support groups, 145
treatment
  cognitive-behavioral therapy, 144–145
  exposure therapy, 144
  medications, 144
  psychotherapy with medications, 144
Anxiolytics, 99–100
APA (American Psychiatric Association), 24
Apathy, 69, 78
Aquaaludes, 100
Arraignment, 47, 55
Arrests in the emergency department, 201
"Art of De-escalation," 172
Assertive Community Treatment (ACT), 52
Attention-deficit/hyperactivity disorder (ADHD),
  120, 125
Atypical antipsychotics, 73, 78
Auditory hallucinations, 62, 64, 68, 69
Autism-spectrum disorders, 133–134, 137
  major characteristics, 130t
Autonomy, 178, 184

B

"Bagging," 98
Barbiturates, 99, 100
Behavior, aggressive, 62. See also Aggressive and dis-
  ruptive behavior in children; Paranoid or aggres-
  sive individuals, responding to
Behavioral Health Link, GA, 211
Benzodiazepines, 144, 147
Bethel, Winston P., 56
Bipolar disorder, 4, 25, 31. See also Depression
  case vignette: Thomas, 84, 88
  defined, 84, 89, 194
  prevalence of in the United States, 5t
  signs and symptoms of, 84, 85t
Blunted or flat affect, 60, 64, 69, 78
Borderline personality disorder, 26, 30
Brain. See also Delirium; Dementia
  affect of some medications on, 105
  affects of substance abuse on, 93
    alcohol, 94–95
Bureau of Justice Statistics, mental health care in correctional institutions, 24–25

C

Campral, 100
Cannabis, abuse and dependence, 96
Cannabis sativa, 96
Cardiac conditions associated with delirium, 106
Case vignettes
  Agnes: developmental disability and sexual as-
    sault, 128–129
  Barbara: paranoid schizophrenia, 180, 181
  Daisy: escalation of a crisis, 171–172
  David: moving to an emergency facility, 196
  Eugene and his family: referral for care, 207
  George: alcohol withdrawal delirium, 104
  Jack: a crisis situation, 160, 162, 170
  Jake: antisocial personality, 154
  James (Snowsuit Man), 176–178
  Jamie: rescue of autistic youth, 132–133
  John: disorientation and agitated behavior, 109, 112
  Kathy: history of multiple suicide attempts, 201
  Keith: schizophrenia: effects of going off medica-
    tions, 2, 7
  Lisa: post-traumatic stress disorder (PTSD), 139,
    142, 145
  Mac: discharged from army due to mental illness, 58
  Mary: depression, 82, 88
  Maya: cutting and child abuse, 121
  Miguel: suicide, 178–179
  Rob: heroin addiction, 99
  Roshanda and her family: transfer to mental health
    center, 210
  Sam: signs and symptoms of a psychotic disorder,
    67, 76
  Sarah: panic attack on a subway car, 145, 146
  Susan: signs and symptoms of psychosis, 75–77
  Thomas: bipolar disorder, 84, 88
  Tony: schizoaffective disorder, 9
  William: alcoholism, 92, 93
  Zachary: aggressive and violent behavior, 116
Centers for Disease Control and Prevention (CDC),
  challenges in regard to mental illnesses, 4
Central nervous system
  affects of cocaine on, 97
  disorders associated with delirium, 106
Central State Hospital (Milledgeville, GA), 21
Cheney, Dick, 14
Children with emotional and behavioral disorders,
  116–127
  abuse and neglect
    child maltreatment, 121, 125
    childhood neglect, 122, 125
    childhood sexual abuse, 122, 125, 128, 129
    immediate action required, 122–123
    physical abuse, 121–122, 126
    signs of, 122t
  adaptive functioning, 118, 125
  aggressive and disruptive behavior
    attention-deficit/hyperactivity disorder
      (ADHD), 120, 125
    behavioral plan, 120–121, 125
    causes of, 120
    conduct disorder, 120, 125

Children with emotional and behavioral
disorders, (cont'd)
 oppositional defiant disorder, 120, 125
 risk factors for, 120t
 case vignette
  Maya: cutting and child abuse, 121
  Zachary: aggressive and violent behavior, 116
 developmental delays, 118, 126
 developmental milestones, deficits in, 118, 126
 engaging caregivers in treatment, 117–118
 global difficulties, 118, 126
 hyperactivity, 118, 126
 impulsivity, 118, 126
 mental retardation, 118, 126
 percentage of American youth suffering from
  severe emotional and behavioral disorders, 117
 psychiatric disorder, 118, 126
 psychoeducation, 120, 126
 resources, 127
 self-injurious behavior
  cutting, 119, 125
  suicide, 118–119
   risk factors for, 119t
   treatment, 119–120
 shortage of services for, 117
 substance use disorders in adolescents, 123
 techniques to engage youths, 124, 124t
Circumstantial thinking, 61, 64
CIT. See Crisis Intervention Team (CIT) programs
Civil commitment laws, 22–23
CMHO (Community mental health officer), 51
Cocaine, 96–97
Cochran, Sam, 163
Cochran and Dupont's continuum of escalation,
 163–165, 165t
 cooperation, 165
 demanding, 164
 generalized acting out, 164
 questioning, 163
 rapport, 165
 recovery, 164
 refusals, 163–164
 specific acting out, 164
 uncertainty, 163
Cognitive-behavioral therapy (CBT), 87, 89
 anxiety disorders, 144–145
Cognitive signs and symptoms, schizophrenia,
 70–71, 71t, 191
Collaborations, mental health and law enforcement,
 46–56
 adjudication, 49, 55
 arraignment and pretrial release/detention hearing, 48
 call histories, 46
 discharge planning, 49, 55
 dispatch, 46
 documentation, 47
 jail, 48–49
 models of collaboration
  Assertive Community Treatment (ACT), 52
  CIT and medical bracelet program, 50
  CIT training for all officers, 50

  community mental health officer (CMHO), 51
  Forensic Assertive Community Treatment
   (fACT), 52
  Mobile Crisis Teams, 51
  new recruit education, 50
  psychiatric emergency response team, 51
 options to defendants, 49
 points of intervention, 46
 police station, 47
 pre-arraignment custody, 47–48
 pre-sentencing investigation report, 49
 resources, 56
 scene of the incident, 47
 screening for suicide, 47
 unmet needs and future directions
  housing issues, 53
  inadequate mental health resources, 52–53
  professional education, 54
  Social Security benefits, Medicaid, and
   Medicare, 53–54
Command hallucinations, 62, 64
Communication, with people with developmental
 disabilities, 135–136
Community approach, treatment of schizophrenia,
 74–75, 78
Community mental health officer (CMHO), 51
Community Service Officer (CSO) unit, 50
Community treatment, 203, 205
Comorbid, defined, 156
Comorbidity (dual diagnosis)
 alcohol or drug use disorder, 101
 defined, 10, 102
 personality disorders, 152
 schizophrenia, 74, 79
Compton, Michael, 12, 45, 81
Compulsions, 141, 147
Concentration and memory difficulties, symptom of
 depression, 83t
Conduct disorder, 120, 125
 prevalence of in the United States, 5t
Conflict statement, assertive intervention, 170
Conventional antipsychotics, 73, 79
Cooperation stage, escalation of a crisis, 165
Coping skills/strategies, 150, 156, 161, 173. See also
 Malingering; Personality disorders
Costs, keeping people in mental hospitals v. prison,
 23–24
Covington, David, 45, 215
Crack cocaine, 96
Criminalization of mental illness, 2, 7, 8, 13–20. See
 also Mental health care in detention
 consequences of incarceration, 16–17
 decriminalization of mental illness, 17
 how mental illness is perceived, 14–15
 mens rea and criminal intent, 14, 19
 mentally retarded individuals in prison, 132
 percentage of mentally ill people in prison, 14
 purpose of the criminal justice process, 13–14
 rate of antisocial personality disorder among prisoners, 152
 resources, 20
 social factors associated with incarceration

economics, 14–15
education, 14
race and other social factors, 15
substance use, 15
Criminalizing the Seriously Mentally Ill: The Abuse of Jails as Mental Hospitals, 21
Crisis Center, Memphis TN, 210–211
Crisis centers, importance of, 38–39
Crisis complexity levels, 166–167, 166t
high-complexity crisis, 167
low-complexity crisis, 166
moderate-complexity crisis, 166–167
Crisis Intervention Team (CIT) programs, 33–45, 75
benefits of the CIT model, 36t
CIT curriculum, 37, 37t, 38t
CIT officers refer people in need of treatment, 40
CIT training for all officers, 50
complexity of law enforcement work, 33–34
decreases use of force and arrests, 40
development of the Memphis CIT model, 35–36
effectiveness of, 39
enhances referral to treatment, 40
families' perspectives on CIT, 41–42
Georgia's experience: a statewide CIT program, 40–41
importance of crisis centers and emergency receiving facilities, 38–39
law enforcement responses to family crises, 34
legal issues, 42
local and state CIT programs, 36
medical bracelet program, 50
mental health-based specialized mental health response, 35, 43
personal characteristics of CIT officers, 37
police-based specialized mental health response, 35, 43
police-based specialized police response, 35, 43
resources, 44–45
"ride-along" program, 40
specialized responses for mental health emergencies, 39
types of partnerships between law enforcement and mental health, 34–35
CSO (Community Service Officer), 50
Cultural competence and mental illness, 186–187
Cutting, 62, 119, 125
Cyclothymic disorder, 85, 89

D

"Date rape" drugs, 100
De-escalation techniques, 160–174
case vignette
Daisy: escalation of a crisis, 171–172
Jack: a crisis situation, 160, 162, 170
Cochran and Dupont's continuum of escalation, 163–165, 165t
cooperation, 165
demanding, 164
generalized acting out, 164
questioning, 163

rapport, 165
recovery, 164
refusals, 163–164
specific acting out, 164
uncertainty, 163
crisis defined, 161
de-escalation defined, 161–162, 173
effects on how one perceives the event, 161
Ellis and Harper's equation, 161
empathy defined, 162, 173
how to de-escalate a crisis situation
active listening defined, 168, 173
emotional labeling, 169
"I" statements, 169
introduce yourself, 167–168
listening, 168
minimal encouragers, 168
reflecting/mirroring, 168–169
restating or paraphrasing, 169
three-step assertive intervention
1. empathy statement, 169–170
2. conflict statement, 170
3. action statement, 170
interference with the communication chain, 162
introduction, 161–163
levels of crisis complexity, 166–167, 166t
high-complexity crisis, 167
low-complexity crisis, 166
moderate-complexity crisis, 166–167
officers successful at de-escalation, 162–163, 162t
putting it all together, 170–172
resources, 174
websites, 174
words of advice, 172
Defendants, 49, 55
Defense attorneys, 47
Deinstitutionalization, 23, 30, 73, 79
Delirium, 104–108
case vignette: George: alcohol withdrawal delirium, 104
collecting information from family or friends, 107, 108
course of, 107–108
defined, 105, 114
due to a medical condition, 106, 106t
engaging people with, 108
populations at risk for, 105
prevalence of, 105
related to substance abuse, 106
resources, 115
risk factors, 105
signs and symptoms
attention problems, 107
disorientation, 107
language disturbances, 107
sundowning, 106–107, 114
treatment, 105, 108
vs. dementia, 110t
Delirium tremens (DTs), 95, 102, 106
Delta-9-tetrahydrocannabinoid (THC), 96
Delusions, 62, 64, 161, 173
defined, 188, 194

Delusions (cont'd)
    delusional disorder, 68, 79
    encountering a delusional person, 188–189
    of grandeur, 62, 64
    from marijuana, 96
    periods of recovery, 189
    and reality, schizophrenia, 192
    signs and symptoms of schizophrenia, 68, 69
Demanding stage, escalation of a crisis, 164
Dementia, 109–113
    Alzheimer's and non-Alzheimer's types of,
        110–111
    case vignette: John: disorientation and agitated be-
        havior, 109, 112
    as a chronic, neurodegenerative disorder, 109, 114
    course of, 111–112
    defined, 109, 114
    engaging and assessing individuals with, 112–113
    resources, 115
    signs and symptoms, 111, 111t
    treatment, 112
    vs. delirium, 110t
Depression, 82–84. See also Bipolar disorder
    case vignette: Mary, 82, 88
    major depression defined, 83, 89
    National Depression Screening Day, 209
    prevalence of in the United States, 5t
    signs and symptoms of major depression,
        83–84, 83t
    symptoms, 83t
Detention. See Mental health care in detention
Developmental delays, 118, 126
Developmental disabilities, 35, 43, 128–138, 161, 173
    ability to achieve one's dream, 130–131
    appearance of, 129–130
    autism-spectrum disorders, 133–134, 137
        major characteristics, 130t
    case vignette
        Agnes: developmental disability and sexual as-
            sault, 128–129
        Jamie: rescue of autistic youth, 132–133
    causes, 130
    as a cluster of disabilities, 129, 130
    code of conduct for first responders and service
        personnel, 131
    communicating with people with, 135–136
    defined, 10, 55, 129, 137
    identifying people with, 134
    multiple developmental disabilities, 130t
    referring to people with, 131t
    resources, 138
    types of, 4
    violence and exploitation of people with, 129
    websites, 138
Developmental milestones, deficits in, 118, 126
Developmental stages, 119, 126
Dextroamphetamine (Dexedrine), 95, 123
Diagnosis. See also Signs and symptoms of
    mental illness
    criteria for psychiatric diagnoses, 59
    defined, 59, 64
    examples of, 59

Diagnostic and Statistical Manual of Mental Disorders
    (DSM-IV), 3, 59, 71
Diathesis-stress model, schizophrenia, 68
Dickof, Mark, 56
Disability, caused by schizophrenia, 72
Discharge planning, 49, 55
Disorders
    diagnosed in children and teenagers, 3, 3t
    diagnosed in later life, 3, 3t
Disorganization (formal thought disorder), 70, 71t, 79
Disruptive behavior disorders, 5t
Disulfiram, 100
D'Orio, Barbara, 206
Driving while under the influence
    of alcohol, 94
    of marijuana, 96
Drug(s). See Medications
Drug abuse and dependence, prevalence of in the
    United States, 5t
DSM-IV (Diagnostic and Statistical Manual of Mental
    Disorders), 3, 59, 71
DTS (delirium tremens), 95, 102, 106
Dual diagnosis: co-occurring diseases, 74, 79
Dupont, Randolph, 163
Durham Center Access, NC, 211
Dusky V. the United States, 28
Dysthymic disorder, 85, 89

E

Economic factors associated with incarceration, 14–15
Ecstasy, 97–98
ECT (electroconvulsive shock therapy), 86–87, 89
Education
    factors associated with incarceration, 14–15
    new recruit education, 50
    professional, 54
    psychoeducation, 87, 90, 120, 126
    training for CIT officers, 41, 50
Egan, Glenn, 32
Elderly, dementia in, 110–111
Electroconvulsive shock therapy (ECT), 86–87, 89
Ellis, Albert, 161
Ellis and Harper's equation, 161
Emergency receiving facilities, 196–206
    case vignette
        David: moving to an emergency facility, 196
        Kathy: history of multiple suicide attempts, 201
    challenges and frustrations, 203
    community treatment, 203, 205
    conclusion, 203–204
    defined, 196, 205
    importance of, 38–39
    law enforcement-mental health interface
        information sharing, 198–199
        mental health history, 199–200
        no-refusal drop-off policy, 198, 206
    long-acting psychiatric medications, 203, 205
    management of agitation in the ED
        arrests in the ED, 201
        weapons in secure areas, 200–201

obtaining a mental health assessment
  dangerousness to self or others, 202
  inability to care for oneself, 202, 203t
  management of suicidal or homicidal
    individuals, 202t
options to obtain mental health assessment
  emergency receiving facilities, 197–198
  mobile crisis team, 198, 205
  petitioning the probate court, 198
  providing referral information to caregivers, 198
partial hospitalization program, 203, 206
resources, 205
Emotional labeling, 169
Emotions, signs and symptoms of mental illness
  affect, 60, 64
  anxiety, 61, 64
  blunted or flat affect, 60, 64
  hypomania, 60, 65
  inappropriate affect, 60–61, 65
  labile affect, 60, 65
  mood, 60, 65
  panic attack, 61, 65
Empathy statement, assertive intervention,
  169–170
Energy decrease, symptom of depression, 83t
Erythroxylon coca bush, 96
Estelle v. Gamble, 24
Exposure therapy, anxiety disorders, 144
Expressed emotion, concept of, 190, 194

F

fACT (Forensic Assertive Community Treatment), 52
Faking a mental illness in prison, 27
Families' perspectives on CIT, 41–42
Family crises, law enforcement responses to, 34
Farmer v. Brennan, 24
FDA (Food and Drug Administration), 191
Firearms and suicide, 179
Flashback, 62, 64
Flight of ideas, 61, 64, 84, 89
"Flight or fight" response, 61
Flunitrazepam, 100
Food and Drug Administration (FDA), 191
Forensic Assertive Community Treatment
  (fACT), 52
Forensic units, defined, 22, 30
Forensics, defined, 22, 30
Formal thought disorder, 61, 64, 70, 79
Frese, Fred, 186–191
Frontline, 21

G

GCAL (Georgia Crisis and Access Line), 211
Gender differences
  antisocial personality disorder and, 152
  frequency of disruptive disorders and, 5
  major depression and, 83
  suicide as cause of death, 179

Generalized anxiety disorder
  course of, 143
  signs and symptoms, 142, 147
Genetic factors, in schizophrenia, 68
Georgia Chapter, NAMI: a statewide CIT program,
  40–41
Georgia Crisis and Access Line (GCAL), 211
Georgia Peace Officer Standards and Training
  (P.O.S.T.), 41
Georgia Public Safety Training Center, 41
Global difficulties, 118, 126
Greek, Milt, 191–193
Guilty thoughts, symptom of depression, 83t
Gustatory hallucinations, 62, 64

H

Hallucinations, 26, 31, 62, 64, 161, 173
  auditory, 68, 69
  command, 189, 194
  defined, 189, 194
  encountering a person experiencing, 189–190
  gustatory, 62, 64
  from marijuana, 96
Hallucinogens, 97–98
Harper, Robert, 161
Haynes, Nora, 45
Health Care for the Homeless, 183
Health disparities, 4, 11
Heightened sensitivity, 190
Heroin, 98
Hochman, Karen, 56
Homeless persons with mental illness
  adaptive behaviors of, 176–177
  case vignette: James (Snowsuit Man), 176–178
  cycle of expected abuse and misunderstanding,
    177–178
  drug users, 177
  interactions with police, 177–178
  noncompliance with medication adherence,
    177, 184
  percentage of homeless people with mental
    illness, 176
  right to autonomy, 178, 184
  stereotypes and biases toward, 178
Homicidal individuals, management of, 202, 202t
Homicide, people with schizophrenia, 72–73
Housing issues, 53
"Huffing," 98
Huntington's disease, 110, 111
Hurricane Katrina, 207, 208
Hyperactivity, 118, 126
Hypnotics, 99–100
Hypomania, 60, 65

I

"I" statements, 169
Ideas of reference, 62, 65
Illusion, 97, 102

Impaired insight, 27, 31, 74, 79
Impulsivity, 118, 126
Inappropriate affect, 60–61, 65
Inhalants, 98
Inpatient care, residential, 212
Insanity
    criteria for, 28
    pleas, 49
Insomnia, symptom of depression, 83t
Interpersonal psychotherapy (IPT), 87, 89

J

Jackson v. Indiana, 28

K

Ketamine, 99
Kotwicki, Raymond, 12, 20, 185

L

Labile affect, 60, 65
Lake v. Cameron, 22
Legal issues and mental illness, 42
Lessard v. Schmidt, 22
Level of Care Utilization System (LOCUS), 212–213,
    212t, 214
    intensive outpatient care, 212
    intensively managed nonresidential service, 212
    nonsecure residential inpatient care, 212
    outpatient care, 213
    recovery maintenance and health management
        services, 213
    resources, 215
    secure residential inpatient care, 212
Listening, de-escalating a crisis situation, 168
Loose associations, 61, 65
Loosening of associations, 70, 79
Louisville, KT, CIT program, 40
LSD (lysergic acid diethylamide), 97
Lushbaugh, David, 45

M

Major depressive disorder, 25, 31. See also
    Depression
    panic disorder and, 143
Malingering. See also Personality disorders
    assessment and diagnosis, 153–154
    defined, 153, 156
    symptoms, 153
Maltreatment of children, 121–123, 125
Mania, 60, 65
Manic episode, 25, 31, 84, 85t, 90
    with amphetamines, 96
Marijuana, 96
MDMA, 97–98

Measurement and Treatment Research to Improve
    Cognition in Schizophrenia (MATRICS), 191
Medicaid benefits, 53–54
    loss of while incarcerated, 16
Medicare, 53–54
Medications
    antidepressants, 86
    antipsychotic, 73–74, 73t, 86
    for anxiety disorders, 144
    atypical antipsychotics, 190, 194
    for borderline personality disorder, 152
    causing behavioral signs and symptoms, 63
    for delirium, 108
    long-acting psychiatric medications, 203, 205
    mood stabilizers, 86, 90
    narcotics/opiates, 98–99
    sedatives, hypnotics, and anxiolytics, 99–100
    street drugs, 190–191
Memphis, TN, pre-booking jail diversion program, 38
Memphis CIT model. See Crisis Intervention Team
    (CIT) programs
Mens rea and criminal intent, 14, 19
Mental health assessment, obtaining
    emergency receiving facilities, 197–198
    mobile crisis team, 198, 205
    petitioning the probate court, 198
    providing referral information to caregivers, 198
Mental health-based specialized mental health
    response, 35, 43
Mental health care in detention, 21–32
    conclusion, 29
    deinstitutionalization, 23, 30
    factors contributing to increase in incarceration
        civil commitment laws, 22–23
        tougher sentencing laws and the cost factor,
            23–24
        treatment in the community, 23
    history of psychiatric hospitals, 21–22
    managing mental health problems
        adjustment difficulties of inmates, 26
        faking a mental illness, 27
        recognizing the problem, 25–26
        respect and awareness, 26–27
    mental health services offered, 24–25
    number of mentally ill in prisons, 22
    resources, 31–32
    right to treatment, 24
    screening inmates for history of mental illness, 25
    transfer to a psychiatric hospital
        incompetence to stand trial, 28
        nonadherence with psychiatric medications,
            27–28
        not guilty by reason of insanity, 28
    transinstitutionalization, 23, 31
Mental health professionals, 4, 11
Mental health resources, 207–215. See also Level of
    Care Utilization System (LOCUS)
    case vignette
        Eugene and his family: referral for care, 207
        Roshanda and her family: transfer to mental
            health center, 210
    costs of mental health programs, 210

inadequate, 52–53
introduction, 208
local crisis and access service systems
    Behavioral Health Link, GA, 211
    Crisis Center, Memphis TN, 210–211
    Durham Center Access, NC, 211
    Georgia Crisis and Access Line (GCAL), 211
    Single Point of Contact System, 211
national-level
    advocacy groups, 209, 214
    National Alliance on Mental Illness (NAMI), 209, 214
    National Depression Screening Day, 209
    National Mental Health Association (NMHA), 209, 214
    National Mental Health Information Clearinghouse, 209, 214
    National Suicide Prevention Lifeline network, 209, 211, 214
resources, 215
Substance Abuse and Mental Health Services Administration (SAMHSA), 208
Mental illness. See also specific illness/disorder
case vignette
    Keith: schizophrenia: effects of going off medications, 2, 7
    Tony: schizoaffective disorder, 9
categories of, 3t
as causes of disability in developed countries, 5
conclusion, 9
defined, 3
diagnosing, 3
groups, 4
myth of dangerousness and violence of people with, 7–8
number of those disorders that are treatable, 41
prevalence of in the United States, 5–6, 5t, 41
resources, 11–12
serious mental illness defined, 11
stigma of, 8–9
Mental retardation, 118, 126, 132, 137
    major characteristics, 130t
Mescaline, 97
Metabolic causes of delirium, 106
Methadone, 99
Methamphetamine, 95
Methaqualone, 100
Methylphenidate (Ritalin), 95
Minimal encouragers, 168
Mobile crisis teams, 51, 198, 205
Montgomery County, PA, jail diversion program, 38
Mood, 60, 65
Mood disorders, 3, 3t, 4, 83
    bipolar disorder, 84, 85t, 89
    cyclothymic disorder, 85, 89
    depression, 82–91
        case vignette: Mary, 82, 88
        major depression defined, 83, 89
        prevalence of in the United States, 5t
        signs and symptoms of major depression, 83–84, 86t
    due to general medical condition, 85

due to substance abuse, 86, 90
dysthymic disorder, 85, 89
engaging and assessing individuals with, 88
leading to suicidal behavior, 119
premenstrual dysphoric disorder, 85t
resources, 91
treatment of
    biological treatments, 86–87, 87t
    psychosocial and social treatments, 87, 87t
Mood stabilizers, 86, 90
Morbidity, from adolescent substance use, 123, 126
Multnomak County, OR, pre-booking jail diversion program, 38

N

NAMI. See National Alliance on Mental Illness (NAMI)
Narcissistic personality disorder, 26, 31
Narcotics, 98–99
Narcotics Anonymous, 100
National Alliance on Mental Illness (NAMI), 17, 75, 198, 205, 209, 214
    Georgia Chapter: a statewide CIT program, 40–41
    purpose and goals of, 42
    report on care in jails and prisons, 21, 22
National Association of State Mental Health Program Directors Research Institute study, 21–22
National Depression Screening Day, 209
National Institute of Mental Health, 191
National Mental Health Association (NMHA), 209, 214
National Suicide Prevention Lifeline network, 209, 211, 214
Negative symptoms, of schizophrenia, 69–70, 69t, 79
Neglect of children, 122, 125
Neurodevelopment, 68, 79
Neurotransmission, 93, 102
Neurotransmitters, 68, 79, 93, 102
    anxiety, 140, 147
"The New Asylums," 21
New Freedom Commission on Mental Health, 4, 8
NGRI (not guilty by reason of insanity), 28
NMHA (National Mental Health Association), 209, 214
No-refusal drop-off policy, 198, 206
Nonadherence, 119, 126
Nonresidential service, intensively managed, 212
Not guilty by reason of insanity (NGRI), 28
Nystagmus, 99, 102

O

Obsessions, 141, 147
Obsessive-compulsive disorder (OCD)
    course of, 143
    signs and symptoms, 141–142, 141t, 147
        compulsions, 141, 147
        obsessions, 141, 147
        pathological doubt, 142, 148
O'Connor v. Donaldson, 23
Olfactory hallucinations, 62, 65
Oliva, Janet, 45

Opiates, 98–99
Oppositional defiant disorder, 120, 125
  prevalence of in the United States, 5t
Outpatient care, 213
  intensive, 212

P

Panic attack, 61, 65
Panic disorder
  course of, 143
  signs and symptoms, 140–141, 141t, 148
Paranoid delusions, 26, 31, 62, 65
  from use of cocaine, 97
Paranoid or aggressive individuals, responding to
  activation of the amygdala, 182, 184
  aggression toward others, 181
  case vignette: Barbara: paranoid schizophrenia,
    180, 181
  characteristics of paranoid people, 180–181
  creating a stable and respectful environment, 182
  as danger to themselves, 181–182
  working with paranoid persons in the commu-
    nity, 181
Paranoid schizophrenia, law enforcement-consumer
  interactions, 186–195
  cognitive difficulties, 191
  cultural competence, 186–187
  delusions and reality, 192
  differences of people with mental illness
    bad drugs: street drugs, 190–191
    concept of expressed emotion, 190, 194
    delusions
      defined, 188, 194
      encountering a delusional person, 188–189
      periods of recovery, 189
    good drugs: atypical antipsychotics, 190, 194
    hallucinations
      command hallucinations, 189, 194
      defined, 189, 194
      encountering a person experiencing, 189–190
    heightened sensitivity, 190
    law enforcement, developing trust over time,
      187–188
  hallmark of schizophrenia, 192
  paranoid schizophrenia defined, 194
  progression of the disease, 192
  resources, 195
  responding to a crisis
    be calm, 192
    caring strategies, 193
    never mention medication, 192
    responding to paranoia, 193
    understand the point of view of the person,
      192–193
Parkinson's disease, 110, 111
Partial hospitalization program, 203, 206
"Partners in Crisis," 40
Pathological doubt, 142, 148
Patton State Hospital, California, 187

PCP, 99
Peer specialists, 55
Personal characteristics of CIT officers, 37
Personality disorders, 3, 3t, 4, 143, 148. *See also*
  Malingering
  antisocial personality disorder
    causes of, 152
    course of, 153
    lack of conscience, sense of remorse, or guilt,
      152–153
    rate of, men *vs.* women, 152
    treatment, 153
  borderline, 151–152
  case vignette
    Jake: antisocial personality, 154
    Maria: attempted suicide: borderline personality
      disorder, 149, 155
  comorbid illnesses, 152
  defined, 25–26, 31, 150, 156
  engaging and assessing individuals with, 154–155
  introduction, 150
  personality defined, 150, 156
  prognosis and treatment, 151–152
  resources, 157
  splitting, 151
  suicidal behavior, 151
Phencyclidine and related substances, 99
Phobias, 141, 148
Police-based specialized mental health response,
  35, 43
Police-based specialized police response, 35, 43
Polypharmacy, 105, 114
Positive symptoms (psychosis), of schizophrenia,
  68–69, 69t
P.O.S.T. (Peace Officer Standards and Training), 41
Post-traumatic stress disorder (PTSD)
  course of, 143
  prevalence of in the United States, 5t
  reacting to individuals with, 145
  signs and symptoms, 142, 142t, 148
Poverty of content of speech, 70, 79
Pre-arraignment custody, 47–48
Pregnancy, opiate use and, 99
Premenstrual dysphoric disorder, 85t
President's New Freedom Commission on Mental
  Health (2003), 208
Pressured speech, 61, 65, 84, 90
Pretrial release/detention hearing, 48
Pretrial release treatment options, 48
Prevalence of mental diseases and addictive disorders
  prevalence defined, 11
  in the United States, 5–6, 5t
Prodomal phase, schizophrenia, 72, 79
Prognosis, 143, 148
Project Link, Rochester NY, 52
Psilocybin, 97
Psychiatric diagnoses. *See also* Signs and symptoms
  of mental illness
  criteria for, 59
Psychiatric disorder, in children, 118, 126
Psychiatric emergency response team, 51

Psychiatric hospitals
  history of, 21–22
  transfer of inmates to
    incompetence to stand trial, 28
    nonadherence with psychiatric medications, 27–28
    not guilty by reason of insanity, 28
Psychiatric illness, 161, 173. *See also* specific illness/disorder
  defined, 11
  first appearance, 4
  major illnesses, 25–26
  treatment, 4
  types of, 4
Psychodynamically oriented psychotherapy, 87, 90
Psychoeducation, 87, 90
Psychomotor retardation, symptom of depression, 83t
Psychosis, 68–69, 79
  with amphetamines, 96
Psychosocial treatments, 4
  for mood disorders, 87, 87t
Psychotherapy
  for borderline personality disorder, 152
  defined, 148
  in detention facilities, 25
  with medications, anxiety disorders, 144
  mood disorders, 87, 87t
Psychotic symptoms, 26, 31, 84, 90, 161, 174

Q

Questioning stage, escalation of a crisis, 163

R

Race and other social factors associated with incarceration, 15
Rap sheet, 47
Rapport stage, escalation of a crisis, 165
Recovery
  defined, 4, 11
  schizophrenia, 75, 79
Recovery maintenance and health management services, 213
Recovery stage, escalation of a crisis, 164
Reflecting/mirroring, crisis situation, 168–169
Refusals stage, escalation of a crisis, 163–164
Residential inpatient care
  nonsecure, 212
  secure, 212
Residual phase, schizophrenia, 72, 79
Resilience, defined, 8, 11
Respiratory conditions associated with delirium, 106
Responding to special populations. *See* Special populations, responding to
Restating or paraphrasing, de-escalating a crisis situation, 169
Risk factors defined, 184
Ritalin, 95

S

Sadness, symptom of depression, 83t
SAMHSA (Substance Abuse and Mental Health Services Administration), 208
Satcher, David, 7
Schizoaffective disorder, 3, 3t, 68, 79, 194
Schizophrenia, 3, 3t, 25, 31, 68–81. *See also* Paranoid schizophrenia, law enforcement-consumer interactions
  aggression in people with, 72–73
  and autism, 134
  case vignette
    Sam: signs and symptoms of a psychotic disorder, 67, 76
    Susan: signs and symptoms of psychosis, 75–77
  causes, 68
  closely related disorders, 68
  course, 72–73
    active phase, 72, 78
    prodomal phase, 72, 79
    residual phase, 72, 79
  defined, 68, 79
  deinstitutionalization, 73, 79
  diathesis-stress model, 68
  disability caused by schizophrenia, 72
  engaging and assessing individuals with, 76–77, 77t
  genetic factors, 68
  impaired insight, 74, 79
  improved attitudes among law enforcement after CIT training, 41
  neurodevelopment model, 68, 79
  prevalence of in the United States, 5t
  recurrence of psychotic symptoms, 72
  resources, 80
  risk factors for, 68
  signs and symptoms
    auditory hallucinations, 68, 69
    cognitive, 70–71, 71t
    delusions, 68, 69
    Diagnostic and Statistical Manual of Mental Disorders (DSM-IV), 71
    disorganization (formal thought disorder), 70, 71t, 79
    less common, 71
    negative symptoms, 69–70, 69t, 79
    positive symptoms (psychosis), 68–69, 69t
  stigma attached to, 74, 79
  suicide in people with, 73
  treatment
    antipsychotic medications, 73–74, 73t
    community approach, 74–75, 78
    dual diagnosis: co-occurring diseases, 74, 79
    percentage of people receiving treatment, 75
    psychosocial, 74–75
    recovery, 75, 79
Schizophreniform disorder, 68, 79
Screening inmates for history of mental illness, 25
Secondary gain, 27, 31
Sedatives, 99–100

Selective serotonin reuptake inhibitors (SSRIs)
  treatment of anxiety disorders, 144, 148
  treatment of depression, 86, 90
Self-care, assessment of individual unable to care for
    oneself, 202, 203t
Self-injurious behavior
  cutting, 119, 125
  suicide, 118–119
    risk factors for, 119t
    treatment, 119–120
Sensitivity, heightened, 190
Sentencing laws, 23
Separation anxiety disorder, prevalence of in the
    United States, 5t
Serotonin, 86, 90
Sexual abuse of children, 122, 125, 128, 129
Shall, Carol, 138
Signs and symptoms of mental illness, 59–66
  aggressive behavior, 62
  akathisia, 63, 64
  case vignette: Mac: discharged from army due to
      mental illness, 58
  combinations of, 59–60
  criteria for psychiatric diagnoses, 59
  cutting, 64
  diagnosis defined, 59, 64
  emotions
    affect, 60, 64
    anxiety, 61, 64
    blunted or flat affect, 60, 64
    hypomania, 60, 65
    inappropriate affect, 60–61, 65
    labile affect, 60, 65
    mania, 60, 65
    mood, 60, 65
    panic attack, 61, 65
  examples of, 59
  perceptions or senses, hallucinations, 62, 65
  resources, 66
  as result of medications, 63
  sign defined, 59, 65
  symptom defined, 59, 65
  syndrome defined, 59, 65
  tardive dyskinesia, 63, 65
  thoughts or beliefs
    circumstantial thinking, 61, 64
    delusions, 62, 64
    delusions of grandeur, 62, 64
    flight of ideas, 61, 64
    formal thought disorder, 61, 64
    ideas of reference, 62, 65
    loose associations, 61, 65
    paranoid delusions, 62, 65
    pressured speech, 61, 65
    tangential, 61, 65
    thought blocking, 61, 65
    thought content, 62, 65
    thought process, 62, 65
    word salad, 61, 65
  understanding by police officers, 59
Single Point of Contact System, 211

Social anxiety disorder
  course of, 143
  prevalence of in the United States, 5t
  signs and symptoms, 141, 148
Social factors associated with incarceration
  economics, 14–15
  education, 14
  race and other social factors, 15
  substance use, 15
Social phobia, 141, 148
Social Security Disability Insurance (SSDI), 53–54
Social treatments, of mood disorders, 87, 87t
Special K, 99
Special populations, responding to, 176–185
  conclusion, 182–183
  homeless persons with mental illness
    adaptive behaviors of, 176–177
    case vignette: James (Snowsuit Man), 176–178
    cycle of expected abuse and misunderstanding,
        177–178
    drug users, 177
    interactions with police, 177–178
    noncompliance with medication adherence,
        177, 184
    percentage of homeless people with mental ill-
        ness, 176
    right to autonomy, 178, 184
    stereotypes and biases toward, 178
  introduction, 176
  paranoid or aggressive individuals
    activation of the amygdala, 182, 184
    aggression toward others, 181
    case vignette: Barbara: paranoid schizophrenia,
        180, 181
    characteristics of paranoid people, 180–181
    creating a stable and respectful environment, 182
    danger to themselves, 181–182
    working with paranoid persons in the commu-
        nity, 181
  people with suicidal thinking or behavior
    case vignette: Miguel: suicide, 178–179
    firearms and, 179
    as leading cause of death for males in
        America, 179
    manifestations of desperation, 179
    protective factors, 179, 184
    risk factors, 179, 184
    strategies for responders, 180
  resources, 185
  special populations defined, 176, 184
  websites, 185
Specific acting out stage, escalation of a crisis, 164
Splitting, 151
SSDI (Social Security Disability Insurance), 53–54
SSI (Supplemental Security Income), 16, 53–54
SSRIS. See Selective serotonin reuptake inhibitors
    (SSRIs)
Stigma, 8–9
  attached to schizophrenia, 74, 79
  defined, 11
Substance abuse and dependence, 92–103

abuse and dependence, differences between, 94
in adolescents, 123
affect on the brain, 93
associated with incarceration, 15
case vignette
    Rob: heroin addiction, 99
    William: alcoholism, 92, 93
comorbidity and dual diagnosis, 101, 102
costs of, 94
delirium related to, 106
diagnosis of, 93
leading to suicidal behavior, 119
lifetime prevalence, 94, 102
resources, 103
screening for, 48
specific substances
    alcohol, 94–95
    amphetamines and like substances, 95–96
    cannabis, 96
    cocaine, 96–97
    hallucinogens, 97–98
    inhalants, 98
    opiates, 98–99
    phencyclidine and related substances, 99
    sedatives, hypnotics, and anxiolytics, 99–100
substance abuse defined, 55
substance dependence as a disease, 93
substance-induced mood disorder, 86, 90
substances (drugs), defined, 93, 102
tolerance, 93, 103
treatment, 100–101
websites, 103
withdrawal, 93, 103
Substance Abuse and Mental Health Services
    Administration (SAMHSA), 208
Substance use disorder, 3, 3t, 25, 31, 35, 44,
    161, 174
anxiety, 143, 148
prevalence of in the United States, 5t
Suicide/suicidal behavior
    case vignette: Miguel: suicide, 178–179
    in children and adolescents, 118–120, 119t
    firearms and, 179
    as leading cause of death for males in
        America, 179
    management of suicidal individuals, 202, 202t
    manifestations of desperation, 179
    in people with schizophrenia, 73
    with personality disorder, 151
    protective factors, 179, 184
    risk factors, 179, 184
    screening for at the police station, 47
    strategies for responders, 180
    suicidal thoughts, symptom of depression, 83t
Sundowning, 106–107, 114
Supplemental Security Income (SSI), related to in-
    carceration, 16, 53–54
Supportive psychotherapy, 87, 90
Surgeon General's Report (1999), 7
Symptom. See Signs and symptoms of mental illness

Syndromes. See also Signs and symptoms of mental
    illness
    defined, 59, 65
    examples of, 59
Synesthesia, 97, 103
System illness, associated with delirium, 106

T

Tactile hallucinations, 62, 65
Tangential conversation, 61, 65
Tangential thinking, 70, 79
Tardive dyskinesia, 63, 65, 73, 80
TCAs (Tricyclate antidepressants), 86
Teenagers, prevalence of mental illness and addictive
    disorders in, 5t
Temporary Assistance for Needy Families, 54
"Therapeutic jurisprudence," 56
Thought blocking, 61, 65, 70, 80
Thought content, 62, 65
Thought process, 62, 65
Thoughts or beliefs, signs and symptoms of
    mental illness
    circumstantial thinking, 61, 64
    delusions, 62, 64
    delusions of grandeur, 62, 64
    flight of ideas, 61, 64
    formal thought disorder, 61, 64
    ideas of reference, 62, 65
    loose associations, 61, 65
    paranoid delusions, 62, 65
    pressured speech, 61, 65
    tangential, 61, 65
    thought blocking, 61, 65
    thought content, 62, 65
    thought process, 62, 65
    word salad, 61, 65
Tolerance for substances, 93, 103
Training, CIT training for all officers, 41, 50
Transinstitutionalization, 23, 31
Tricyclate antidepressants (TCAs), 86

U

Uncertainty stage, escalation of a crisis, 163
U.S. Department of Health and Human Services'
    Children's Bureau, incidence of child maltreat-
    ment, 121
U.S. Supreme Court
    competency to stand trial, 28
    criteria for confinement of nondangerous per-
        sons, 23
    on medical care for prisoners, 24

V

Vascular dementia, 110, 114
Visual hallucinations, 62, 65

W

Washington, Earl, Jr., 132
Weapons
    carrying into secure areas by officers, 200–201
    firearms and suicide, 179
Withdrawal symptoms, 93, 103
    alcohol, 94
    of detainees, 48, 55
    opiates, 98–99
    sedatives, hypnotics, and anxiolytics, 100
Wood, Keith, 20

Woody, Michael, 172
Word salad, 61, 65, 70, 80

X

Xanax, affect of with alcohol, 92, 95

Y

Youth Risk Behavior Survey (2004), 118

CPSIA information can be obtained
at www.ICGtesting.com
Printed in the USA
JSHW040750081220
10043JS00008B/124